MEDIEVAL MISOGYNY AND THE INVENTION OF WESTERN ROMANTIC LOVE

Presented to Purchase College
by
Gary Waller, PhD Cambridge

State University of New York
Distinguished Professor

Professor
of Literature & Cultural
Studies, and Theatre &
Performance, 1995-2019
Provost 1995-2004

M·E·D·I·E·V·A·L

and the Invention

THE UNIVERSITY OF CHICAGO PRESS

M·I·S·O·G·Y·N·Y

of Western Romantic Love

R. HOWARD BLOCH

Chicago & London

R. HOWARD BLOCH, professor and chair of the department of French at the University of California, Berkeley, is the author of *Etymologies and Geneologies* and *The Scandal of the Fabliaux,* also published by the University of Chicago Press.

The University of Chicago Press, Chicago 60637
The University of Chicago Press, Ltd., London

© 1991 by The University of Chicago
All rights reserved. Published 1991
Printed in the United States of America
00 99 98 97 96 95 94 93 92 91   5 4 3 2 1

Library of Congress Cataloging-in-Publication Data

Bloch, R. Howard
    Medieval misogyny and the invention of Western romantic love / R. Howard Bloch.
        p.   cm.
    Includes bibliographical references and index.
    ISBN 0-226-05972-3. — ISBN 0-226-05973-1 (pbk.)
    1. Women—History—Middle Ages, 500–1500. 2. Misogyny—Europe—History. 3. Patriarchy—Europe—History. 4. Love—History.
    I. Title
    HQ1143.B56   1991
    305.4'09'02—dc20   91-12699
                                                                            CIP

∞ The paper used in this publication meets the minimum requirements of the American National Standard for Information Sciences—Permanence of Paper for Printed Library Materials, ANSI Z39.48-1984.

This book is dedicated to my mother, Virginia R. Bloch,
and to the memory of my father, Bertram H. Bloch, 1913–1990

C O N T E N T S

ACKNOWLEDGMENTS

Much of what is to be admired in this book results from the attentive listening and engaging responses of those who attended my seminars at the University of California, Berkeley, and the Newberry Library, Chicago, as well as from careful readings by friends and others who expressed concern for my social and domestic well-being. This, then, is a delicious opportunity to express my thanks to Peter Allen, Albert Ascoli, George Beech, Charles Bernheimer, Leo Bersani, Daniel Boyarin, Adam Bresnick, Catherine Brown, Kevin Brownlee, Caroline Bynum, Jane Chance, Susan Crane, Carolyn Dinshaw, Shoshana Felman, Dolores Frese, Sepp Gumbrecht, Penny Shine Gold, Janice Butler Holm, Sylvia Huot, Sam Kinser, Anne Knudsen, Alexandre Leupin, Leo Lowenthal, Stephen G. Nichols, Nancy Regalado, Mary Beth Rose, Tilde Sankovitch, David Stern, Tom Stillinger, Mogens Trolle Larsen, Sylvia Tomasch, and Eugene Vance. The group around *Representations* is, of course, an enduring source of intellectual pep, and the evening discussion of my original paper on misogyny in Mike Rogin's living room in the presence of Jacques Revel produced a fracas for the ages. So too, the published response to this paper in the *Medieval Feminist Newsletter* marked the beginning of a salutary dialogue whose effects upon the pages that follow are the very stuff of meaningful intellectual exchange; for this I am grateful to Elizabeth Clark, Wendy Clein, Elaine Hansen, Peggy Knapp, Marshall Leicester, Linda Lomperis, Carol Neel, and Helen Solterer. Where the actual preparation of the book is concerned, I am indebted to Lys Ann Shore, whose expert copy editing and knowledge of medieval sources made the final version more precise than at the outset, and especially to Katharine Streip, whose assistance in every aspect of the current endeavor—from the sleuthing of elusive sources and the proofing of tangled prose to astute criticism of substance—was without equal. Finally, I am saddened that Joel Fineman did not live to see the final product of a dialogue that benefited more than a little from his wacky, generous brilliance.

This book has aroused some controversy even before its publication. Much of the reaction, which came in the form of responses to an article originally published in *Representations*, has been highly constructive, and indeed has had a determining effect upon that which follows.[1] The tone and the insistence of some scholars, however, reveal what I can only take to be a certain disapproval of the topic, seen to be morally inadmissible. Such a consequence is surprising. Surprising, first, because I conceived of my essay from the outset as an essentially feminist project; second, because one of the defining presumptions of feminist analysis is the omnipresence of misogynist attitudes within our culture; and third, because such disapproval can only be based upon the assumption that writing about misogyny automatically constitutes an endorsement of it. Nothing could be further from my intention. Nor is anything less logical than supposing that the choice of a subject for critical treatment means advocacy. The designation of antifeminism as a legitimate topic for study no more implies an espousal of its obviously unacceptable terms than the sociologist's study of poverty entails an apology for abjection, the historian's study of the Nazi or Stalinist past a call to authoritarianism, or the medical researcher's study of cancer a welcome to disease.

If I present antifeminism as a topic for discussion, it is because I think it is a mode of thought often taken for granted; one that, when acknowledged, is often analyzed superficially, even in the languages of anthropology and psychoanalysis, which tend to naturalize rather than inhibit it; and, finally, one that works most insidiously when occulted. It cannot, in other words, simply be washed away by assuming that it is always already there or by the best moral intentions. On the contrary, a failure to recognize the topic can itself be a source of misogyny by leaving the way open to the kinds of unconscious complicities to which none of us is immune. "Misogyny," as Frances Ferguson and I wrote in an earlier volume, "seemed to us to emblematize the problem that representation poses when it creates oppositions between what we perceive and what we endorse. And in that sense, it provides the occasion for a discussion of the limits of idealism, or of a conflict between authors and readers comparable to the conflict between misogynists and the women who are

1

misrepresented by its pervasive and perfidious, but often unrecognized, images."[2] This book concerns itself even more deeply with the problems of enacting an easy fit between representation and what one might think of as a political will.

Since much contemporary feminist thought assumes the diverse cultural forms of the West to have been misogynistic from the beginning, and since some feminists have reacted disapprovingly to my recognition of the topic of misogyny, I can only speculate that this contradiction entails a question of voice. Indeed, those who have read my early work or listened to my lectures on this subject often pose one or another version of the question, "Where do I situate myself with respect to the subject?" To which I can only reply that I am a self-identified gendered male, who is prevented out of a deep respect for the variety of feminisms from speaking for *a* feminism; and, more important, prevented out of respect for the ability of women to speak for themselves from adopting the voice of a woman, to speak or "to read like a woman" in the phrase made popular by Jonathan Culler.[3] For, as both men and women are becoming increasingly aware, the ventriloquistic imitation of someone else's voice can turn out, in this hyperflorescent moment of the prehumiliated sublime, to be either a strategy of seduction or a usurpation of that person's power. Moreover, the quick move from "speaking like a woman" to the supposition that only a woman can speak *about* a woman, to an essentialized notion of woman *as* truth—yet another version of the Eternal Woman, which I discuss by way of conclusion (chapter 7)—places such a gesture firmly within one of the strong currents of Western misogyny from Plato at least to Nietzsche. Thus I have no choice that would not be as politically disenfranchising to women as the urge to "speak like a woman" finally is. Nor is this perspective necessarily such a bad one from which to approach a subject that is often too painful for many women to face head on. As a male, I am keenly aware not so much perhaps of what it feels like to be the victim of misogyny as of the many ruses of speech that even the most ardently feminist, sexually "correct" men use in order to continue to act as men have always acted. (In *New French Feminisms*, Gisèle Halimi, discussing what she calls "Doormat-Pedestal tactics," quotes Sacha Guitry, who "is willing to admit that women are superior to men as long as they do not seek to be equal.")[4]

My approach to the topic stems from what I recognized early on to be a repetitive monotony in what misogynists had to say about women from the church fathers on, and which has hardly varied in almost two thousand years. This is not an original perception but one that dates from the early fifteenth century and the first sustained attempt to counter the pernicious effects of misogyny on the part of Christine de Pizan. "Judging from the treatises of all philosophers and poets and from all the orators . . . ," writes the apologist for women in the Quarrel of the *Romance of the Rose,* "it seems that they all speak from one and the same mouth."[5] But, more important, alongside the monotonous persistence into the current era of the topoi of misogyny established in the first centuries of Christianity, I discovered that most previous histories of misogyny seemed to be simple summations or rehearsals of that repetition; and such a tactic leads to a common strategic error—that is, the equation of the uniformity of the discourse with its inevitability.[6] For example, in writing about the Quarrel of the *Rose,* Blanche Dow tends to assume that what is widespread is eternal, and what is eternal is natural: "It is a recurring quarrel, and is no more than one expression of the eternal struggle between the forces of naturalism and those of classicism, between the opposing definitions of art, two conflicting moral concepts, a struggle between elements which are always present in the human mind and in the social order. . . . The 'Quarrel of the *Rose*' involves an argument which is universal and ageless."[7] Marie-Thérèse d'Alverny, the author of an excellent study of the misogyny of medieval theologians and philosophers, expresses a similar resignation before the monolithic quality of the material: "We must then resign ourselves to a harsh exposition, illustrated by texts that lack variety and that reveal only an approximate image of the real attitude of the men we will cite."[8] Katherine Rogers, who has written a more general history of literary misogyny, is also aware of how easily the acknowledgment of universality promotes a blindness that naturalizes: "The view that women are inferior to men and therefore should be subordinated to them is not in itself misogynistic, because it was almost universally held until modern times."[9]

All of this made it clear to me from the outset that any effective strategy for resisting antifeminism must be twofold.

First, in exploring the pitfalls and paradoxes of this socially sanctioned discourse, it is not enough simply to recite once again the history of a tort, a litany of woe. Given the persistence of the topoi of antifeminism, moral righteousness and counterexamples—both medieval and modern—have historically never been enough, or even very effective. One must push the antifeminist clichés to their limit in order to unmask their internal incoherences—to deconstruct, in short, whatever will not go away simply by exposure or by wishing that it were not so. To that end the present essay is an attempt to say to all those responsible for the particular articulation of antifeminism under which our culture still labors—to Tertullian, Jerome, Chrysostom, Ambrose, Augustine, Gregory of Nyssa, Novatian, Methodius, Clement of Rome, and Clement of Alexandria, as well as their intellectual and literary heirs of the nineteenth century—that where a certain vision of woman is concerned, "you are not only wrong, you also contradict yourself."

This is why it is so important, second, to distinguish between language and action, words and deeds, in dealing with the question of misogyny. Here again, Christine de Pizan serves as our best guide. In her insistence upon the repetitiveness of misogynists she acknowledges the important role played by language in coming to grips with antifeminism. Misogyny is the expression of a negative opinion. Concerning what is perhaps the most virulent anti-matrimonial tract of the late Middle Ages, Jehan Le Fèvre's *Lamentations de Matheolus,* Christine confesses that "just the sight of this book . . . made me wonder how it happened that so many different men—and learned men among them—have been and are so inclined to express both in speaking and in their treatises and writings so many wicked things about women."[10] That is, using her own terms and leaving aside for the moment the unknowable affective element of antifeminism as well as the social status of actual women at any given moment, misogyny is a way of speaking about, as distinct from doing something to, women, though speech can be a form of action and even of social practice, or at least its ideological component. Such a distinction between words and deeds, where relations between the genders are concerned, is the necessary foundation of a dialectical, historically informed, political understanding of the phenomenon, an understanding which otherwise would remain hopelessly enmeshed in the literalism of a false ideology, a literalism that risks taking gender difference rather than the oppressive exercise of power by either sex for the true historic cause of social injustice. Thus I have been careful throughout this book to distinguish between the alienating speech acts made by the self-identified misogynists I quote and my definition of what they are doing. I have not used the phrase "Woman is . . ." without bracketing it by something like, "according to the discourse of medieval misogyny. . . ." For only by making such a distinction can one begin to identify not only the obvious forms of misogyny, but the more subtle, invisible manifestations of its grand themes, some of which even look like the opposite of antifeminism (see chapter 6).

Here lies another important difference between previous modern histories of misogyny, some of which may be unconsciously complicit with the phenomenon they describe, and the present attempt to undo it. My conclusion broadens Christine's perception concerning "so many wicked things about women" said by "so many different men" to include the alienating effects of both negative and positive predication. Whether good or bad, laudatory or deprecatory, the reduction of Woman to a category implies in our culture—and this because of a historic real imbalance of possessory power—an appropriation that is not present when identical generalizing statements are applied to man or men. I propose, then, a definition of misogyny as a speech act in which woman is the subject of the sentence and the predicate a more general term; or, alternatively, as the use of the substantive *woman* or *women* with a capital *W*. Even the sentence "All women are different" is included in such a definition, since there are among women, as among men, points of resemblance that reduce such a statement to a violating generalization akin to the notion, never very far behind, that "Woman is undefinable," is a question or an enigma (see chapter 7).[11] "We talk about 'women' and 'women's suffrage,'" Millicent Fawcett, the nineteenth-century British feminist, is quoted as saying, "we do not talk about Woman with a capital *W*. That we leave to our enemies."[12] More recently, Judith Butler has sought to extend the proscription of the word *woman* to *women* as well.[13]

This means that the contrary of misogyny is neither a corresponding negative generalization about men (which culturally would not produce the same effect) nor the love of all women (a pretense that is merely another form of misogyny), but something on the order of a perception of women as individuals, or the avoidance of general statements such as "Woman is . . ." or "Women are . . . ."[14] For the effect of a speech act such that woman is the subject of the sentence and the predicate a more general term, that effect which dwells in the zone where the use of words produces the most basic elements of thought—and thought authorizes action, is to make of woman an essence, which, as essence, is eliminated from the world historical stage. This is precisely why the discourse of misogyny seems so repetitive, is so culturally constant, and seems to lack an internal history. Its purpose—to remove individual women from the realm of events—depends upon the transformation of woman into a general category, which, internally at least, appears never to change.

To say that the discourse of misogyny seems to have no internal history is not to say that this way of speaking, and thus of thinking and acting, does not have a history or that it is "only a text"—as patristic and medieval misogynists and their modern counterparts maintain that it is—or that its effects are not real. It is not to imply that there have been no changes in the ways misogyny has been received, understood, assimilated, or pressed ideologically in the service of social practice. It is not to say misogyny has not been different in other cultures or has not been used in different ways in the course of the Christian era (though even here one can point to a rather singular purpose, which is subjugation). It *is* to say, above all, that any essentialist definition of woman, whether negative or positive, whether made by a man or a woman, is the fundamental definition of misogyny. It *is* to say that such essentialist definitions of gender are dangerous not only because they are wrong or undifferentiated but, once again, because historically they have worked to eliminate the subject from history. "'Woman' as a collective noun is as full of traps as it is convenient . . . ," writes Sheila Ryan Johansson. "Over time men have changed their minds again and again about who and what 'Woman' is. . . . Most often it has been those hostile to women who have written of 'Woman' and their true unchanging essence. Descriptions and analyses of the eternal feminine have usually been put forth by those anxious to justify continuance of various forms of social and legal restrictions."[15] Thus the very lack of an internal history of antifeminism implied by the use of the eternalizing, essentializing substantive *Woman,* or by the use of *woman* or *women* in a universalizing proposition, is intimately bound to its specific social effects.

Again, what is called for is not the repression of the topic but its critique, analysis that would undermine rather than confirm its historic power. For, to repeat, any attempt merely to trace the history of antifeminism without deconstructing it—without exposing its inner tensions and contradictions—is hopelessly doomed, despite all moral imperative, to naturalize what it would denounce. The definition I propose suggests, in contrast, that the tenacity as well as the uniformity of the topoi of antifeminism are significant in and of themselves. In fact, these characteristics provide one of the most powerful ways of critiquing it precisely because the problem of defining misogyny remains indissociable from its seeming ubiquity or from the essentializing definitions of woman apparent in the writings of almost all who adopt this way of addressing the question of the feminine, from the earliest church fathers to Chaucer.

So persistent is the discourse of misogyny in the Middle Ages that the uniformity of its terms furnishes an important link between this period and the present, rendering the topic even more compelling because, as we shall see, such terms still govern (consciously or not) the ways in which the question of woman is conceived—by women as well as by men. This is by no means an obvious point, and in order to make it I shall refer not only to the canonical antifeminists of the Middle Ages, but to their spiritual heirs—the philosophers, novelists, medical specialists, social scientists, and critics of the nineteenth century, whose own particular brand of Romantic and naturalistic misogyny carries a large charge of unexamined attitudes from the medieval, and even the patristic, past.

If the title *Medieval Misogyny* seems redundant, it is because the topic of misogyny, like the mace or chastity belt, participates in a vestigial horror practically synonymous with the Middle Ages and because one of the assumptions governing our perception of the early Christian and medieval period is the viral presence of antifeminism. This view does not emanate from the nineteenth-century revival of medievalism, from contemporary feminism, or even from recent interest in the study of women in medieval culture. Christine de Pizan complains in the *Cité des dames* (1405): "I could hardly find a book on morals where, even before I had read it in its entirety, I did not find several chapters or certain sections attacking women, no matter who the author was."[16] The denunciation of women, as Christine acknowledges, constitutes something of a cultural constant. Reaching back to the Old Testament and to ancient Greece and extending through classical Hellenic, Judaic, and Roman traditions all the way to the fifteenth century, it dominates ecclesiastical writing, letters, sermons, theological tracts, and discussions and compilations of canon law; scientific works, as part of biological, gynecological, and medical knowledge; folklore and philosophy. The discourse of misogyny runs like a vein—Christine's "several chapters or certain sections" of almost every "book on morals"—throughout medieval literature.

Like allegory itself, to which it is peculiarly attracted, antifeminism is both a genre and a topos, or, as Paul Zumthor might suggest, a "register"—a discourse visible across a broad spectrum of poetic types.[17] Examples are to be found in classical Latin satire and in the satires of the High Middle Ages—John of Salisbury's *Policraticus,* Walter Map's *De nugis curialium* (especially the Letter of Valerius to Rufinum), Andreas Capellanus's *Art of Courtly Love* (Book III)—as well as in the *Quinze joies de mariage* and the *Lamentations de Matheolus* denounced by Christine. The little-known subgenre of debate poems, popular in the thirteenth century and involving the virtues and vices of women ("Le Sort des dames," "Le Bien des fames," "Le Blastagne des fames," Le Blasme des fames"), participates in the antifeminism of popular forms, not the least of which is the hermetic fifteenth-century *Malleus maleficarum*. Misogyny is, moreover, virtually synonymous with the works grouped under the rubric of "les genres du réalisme bourgeois": the comic tale or fabliau (including Middle English and Italian versions); the animal fable (*Roman de Renart*); the comic theater or farce. It is also associated with certain mixed or unclassifiable types like the *chantefable Aucassin et Nicolette* or Adam de la Halle's *Jeu de la feuillée* and, of course, Jean de Meun's portion of the *Roman de la rose*. It was this last work which sparked France's first literary quarrel, involving both the question of poetic interpretation and that of woman in a sexual/textual scenario, that would last through the medieval period into the neoclassical age (see chapter 2). Further, as we shall see in chapters 5–7, even those types which historically have been considered to be the opposite of, or liberating from, the dark age of medieval antifeminism—the courtly romance, lyric, and lay— maintain a complicated relation to the hegemonic negative images of the feminine that dominated the earlier period.

If the expression "invention of Western romantic love" seems like a contradiction, it is because we so often assume love as we know it to be natural, to exist in some essential sense, that is, always to have existed. Nothing, however, could be further from the truth. For love, unlike the discourse of misogyny of the Christian West, has an internal history expressed both as an evolutionary shift and a difference from itself. The terms that serve to define, or mediate, what we consider to this day to constitute romantic involvement were put into place definitively—at least for the time being—sometime between the beginning and the middle of the twelfth century, first in southern and then in northern France. Along with the revival of cities, the return of money, and growth of long-range trade with the East; along with the reconstitution of monarchy and the legal institutions of the monarchic state; along with the reconquest of territories that had since the disintegration of the Carolingian Empire escheated to local feudal lords; along with the revival of classical literature and the rise of a poetry in the vernacular—all manifestations of what C. S. Lewis characterized as one of the few moments of true cultural mutation the West has ever known—there occurred the most significant shift in the articulation of the feminine and of sex since the patristic invention of gender in the first centuries of the Christian era. As C. S. Lewis, Robert Briffault, Denis de Rougemont, Reto Bezzola, Irving Singer, and others maintain, the notion of romantic fascination that governs what we say about love, what we say to the ones we love, what we ex-

pect them to say to us, (and to say they say), how we act and expect them
to act, how we negotiate our relation to the social—in short, the hygiene
that governs our erotic imagination right down to the choice of whom
we love or the physical positions we use to express it—did not exist in Judaic, Germanic, Arabic, or Hispanic tradition, in classical Greece or Rome, or
in the early Middle Ages.[18] Romantic love as we know it did not come
into being until what is sometimes called the renaissance of the twelfth century.

The chapters that follow seek to situate and to relate two moments of
rupture or disjunction in the history of sexuality in the West. The first,
which occurred between the first and fourth centuries (some say as early as
Paul and others as late as Augustine), is characterized by an articulation of
gender quite different from that of Stoic, Judaic, Platonic, Aristotelian,
Gnostic, Manichaean, or late Roman tradition. Indeed, the Christian construction of gender is composed of elements to be found in preexisting or
surrounding cultures, but not in quite the combination that was passed to
the Middle Ages and has lasted until the current era. More precisely, we find
in the writings of the early church fathers: (1) a feminization of the flesh,
that is, the association, according to the metaphor of mind and body, of man
with *mens* or *ratio* and of woman with the corporeal; (2) the estheticization
of femininity, that is, the association of woman with the cosmetic, the
supervenient, or the decorative, which includes not only the arts but what
Saint Jerome calls "life's little idle shows"; and (3) the theologizing of
esthetics, or the condemnation in ontological terms not only of the realm of
simulation or representations, of "all that is plastered on" in Tertullian's
phrase, but of almost anything pleasurable attached to material embodiment. Nothing in prior tradition rivals the asceticism of early Christianity,
according to which only the renunciation of the flesh holds the promise of
salvation. The shape of this initial articulation of gender is the subject of the
first two chapters, which also seek to define the crucial role played by literature and poetics in the definition of gender in the West and in the dissemination of that definition upon the stage of history and within the
context of a social and material base.

Here a word of caution is in order. The initial chapters are not about
women in the Middle Ages. They do not seek to uncover the suppressed
voice of women; they do no present a rounded portrait of women, of the
images of women, or even of the social status and roles of medieval women.
That has been done by others far better than I could do. Instead, they are

about one particularly negative version of the feminine, which happens also to be particularly influential upon the question of gender still today. Above all, I do not want to deny the existence, alongside the discourse of misogyny, of a myriad galleries of good women stretching from Augustine's portrayal of the martyrs Felicity and Perpetua or Gregory of Nyssa's portrait of his sister, to Christine de Pizan's *Cité des dames* or Chaucer's *Legend of Good Women*. Nor do I wish in the least to diminish the importance of female spirituality in late Classical and medieval culture. On the contrary, I seek in chapter 3 to answer the question of how those who thought so intensely about gender in the first four centuries of the Christian era were able almost to a man to assert that woman is both good and bad, is at once the "Bridge of Christ" and the "Devil's Gateway."

In chapter 4 I focus upon the topic of virginity, which lies at the core of the medieval discourse of misogyny. As a defining constant of both theological and literary works, it enables us to make a connection between the patristic writings of the earlier period and the courtly literature of the twelfth and thirteenth centuries. As we shall see in chapters 5 and 6, the obsession with chastity among both Church Fathers and poets leads to the conclusion that this second crux in the history of the relation of the genders represented not so much a break with the Early Christian articulation of sexuality as an inversion of its terms, a transformation of antifeminism into woman worship. It is my claim that the asceticism of the earlier period, synonymous with the deprecation of the feminine, was, in the High Middle Ages, simply transformed into an idealization both of woman and of love according to which: (1) desire was secularized, or the passion reserved in Christianity for divinity became legitimately focused upon a supposedly mortal human being; (2) secular love became impossible or, as Denis de Rougemont and others have noted, it became by definition "unhappy," "romantic"; and (3) impossible love became noble, and suffering the mark of social distinction.

This shift cannot be accounted for, as so many have tried to do, by single-factor explanations, such as the influence of Celtic folk rituals, Eastern religions, Albigensian heresy, Platonic philosophy, or Arabic or Hispanic poetry. It cannot be seen merely as a manifestation of the secularization of society at the time of the Gregorian Reform, for a similar evolution took place both in secular culture and in the ecclesiastical sphere, where it was most keenly expressed in terms of the Mariolatry accompanying new forms of piety in the late feudal era. Nor can the invention of romantic love adequately be understood as a by-product of a general "warming" of the cultural climate in twelfth-century Poitou and the South. Indeed, as we shall see in chapter 7, only an analysis of the specific social, legal, and economic determinants of this seemingly radical change in the politics of gender can account for the appearance of what since the late nineteenth century has been called "courtliness" or "courtly love."[19] The coming into being of Western romantic love was part of a particular moment in the history of misogyny—a moment at which, because of contemporaneous changes in both the forms of property and relations of power between the genders, the debilitating obsession with woman as the source of all evil became inverted into a coconspiring obsession with woman as the source of all good.

Thus we seem to be caught between a redundancy and a contradiction. On the one hand, a disparaging of woman is asserted to lack internal history. On the other hand, an idealization of woman appears to possess too much history, or to be overdetermined by it. In fact, the terms of our equation are not as simple as they might seem. As both psychoanalytic and feminist criticism have confirmed, the relation of the competing discourses on the feminine—the misogynistic and the courtly—is a good deal more complicated than one of simple opposition. For, to repeat: it is not exactly that misogyny is without history, but the denial of history to women entails an abstraction that also denies the being of any individual woman, and is therefore the stuff of a disenfranchising objectification. Conversely, the articulation of love as an ideal, which is what we mean by romantic love, *is* the product of a historical process, of material conditions and of a contingent set of circumstances and even personalities, belonging to a specific time and place. A certain way of thinking about history, no matter how big the scale, implicates what the French call "la petite histoire." But this is jumping the gun a bit; and though readers might want to believe me out of either the political correctness or the deconstructive perversity that such an equation implies, we have a good deal of territory to cover before they will be called upon to concede that negative and positive fetishizations of the feminine work to identical effect, and that their seeming polarity is the product of material conditions that have pertained since the end of what Marc Bloch terms "the first feudal age" and Georges Duby the "watershed years" of the early modern era.

MOLESTIAE NUPTIARUM AND THE YAHWIST CREATION

The persistence—in theological, philosophical, and scientific tracts; in literature, legend, myth, and folklore—of so many of the earliest formulations of the question of woman, from the church fathers to the nineteenth century, means that anyone wondering where to begin to understand the Western current of antifeminism must recognize that it is possible to begin just about anywhere. We begin our study with a passage from among the many antimatrimonial tirades of Jean de Meun's *Roman de la rose:*

Ha! se Theofrastus creüsse,
ja fame espousee n'eüsse.
Il ne tient pas home por sage
qui fame prent par mariage,
soit bele ou lede, ou povre ou
    riche,
car il dit, et por voir l'afiche,
en son noble livre *Aureole,*
qui bien fet a lire en escole,
qu'il i a vie trop grevaine,
pleine de travaill et de paine.

Ha! If I had only believed Theophrastus,
I would never have taken a wife. He
holds no man to be wise who takes a
woman in marriage, whether ugly or
beautiful, poor or rich. For he says, and
you can take it for truth, in his noble
book Aureole, *which is good to read in*
school, that there is there a life too full of
torment and strife.[1]

Though the Theophrastus referred to—identified alternately as the author of the *Characters* and as a pupil of Aristotle—and his *livre Aureole* are mentioned by Jerome in *Adversus Jovinianum* (I, 47), they are otherwise unknown, which does not prevent their being cited by almost every antimatrimonial writer of the Middle Ages.[2] Together they constitute an absent *locus classicus* of the topos of *molestiae nuptiarum,* the pains of marriage, which was read, Jean maintains, "in school."

Of what do the pains of marriage consist?

This question brings us to one of the grand themes of gender, which passes in the High Middle Ages from Christian orthodoxy to vernacular culture:

qu'il i a vie trop grevaine,	*That there is there a life too full of*
Pleine de travaill et de paine	*torment and strife and arguments and*
et de contenz et de riotes,	*riotousness because of the pride of foolish*
par les orgueuz des fames sotes,	*women—and dangers and reproaches*
et de dangiers et de reproches	*which they do and say with their mouths,*
qu'el font et dient par leur	*and requests and complaints which they*
boches,	*invent on many occasions. It takes a*
et de requestes et de plaintes	*great effort to keep them and to hold back*
qu'el treuvent par achesons	*their foolish wills. (Rose, vv. 8539–48)*
maintes.	
Si ra grant paine en eus garder	
Por leur fous volairs retarder.	

According to the topos of the *molestiae nuptiarum*, wives are portrayed as contentious, prideful, demanding, complaining, and foolish; they are pictured as uncontrollable, unstable, and insatiable: "si ra grant paine en eus garder / Por leur fous volairs retarder." To push a little further, one cannot help but notice the extent to which the pains of marriage involve verbal transgression, so that the reproach against women is a form of reproach against language itself—"that which is said by the mouth" ("qu'el font et dient par leur boches"), or more precisely, *contenz* (contention, garrulousness, bickering, and quarrels), *reproches* (criticism, reproach), *plaintes* (complaint), *requestes* (demands), *orguelz* (pride). A wife is depicted as a constant source of anxiety and dissatisfaction, an anxiety expressed—or, as the text suggests, "composed"— with words: "qu'el *treuvent* par achesons maintes." The protest against women as a form of verbal abuse, addressed to "anyone who marries," is thus posited as universal.[3]

Here we touch upon one of the touchstones of the genre which is latent, of course, well before the thirteenth century and even before the Christian era—the link of the feminine to the seductions and the ruses of speech. It is to be found, for example, in Homer's sirens who implore the wandering Odysseus to "Bring your ship in so that you may listen to our voice. / No one has ever sped past this place in a black ship / Before he listened to the honey-toned voice from our mouths." It is present in Hesiod's version of the simultaneous creation of woman and "lying speech" in the figure of Pandora, "this ruin of mankind" molded from the earth as part of Zeus's vengeance for the theft of fire.[4] The view of woman as the one who through speech sowed discord between man and God lies at the core of the narrative of the Fall, the Old Testament association of the feminine and verbal allurement. Nowhere, however, is the cosmic misogyny of the classical world—a world that includes the terrible figures of the Furies, the Harpies, the Fates, but at least accords woman a powerful place in the order of nature—nowhere is the founding antifeminism of the Genesis story more powerfully domesticated (literally, taken into the home) than in the late Latin and Christian world where wives are the equivalent of an annoyance of speech implicit to everyday life. With the first centuries of our era antifeminism becomes synonymous with anti-marriage literature. Juvenal, for example, claims that it would be "impossible for a lawyer, a public crier, or even another woman, to speak, so abundant is the sea of a wife's words," which he compares to a "cacophony of cauldrons and bells."[5] "What if a husband is moderate but his wife is wicked, carping, a chatterbox, extravagant (the affliction common to all womankind), filled with many other faults, how will that poor fellow endure this daily unpleasantness, this conceit, this impudence?" asks John Chrysostom. "The man who does not quarrel is a bachelor," Saint Jerome seems to answer.[6]

The notion that women are by nature more talkative than men is, of course, a staple of antifeminist prejudice, one of "our culture's deep roots in medieval culture," in the phrase of Eleanor McLaughlin.[7] And lest one think that such abusive language about women as verbal abuse is restricted to the Middle Ages, it is only necessary to scan the canonical misogynistic texts of subsequent centuries to see that neither the association of woman with verbosity nor the specific terms of the cliché have changed very much. The topos of the garrulous female is a persistent feature of the discourse of antifeminism in the West. That guardian of literary probity of the seventeenth century, Boileau, for example, repeats the tiresome traditional list of the *molestiae nuptiarum*. Marriage, he claims, holds the promise of unceasing contradiction, argument, scolding, and harangue. Worse, the verbal abuse to which the husband submits implies the use of terms not to be found in the dictionary, as woman herself becomes the equivalent of a neologism and marriage threatens the purity of the French language. Boileau's own pen "tracing these words alphabetically," he claims, "might increase by a tome the Richelet Dictionary."[8]

The topos of the talkative female is particularly prevalent in the century directly preceding our own. A medical encyclopedia from the early 1800s, under the entry "Femme," characterizes women as being instinctually given to conversation.[9] Jules Barbey d'Aurevilly in *Les Bas-bleus* (1878), a vitriolic tract against women writers, transforms the classical and medieval topos of the garrulous wife into the woman who writes too easily and too much: "Ah! quand les femmes écrivent, c'est comme quand elles parlent! Elles ont la faculté inondante; et comme l'eau, elles sont incompréhensibles" ("Ah! when women write, it is like when they speak! They have the ability to inundate; and like water, they are incomprehensible"). P.-J. Proudhon, whose *De la Justice dans la Révolution et dans l'Eglise* (1858) contains an enormous pseudoscientific and legal justification for the political disenfranchisement of women, attributes what he judges to be a certain decadence in the arts to female loquacity, which he calls "literary nymphomania" ("une espèce de nymphomanie littéraire"). This is a theme to which we shall return in chapter 2.[10] Cesare Lombroso, whose *La Femme criminelle et la prostituée* had a tremendous influence at the end of the nineteenth century, roots the belief that women naturally talk more than men in his own version of impressionistic biologism. He makes the claim, for example, that science proves that female dogs bark more than the male of the species, that young girls are more precocious in their speech than boys, and that old women continue to speak later in life than old men. Lombroso offers a series of proverbs as abundant as the words of the garrulous women he denounces in order to back up the wisdom of science with that of popular belief. His presentation of folk sayings from practically every region of Italy, France, and even China resembles nothing so much as Sganarelle's list of the women whom Don Juan has seduced: two from Tuscany ("Fleuve, gouttière et femme parleuse chassent l'homme de sa maison," "Trois femmes parleuse chassent l'homme de sa maison"); one from Venice ("Deux femmes et une oie font une foire"); three from Sicily ("Discours de femme et cris de perroquet," "Deux femmes et une poule font un marché," "Trois femmes font une foire"); one from Naples ("Une femme et un perroquet révolutionnent Naples"); one from Umbria ("Sept femmes et une pie, c'est une foire complète"); one from Bologna ("Trois femmes et un chat c'est un marché complet"); one from Milan ("Deux femmes et une oie font un marché"); one from France ("Deux femmes font un plaid, trois un grand caquet, quatre un marché complet"); and one supposedly from China ("La langue est l'épée des femmes qu'elles ne laissent jamais rouiller").[11]

Woman as Riot

According to the medieval topos of talkative women, which is no doubt motivated by the desire to silence them, wives are portrayed as perpetual speech with respect to which no position of innocence is possible. Woman is conceived as an overdetermined being with respect to which man is always at fault. If she is poor, one must nourish, clothe, and shoe her: "Et qui veust povre fame prendre, / a norrir la l'esteut entendre / et a vestir et a chaucier" (*Rose,* vv. 8549–51). But if she is rich, she is uncontrollable:[12]

et s'il tant se cuide essaucier	*And if one thinks he can escape by taking*
qu'il la prengne riche forment,	*a rich one, he will suffer great torment*
au soffrir la ra grant torment,	*again—so arrogant and prideful will he*
tant la trove orgueilleuse et fiere	*find her, so outrageous and full of*
et seurquidee et bobanciere.	*presumption.* (*Rose,* vv. 8552–56)

If a woman is beautiful, all desire her (*Rose,* vv. 8557–66), and she will in the end be unfaithful; yet if she is not beautiful, she will need all the more to please and, again, will eventually betray: "Maintes neïs par eus se baillent, / quant li requereür defaillent" ("Many will give themselves willingly when suitors lack," vv. 8629–30). If she is reasonable, she is subject to seduction ("Penelope neïz prendroit / qui bien a lui prendre entendroit; / si n'ot il meilleur fame en Grece" ["One could take Penelope herself, and there was no better woman in Greece," vv. 8575–77]); yet if she is irrational, she becomes the victim, like Lucretia, of madness and suicide (v. 8578).

Nor is such a view restricted to the Romance vernacular. The original source is, again, Jerome: "If a woman be fair she soon finds lovers; if she be ugly, it is easy to be wanton. It is difficult to guard what many long for. It is annoying to have what no one thinks worth possessing." Isidore of Seville proffers the same motif in the seventh century. John of Salisbury repeats it almost verbatim in the twelfth: "A beautiful woman is quick to inspire love; an ugly one's passions are easily stirred. What many love is hard to protect; what no one desires to have is a humility to possess."[13] Yet even possession is no guarantee against the agony of overdetermination, for marriage is conceived as a constant struggle for mastery, over who possesses what. "If you entrust your whole establishment to her," John warns, "you are reduced to a state of servitude; if you reserve some department for your personal direction, she thinks you lack confidence in her. . . . If you admit beldames, goldsmiths, soothsayers, tradesmen in jewels and silks, her chastity is imperiled; if you shut the door on them there is your unjust suspicion. After all, what does a strict guard avail, as a lewd wife cannot be watched and a chaste one does not have to be?"[14] Chaucer echoes the motif in the Wife of Bath's reproach of all such reproaches: "Thou seist to me it is a greet meschief / To wedde a povre womman, for costage; / And if that she be rich, of heigh parage, / Thanne seistow that it is a tormentrie / To soffre hire pride and hire malencolie."[15] Woman by definition finds herself in a position of constant overdetermination, or movement. She is, as Jean contends, full of "contenz et . . . riotes"; and also, as Jehan Le Fèvre, author of the fourteenth-century translation of the *Lamentations de Matheolus,* adds, of "tençon rioteuse."[16]

Woman as riot is a topos in medieval literature and has a special sense in Old French. The word itself, meaning chaos or upset, also refers to a kind of poetic discourse belonging to the rich tradition of nonsense poetry—the *fatras, fatrasie, dervie, sotie,* and *farce*—as well as to the more specific type known as the *Riote del monde,* of which one example is the prose *Dit de l'herberie* and another the fabliau entitled "La Rencontre du roi d'Angleterre et du jongleur d'Ely." This last, placed in the context of the *molestiae nuptiarum,* enlarges somewhat the terms of the analogy between woman as abundant speech and her portrayal as overdetermined. For that which is characteristic of the female in the medieval learned conception of gender, as well as in popular belief, is transformed in the comic debate between king and jongleur into a conundrum involving the inadequacy of words to their referents, or of the signifier to the signified. After a series of nonsensical parries capped by the poet's reminder that "one often hears a fool speak sanely, and the wise man is the one who speaks wisely,"[17] the crafty jongleur—in anticipation of the fool of Renaissance drama—seeks to teach the king a lesson about language in general:

Et tot vus mostroi par ensample	*And I will show you by examples that are*
Qu'est si large et si aunple	*so general and compelling and so full of*
Et si pleyn de resoun,	*reason that one cannot fail to agree. If*
Que um ne dira si bien noun.	*you are a simple and wise man, you are*
Si vus estez simple et sage	*taken for a rogue;. . . . If you like*
houm,	*women and speak often with them,*
Vus estes tenuz un feloun;. . . .	*frequent them, and praise and honor*
Et si vus les femmes amez,	*them, . . . someone will say: "Look at*
Et ou eux sovent parlez	*that evil pimp who knows his work and*

Et lowés ou honorez . . .
Donques dirra ascun pautener:
"Veiez cesti mavois holer,
Come il siet son mestier
De son affere bien mostrer".
Si vus ne les volez regarder
Ne volenters ou eux parler,
Si averount mensounge trové
Que vus estes descoillé! . . .

shows it." If you do not look at them or
willingly talk with them, they will find
the lie to prove that you are
castrated! . . . (Recueil, vol. 2, 249)

Jean de Meun's vision of women as overdetermined is thus complicated by the fabliau's positing of the problem of overdetermination in terms of subjective vision and, more precisely, of the prejudicial subjectivity of all speech acts where relations between the genders are concerned. There is, the anonymous poet asserts, no possibility of an objective regard upon the opposite sex and, therefore, no innocent place of speech. The mere fact of speaking to women makes one a pimp; a refusal to speak or even to look is the sign of a eunuch.

Thus, what began in our initial example as women's fickleness translates into the impossibility of a husband's ever replying adequately to the abundance of his wife's words, which are motivated by what is imagined to be the overdetermined nature of the feminine. Again, the source is Jerome: "Then come curtain-lectures the live-long night: she complains that one lady goes out better dressed than she: that another is looked up to by all: 'I am a poor despised nobody at the ladies' assemblies.' 'Why did you ogle that creature next door?' 'Why were you talking to the maid?' 'What did you bring from the market?' 'I am not allowed to have a single friend, or companion'." Yet none of the medieval misogynists is innocent where such a view is concerned, least of all Pope Innocent himself, who seeks to demonstrate not only that a married woman is the source of anxiety through her jealousy of others, but that no reply to her garrulous gossiping will ever be sufficient: "'This woman,' she says, 'goes out better dressed, that one is honored by everybody; but poor little me, I'm the only one in the whole group of women that they scorn— they all look down their noses at me.' She wants all his attention and all his praise; if he praises another she takes it as humiliation. He must like everything she likes, hate everything she spurns. She wants to master, and will not be mastered. She will not be a servant, *she* must be in charge. She must have a finger in everything."[18]

This changes somewhat our paradigm, since the assumed inadequacy of

women, expressed as an ever present overdetermination, becomes indissociable from the inadequacy of words; or, as the anonymous author of *La
Ruihote del monde* suggests, of speech in general:

S'il se taist, il ne set parler;	*If a man is quiet, he is accused of not*
S'il parole, vés quel anpallier,	*knowing how to speak; if he speaks, of*
Il ne cese onques de	*being a loudmouth who never shuts*
plaidier. . . .	*up. . . . If he sings well, he is taken for a*
S'il cante bien c'est un	*jongleur; and if he uses nice phrases, for a*
jongleres;	*trouvère.*[19]
S'il dist biaus dis, c'est uns	
trouveres.	

The riotousness of woman is, in the medieval thinking of the question, linked
to that of speech, indeed, seems to be a condition of poetry itself. And if the
reproach against the wife is that she is a bundle of verbal abuse (*contenz, riotes,
reprouches, requestes, plaintes*), such annoyances make her at least the fellow-
traveler of the poet. Because of the inadequacies of language that she is imagined to embody, she is in some fundamental sense always already placed in the
role of a deceiver, trickster, jongleur. Here the story of the king's attempt to
buy the poet's horse and the image of the horse sale are central, and indeed
crop up often in the context of the *molestiae nuptiarum:*

"Vendras tu ton roncyn à moy?	*Will you sell me your horse?—Yes, more*
—Sire, plus volenters que ne le	*willingly than I would give it.—For how*
dorroy.	*much will you sell it?—For as much as*
—Pur combien le vendras tu?	*you will give me.—And for how much*
—Pur taunt com il serra vendu.	*will I have it?—For as much as I shall*
—Et pur combien le vendras?	*receive.* (*Recueil*, vol. 2, 244)
—Pur taunt come tu me dorras.	
—Et pur combien le averoi?	
—Pur taunt comme je	
recevroy."	

A wife, as deceiver, is conceived to be like a horse that one cannot inspect
before the sale; and, like language, she is imagined, as Jean de Meun implies,
to be a cover which hides "that she might not displease before being wed."[20]
Chaucer, echoing Jerome, concurs: "Thou seist that oxen, asses, hors, and
houndes, / They been assayed at diverse stoundes; . . . But folk of wyves
maken noon assay, / Til they be wedded. . . ."[21] Nor, as Innocent III con-

tends, is it possible to separate the motif of horse trading from that of overdetermination. "There are three things," Innocent writes, "which keep a man from staying home: smoke, a leaky roof, and a shrewish wife. . . . If she be beautiful, men readily go after her; if she be ugly, she goes as readily after them. It is hard to keep what many want, and annoying to have what no one cares about. . . . When you buy a horse, an ass, an ox, a dog, clothes and a bed, even a cup and a pitcher, you first get a chance to look them over. But no one displays a bride, lest she displease before the marriage."[22]

Here the assumption is, of course, that woman is the equivalent of the deception of which language is capable, a prejudice so deeply rooted in the medieval discourse on gender that it often even passes unnoticed. The morals tacked on to the end of many fabliaux, and even the *Fables* of Marie de France, attest to the naturalized, almost reflexive, status of the topos, which is also written all over the *Quinze joies de mariage* as well as the *Roman de la rose*. "But there is no man in this country who is so smart and who can remain so alert that he cannot be tricked by a woman," concludes the anonymous author of the fabliau "La Saineresse."[23] "It has often happened this way: many a woman has advised her husband so that it comes back to dishonor him; many women suggest doing something that is disadvantageous to others," writes Marie de France.[24] A husband "will be served with lies and will graze upon them," echoes the author of *Les Quinze joies de Mariage.*[25]

The thirteenth-century subgenre of short poems devoted exclusively to the question of the virtues and vices of women—such as "Le Sort des Dames," "Li Epystles des femes," "L'Evangile as fames," "Le Blastange des fames," "Le Blasme des fames"—covers the repetitive range of recrimination and ironical defense against the charge of verbal falseness. One such example, "De Dame Guile," contains, in fact, a "reverse" or "negative" blason of the woman—everywoman—which equates her body parts with falseness and deceit: "I will begin with the head: she wears a braid of foolish pride and a plait of false seduction. She wears a hat of cowardice, and her hair-do of trickery is interwoven with deceit. Her locks are of melancholy. And the dress she wears is not of silk or of beaten gold, but of false envy bordered with fakery which does not permit honesty."[26] "De la Femme et de la pye" as well shows how culturally ingrained some of the proverbs and comparisons of the current era really are: "With the chatter of a magpie one is led to the deceptiveness of a fox or a cat; with words a woman drives many a man crazy and masters him completely."[27]

Finally, a corollary of the topos of the talkative female, the woman as
liar, occupies pride of place within the often confused mixture of supposedly
scientific principle and the folklore of gender that resurfaces in the discourse
of misogyny of the past century. It is not only written all over the novel, but
also permeates philosophical and sociological literature. Schopenhauer links
womanly dissimulation to natural selection. "As the weaker sex," he asserts,
"they are driven to rely not on force but on cunning: hence their instinctive
subtlety and their irradicable tendency to tell lies."[28] So too, Schopenhauer's
spiritual successor Nietzsche asks, "What is truth to woman? From the beginning, nothing has been more alien, repugnant, and hostile to woman than
truth—her great art is the lie, her highest concern is mere appearance and
beauty. Let us men confess it: we honor and love precisely *this* art and *this*
instinct in woman." Cesare Lombroso holds that there is no need to demonstrate that lying is "habitual, physiological" in women; rather, physiology is
"consecrated by popular belief," the noted criminologist maintains.[29] "Lying
is instinctive," rooted in woman's arrested ("atavistic") development and in
her need to hide the fact of menstruation: "It is well known that during her
period a woman is more given to lying, to inventing insults and fantastic
tales."[30] The association of woman with the seductions both of speech and of
the flesh is, of course, as ancient as Genesis itself, and any attempt to deal with
it cannot avoid coming to grips with the Creation story.

Genesis and the Yahwist Version of Creation

One of the great facts of cultural amnesia, which has only recently begun to
creep back into memory, is that the Bible contains not one but two stories of
Creation. The first (Genesis 1:27), known as the "priestly" version, suggests—to the extent possible, and anything is possible in the mind of God,
Augustine reminds us,—the simultaneous creation of man and woman, undifferentiated with respect to their humanness, and whose equality is attested
by a common designation. Both sexes are subsumed under the singular term
homo, and the relation between the terms that distinguish them, the attributes
of gender, come as close as language can to a referential and syntactic equivalence through the two adjectives modifying the same pronoun: "Et creavit
Deus hominem ad imaginem suam: ad imaginem Dei creavit illum, masculum
et feminam creavit eos" ("And God created man in his image; in the image of
God he created him, masculine and feminine he created them").[31] The sup-
pression of the story of the simultaneous creation of man and woman has far-

reaching implications for the history of sexuality in the West. Who knows? If the spirit of this "lost" version of Creation had prevailed, the history of the relation between the genders, beginning for example with the Fall, might have been otherwise. Yet the priestly Genesis has been all but forgotten except for recent attempts among feminist biblical scholars to apply the force of what is seen as an original egalitarian intent. That it has not endured is itself the story as well as the effect of a textual repression indissociable from the story of the sexual repression contained in the version that dominates.[32] For despite the fact that the priestly Genesis, which confirms the simultaneous coming into being of the sexes and assumes them to be equal, comes *before* the more sexist account of their difference, it is the so-called Yahwist account of Creation (Genesis 2:7) that, culturally at least, was most readily appropriated in the patristic and medieval period:

> And the Lord God formed man of the slime of the earth, and breathed into his face the breath of life; and man became a living soul. . . .
> And the Lord God said: It is not good for man to be alone; let us make him a help like unto himself.
> And the Lord God having formed out of the ground all the beasts of the earth, and all the fowls of the air, brought them to Adam to see what he would call them: for whatsoever Adam called a living creature the same is its name. And Adam called all the beasts by their names, and all the fowls of the air, and all the cattle of the field: but for Adam there was not found a helper like himself. Then the Lord God cast a deep sleep upon Adam: and when he was fast asleep, he took one of his ribs, and filled up flesh for it. And the Lord God built the rib which he took from Adam into a woman: and brought her to Adam. And Adam said: "This now is bone of my bones and flesh of my flesh; she shall be called woman, because she was taken out of man." (Genesis 2:7, 18–23)

According to the Yahwist Genesis, not only is the creation of the genders an *ad seriatim* process, but that process itself is dependent upon both the association of sexual difference with an original eponymic moment—the naming of things—and the derivational relation of the designations of gender. In the Yahwist account the creation of woman is linked to a founding linguistic act. Adam is said to be the first to speak, the namer of things; and woman, or the necessity of woman, her cause, seems to arise from the imposition of names.[33] The designation of things, a primal instance of man's exertion of power over them, and the creation of woman are coterminous. Further, according to this second version of the creation of the genders, woman is by definition a deriva-tion of man who, as the direct creation of God, remains both chronologically antecedent and ontologically prior. Medieval commentators—Philo Judaeus, Chrysostom, Jerome, Augustine—focus upon the Yahwist Creation, and they understand the sequential coming into being of the genders in a highly hierarchized way. Such an interpretation constitutes the founding instance of the "phallogocentric" logic that has dominated Western thought on gender ever since. That is, in the phrase of Mary Nyquist, "when it comes to paired or coupled items, that which is temporally later is also, frequently, regarded as being secondary in the sense of derivative or inferior." Or, according to Mar-garet Miles, "the 'order of creation'—man first, woman second—was understood to reflect cosmic order and to stipulate social order."[34]

The Yahwist account of Creation conceives woman, who comes from man, to be secondary, a supplement, or, in the Pauline prescription, "man the image of God, woman the image of man" (1 Corinthians 11:7–8).[35] And just as words are assumed to be the supplements of things, which are brought nameless to Adam, so woman is inferred as the supplement to, the "helper of," man. "It is not good that *any* man should be alone," writes Philo Judaeus in the first century. "For there are *two* races of men, the one made after the (Di-vine) Image, and the one moulded out of the earth. . . . With the second man a helper is associated. To begin with, the helper is a created one, for it says 'Let us make a helper for him'; and in the next place, is subsequent to him who is to be helped, for He had formed the mind before and is about to form its helper." Or John Chrysostom (A.D. 345–407): "Formed first, man has the right to greater honor. Saint Paul marks this superiority when he says: 'the man has not been created for woman but the woman for the man'" (1 Corinthians 11:9). Gratian, nearly eight hundred years later, shows how easily chronology can be converted into logic: "It is not for nothing that woman was created, not from the same matter as that of which Adam was created, but from Adam's rib. . . . It is because God did not create in the beginning a man and a woman, nor two men, nor two women; but first man, and then woman from him. . . . It is natural that women serve men, as sons their parents, because it is just that the inferior being serve the superior one."[36]

Thus the imposition of names and the creation of woman are not only simultaneous but analogous gestures implicated in each other, their mutual implication translated even in the concreteness of the creational language (Genesis 2:23), "hoc nunc os ex ossibus meis, et caro de carne mea," and in the play of the name itself: "Haec vocabitur virago, quoniam de viro sumpta est"

("This now is bone of my bones and flesh of my flesh; she shall be called woman because she was taken out of man"). Medieval exegetes, who were acutely
aware of the derivational quality of the words for gender, and who therefore
used it to substantiate the derivational relation of the genders, made much of
the Hebrew *isha* from *ish* and the Latin *virago* from *vir* (just as Milton will
have it that "woman is her name, of man / Extracted").[37] Isidore of Seville
claims that the word for man, *vir*, is a function of his superior force, while the
word for wife, *mulier*, derives from her greater softness.[38] Such deadly serious
wordplay continues after—is even used to substantiate—the Fall. "Then,
too, we are all born weeping to express the misery of our nature," Innocent III
writes. "It is observed that the boy cries 'Ah' just after birth, the girl cries 'E'.
Whence the common verse: 'They are crying 'E' or 'Ah,' / All of them born of
E-va.' For what is the name 'Eva,' when examined carefully, but *Eu!* plus *Ah!*
—these words being interjections of sorrow or great pain. For this reason,
before the Fall the female was called 'wo-man' ('made from man'), but after
the Fall she deserved to be called 'Eva'. . . ."[39]

Adam's chronological priority implies a whole set of relations that strike
to the heart not only of medieval sign theory but also of questions of ontology
that make it apparent that the Fall, commonly conceived to be the originary
moment—the cause and justification—of medieval antifeminism, is merely a
fulfillment or logical conclusion of what is implicit in the Creation of Adam
and then Eve. For the woman of the Yahwist version, conceived from the beginning as secondary, derivative, supervenient, and supplemental, assumes,
within the founding articulation of gender of the first centuries of Christianity, the burden of all that is inferior, debased, scandalous, and perverse.

Adam, first of all, has what medieval philosophers called substance. His
nature is essential; he is imagined to possess Being—Existence. "All good is
from God," Augustine affirms, "hence there is no natural existence which is
not from God."[40] Eve, on the other hand, is imagined to come into being as a
part of a body more sufficient to itself because created directly by God and to
whose wholeness she, as part, can only aspire. Thus, as the by-product of a
part of the essential, she from the outset partakes of the accidental, associated
with a multiplicity of modes of degradation implicit to her coming into being
as becoming.

If Adam exists fully and Eve only partially, it is because he participates in
what is imaged to be an original unity of being, while she is the offshoot of
division and difference. This association translates even into what might be
thought of as a medieval metaphysics of number, according to which, under

the Platonic and Pythagorean schema, all created things express either the principle of self-identity (*principium ejusdem*) or of continuous self-alteration (*principium alterius*). The first is associated with unity, the monad; the second with multiplicity, dyadic structures. Also they are specifically gendered, the monad being male, the dyad female. "It must be said," we read in a fragment from Eudorus, "that the Pythagoreans postulated on the highest level the One as a First Principle, and then on a secondary level two principles of existent things, the One and the nature opposed to this. . . . One of them is called by them ordered, limited, knowable, male, odd, right, and light; the one opposed to this is called disordered, unlimited, unknowable, female, left, even, and darkness."[41] Of the two principles, "one expresses stability, the other endless variation," writes Boethius. "Here is change and alteration, there the force of fixity. Here, well determined solidity, there the fragmentation of infinite multiplicity."[42] The oneness that Adam once enjoyed, the uniqueness of singularity, is indistinguishable from the oneness that is the founding principle and guarantor of grammar, geometry, philosophy, and implicitly of theology, since God is defined as the nature of one, that which is universal and eternal. The word *universe* comes from *unus*, Augustine maintains in *De ordine,* and "it is only when the soul is unified that it understands the beauty of the world." Unity, another word for Being, is synonymous with the goal of philosophy or with truth. "Philosophy as a discipline itself already contains this order of knowledge, and it need not discover more than the nature of one, but in a much more profound and divine sense."[43] "Unity, moreover," writes Tertullian, "is everything which is once for all." And according to Anselm of Canterbury, only the One is necessary, and therefore worthy of love.[44]

Here we behold one of the great topoi of gender in the West at least since Augustine, according to which man is undivided, asexual, pure spirit, while woman remains a divided being whose body does not reflect the reality of the soul. With this consequence: that if man remains fully human because he is the image of God while woman is human only in part, the specifically human comes to signify, is elided to, the side of the masculine. Woman is conceived to be human only in that part of her which is the soul, and which, as we shall see, makes her a man (chapter 4). "This image of God," writes Gratian, "is in the man (in the male sex), unique created being, source of all other human beings, having received from God the power to govern in his stead, because he is the image of a unique God."[45] The Yahwist version of the Creation story serves, of course, as the basis of what is known as the "household code" of early Christianity, to which we shall also return. Let it suffice for the present to insist simply on how deeply this distinction between the genders, by which man is conceived as unity and woman as difference, is ingrained in the medieval West—so deeply, in fact, that even women internalize it. "For woman is weak, and looks to man that she may gain strength from him," writes Hildegard of Bingen, "as the moon receives its strength from the sun; wherefore is she subject to the man, and ought always to be prepared to serve him."[46]

This is another way of saying that Adam possesses form and is the equivalent of an Idea, for whatever has unity and existence also has form. "All existing things would cease to be if form were taken from them, the unchangeable form by which all unstable things exist and fulfill their functions in the realm of number," asserts Augustine in a formula that appears almost everywhere.[47] That is, man is form or mind, and woman, degraded image of his second nature, is relegated to the realm of matter.[48] A love of the One and a scorn of multiplicity translates, in other words, into a privileging of form and a devaluation of the corporeal that is specifically gendered.[49] Put simply, man is associated throughout the period in question with spirit or soul formed directly by God, partaking of his divinity, while woman is assumed to partake of the body, fleshly incarnation being by definition the sign of humanity's fallen condition. Isidore of Seville claims that the word *femina* comes from the female femur, which differs from that of the male, despite the fact that some reckon that the Greek etymology derives from "the force of fire" since the female of the species, whether woman or animal, desires more strongly than the male.[50]

Thus in the misogynistic thinking of the Middle Ages there can be no distinction between the theological and the sexual. Woman is a limit case of man, and as in Platonic thought, she remains bound by the material, by flesh and lust.[51] "For the groundwork of this corporeal beauty," Chrysostom writes, "is nothing else but phlegm, and blood, and humor, and bile, and the fluid of masticated food."[52] "Man was formed of dust, slime, and ashes; what is even more vile, of the filthiest seed," Innocent III echoes in what is a cliché of the age. "He was conceived from the itch of the flesh, in the heat of passion and the stench of lust, and worse yet, with the stain of sin."[53]

Though mankind in general is from such a perspective condemned, woman comes to embody the material corruption associated with the flesh and in which the theological and the gynecological blend. If all humans participate by definition and from the beginning in the sinfulness of the corporeal, woman is the efficient cause of such iniquity even before birth.[54]

The association of woman with the material, or with incarnation itself, is an idea that has a long heritage and is still very much with us. Naomi Schor has traced the ways in which the link of man to the realm of the Universal and of woman to the particular is rendered, within the philosophical misogyny of the nineteenth century, into an affiliation of man with abstraction, and thus a capacity for philosophy, and of woman with details, and thus a natural disposition toward the accessory, the ornamental, and style.[55] "To the extent that man relates to the species and to general things, woman remains attached to the individual thing and fixated upon particular objects," wrote J. J. Virey in a discourse that won the prize of the Société des Sciences, Lettres et Arts de Mâcon in 1809.[56] Hegel repeats virtually the same topos in *The Philosophy of Right:* "Women are capable of education, but they are not made for activities which demand a universal faculty such as the more advanced sciences, philosophy and certain forms of artistic production. Women may have happy ideas, taste and elegance but they cannot attain to the ideal."[57] Proudhon, who adopts the Aristotelian concept of conception whereby the man contributes the form and the woman the matter in the process of generation, claims that men possess the "germe" that is the equivalent of genius. Children, eunuchs, and women are, however, deprived of ideas: "She does not generalize at all, does not synthesize. Her mind is anti-metaphysical. . . . Woman does not philosophize."[58] That sorcerer's apprentice Michelet, in attempting explicitly to distance himself from Proudhon, seems merely to come at the same prejudice from a different point of view in asserting that woman "is productive by her influence upon man, both in the ideal and in the real. But her thought seldom attains a strong reality; and that is why she has created so little."[59] For Lombroso woman's affinity for detail and her supposed inability to philosophize are a function of an arrested evolutionary development: "One finds another proof of the inferiority of the feminine mind in its inferior power of abstraction and in its great preciosity. The intelligence of woman is seen to be defective where the highest form of mental evolution is concerned, the faculty of synthesis and of abstraction; she excels, in contrast, through subtlety of analysis and in the clear perception of details." The more one pushes a woman toward abstraction, he maintains, the more prone she becomes to neurosis. Then too, the assumption that woman is less naturally disposed to philosophy implies that she is less adapted to writing. We have already seen that for a mainstream misogynist like Lombroso women are associated with abundant orality, which further excludes writing because "their graphic centers are less well developed." If women must write, they are enjoined to write letters, conceived as the written form of conversation, which "conforms to their character and, once again, satisfies their need for speech."[60]

The Realm of the Senses

The patristic articulation of gender assumes a relationship of male to female built upon the analogy of the world of intelligence to that of the senses. Such an idea has, of course, deep roots in Platonic tradition. Yet it was Philo Judaeus (c. 20 B.C.–c. A.D. 50) who, under the influence of models of interpretation of Alexandrian Middle Platonism of the first century B.C., transformed the Genesis story into an "allegory of the soul in which man is mind and woman sense perception."[61] Philo, recalling the Creation of Eve, recasts the philogenetic argument concerning her supervenient status into an ontological claim for the superiority of mind over body, and this claim is analogous to the superiority of man over woman. "To begin with, the helper is a created one, for it says, 'Let us make a helper for him'; and in the next place, is subsequent to him who is to be helped, for He had formed the mind before and is about to form its helper. In these particulars again, while using the terms outward nature, he is conveying a deeper meaning. For sense and the passions are helpers of the soul and come after the soul."[62]

The status of woman is analogous to that of the senses within the cognitive realm. Man as mind and woman as sensory perception are mutually exclusive: "it is when the mind (Adam) has gone to sleep that perception begins, for conversely when the mind wakes up perception is quenched." Woman, formed of flesh from the rib, remains bound by the corporeal. "'He built it to be a woman, (Gen. ii, 22)'," Philo continues, "proving by this that the most proper and exact name for sense-perception is 'woman'."[63]

The Philonian distinction, which may resonate with the Old Testament relation of Abraham to Sarah or of Lot to his wife, is indeed another version or aspect of the contrast between form and matter, activity and passivity, soul and flesh, which are gendered male and female from the beginning. Man is associated with intelligence—*mens, ratio,* the rational soul—and woman, with *sensus,* the body, the animal faculties, appetite. According to Philo, she is allied with the serpent, which symbolizes pleasure. Origen follows the Philonian lead, as do Gregory of Nyssa, Ambrose, Augustine, and, later, John Scotus, Hugh of Saint-Victor, Gilbert of Poitiers, and Saint Bernard. For all of these men, the male-female dualism becomes assimilated into a distinction between the mind and the senses according to which woman, in the phrase of Rosemary Ruether, assumes the burden of "carnality in the disorder of sin."[64] Carolyn Bynum too articulates this distinction succinctly in a series of oppositions that capture much of the material under discussion: "*Male* and *female* were contrasted and asymmetrically valued as intellect/body, active/passive, rational/irrational, reason/emotion, self-control/lust, judgment/mercy, and order/disorder."[65]

The mind/senses distinction is, of course, the foundation of a conjugal typology, according to which woman, the "body" of man, is necessarily subordinate to him as the passions are subject to the intellect. Hence the repeated invocation—the basis of the "household code"—for the man to rule the woman as reason controls the bodily appetites.[66] Already in Ephesians 5:21 Paul enjoins wives to "submit yourselves unto your own husbands, as unto the Lord. For the husband is the head of the wife, even as Christ is the head of the church; and he is the saviour of the body." Augustine too maintains in the *De Genesi contra Manichaeos* that "the subjugation of woman is in the order of things; she must be dominated and governed by man just as the soul should regulate the body and virile reason should dominate the animal part of the being. If a woman dominates man, and the animal part dominates reason, the house is turned upside down."[67] And Aquinas, discussing two kinds of subjection, distinguishes between slavery, "in which the ruler manages the subject for his own advantage," and "domestic or civil" subjection, "in which the ruler manages his subjects for *their* advantage and benefit. . . . Such is the subjection in which woman is by nature subordinate to man because the power of rational discernment is by nature stronger in man."[68]

Here we touch upon one of the key internalized anxieties underlying the projection of the faculty of appetite upon the woman and the corresponding injunction to containment—the fear attached to the uncontrollability of the body, of its members and its drives. The distrust of woman in the writings of the early church fathers is at least partially attributable to a refusal of, a barrier against, the contumacious presence of the body. Page Du Bois maintains that "much of the misogynist's discourse centers on women's bodies" and that this "fear of women's corporeality, this intense misogyny and the witch-hunting contemporaneous with it, lie behind the presence of Renaissance Eves, Circes, and Didos in epic poetry."[69] I would differ with Du Bois, however, to the extent of diminishing, at least for the medieval period, the distinction between the notion of woman and of woman's body, since for the fathers they were practically synonymous. The fear of femininity, identified with the fac-

the woman's part

ulties of cognition and expression that could bring such a fear to consciousness, is not only a generalized, abstract fear of sensuality, but a mistrust of the
senses—a fear of the woman as body, the body as woman. In other words, it is
the fear of the woman in every man's body. For if woman as sensitive soul is
allied with sensuality, that is, with the possibility of engendering concupiscence, then even to perceive her, as Chrysostom claims, menaces to deprive
the soul of reason:

> Hence how often do we, from beholding a woman, suffer a thousand
> evils; returning home, and entertaining an inordinate desire, and
> experiencing anguish for many days; yet nevertheless, we are not made
> discreet; but when we have scarcely cured one wound, we again fall into
> the same mischief, and are caught by the same means; and for the sake of
> the brief pleasure of a glance, we sustain a kind of lengthened and
> continual torment. . . . The beauty of woman is the greatest snare. Or
> rather, not the beauty of woman, but unchastened gazing![70]

The disenfranchising alliance of woman with the senses as opposed to mind,
with the body as opposed to the soul, has far-reaching implications within the
hierarchized ontological oppositions that dominate medieval thought,
culture, and society. So deep and pervasive, in fact, is this distinction that it
finds even an abstract, structural expression in what is for the Middle Ages the
analogy of analogies, that of the letter versus the spirit. This conception provides not only a category of thought, but something on the order of a mental
structure, a mode of interpretation according to which other categories can
be understood. The contrast between the letter—on the side of the body, the
senses, the temporal, and the worldly—as opposed to the spirit, which is on
the side of mind, form, and divinity, is in the early centuries of Christianity a
means of understanding the world and of constituting community. It functions to create an opposition between female and male that relegates the
feminine, and ultimately woman, to the inferior side, and it also works as the
ideological sign of identity of the Christian: to be on the side of the spirit is to
understand without the aid of the senses, to know without perceiving, that is,
without the participation of the body, to always already have known.[71] To
seek to know through the senses, however, is to remain on the side of the
letter, the law, and ultimately the non-Christians, the pagans and Jews. This
explains, I think, the association throughout the Middle Ages as well as much
later between the repression of heresy and antifeminism.[72] Those who don't
believe, who remain on the side of the letter, the body, and the senses, are

perceived to be women, and women, those who do not give up the feminized principle of the body, tied to the letter of the law, are, finally, heretics.

The "genderized" opposition of the letter to the spirit can also be seen to participate in what I have defined elsewhere as a radical privileging of the signified over the signifier in the Christianized Platonism of the West. "One must estimate things signified more than their signs," writes Augustine, "for everything that exists for another is necessarily less noble than that for which it is ordered. . . . One must give words less value than the objects for which we use them."[73] Similarly, one values a thing over its image, and even its mental image over its material embodiment, the "word which we speak in our heart," in Augustine's phrase, over any concrete instance of language in any particular tongue.[74] Under such a paradigm the letter or the word can never be adequate to its object. As in the lesson of the Jongleur d'Ely with which we began, words will never suffice to describe the body, but will always produce a superfluity, which in the thirteenth-century "Sort des Dames," is expressed specifically in terms of the insufficiency of ink and paper to a woman's body:

De ci jusqu'au mont Saint-   *If from here to Mont Saint-Michel were*
  Michiel,   *ink and paper, and all those who go that*
Devenoit enque et parchemin,   *way were to write forever, they could*
Et tuit cil qui vont par chemin   *never capture the shape of your body; the*
Ne finoient jamès d'escrire,   *one who made it was certainly a fine*
La moitié ne porroient dire   *mason.*[75]
De vostre gent cors la façon:
Qui le tailla fu bon maçon.

The privileging of the signified over the signifier may seem like a minor philological point unrelated to the question of gender. Yet one must bear in mind that the question of the sign is, in the period under scrutiny, fundamental to the thinking of all other philosophical and theological issues. The millennium between the early centuries of Christianity and the Renaissance, an era of wide cultural divergence and political fragmentation, is unified perhaps only by the extent to which speculation about the nature of representations was fundamental to speculation about the wider universe. Not only was medieval culture a culture of the Book, its epistemology one of the Word and of words, but also disciplines that today are considered primary were subordinate to the *artes sermocinales*.[76] Further, one of the governing assumptions of the verbal epistemology of the medieval West is the assimilation of the verbal and the social. The orders of language and of society were considered to be connatural. This is a question of more than Cicero's simultaneous foundation of the city and of rhetoric, more than Varro's common origin of speech and the law, more than the patristic association of Hebrew letters and the reception of the law through Moses, more than John of Salisbury's idea of language as the sine qua non of social life, more than Aquinas's notion of language as the expression of man's social nature. Historically and logically related, the order of language and society are ontologically intertwined, as seen in the Platonic theme of man the microcosm of the greater universe, which is itself often represented as a written text (as in Bernard Silvestris, Godfrey of Saint-Victor, Albert the Great, Bonaventure, Aquinas, Jean de Meun).

What this means is:

1. It is impossible to separate the discrediting of the material world and especially the disparagement of signs from the deep medieval distrust of the senses. "Through the five senses, as through open windows, vice has access to the soul," Jerome writes. "The metropolis and citadel of the mind cannot be taken unless the enemy have previously entered by its doors. The soul is distressed by the disorder they produce, and is led captive by sight, hearing, smell, taste, and touch."[77] Nor, once the windows and doors have been opened, is it possible to exclude the pleasures of the senses.

2. Such a mistrust of the senses can only be construed as a mistrust of the feminine. Thus Jerome warns that "if any one delights in the sports of the circus, or the struggles of athletes, the versatility of actors, the figure of women, in splendid jewels, dress, silver and gold, and other things of the kind, the liberty of the soul is lost through the windows of the eyes, and the prophet's words are fulfilled: 'Death is come up into our windows' [Jer. xi. 21]. Again, our sense of hearing is flattered by the tones of various instruments and the modulations of the voice; and whatever enters the ear by the songs of poets and comedians, by the pleasantries and verses of pantomimic actors, weakens the manly fibre of the mind."[78]

3. The analogy established between woman and the letter can be translated into specifically social terms, which necessarily imply a disenfranchising exertion of the power of men over women. It is an easy, almost self-evident, step from, say, the Yahwist version of Creation to the ecclesiastical denial of authority to women within the church. Timothy may be the first, in fact, to make such a move explicit: "Let the woman learn in silence with all subjection. But I suffer not a woman to teach, nor to usurp authority over the man, but to be in silence. For Adam was first formed, then Eve" (1 Timothy 2:11).

But the principle is general and operative even within discursive realms that seem to exclude women altogether. In the sacramental theology elaborated by Augustine, for example, the relation of the signified to its sign is cast as a relation of the speaker to his word that is also given an explicitly familial cast in the relation of Father to Son, who occupies the position of the woman with respect to the man. "Hence, the Father and the Son together are one essence, one greatness, one truth, and one wisdom," writes Augustine. "But the Father and the Son together are not one Word, because they are not together one Son. For as Son expresses a relationship to the Father and is not spoken of in respect to Himself, so the Word, when it is also called the Word, expresses a relationship to Him whose Word it is."[79] The goal of Augustine's theology of the sign, and of history, is precisely a transcendence of the body by a journey through perception and cognition toward the male-defined *intellectio* that he associates with a union of parent and child. This union, which is indistinguishable from the sacrament itself, not only implies a return of the Son to the Father, but represents a convergence of the form of knowledge with its object, a recuperation of the names that are "the images of things."[80] Thus, the paternalized relation between father and son, between the speaker and his word, implies an ontological priority of origin to effect, of engenderer to engendered, which, in philosophy, is expressed as a priority of the genre over its species.

Indeed, within the somewhat rarefied terms of medieval realism, with its elaborate tree of the subsistent categories of the real, this translates into the superiority of the genre over the species it contains—a relation couched, moreover, not only in linguistic terms, for the species can be predicated of its genre though the reverse is not true, but in specifically political terms as well. "Subject, therefore, the *special* is to the *general* (because the general is prior)," writes Tertullian, "and the *succedent* to the *antecedent,* and the *partial* to the *universal:* (each) is implied in the word itself to which it is subject; and is signified in it, because contained in it."[81] Or, where the genders are concerned, the woman represents a species of the genre of man, who literally has engendered her, and to whose substance she merely returns through marriage. "For when two are made into one flesh through the marriage-tie, the 'flesh of flesh and the bone of bones' is called the *woman* of him of whose *substance* she begins to be accounted by being made his *wife.*" Further, even within the realm of the feminine, the wife, according to Tertullian, is a species of woman, wifehood, as it were, yoked to womanhood: "Thus *woman* is not by nature a name of *wife,* but *wife* by condition is a name of *woman.* In fine, *woman*hood is predicable apart from *wife*hood; but *wife*hood apart from *woman*hood is not, because it cannot even exist."[82] We have come a long way from the *molestiae nuptiarum* by entering the arcane realm of the properties and differences that determine what, with respect to truth, can be predicated or said of anything that exists, including man and woman. The predicables are germane, however, to the extent to which the differences between degrees of existence that they confer imply differences of power. The notion of woman as a species of man and of the wife as a species of woman serves ideologically to naturalize the Pauline dictum that "man is the head of woman." It is an easy move from Tertullian's categories of subsistence to the assumed power of husbands over wives, and more generally to the control of men over women: "If 'the man is the head of the *woman*,' of course (he is) of the *virgin* too, from whom comes the *woman* who has married."[83]

EARLY CHRISTIANITY AND THE ESTHETICIZATION OF GENDER

My claim is that we cannot separate the concept of woman as it was formed in the early centuries of Christianity from a metaphysics that abhorred embodiment; and that woman's supervenient nature is, according to such a mode of thought, indistinguishable from the acute suspicion of embodied signs—of representations.[1] As Philo Judaeus maintains, woman's coming into being is synonymous not only with the naming of things, but with a loss—within language—of the literal: "'And God brought a trance upon Adam, and he fell asleep; and He took one of his sides' and what follows (Gen. ii, 21). These words in their literal sense are of the nature of a myth. For how could anyone admit that a woman, or a human being at all, came into existence out of a man's side?"[2] So too does John Chrysostom locate the necessity of interpretation precisely in the creation of woman from Adam's rib:

> Notice the considerateness of Sacred Scriptures in the words employed with our limitations in mind: "God took one of his ribs," the text says. Don't take the words in human fashion; rather interpret the concreteness of the expressions from the viewpoint of human limitations. You see, if he had not used these words, how would we have been able to gain knowledge of these mysteries which defy description? Let us therefore not remain at the level of the words alone, but let us understand everything in a manner proper to God because applied to God. That phrase, "he took," after all, and other such are spoken with our limitations in mind.[3]

The third-century Greek saint, Methodius, deferring to Paul, concurs: "The text in Genesis reads as follows: *And Adam said: This now is bone of my bones, and flesh of my flesh; she shall be called woman, because she was taken out of man* . . . . The Apostle, then, in considering this same passage, does not now, as I have said, want it to be taken literally in a natural sense."[4] The fathers thus identify a loss of literalness, and the consequent necessity of interpretation, with the creation of Eve, or with the appearance of gender difference. The origin of commentary is assimilated to the origin of woman.

Since the creation of woman is synonymous with the creation of metaphor, the relation between Adam and Eve is the relation of the proper to the figural, which implies a derivation, deflection, denaturing, a tropological turning away. The perversity of Eve, as it is imagined in the early centuries of the Christian era, is that of the lateral: as the outgrowth of Adam's flank, his *latus,* she retains the status of *translatio,* of translation, transfer, metaphor, trope. She is side-issue.

How are we to understand this seeming contradiction—the association of woman with both the material and the figural? Is it simply one of the plethora of incoherences and paradoxes that riddle the discourse of misogyny? Can such an apparent contradiction be redeemed in the way, say, that Augustine understood metaphor to work? That is, to point, despite the degraded nature of signs, in the direction of the truth that remains inaccessible to material representations. Indeed, the founding father of medieval sign theory sought in places to remove the Creation from the physicality of embodiment, claiming that when God spoke in Genesis, "these words of God were prior to all vibration of air, prior to all voice of the flesh or of the cloud."[5] He acknowledges too that where biblical exegesis is concerned, metaphor can function to explain the seeming illogicalities of a literal reading.[6] This would mean that Eve, as a figure of the figural, stands for the division of unity of which metaphor itself, in the terms that Augustine understood it, is an attempt at recuperation. And yet, neither the assimilation of the paradox nor its resolution recognizes the fact that the question of woman as formulated in the early centuries of Christianity implies the same kind of contradiction that we identified earlier in terms of overdetermination, and which is such an integral feature of the articulation of gender in the West. I think it can be shown that the answer lies in the way in which the figural is here understood, which represents another of those slippages of frame which seem to occur whenever such polarities become gendered. That is, the figural is capable of pointing in the direction of truth as long as it remains outside of any specific sexual context; the moment it is elided to the side of the feminine, however, the figural is divested of its capacity to transcend material signs. It slips to the side of mere physicality—the figure as ornament or decoration.

Cosmetic Theology

Marcia Colish has written a brilliant article on the topic of "cosmetic theology," in which she suggests that the early fathers' appropriation of the Stoic (and before that, Cynic) attempt to ally ethics, nature, and reason involved a shift from concern with masculine modes of self-presentation, such as dress and hairstyle, to an obsession with an esthetics of femininity. This move involved the appearance of an entirely "new genre of Christian hortatory literature addressed to women."[7] Thus, one finds among the Stoics, who criticized men and women alike for overconcern with personal appearance, the belief that the true sage remains unshaven. He should not pluck his eyebrows or pubic hair, or do anything that alters the nature of the body for the sake of drawing the attention of women or of other men; on the contrary, the more uninterested he is in appearance, the more detached he is from the world, and therefore the wiser he is—or appears. One also finds a concern with masculine adornment in the Syriac *Disdascalia apostolorum*, where the warning against makeup and style addressed to husbands resembles nothing so much as that which in Christian tradition will be directed toward wives.[8] Then too, gnostic, Platonic, and Manichaean traditions carry a certain disparagement of the physical that implies a distrust of the cosmetic. The pseudepigraphical myths contain here and there an association of woman with decoration.[9] Yet nothing comes close to matching Tertullian's campaign against the relative moral equality of the sexes among the Stoics, or against the belief according to which men and women were equally dangerous agents of seduction. Nothing before this first of the Latin Christian authors (A.D. 155–220) matches the virulence with which he shifts the ethical burden of sexuality toward woman, making her the passive agent—and this by natural condition and not by conscious moral choice—of the seduction of males. As Colish maintains, Tertullian, using biblical, apocryphal, and classical sources, "turned the Stoics inside out." He articulated the link between the derivative nature of the female contained in the Yahwist version of Creation and that of figural representation in a way that has continued to dominate thought on gender well into our own age.[10]

The writers of the first centuries of Christianity—Paul, Clement of Alexandria, Tertullian, John Chrysostom, Cyprian, Novatian, Ambrose, Philo, Jerome—were obsessed by the relation of women to decoration. They were fascinated by veils, jewels, makeup, hairstyle, and hair color—in short, by anything having to do with the cosmetic. Their fascination is of a piece with the patristic devaluation of the material world, which comes to be seen as a mask, a mere cosmetic reproduction.[11] For the second-century apologist, as for no one before him, woman is a creature who above all else and by nature covets ornamentation:[12]

> *You* are the devil's gateway: *you* are the unsealer of that (forbidden) tree: *you* are the first deserter of the divine law: *you* are she who persuaded him whom the devil was not valiant enough to attack. *You* destroyed so easily God's image, man. On account of *your* desert—that is, death— even the Son of God had to die. And do you think about adorning yourself over and above your tunic of skins? Come, now; if from the beginning of the world the Milesians sheared sheep, and the Serians spun trees, and the Tyrians dyed, and the Phrygians embroidered with the needle, and the Babylonians with the loom, and pearls gleamed, and onyx stones flashed; if gold itself also had already issued, with the cupidity (which accompanies it), from the ground; if the mirror too, already had licence to lie so largely, Eve, expelled from paradise, (Eve) already dead, would also have coveted *these* things, I imagine! No more, then, ought she *now* to crave, or be acquainted with (if she desire to live again), what, when she *was* living, she had neither had nor known. Accordingly, these things are all the baggage of woman in her condemned and dead state, instituted as if to swell the pomp of her funeral.[13]

If man's desire for ornament, or for that which is secondary, is analogous to his desire for woman, it is because woman is conceived as ornament.[14] She is, by her secondary nature, associated with artifice and decoration. The mildest version of the paradigm is found in the often repeated licence for men to pray with bare heads while women are enjoined to be veiled—and in its corollary, that woman herself is covering or veil. "But if a woman nourish her hair, it is a glory to her," writes Paul, "for her hair is given to her as a covering" (1 Corinthians 11:15).

One can, of course, seek the historical causes for the Pauline prescription in the effort to instill decorum into Christian worship as opposed to what was perceived as the orgiastic, pneumatic frenzies of the pagan cults. One can see in it the external sign of modesty, which, as an identifying factor, served to unite the early Christian community.[15] And it has even been suggested that the dress code that required women engaged in worship to look "proper" is in fact a sign of liberation.[16] But neither the assessment nor the moralizing of

such causes belies the fact that, according to Tertullian, woman naturally decorates herself and is by nature decoration: "Female habit carries with it a
twofold idea—dress and ornament. By 'dress' we mean what they call 'womanly gracing'; by 'ornament,' what it is suitable should be called 'womanly *dis*-
gracing.' The former is accounted (to consist) in gold, and silver, and gems,
and garments; the latter in care of the hair, and of the skin, and of those parts
of the body which attract the eye. Against the one we lay the charge of ambition, against the other of prostitution."[17] It is tempting to equate such
hostility towards women with a more generalized horror of the flesh. And
this is certainly not lacking here. "And so we are trained by God for the purpose of chastising, and (so to say) emasculating, the world," Tertullian attests.
"We are the circumcision—spiritual and carnal—of all things."[18] Yet it is not
the flesh that Tertullian denounces. On the contrary, there seems to be little
difference between the materialism of the body and of its clothes; moreover,
the draping of the flesh with "dress and ornament" is the equivalent of seduction: "The only edifice which they know how to raise is this silly pride of
women: because they require slow rubbing that they may shine, and artful
underlaying that they may show to advantage, and careful piercing that they
may hang; and (because they) render to gold a mutual assistance in meretricious allurement."[19] To decorate oneself is to be guilty of "meretricious
allurement," since embellishment of the body, or the attempt "to show to advantage," re-creates and is the sign of an original act of pride that is the source
of potential concupiscence. This is why Tertullian is able to move so quickly
and naturally from the idea of dress to a whole range of other associations—
between transvestism and the monstrous, or between the toga and lust, adultery, cannibalism, intemperance, and greed.[20] It is as if each and every act of
clothing an original nakedness of the body, and not the weakness of the flesh,
were a corrupting recapitulation of the Fall entailing all other perversions.
"Just as the serpent deceived Eve," writes Clement of Alexandria, "so, too, the
enticing golden ornament in the shape of a serpent enkindles a mad frenzy in
the hearts of the rest of womankind, leading them to have images made of
lampreys and snakes as decorations."[21]

That which is secondary, artificial, and thus assimilated to woman is considered to participate in a supervenient and extraneous rival Creation that in
the thought of the fathers can only distract man's attention from God's original "plastic skill": "Whatever is born is the work of God," Tertullian
maintains. "Whatever, then, is plastered on (that), is the devil's work. . . . To
superinduce on a divine work Satan's ingenuities, how criminal it is!"[22]

"They are laying hands on God when they strive to remake what He has made, and to transform it, not knowing that everything that comes into existence is the work of God; that whatever is changed, is the work of the devil," Cyprian concurs.[23] The decorative not only constitutes, as in the case of gold, an artificial investment of value, with all that such intention implies by way of potential concupiscence, but is a literal adding to the "weight" of creation. "When a woman interweaves her clothing with gold," Novatian warns, "it's as if she thought it of value to corrupt her vesture. What are stiff metals doing among the delicate threads of the woven fabric? These metals only weigh down drooping shoulders and expose the wantonness of an unhappily proud spirit. Why are women's necks concealed and loaded down with imported stones, whose cost, exclusive of jeweler's fee, exceeds an entire fortune? Such women do not adorn themselves—they merely make a show of their own vices."[24]

If clothes are at once the sign, the effect, and a cause of the Fall,[25] it is because, as artifice, they are conceived, like woman in the Yahwist Creation, to be secondary, collateral, supplemental. Dress is unnatural since, like all artifice, it seeks to add to or perfect the body of nature or God's creation:

> That which He Himself has not produced is not pleasing to God, unless
> He was *unable* to order sheep to be born with purple and sky-blue
> fleeces! If He was *able,* then plainly He was *unwilling:* what God willed
> not, of course, ought not to be fashioned. Those things, then, are not
> the best by *nature* which are not from God, the *Author* of nature. Thus
> they are understood to be from *the devil,* from *the corrupter* of nature: for
> there is no other whose they *can* be, if they are not God's; because what
> are not God's must necessarily be His rival's.[26]

Women who make up, Clement of Alexandria maintains, insult the Creator "who, in their opinion, has not made them beautiful enough"; their made-up bodies are not more beautiful, but bear the outward signs of inner disease— the marks of adultery comparable to the tattoos that betray the fugitive.[27]

As a re-creation, the artificial implies, Tertullian maintains, a pleasurable surplus that is simply inessential: "Thus (a thing) which, from whatever point you look at it, is in *your* case superfluous, you may justly disdain if you have it not, and neglect it if you have. Let a holy woman, if naturally beautiful, give none so great occasion (for carnal appetite)."[28] Tertullian does not, of course, seek to determine how something can be "naturally beautiful," much less to wrestle with the supervenient status of his own thought upon the superficial.

On the contrary, one of the salient features as well as one of the ironies of such antifeminist discourse is that it often becomes rhetorical or ornamental in direct proportion to its denunciation of woman as ornament.[29] Further, Tertullian's indictment of the artificial not only condemns what we think of as the realm of the esthetic, "adulteration with illegitimate colours," but also extends to any investment of nature with human intention.[30] Here, it must be said, we are carried far beyond the notion of women as deceitful. In essence, all artists, builders, and craftsmen sin, by definition, through their imitation of the natural. "What playhouse constructed by human hands," the third-century Novatian asks, "can be compared to works such as these [works of nature]? Playhouses can be constructed with huge masses of stone, but the mountain crests are higher. The paneled ceilings may glisten with gold, but are no match for the glorious splendor of the stars. Human works lose their wonder for the man who knows that he is a son of God. The man who has admiration for anything other than God loses some of his dignity."[31]

Early patristic thought on gender can be said to be Manichaean not only in its reliance upon radical binary oppositions between good and evil, spirit and matter, but also in its tendency to operate such violent exclusions wherever the fathers focus their attention. Thus even within the realm of nature one finds a constant comparison between iron and gold, both natural products, in which iron takes on the valence of a use-value par excellence, while gold is perverse because its worth has been created. "So true is it that it is not intrinsic worth, but rarity, which constitutes the goodness (of those things): the excessive labour, moreover, of working them with arts introduced by the means of the sinful angels, who were the revealers withal of the material substances themselves, joined with their rarity, excited their costliness, and hence a lust on the part of women to possess (that) costliness."[32] The affinity between gold, the product of excess labor, "the arts," and women constitutes an economic nexus taken as a given; their natures, by definition conceived to be inessential and antinatural, attract each other because they partake in a scandalous excess that offends.[33] "Let us cast away earthly ornaments if we desire heavenly," Tertullian urges. "Love not gold; in which (one substance) are branded all the sins of the people of Israel. . . . But Christians always, and now more than ever, pass their times not in gold but in iron: the stoles of martyrdom are (now) preparing."[34]

The contexts and motivations of the association between women, ornament, and artistry may differ. For Tertullian it represents a problem of sexual ethics; for Ambrose, a privileged instance of the problem of deception; for

Jerome, a weapon against heresy. Nonetheless, the feminization of the esthetic is a topos to be found practically everywhere, so insistently repeated as to absorb the double indignity of sexism and banality.[35] "What madness is here," Ambrose asks, "to change the fashion of nature and seek a painting?"[36] Yea, not even an original painting, but a forgery, one of those palimpsests with which medieval writers were so familiar. Women, the famous teacher of Augustine claims,

> erase that painting by smearing on their complexion a color of material whiteness or by applying an artificial rouge. The result is a work not of beauty, but of ugliness; not of simplicity, but of deceit. It is a temporal creation, a prey to perspiration or to rain. It is a snare and a deception which displeases the person you aim to please, for he realizes that all this is an alien thing and not your own. This is also displeasing to your Creator, who sees His own work obliterated. Tell me, if you were to invite an artist of inferior ability to work over a painting of another of superior talent, would not the latter be grieved to see his own work falsified? Do not displease the artistic creation of God by one of meretricious worth. . . . He commits a serious offense who adulterates the work of God.[37]

Women who make themselves up, Chrysostom asserts, "insult the Creator who evidently did not, in their opinion, make them beautiful enough."[38]

From the estheticizing of the feminine among the early church fathers, which implies always a scandalous dressing of the naked body of nature, a decoration synonymous with the Fall, emanates an entire range of perverse terms associated with "meretricious garbs and garments." In particular, the church fathers move quickly, by association, from sins of imagination, such as vainglory and pride, to the symbolic (artifice, idolatry) and the erotic (allurement, voluptuousness, concupiscence, fornication, adultery), as if representation itself were, always and already, an offense within the givens of the Pauline dictum, "The letter killeth, but the Spirit giveth life." "Know you not that the unjust shall not possess the kingdom of God? Do not err: Neither fornicators nor idolaters nor adulterers," Paul warns, in what is also a leitmotif (1 Corinthians 6:9; see also 10:7–8). "Hence Paul saith," John Chrysostom repeats, "that 'she who liveth in pleasure is dead while she liveth.' Again, to go to the theatres, or to survey the horse-race, or to play at dice, does not seem, to most men, to be an admitted crime; but it introduces into our life an infinite host of miseries. For spending time in the theatres

produces fornication, intemperance, and every kind of impurity. The spec-
tacle of the horse-race also brings about fightings, railings, blows, insults
and lasting enmities. And a passion for dice-playing hath often caused blas-
phemies, injuries, anger, reproaches, and a thousand other things more
fearful still."[39] Clement of Rome, supposedly the disciple of Peter the
Apostle, attempts to list the "thousand other things":

> In those who are truly believers and "in whom the Spirit of Christ
> dwells"—in them "the mind of the flesh" cannot be: which is
> fornication, uncleanness, wantonness; idolatry, sorcery; enmity,
> jealousy, rivalry, wrath, disputes, dissensions, ill-will; drunkenness,
> revelry; buffoonery, foolish talking, boisterous laughter; backbiting,
> insinuations; bitterness, rage; clamour, abuse, insolence of
> speech; malice, inventing of evil, falsehood; talkativeness, babbling;
> threatenings, gnashing of teeth, readiness to accuse, jarring,
> disdainings, blows; perversions *of the right*, laxness *in judgement*;
> haughtiness, arrogance, ostentation, pompousness, *boasting* of family, of
> beauty, of position, of wealth, of an arm of flesh; quarrelsomeness,
> injustice, eagerness for victory; hatred, anger, envy, perfidy, retaliation;
> debauchery, gluttony, "overreaching (which is idolatry)," "the love of
> money (which is the root of all evils);" love of display, vainglory, love of
> rule, assumption, pride (which is called death, and which "God fights
> against"). Every man with whom are these and such like things—every
> such man is of the flesh.[40]

This nexus of ideas suggests that the representation of woman as ornament is an integral part of a broader paradigm, or that her imagined secondariness is equated with that of symbolic activity. The deep mistrust of
the body and of materiality defined by their accessibility to the senses
constitutes, in fact, a commonplace of what we know about the Middle
Ages—something that might be considered a cultural constant alongside,
and indeed allied with, that of the estheticization of gender. "There are
indeed," Augustine writes, "some things which are changeable, but not
visible, as our thoughts, our memories, our wills, and every incorporeal
creature, but nothing is visible that is not at the same time changeable."[41]
The temporary, contingent nature of all matter extends in particular to signs,
which are but the representations of a material world that is already representation. God produced signs, Augustine writes, "in order to signify His
presence, and to reveal Himself in them, as He Himself knows it to be

fitting, but without appearing in that substance itself by which He is, and which is wholly unchangeable."[42] If, as Tertullian claims, "all things that are not of God are perverse," and if, as Augustine maintains, God is not in signs, then not only are signs perverse, but words or verbal signs stand as a particularly degraded excess. They stand as a constant reminder of the secondary and supplemental nature of all "the arts." "With the word the garment entered," Tertullian asserts, implying that language is a covering that, by definition and from the start, is so wrapped up in the decorative as to be essentially perverse.[43] For where numbers signify permanence, reason, and order, language implies only corruption.[44] Words are to images in the mind as the corporeal or sensitive is to the domain of the spirit; they are secondary, derivative, supplemental, rival, and potentially confusing semblances that rely upon the fallible function of sound. "Words only teach us other words," Augustine insists, "less than that, a sound and a simple noise of the voice."[45] "Words are called words," the seventh-century Isidore of Seville suggests in his *Etymologies,* "because they make the air vibrate."[46]

More precisely, the mistrust of woman because of her alliance with the senses, and the mistrust of the senses because of their alliance with the cosmetic or decorative, can also be translated in a deep distrust of poetry, which, like all representational pleasures, Jerome insists, is directly threatening to mind and to man: "If any one delights in the sports of the circus, or the struggles of athletes, the versatility of actors, the figure of women, in splendid jewels, dress, silver and gold, and other things of the kind, the liberty of the soul is lost through the windows of the eyes, and the prophet's words are fulfilled: 'Death is come up into our windows' [Jer. ix. 21]. Again, our sense of hearing is flattered by the tones of various instruments and the modulations of the voice; and whatever enters the ear by the songs of poets and comedians, by the pleasantries and verses of pantomimic actors, weakens the manly fibre of the mind."[47]

Thus we have seen that in the early centuries of Christianity among the church fathers, the flesh becomes gendered as specifically feminine, and the female gender is estheticized in a way, and to a degree, that it had not been in previous tradition. At the same time the realm of esthetics is theologized, with the result that whatever belongs to the realm either of the feminine or of the esthetic is devalued within an ontological perspective according to which everything conceived to exist beyond the flesh, and thereby gendered masculine, alone has a claim to full Being. In the remainder of this chapter, we shall explore the specifically literary effects of this estheticization of gender as expressed among selected Latin and vernacular satirists of the High Middle Ages as well as among poets and thinkers of the nineteenth century.

Misogyny and the Literary: The Question of Reading

If much of the material we have encountered so far seems to be all of a piece, if it seems repetitious to the point of monotony, this is first of all because the teachings of the church fathers on the subject of women were passed to the Middle Ages in collections or *florilegia,* where they were read, cited, and repeated in other works. Yet there is a more compelling reason: the discourse of misogyny is always to some extent avowedly derivative; it is a citational mode whose rhetorical thrust displaces its own source away from anything that might be construed as personal or confessional. No one admits to antifeminism. No one says, "I am a misogynist." On the contrary, he tends, like the fathers, to quote what others have said about women (especially Paul); or, as in medieval examples, to cite the sacred authorities whose own source, as often as not, is the absent (and possibly nonexistent) Theophrastus with whom we began—and whose own citational *locus classicus* is to be found in Jerome.

The deflected nature of medieval and modern antifeminism accounts for the difficulty of locating this particular crime of thought, which always implies a problem of voice. The antifeminist speaks of the other in terms that bespeak otherness, through the voice of the other; this defining tautology emphasizes the elusiveness of the phenomenon as well as the relevance of the questions of reading and reception. To be more precise, I think it can be shown that where antifeminism is concerned the question of interpretation is crucial. Indeed, the beginning point of resistance to antifeminism, it seems, is a recognition of just how easily the phenomenon is deflected toward, transformed into, one of interpretation, of how profoundly the historic pro- and antifeminist debates have been determined by questions of reading: Who speaks? In what voice? With what intention?

I am not claiming that misogyny is merely a question of interpretation, of reading texts in one way or another, of understanding the condition of individual women at any given historic moment as a matter simply of perspective. On the contrary, my claim is that misogyny in our culture consists of a series of specific associations between the esthetic and the feminine, which in essence turns women into a text to be read, and thus to be appropriated. I seek to determine why the question of woman has traditionally been so enmeshed in that of reading in the literary history of the West. Further, I maintain that only by acknowledging that the question of interpretation historically has imposed itself between the detractors and the defenders of women in every "querelle des femmes" can the critic avoid simply repeating the terms that such debate has taken many times before. Otherwise one remains trapped in a false ideology that would confuse gender and politics, or in simplistic gender baiting that is more often than not mere name calling.

To ignore the importance of the question of interpretation is in a profound way merely to repeat France's first literary debate, the Quarrel of the *Romance of the Rose,* without realizing that Jean de Meun's work, which Christine de Pizan herself calls a "tresdeshonneste lecture en pluseurs pars" ("most dishonest reading in several parts"), may be less important for what it actually contains than for what surrounds it—what those who use it as a focal point around which to argue the question of woman have to say about it.[48] Indeed, the history of the reading of Jean's text not only offers a key to our understanding of the resurgence of the asceticism of the fathers in the antifeminism of the vernacular poets of the late Middle Ages, but also constitutes one of the important senses in which antifeminism can be historicized.[49] Again, because misogyny is a citational mode, its history resides primarily in the *differences* between the various things said through time about such texts, or in the problems of interpretation and use. Discussion of the misogynistic work, which becomes critical at certain moments in the history of sexuality, is a map of a certain kind of charged misreading that serves at any given cultural moment to define the permissible limits of gender relations.

It is above all around the question of woman that questions of language and of literature are debated passionately between the thirteenth and fifteenth centuries, and really until the seventeenth century, whose "querelle des femmes" and "querelle des anciens et modernes" can be seen to constitute continuations of the Quarrel of the *Rose.*[50] Not only was this exchange of texts and letters France's first literary quarrel, but the terms of the debate turned specifically around the enmeshed issues of woman and interpretation. Christine de Pizan, the first to take the side of women against Jean de Meun's antifeminism, focuses specifically upon authorial intention, voice, and the relation of poetic representation to social base, as seen in a sarcastic response to Jehan de Montreuil (Jehan Johannez) concerning the *Rose:*

> Et la laidure qui la est recordee des femmes, dient pluseurs en lui
> excusant que c'est le Jaloux qui parle, et voirement fait ains comme Dieu

parla par la bouche Jeremie. Mais sans faille, quelxque addicions
mençongeuses qu'il ait adjoustees, ne peuent—Dieu mercy! en rien
amenrir ne rendre empirees les conditions des femmes.

> *And many say in excusing the ugly things that are said there of women that it
> is the Jealous Husband who talks, as if truly God were speaking through the
> mouth of Jeremiah. But without a doubt, whatever untruthful things he has
> added to the pile cannot—thank God!, either improve or render worse the
> condition of women.*[51]

Or, as in the Latin letter of Jean de Montreuil to Gontier Col, the questions of
women and of reading are so thoroughly intertwined as to displace the phenomenon of misogyny away from a definable, stable, textual reality toward
the reading subject:

> Nonetheless our censors curse, hate, scorn, and attack him in a shameful
> way, having read him, studied, and understood him badly: this is what is
> intolerable! What arrogance! What rashness! What audacity! These
> people who admit themselves to only having read superficially, by bits
> and with no concern for context; here is how they rush in, like drunks
> arguing at the dinner table, to blame, reproach, and condemn abitrarily
> and at their whim such an important work, conceived and edited in so
> many nights and days, at the price of so much effort and with such
> constant application, as if such an important text weighed no more in
> the balance than the song of a jongleur, the work of one day.[52]

Jean de Montreuil's concern is not merely a rhetorical ruse, it poses a key issue
concerning the question at hand: the extent to which the alliance of woman
with the material, with the senses, with the superficiality of signs and artifice,
lies at the root of a deep identification between the feminine and the literary.

The Lamentations de Matheolus *and Logical Trouble*

The seductiveness of the feminine is for the medieval Christian West virtually
synonymous with delusiveness of language embodied in rhetoric, whose seduction, that of "mere words, worse than that of empty noises" (Augustine),
recapitulates the original sin—that "she," in the words of John Chrysostom,
"believed in the one who professed mere words, and nothing else."[53] Here
there is no better illustration than the fourteenth-century *Lamentations de
Matheolus* by Jehan Le Fèvre, a translation from the Latin of the *Liber Lamen-
tationum Matheoluli,* and indeed a summa of what we have seen with respect

to gender up until now. Jehan, who was known by the participants in the Quarrel of the *Rose* as well as by Chaucer, was, according to his modern editor, a cleric who bore the title of *magister,* who lived in Paris "where he denied himself no pleasure." The assertion in the poem is that he married a widow, which placed him in a position of bigamy—the object of the old attack against remarriage, which dates from the early centuries of Christianity—and thus he was relieved of clerical support, privileges, and immunities, according to church councils (such as that of Lyon, 1274) and bulls.[54]

Mathieu, the antiheroic narrator of the *Lamentations,* does not lament because he has married a woman who had been married before, although he identifies himself as "Le plus chetif de tous clamés / Pour ce que je suy bigamé" ("Proclaimed the most miserable of all because I am bigamous" [1, vv. 1074–75]). Instead, his main concern is that his perceptual functions have been troubled, as John Chrysostom claims is inevitable, by a gaze:

Je me plaing, car par la *veüe*
Fu ma science deceüe.
Beauté par l'uel mon cuer
  navra,
Dont jamais jour repos
  n'avra. . . .
Las! povre moy, quant tant
  amay,
Que par amours me bigamay;

I complain, for by vision was my knowledge deceived. Beauty wounded my heart through my eye, and because of which I will never be at peace. . . . Alas! poor me, when I loved so much that by love I became bigamous. (1: vv. 647–50, 657–58)

Beauty, however, has turned to its opposite:

Las! or ay le cuer trop marri.
Car orendroit est tant ripeuse,
Courbée, boçue et tripeuse,
Desfigurée et contrefaite
Que ce semble estre une
  contraite.
Rachel est Lya devenue,
Toute grise, toute chenue,
Rude, mal entendant et
  sourde,
En tous ses fais est vile et
  lourde;

Alas! now my heart is really sad, for she is now so mangy, stooped, humpbacked and pot-bellied, disfigured and undone that she seems to be a deformed person. Rachel has become Leah, all gray, white-haired, rough, senile, and deaf. In all she does she is heavy and vile; her chest is hard and her breasts that used to be beautiful, are wrinkled, black, spotted like the wet bags of a shepherd. (1, vv. 672–85)

> Le pis a dur et les mamelles,
> Qui tant souloient estre belles,
> Sont froncies, noires, souillies
> Com bourses de bergier
>   mouillies

The difference between a happy former state and the present state of bigamous torture is a result of the seductions of vision ("Je fuy seduis et afollés /
Par doulx regars, par beau langage" ["I was seduced and maddened by sweet
looks and words" (1, vv. 570–71)]) that has become inverted: "Mon impotence est anoncie" ("My impotence is exposed" [1, v. 1349]). It is, in
fact, impossible to tell whether a loss of beauty has diminished desire or
diminished desire has caused the beloved to appear less desirable; whether
or not, in other words, it was a trouble of perception that produced desire in
the first place. For vision is certainly at stake in Mathieu's seduction:

> Mieulx me venist mes yeux   *I would have done better to shield my*
>   bander   *eyes the day I first saw her and so*
> Au jour que premier l'avisay   *esteemed her beauty and her sweet an-*
> Et que sa beauté tant prisay   *gelic face covering sophisticated woman.*
> Et son doulx viaire angelique   (1, vv. 626–30)
> Dessoubs la fame sophistique.

Here the connection is established between bigamy, seduction, and sophistication. Woman, feminine or sophisticated beauty, is imagined to seduce
not only because she appeals to the senses but also because she corrupts
them, one by one:[55]

> Mes cinq sens sont mortifiés;   *My five senses are mortified, my eyes*
> Mes yeuls ne peuent   *cannot see. . . . I cannot taste or smell*
>   regarder, . . .   *anything, nor can I feel anything with*
> Je ne puis a goust savourer   *my hands as I used to be able, but less;*
> Ne je ne puis rien odourer,   *and my ears don't hear a thing.* (1,
> Si ne sçay taster de mes mains   vv. 1510–16)
> Tant com je souloie, mais
>   mains,
> Et de mes oreilles n'oy goute;

Nor can Jehan's vision of the corruption of vision be restricted to the literary
domain, for it corresponds remarkably to at least one of the ways in which

desire was understood in medieval medical texts. In the *Lilium medicinae*, Bernard of Gordon, who became professor of medicine at the university of Montpellier in 1285, claims, for example, that the source of the disease called "'heroes' [Eros] is a melancholic anxiety caused by the love for a woman" and that "the cause of this disease [*passionis*] is the corruption of judgment by means of the ardent attachment to form and figure."[56]

Thus we meet a paradox: before marriage the senses are seduced and distorted by desire; yet after marriage they are distorted by abuse, or by the tears of lamentation that alter vision. There is, then, according to Jehan Le Fèvre, no moment at which woman does not trouble vision and distort and destroy the senses, for the seducing sophistication of the feminine is conceived to be synonymous with that of illusion itself. Women are by definition sophisticated (dirty, illusory), and are posited as that which exists in distinction to reason. Moreover, if, as Mathieu admits, "By her sight my knowledge [*science*] was troubled," it is because woman is conceived as that which escapes logic. This is why the author of the *Lamentations* is obsessed by the "Lai d'Aristote," a work which for the Middle Ages represented a parable of the triumph of woman over philosophy, for it ends with a seductress riding the great philosopher like a horse.[57] Indeed, according to Mathieu, woman is more powerful than the Perihermenias, the Elench, the Prior and Posterior Analytics, mathematics, and logic. "What will the logicians have to say about their ancient sophisms," he asks, "when they see their doctor and their leader more confused than any crazed fool. . . . Alas! What will philosophy have to say when the great master is deceived by the figure of amphibology?"[58]

Woman is portrayed in this most virulent antifeminist vernacular work of the Middle Ages, which can be considered to have sparked the Quarrel of the *Rose*, as the one whose interference with univocal meaning is equated with noise, or with the defining secondariness of material words with respect to Being in the original Yahwist version of the Genesis story (see chapter 1):

Pourquoy sont femmes plus
noiseuses,
Plaines de paroles oiseuses
Et plus jangleuses que les
hommes?

Why are women more noisy, full of foolish words, and more garrulous than men? Because they are made of bones and our persons are made of clay: bones rattle louder than earth. (2, vv. 241–46)

Car elles sont d'os et nous
  sommes
Fais de terre en nostre
  personne:
L'os plus haut que la terre
  sonne.

Thus we are faced with another of the slippages characteristic of the discourse of misogyny: when, within the order of Creation, there is a distinction between the spiritual and the material, woman falls to the side of matter; when, however, both men and women are considered in their materiality, woman again is displaced toward the less noble substance—bone rather than earth.

Jehan's diatribe is a version of the topos of the woman as "the one who speaks without ever saying anything" (Boileau).[59] It reduces her, moreover, to the category of the sophism by equating her with a false logic that vanquishes both grammar and dialectics: "En ce fu grammaire traïe / Et logique moult esbaïe" ("In this was grammar betrayed, and logic quite confounded" [1, vv. 1105–6]). Together grammar and logic constitute within the medieval language arts (the trivium) the sciences of the true, respectively of rectitude of expression and of correct propositions.[60] Woman, however, here signifies the opposite of the truth: "Femme de verité n'a cure" ("Woman does not care about truth" [1, v. 966]). More precisely, she becomes, in the antifeminist thinking of the High Middle Ages, associated with the third element of the trivium—rhetoric, the art of persuasion, which by the thirteenth century was synonymous with poetics.[61] Woman is figured as the sophist, the dissimulator (1, v. 1027), the seducer with false arguments or subtlety: "Oultre les tençons et les limes / Par cinq manieres de sophismes / La femme maine l'omme a methe" ("In addition to arguments and quarrels woman brings man to his end with five kinds of sophism" [1, vv. 843–45]). The word *methe* is interesting in and of itself. From Latin *meta*, it means a mark or boundary, an end, period, or turning point. But the resonance of *methodium* (a witty conceit, jest, or joke) is also present, as is that of *metus* (fear). Moreover, careful readers, aware of the extent to which medieval vernacular poets loved wordplay, cannot help but recognize in *methe* a part of the poet's name—Mathieu of Matheolus—who was brought by woman to his end. And why not all four—end, joke, fear, and the name of the poet? After all, if woman is imagined to be the sign of an always present bigamy, she is also the figure of ambiguity ("figure d'amphibolie" [1, v. 1144])—the one who through the ruse that is her power works against logic and grammar (*methodice*) to trouble the senses with sophisms. In speaking, sight is deceived by sophism: "Avec la langue est la veüe / Par le sophisme deceüe" (1, vv. 903–4). Touch is touched by specious argument: "Femme dit que la touche ment / Et confute l'atouchement / Par argument et par fallace" (1, vv. 967–69). Falsehood and truth, dream and waking reality, become confused through the agency of woman as sophism (1, vv. 850–85). Here we have come full circle, since the alliance of woman with rhetoric against grammar and logic places her on the side of the poet, the imitator whose creation, because it rivals the Creation, is but simulation, the one who dissimulates through the clever use of language.[62]

The Latin Satirists and the Rhetoric of Self-Contradiction

If one were to pose the question made famous by Freud at the end of the last century, "What does a woman want?" within the context of medieval antifeminism, the answer would be clear: "A woman wants to speak." She is aligned, as we have seen, with the senses, the body, and the material, portrayed as pure appetite (economic, gastronomic, sexual), and such a portrayal cannot be disassociated from the desire to speak any more than in medieval sign theory the linguistic can be separated from the corporeal. "Furthermore, not only is every woman by nature a miser, but she is also envious, and a slanderer of other women, greedy, a slave to her belly, inconstant, fickle in her speech, . . . a liar, a drunkard, a babbler, no keeper of secrets," writes Andreas Capellanus, the supposed author of *The Art of Courtly Love*, the third book of which contains an antifeminist tirade. "Even for a trifle a woman will swear falsely a thousand times. . . . Every woman is also loud-mouthed. . . . When she is with other women, no one of them will give the others a chance to speak, but each always tries to be the one to say whatever is to be said and to keep on talking longer than the rest; and neither her tongue nor her spirit ever gets tired out by talking. . . . A woman will boldly contradict everything you say."[63] More than mere encumbering ambiguity, she is defined above all as embodying the spirit of contradiction: "Je ne sçai de chose passé / Ne du temps present rien retraire / Qu'elle ne die le contraire" ("I know how to say nothing, past or present, that she does not say the opposite" [*Lamentations*, 1, vv. 1300–1302]). As man's copy or image, his double, she doubles per-

niciously everything he says: "Elle est de trop parler isnelle / Et en parlant a
double ment, / Pourquoy je peris doublement" ("She is too quick to speak;
and in speaking she lies twice, by which I perish doubly" [1, vv. 1291–93]).
Woman in the sense that Jehan Le Fèvre understands her is the analogue of
the poet in the sense that even Marie de France defines her—a glossator.[64]
"Elle glose toujours le pire" (1, v. 1179), Jehan contends, which, in our am-
bivalent, bigamous reading, means: "She always glosses the worst," "She
desires the worst."

The portrayal of woman as endless garrulity or as contradiction would
not be so significant, however, if it were not for the defining rhetorical context
of all antimatrimonial literature, which seeks to dissuade from marriage and
to do so precisely by speaking, often at great length. How, it may be asked,
does the desire of women to speak differ from that of a writer like Walter Map,
author of the "Dissuasion of Valerius to Rufinus the Philosopher that he
should not take a Wife," one of the prime antimatrimonial satires of the High
Middle Ages? Walter repeats, through the voice of Valerius, in the space of
only two pages:

> *I am forbidden to speak, and I cannot keep silence.* I hate the crane and
> the screech-owl's voice, I hate the owl and the other birds that dismally
> shriek their prophecies of the woes of winter and mud. And you, you
> scoff at my bodings of loss to come, true bodings, if you persist. *So I am
> forbidden to speak—I the prophet of truth,* not of my own will. . . .
> You love the Gnathos and the comedians who whisper of pleasant
> enticements to come, and above all Circe who pours for you full
> draughts of joy, with the perfume of the sweetness you sigh for, to
> delude you. Lest you be turned into a sow or ass, *I cannot keep silence.*
> To you the cupbearer of Babel holds out the honeyed poison; it
> goes down sweetly and gives delight and brings on the heat of your
> spirit; therefore *I am forbidden to speak.*
> I know that at the last it will bite as an adder, and inflict a wound
> that no antidote can cure; therefore *I cannot keep silence.*
> You have many advocates of your desire, to the peril of your life,
> and those most eloquent: me only you have, the *tongue-tied preacher of
> bitter truth,* which sickens you: therefore *I am forbidden to speak.*
> The foolish voice of the goose was chidden amidst the swans which
> are only taught to please; yet that voice enabled the senators to rescue
> Rome from fire, her treasures from pillage, themselves from the enemy's

darts. Peradventure you too will understand, as they did—for you are wise—that the swan's melody is of death to you, and that the goose's scream is salvation: therefore *I cannot keep silence.*

You are all on fire with your passion, and, led astray by the beauty of a comely head, you fail to see that what you are wooing is a chimaera. . . . therefore *I am forbidden to speak.*

Ulysses was enchanted by the concert of the Sirens, but because "the Sirens' voice and Circe's cup he knew," he forced himself, by the bonds of virtue, to shun the whirlpool. . . . Therefore *I cannot keep silence.*

Finally, that fire of yours which the opposing side shares with you is stronger than that which inflames you against me. Lest the greater draw to it the less, and I perish—therefore *I am forbidden to speak.*

If I may speak in that spirit which makes me yours, let the two fires be weighed in any balance, just or false, and let the result turn to the peril of my head, whatever you do, whatever you decide: you should make allowance for me who, in the impatience of my affection, *cannot keep silence.*[65]

Here resides one of the profound paradoxes attached to the discourse of misogyny. That is: if woman is defined as verbal transgression, indiscretion, and contradiction, then Walter Map, indeed any writer, can only be defined as a woman. And we can only assume too that the Walter to whom the *Art of Courtly Love* is addressed is no less fickle than Andreas accuses all women of being: "A woman is just like melting wax, which is always ready to take a new form and to receive the impress of anybody's seal. No woman can make you such a firm promise that she will not change her mind about the matter in a few minutes."[66] Indeed what are the antimatrimonial tracts of the late classical and medieval period if not attempts at persuasion? Walter Map is highly conscious of the rhetorical context of his *dissuasio.* "I see you by this time tired out and running through what you are reading with all the haste you can, not weighing the sense but on the lookout for figures of speech . . . " he warns Valerius, "and you must not expect from me the rouge and raddle of the orator (of which I mournfully confess I know nothing) but be content with the goodwill of the writer and the honesty of the written page."[67]

Walter Map's artful pretense of honesty—"the honesty of the written page"—is the ultimate ruse, since the works that bemoan the instability of women are attempts to achieve what they denounce. They perform what they seem most to reject. Put another way, the author tries to do to his interlocutor precisely what he accuses women of doing: to deceive with words, to provoke contradiction, and to seduce with that which is defined as the essence of the feminine, the ruses of rhetoric.[68] All of which means too that the reader to whom the work is addressed can hardly be other than a woman, as defined in Andreas's own terms: the one subject to persuasion. "Woman is commonly found to be fickle, too, because no woman ever makes up her mind so firmly on any subject that she will not quickly change it on a little persuading from anyone." The antifeminist writer uses rhetoric as a means of renouncing it and by extension woman; he "cheats," in the phrase of Andreas, "one trick with another."[69] This is perhaps the greatest ruse of all, for the confession of contradiction, which Walter Map equates with "the goodwill of the writer and the honesty of the written page," is no less of an aporia than Andreas's concluding advice:

> Now this doctrine of ours, which we have put into this little book for you, will if carefully and faithfully examined seem to present two different points of view. In the first part . . . we set down completely, one point after another, the art of love. . . . If you wish to practice the system, you will obtain, as a careful reading of this little book will show you, all the delights of the flesh in fullest measure. . . . In the latter part of the book . . . we added something about the rejection of love. . . . If you will study carefully this little treatise of ours and understand it completely and practice what it teaches, you will see clearly that no man ought to mis-spend his days in the pleasures of love.[70]

Thus the book is all that it claims to reject: contradiction, deceit, seduction, a source of mischief and mistrust. "We know that everything a woman says is said with the intention of deceiving, because she always has one thing in her heart and another on her lips," Andreas inveighs in a phrase whose own irreducible ambiguity warns against nothing so much as itself.[71]

This is a way of suggesting that the reader's own strategy can only be one of mistrust of the writer and of the text, which returns us to the problem of reading. How do we distinguish, finally, persuasion from dissuasion? How do we tell the difference, for example, between Andreas's prescription that "if you want a woman to do anything, you can get her to do it by ordering her to do the opposite" and the opening injunction to the reader of Book III, "Friend Walter," to "read this little book, then, not as one seeking to take up the life of the lover, but that, invigorated by the theory and trained to excite the minds of women to love, you may, by refraining from so doing, win an eternal recompense"?[72] There is no way of determining with certainty Andreas's intent, whether to urge to convince or desist, and ultimately whether he wants us to take literally the warning against love or to be seduced by the letter. He, and any other author for that matter, performs that which he denounces Eve for having done: he seduces, in Tertullian's phrase, "by mere words," and disobeys his own injunctions. The danger of the feminine, according to this understanding of misogyny, is that of the undecidability of poetry itself. The medieval portrayal of marriage as verbal abuse—the *molestiae nuptiarum* with which we began—is, as Boileau affirms in his tenth satire, a "text which everyone glosses" (*gloss* still carrying the semantic valence of *desire*) and, moreover, constitutes "the immortal archives of the ills of Sex" that is classicism's legacy from the "naive" Middle Ages.[73]

The Romantic and Symbolist Past

The feminization of the esthetic, which is evident both in the patristic association of woman with the supplementary modes of representation and in her assimilation to the poetic, has a long history in the West. Indeed, many of the founding topoi of medieval antifeminism resurface within the re-theologized misogyny of the nineteenth century. What can only be described as a widespread and pervasive fear of the feminine haunted the immediate past no less than the early centuries of Christianity and was often conceived in similar terms. One finds, for instance, the notion of woman as the contrary of reason in, say, the moral philosophy of Proudhon.[74] One finds the topos of woman as riot translated into Michelet's widely circulated belief that "she cannot be contained."[75] Then too, inherited presuppositions concerning woman and embodiment, the relation of woman as the particular to man as the universal, appear in more recent assumptions about woman's natural affinity for detail and her unfitness for abstraction in contrast to man's natural capacity for philosophy. Such modern versions of the theological equation of man with mind and woman with the senses culminate inevitably, as in the medieval case, in the assimilation of the feminine with the poetic. The ultimate expression of this idea is to be found in Baudelaire, for whom the woman represents a force of antinature: "Idole, elle doit se dorer pour être adorée" ("Idol, she must make herself up to be adored"). Woman, like the male dandy, is naturally drawn to ornamentation and the arts, and she incarnates the artificial since her body, through makeup, "borrows from all the arts in order to rise above nature."[76] For Baudelaire, the feminine body is a work of art, woman an artistic invention:

> All that a woman wears, all that enhances her beauty, is part of her; and artists who have set out intentionally to capture this enigmatic being become as passionate about the *mundus muliebris* as about the woman herself. Woman is without doubt a light, a look, an invitation to happiness, sometimes a word; but she is above all a general harmony, not only in her bearing and in the movement of her limbs, but also in the chiffons, the silks, the vast and undulating clouds of cloth in which she envelops herself, and which are like the attributes and the pedestal of her divinity; in the metal and mineral which snake around her arms and her neck, which add their sparkle to the fire of her glances, or which chatter softly around her ears. What poet would dare, in the portrayal of pleasure caused by the apparition of a beauty, separate the woman from her clothes?[77]

The woman, who disappears into the evanescent *mundus muliebris* that surrounds her, loses all specificity: her body, her beauty, her clothes, and her jewels are subtilized into sensation or the representation of sensation, which replaces the woman in herself ("la femme elle-même"). More radical still— and here one can only marvel at the paradox of the woman incapable of abstraction subtilized into a pure abstraction—Baudelaire's woman is transformed into the equivalent of esthetic principle: "a light, a look . . . sometimes a word . . . above all a general harmony . . . an apparition." This transformation is synonymous with the Baudelairian esthetics of invisible correspondences.[78]

Mallarmé too recognizes the intertwining of the feminine, the decorative, and the specifically literary. In justifying writing a fashion column addressed to women, he relies upon the old analogy between literature as the leisure activity that decorates the otherwise serious cares of life—literature as the cosmetic of the soul—and the feminine-gendered activities of self-decoration and reading: "all women love verses as well as perfumes and jewels or even the characters in a story as much as themselves. To please them or to be worthy of it: I know of no ambition, a veritable triumph if one succeeds, which better crowns a work of poetry or prose. One repeats, not without truth, that there are no more men readers; I agree, they are all women. Only a lady, in her isolation from politics and other morose cares, has the necessary leisure in order, once her dressing is done, to feel the need of adorning the soul as well."[79]

The modern estheticization of the feminine has as a corollary a plethora of subsidiary clichés concerning woman and creativity. The first of these is the topos of the rarity and the inferiority of serious women artists, composers, and writers in the traditional thinking of the West. "Women have been absent neither from the field of painting nor of letters," writes Paul Valéry, "but, in the order of the more abstract arts they have not excelled. I say of an art that it is more abstract than another when it requires more imperatively than that other art the intervention of completely ideal forms, that is forms not borrowed from the world of sense . . . the more abstract an art, the fewer women there are who have made a name for themselves in that art."[80] Second, the alliance of woman with the esthetic sustains the widespread belief that when women do engage in the arts, their engagement is somehow to be taken less seriously. We have already seen that for Cesare Lombroso women are associated with abundant orality—loquacity, gossip—with speech to the exclusion of writing because, as he maintains, "their graphic centers are less well developed" (see chapter 1). If women must write, the noted criminologist maintains, they are enjoined to write letters, conceived as a graphic form of conversation that "conforms to their character and, once again, satisfies their need for speech." This is another way of saying that women's writing is less serious, more superficial, or allied with that which is considered to be the surface of writing—ornament, style, rhetoric, which pleases without acceding to truth. For J. J. Virey, she represents a "patina of elegance spread over all discourses, the disguising of too harsh truth behind delicate ornaments," as we encounter the old topos linking women to makeup and self-decoration, as in the medieval example, and to the decorative arts as opposed to philosophy. "Song, dance, painting, poetic ornaments of language are born from this same source, which also gave us our taste for makeup [*parure*] and everything which has to do with it," Virey continues, in a cliché full of social implications as well: "Manners and good breeding are established by women, while principles and laws are settled by men."[81]

Thus, whereas the church fathers' relegation of woman to the realm of esthetics and their condemnation of the artificial are rooted in a metaphysical fear of the flesh, the ghost that haunted the nineteenth century, as Naomi Schor has demonstrated, remains internal to esthetics and has to do precisely with the assimilation of the feminine to the decorative detail. That is, to the extent to which woman is allied with the particular, the partial, the part, the contingent, the fleeting, smallness of scale, her threat is not so much luring man to eternal perdition as causing loss of measure in the here and now, and which is couched in specifically social terms. To be overcome by details, as in realistic art or the mnemonic art—in Baudelaire's example—of Constantine Guys, is to be overcome by the mob: "An artist having the perfect feeling for form, but accustomed to relying above all on his memory and his imagination, finds himself overwhelmed by a riot of details, each of which demands justice with the fury of a crowd bent on absolute equality. All justice is thus violated; all harmony destroyed, sacrificed; many a trifle becomes enormous; many a triviality usurps all. The more an artist bends with impartiality toward the detail, the greater the anarchy that reigns. Whether he be long-sighted or short-sighted, all hierarchy and all subordination disappear."[82] Nor is Baudelaire eccentric in his juxtaposition of the esthetics of the detail with civil chaos, for here as well we find the profound Nietzschean problematic of woman as superficial and at the same time a source of disorder. "Man thinks woman profound—why?" the philosopher asks in *Twilight of the Idols*. "Because he can never fathom her depths. Woman is not even shallow."[83] The question of the relation of woman to truth is as complicated for Nietzsche as that of her relation to nature is for Baudelaire. For despite the seeming exclusion of the feminine-as-surface from truth, in keeping with the alliance of man with the idea and woman with embodiment, woman can come to represent a higher truth of antitruth associated, as among the fathers, with deceit, illusion, ruse. According to Nietzsche, to the extent that truth has become occulted by Christianity, it "becomes more subtle, more insidious, more evasive,—it becomes a woman, it becomes Christian."[84]

Nietzsche displays the same kind of impossible reasoning that we have seen elsewhere. Again, one of the enduring truths about the binary exclusionary logic of the discourse of misogyny is that its exclusions operate wherever focused; by their prejudicial illogicality they constitute a series of double binds that cannot be disentangled. We have seen, for example, that within the realm of philosophy, woman (as abstraction) is excluded from abstraction because her essence is located in the partial and the particular, which takes on the valence of the oral, conceived as contingent or fleeting—an instance of *parole* as opposed to the more enduring *langue*. If, however, woman writes, her writing again falls on the side of the transitory. It is literature, rhetoric, as against philosophy. Even within literature, however, not only do certain genres (such as the epistolary) accommodate the feminine better than others, but there is such a thing as a "feminine style," which in its insistence upon manner, melody (Baudelaire's harmony), color, grace, elegance, and curve in distinction to line, depth, truth, and force represents another instance of the traditional alliance between woman and the decorative versus man and the ideal. Barbey d'Aurevilly claims that one can recognize a book written by a woman by its "lack of vision, of depth, of originality, of enflamed vigor; virile qualities that women lack because they have others, grace, elegance, finesse, soft color, tenderness, surprise, vivid sensation."[85] Nonetheless, one can detect in Mme. de Staël's style "that virile genuis in an overly masculine woman's body": "the distinction which grazes originality the way grace touches force! a style full of color and of melody, and a word choice rarer than the style which crowns it with diamonds, the word which she seeks out and which she loves, the ornamentation [*parure*] of her woman's sentence, which has the same contours as she does, but which lacks the links, the articulations, the animally powerful procedure of the sentence of men of genius."[86]

The contrast between the straight, forceful, truthful language of man and the gracious, curvaceous, refined language of woman is more than simply a contrast between styles: it is a contrast between what is conceived to be style and its lack, distinguishing what can be defined as the literary and the non-literary. Thus, if woman is excluded from the realm of ideas or of the ideal, she is nonetheless associated with that of the imaginary. And here we skate dangerously close to that strange mixture of science and folklore that characterizes much nineteenth-century literary history, and, in particular, the nineteenth century's history of the Middle Ages. Michelet, for instance, finds in the world of women, isolated in huts throughout the medieval forest, a perfect medium for the cultivation of the pagan imagination. This "peculiar, delicate, world of fairies and sprites is made for the feminine soul." According to Michelet's own fantasy of literary history, "as soon as the great era of saints' lives ended, this older and more poetic legend came secretly, imperceptibly, to the fore. It is the treasure of women, which fondle and caress it; for the fairy is a woman too, a fantastic mirror in which she sees herself beautified."[87] The world of woman is the world of decorative luxury—"clothes, stoles, carpets of soft sweetness and mysterious harmony . . . a world of treasures, silk, sugar, a myriad of powerful herbs"—which "conquers all through an easy war of love and maternal seduction."[88]

There is much here to suggest the topos—about which we will have a good deal to say by way of conclusion (see chapter 7)—of woman the bringer of culture, the civilizer identified with "the world of decorative luxury," who

represents for the Middle Ages a Renaissance in germ. For it is assumed widely among nineteenth-century literary historians that literary style or manner,
the essence of poetic elaboration, was a product of the Renaissance, an impor-
tation from Italy, and that, like imagination itself, it was a feminine
invention.[89] The natural affinity of women for the decorative finds an analogue in baroque esthetics. "Catherine, and then Marie de Médecis," writes
J. J. Virey, "imported into France, among other vices from Italy, the taste for
magnificence, and this prerogative of their family, this delicate sentiment in
letters and arts of which they especially accelerated the development. But they
made into fashion at the same time this mania for wittiness [*bel esprit*] and for
the grotesque, and this manneristic tone which had already infected Italian
literature. One no longer flaunted erudition, but abused thought."[90] In the
occulting of erudition by abused thought one recognizes, of course, another
instance of the displacement of philosophy by the rhetoric which, measured
against grammar, from the late Latin rhetoricians on was conceived in terms
of linguistic abuse. Woman is, through the style to which she is imagined to
be naturally drawn and which she embodies, on the side of antitruth, excessive loquacity, and the poetic, which, according to Proudhon, replaced the
masculine idea and can only represent a decline: "All advanced literature, or, if
one prefers, developing literature, can be characterized by the movement of
the *idea,* its masculine element; all literature in a state of decadence is recog-
nizable by the obscuring of the idea, replaced by an excessive loquacity, which
only emphasizes the falseness of the thought, the poverty of moral sense,
and, in spite of the artifice of diction, the nullity of style."[91] How close the
nineteenth-century misogynists are in spirit to Jerome, for whom, it will be
remembered, "whatever enters the ear by the songs of poets and comedians,
by the pleasantries and verses of pantomimic actors, weakens the manly fibre
of the mind."

"Devil's Gateway" and "Bride of Christ"

In the last chapter we explored some of the ways in which the early Christian setting of gender in the first four centuries of our era resurfaced in both the Latin and the vernacular literary tradition of the High Middle Ages. Having seen how closely the idea of woman is allied with the supervenient and the contingent, with the realm of the senses, with the decorative or cosmetic, and with symbolic activity in general, we linked such an estheticization of the feminine to the topos of the *molestiae nuptiarum*. More precisely, we saw that the reproach against wives synonymous with the varieties of verbal abuse—garrulity, argumentativeness, the spirit of contradiction, indiscretion, lying, and seduction with words—is virtually identical to the medieval reproach against rhetoric for being uncontrollable, untruthful, appealing, and deceptive to the senses. The simultaneous reproach against rhetoric and wives leads inevitably, as we saw, to essential issues of voice, literary hermeneutics, and gender that remain deeply imbricated in the thinking of the West.

To demonstrate just how such a paradigm is played out in a medieval vernacular text, we began with what is perhaps the most excessive example of its kind—Jehan Le Fèvre's *Lamentations de Matheolus*, where woman is portrayed as a kind of false logic, a sophism, that vanquishes both grammar and dialectics, the sciences of the true. And it is here that we encountered a number of inconsistencies, contradictions, or paradoxes within the medieval reception of the early Christian articulation of gender. If woman is presented as infinitely garrulous, how is it that the male misogynist is able to speak at such length about her loquacity? Or, given that the antimatrimonial impulse is to some degree always situated within the rhetorical context of persuasion, or rather of dissuasion, which means that woman is pictured as fickle, how is it possible to imagine the supposed object of his entreaties as other than feminine? Put another way, the author seeks to do to his interlocutor precisely what he projects upon women: to deceive with words, to provoke contradiction, and to seduce with what is defined as the essence of the feminine, the ruses of rhetoric. This final wrinkle is implicit to the antifeminist performative: if woman is presented as contradictory, the opposite of logic, against the male adherence to a unified truth that is in the words of Augustine "once and for all," then the misogynist, by transgressing the difference he establishes, contradicts himself or again acts like the woman he censures for being inconsistent.

The Paradox of Equality

In this chapter we will explore yet another defining contradiction of the early Christian discourse on gender, which can be traced back to the patristic period and has implications for our understanding of vernacular literature that reach far beyond the identification of women with rhetoric or decoration. Put in simplest terms, all that we have seen until now by way of a negative portrait of women and of femininity, including the identification of woman as the source of all evil, is juxtaposed throughout the period in question with an equal and opposite discourse of Christian thought on gender, which maintains the equality of the sexes. And this is true from the beginning, since the founding articulation of equality is to be found in Paul, Galatians 3:28, where it is written: "There is neither Jew nor Greek, there is neither bond nor free, there is neither male nor female: for ye are all one in Christ Jesus." We find, of course, an important distinction between the words of Jesus, who relativizes the importance of sexual difference, proclaims the equal dignity of all beings, and displays little of the sexism of the household code, and, say, the pastoral letters of Paul whose ascription is certain and the so-called pseudo- or deutero-Paul. There is a difference between the Pauline formulas and subsequent elaborations of the attributes of gender by Tertullian, Chrysostom, Ambrose, or Jerome, just as there are nuances between the most adamantly misogynist fathers and the more moderate Augustine. Nonetheless, if one takes seriously the Pauline prescription of equality, one is potentially apt to believe, with Jo Ann McNamara, that "patristic writers were committed to the doctrine that with God there is neither male nor female," and that "despite the personal proclivities of many of its formulators, the logic of the Christian doctrine required a commitment to sexual equality."[1] Despite the enormity of the irony, almost all patristic writers maintain the rule of equality, the Pauline principle of "Oneness in Christ," alongside an omnipresent anti-feminism.

Further, if one follows to its conclusion the logic of the new religion of the meek, according to which "the last shall be first, and the first last" (Matthew 20:15), then women possess the potential not only to equal but even to surpass men. Indeed, to the extent that the frailty of the flesh is elided to the side of the feminine, it entails, through the inversion of the values of weakness and strength synonymous with early Christianity, the possibility of women being stronger than men. Since the coming of Christ, complains Chrysostom, "women outstrip and eclipse us."[2] The literature of the early fathers is filled with examples of heroic feminine martyrs, of women whose triumph is considered to be all the greater because of their gender.[3] Paul maintains in Romans 5:20 that "where sin abounded, grace did much more abound"; and of the thirty-six names he cites in Romans 16 for valorous effort in the Christian cause, sixteen are the names of women. Augustine, in speaking of Felicity and Perpetua, claims that "the crown is all the more glorious when the sex is weaker, and the soul shows itself assuredly more virile in women when they do not succumb to the weight of their fragility."[4] Thus women are considered special candidates for salvation, since, according to the dichotomy that places man on the side of the spirit and woman on the side of the senses and seduction, men, strictly speaking, have less to overcome in order to be redeemed.[5] Here too we touch upon an area that defines more powerfully than any other the appeal of Christianity to women, for not only is the woman who is saved more holy than her male counterpart, but it is a woman who carries the possibility of salvation. Mary, the redeemer of Eve who liberates her from the malediction of the Fall, is one of the great themes of the formative Christian era and a mainstay of Christianity's attraction. "Come, virgins, to the side of the Virgin," we find written in a pseudo-Augustinian sermon, "come women, to the side of this Woman; come mothers, to the side of this Mother; come you who give your breast to the side of this one who gives hers; come young women to the side of this young woman. Mary has passed through all the states of woman in Jesus Christ our Lord in order to welcome all women who seek her. The new Eve, who remains a virgin, has restored the condition of all women who come to her side."[6]

One finds among the fathers many positive depictions of women alongside the more abstract negative portrayal of femininity. The heroines praised in Gregory of Nazianzen's (A.D. c. 330–390) portrait of his sister Gorgonie leave little doubt about the equality—even the superiority—of the female woman, in the struggle for salvation, you have surpassed the courage of men, and you have proven that the body alone makes the difference between man and woman and that the soul is the same."[7] Gregory of Nyssa glorifies his sister Macrina whose virtues he refuses to allow to "disappear behind the veil of silence."[8] Cyprian lauds a woman named Bona "who was dragged by her husband to sacrifice, who did not pollute her conscience," but showed heroic resolution to the end.[9] Jerome praises Marcella's philosophical understanding, and the ascetic probity of Paula as well as her daughters Blesilla and Eustochium; Palladius does the same for Melania the Elder ("most erudite") as well as her granddaughter Melania the Younger, who supposedly instructed the emperor Theodosius.[10] Finally, there is no more moving portrait of courage than Augustine's narrative of the martyrdom of Felicity and Perpetua, who tend their children even in prison. "Do not the combined names of these two women," Augustine asks, "designate the grace which awaits all saints? For why do martyrs endure all except to enjoy a perpetual felicity?"[11]

How is it that the church fathers simultaneously affirm the view of woman as the source of evil, the "Devil's gateway," and as a mediator and even more, the symbol of the union of the soul with Christ, a source of redemption, the "Bride of Christ"? "The man is the head of the woman," on the one hand; "neither male nor female: for ye are all one in Christ," on the other. How is it possible to reconcile the radical disenfranchisement implicit in the household code with the equally radical affirmation of sexual equality? Or, to focus upon contemporary understanding of the patristic period, how is it possible to accommodate the double truth of women's equality according to the order of redemption and her inequality according to the order of creation with the widespread belief that where marriage and sexuality are concerned Christianity abolished the ethical double standard? How is it possible, finally, to view as personally liberating an asceticism that, by current moral standard at least, seems to deny the integrity of the person?[12]

The answer to the question we have posed has three parts, the first two of which are determined by the weight of previous scholarly tradition and the third by the attempt to recast the seeming contradiction in different terms. The first is a matter of dates: When did such conflicting attitudes come about? The second concerns source: From where did these attitudes come? And the third addresses from a social and economic perspective the issues of how and why.

When?

Scholars disagree about exactly when the disjunction of which we speak came about. Some locate its earliest expression in Paul's letters, others more precisely in the Paul of the Inter-Time, that is between Galatians 3:28 and 1 Timothy 2:15.[13] Still others situate the decisive moment after Paul: in Philo's exegesis of Genesis assumed to have been written around A.D. 40, or in the Philonian reception of Middle Platonism;[14] in the last third of the first century with the reception of Colossians written by a disciple of Paul; at about the same time as a result of the influence of Aristotle's *Politics;*[15] between the second and third centuries with Tertullian;[16] in 325 with the Council of Nicaea and the exhortation to follow Mary;[17] in the latter part of the fourth century with the transformation of Christianity into an official state religion; in the first quarter of the fifth century with Jerome and the Jovinian controversy;[18] or a little later with Augustine and his struggle not only against heresy (Donatist and Pelagian) but against his own will.[19]

Thus it is difficult to determine when Christianity became divided between the possibilities of salvation and pleasure and, at the same time, between attitudes of sexual equality versus subordination of the female to the male. Indeed, it is next to impossible to say at what precise moment sex became "identified as something intrinsically evil" and "as the controlling element in morality,"[20] for there is no single figure or event that can be said to be decisive, and no year, decade or even century that unequivocally marks the difference, where the question of sexual renunciation is concerned, between Christianity and either other cultures or its own past.[21] On the contrary, all that we can know points to the crystallization across a period of some three hundred years of both a doctrine of asceticism and techniques of self-repression, which grew progressively through a series of elaborations and stages. This means that disagreement about the determining moment in the conflict itself is not only irresolvable, but also, finally and almost inevitably, just a part of the seemingly broader question of origin.

From Where?

Those who seek to trace the roots of Christian asceticism look first to the weight of pagan tradition—Eastern, Hebraic, Hellenic, and Roman. Some, for example, see in the Eastern fertility cults a cluster of associations between femininity and production that will later surface in Greek culture in the form of an association between women and the uncontrollability of reproductive sexuality. Or they see in the mysticism of the Attis cult, which derives its force from the dramatic imitation of an act of self-castration, a prototype of the Christian renunciation of the flesh (one that may have survived as a fear of witchcraft).[22] Others maintain, along the same lines, that the Old Testament itself represents an attempt to overcome more ancient nature religions, to desexualize fertility cults, more precisely, to resist the feminine deities of pagan religion by replacing them with a god that is altogether beyond sexuality.[23] Then too, as we saw in chapter 1, a plausible case can be made for the contribution of the Genesis story of the Fall to the later patristic formulation of the question of gender, and in particular its role in the ideological substantiation of the household code.[24] Christianity rejected the Judaic practices of divorce, polygamy, and remarriage (the levirate or sororate) in what might be seen as a refusal of reproductive sexuality symptomatic of a broader renunciation of the body. Judaism itself produced in the century before Christ its own version of an ascetic community among the Essenes, who rejected both private property and sexual contact.[25] There is, morever, much in Jewish folk wisdom to warn of the ruses of women. And yet, although there are elements in the Old Testament that will later be appropriated by the church fathers, and although ancient Jewish culture was no doubt every bit as patriarchal as any in the Middle East of the time, canonical Judaism did not dwell upon the Yahwist version of Creation; the hostility toward women apparent, for example, in Paul; or the theologized version of antifeminism characteristic of the fathers of the church.

In assessing the elements of Greek culture that might be identified with the Christian position, one thinks, again, of a reaction against matriarchy that, as in the Old Testament example, is considered somewhat mythically to lie at the headwaters of subsequent antifeminism.[26] A glorification of virginity can be deduced from the presence of virgin priestesses in the religious life of the Greeks, who maintained a keen sense of the potential dangers of overindulgence in sex and a sense of self-restraint, which manifests itself in terms of a fear of the feminine.[27] The Platonic mistrust of the flesh, of the senses, and of sensuality, as well as of the superficiality of representations, no doubt influenced the fathers. Plato's distinction between the life of the philosopher and family life is one source of later condemnations of marriage, which can easily be identified with the topos of the *molestiae nuptiarum* (see chapter 1); and the Platonic indictment of poetry and images certainly can be seen to contribute to the atmosphere of anathema, which in Christianity hangs over cosmetics and the decorative. Aristotle too expresses a distrust of pleasures, both sex and eating, which are to be avoided because they are beyond the pale of reason. Elizabeth Schüssler Fiorenza maintains that the adaptation in Aristotle's *Politics* of the relation pertaining between masters and their slaves to the question of gender was the deciding factor in the definitions of "woman's nature" and "woman's proper sphere," which thus found their determining political background well before the Christian era. Aristotle's political philosophy, revitalized in Neopythagorean and Stoic philosophy and integrated to Hellenic Judaism in the writings of Philo and Josephus, which stressed the relation between the state and household management, played an important role in the formulation of the household code.[28] The Pythagoreans accepted the Aristotelian rejection of sexual pleasure, and the church of the third century would draw upon their beliefs in its campaign in favor of celibacy. Stoic thought as well furnished the church fathers with arguments against the flesh and in favor of an ideal of life in accordance with nature. We have already acknowledged Tertullian's debt to the Stoic denigration of decoration, which he transformed in *De cultu feminarum* into the first expression of "cosmetic theology" (see chapter 2).[29]

One must be careful not to confuse the theologized misogyny of the Christian era with the at once more magical and more physiological misogyny of the Hellenic world. Nonetheless, Greek medicine offers models of sexual containment and sexual difference that no doubt served to substantiate subsequent ideological prejudice and to justify Christian celibacy. Galen associated maleness with self-control and femaleness with a lack of self-restraint. Soranus maintained that "all excretion of seed is harmful in females as in males. Virginity, therefore, is healthful, since it prevents the excretion of seed. . . . Men who remain chaste are stronger and better than others and pass their lives in better health, correspondingly it follows that for women too virginity in general is healthful."[30] Aristotelianism, and especially the physical Aristotle of *On the Generation of Animals*, provided a model of reproduction that roots the inequality of the genders in the biological difference between a male, associated, as in Christianity, with form, and a female of the species, associated with matter. In the Aristotelian physiological tradition, which permeates the domains of law and theology as well as medicine and stretches all the way from Greece to the High Middle Ages and Aquinas, and even to Freud, the woman represents an imperfect version of the male, a "misbegotten male."[31] Finally, the contribution of the Hellenic world to Western asceticism passed via Greek literature, which is perhaps less important for the Middle Ages, but which contains nonetheless many examples of the topoi we have discussed in relation to medieval misogyny.

In the Latin tradition one finds in Lucretius a condemnation of ornament and warnings against bodily decoration alongside the Platonic definition of sexual desire as a trouble of the senses, especially of vision, and a threat to the *ataraxia* or spiritual detachment that was also the goal of Stoic philosophy.[32] Virgil voices a familiar cliché concerning the fickleness of women: "Varium et mutabile semper femina" (*Aeneid,* IV, 659). Then too, the search for expressions of antifeminism in Roman culture leads inevitably to Juvenal's sixth satire, which is as virulent a diatribe against woman and marriage as can be found in the ancient world. There woman is depicted as without scruples, unfaithful, uncontrollable, endlessly garrulous and quarrelsome, and filled with lust for decoration. And again, though elements of the great Latin naturalist and the satirist can be found in the medieval discourse of misogyny, neither Lucretius's physical model of sexuality as the excitement of atoms nor Juvenal's caricature of domestic life as perpetual discord is theologized in quite the way that these ideas will be in Christian culture.

Among the possible sources within the climate of Christianity, though not strictly speaking Christian, one can point to the pseudepigraphical myths: the Book of Enoch, the Book of Jubilees, and the Testament of Reuben from the Testaments of the Twelve Patriarchs, which associate women with adornment, lust, seduction, fornication, and prostitution. Bernard Prusak maintains, for example, that there is a direct line between the Apocrypha, the teachings of Clement of Alexandria and Origen, and Tertullian's Catholic and Montanist works.[33] Students of the late Roman Empire stress, further, the important role played in the first five centuries of our era by the major heresies, which not only permeated the writings of the fathers but also often produced a reaction crucial for the crystallization of early Christian attitudes towards gender. The repression of heresies by the orthodox church often served as a means of defining doctrine, which also can be said to have integrated heretical teaching. Tertullian, for example, was one of the chief opponents of Montanism (mid-second century) which held that the kingdom of God was imminent, and accorded to women a power of prophecy and a liberty to teach that scandalized the "mainstream" church enough to suppress such an expression of feminine spirituality. The Encratites of Syria (mid-third century) preached, in the words of Peter

Brown, that "the end of the present age was to be brought about by the boy-cott of the womb."[34]

Gnosticism represented at once a more complicated and a more interest-ing movement, which can be seen as both pro- and antifeminist in the way that the dominant contradictory attitudes of Christianity (to which it con-tributed both directly and by way of reaction) would eventually emerge as the dichotomy surrounding woman as the "Bride of Christ" and "the Devil's gateway." Gnosticism contained, first of all, a strong component of as-ceticism, according to which sexual relations constituted the "prototype of all moral offenses" (James Brundage) and the flesh was gendered feminine.[35] The followers of Valentinus, a contemporary of Tertullian, associated the female with a lack of shape and direction and the male, as in both the dominant patristic and Aristotelian traditions, with form. The goal of gnosticism, which recognized the mind/body split as a gendered one, was the reintegration of the woman, "the perpetual inferior other, into her guiding principle, the male."[36] Marcion and the Marcionites too rejected the created world; devoting themselves to asceticism, they preached a du-alism that links the feminine to the order of creation—matter and the world—while maleness is affixed to a more transcendent reality. The gnostic *Gospel according to the Egyptians* contains a saying of the savior to the effect: "I have come to destroy the works of the female, by the 'female' meaning lust, and by the 'works' birth and decay." The pseudo-Clementines maintain that "the present world is female, as the mother brings forth the souls of children, but the world to come is male, as a father receiving his children."[37] Thus we find in gnosticism a theologizing of gender that subtends the patriarchal paradigm of subsequent Christian tradition. But gnosticism, as Elaine Pagels has shown, also contained elements that can be taken to be profeminine; in particular, it recognizes in Eve the spirit of redemption. The gnostic *Reality of the Rulers* identifies the woman with life and with the principle of spiritual awakening.[38] Indeed, gnosticism included within the Godhead female elements, more precisely, a Trinity that consisted of "the Father, the Mother, and the Son"; and, like the Montanists, the gnostics were willing to recognize the equality of the sexes for those who had redeemed themselves from sexuality, the proof being that women prophesied at least about the created world (as opposed to the world to come, a subject reserved for male prophets) and were, at least in the case of the heretic Marcion, reported to have been allowed to serve in the priesthood and to baptize. Again, such actual sexual egalitarianism drew strong resistance which can be confused with the antifeminism of orthodox churchmen. Tertullian was one of the opponents of gnosticism. He complains in his treatise *On the Prescription of Heretics:* "These heretical women—how bold they are! They have no modesty; they are audacious enough to teach, to engage in argument, to perform exorcisms, to undertake cures, and maybe even to baptize."³⁹ Finally, in considering the reaction against heresy as a catalyst to antifeminism, one cannot fail to mention other groups: the Manichaeans, who maintained a dualism of the spirit and flesh similar to that of the gnostics and scandalized the orthodox because the followers of Mani allowed women to participate in public debates; the Arians, who reserved for Mary a more prominent role in the drama of the Incarnation; and the Jovinians, who denied not only that Mary remained a virgin during and after birth, but also that the celibate life of monks was any more virtuous than that of the ordinary married Christian practicing sexual intercourse. The doctrines of Jovinian elicited what was to remain one of the most influential antifeminist attacks of the Middle Ages, one that constituted the prime source of medieval antimatrimonial literature, the *Adversus Jovinianum* of Saint Jerome.⁴⁰

We have identified some of the potential sources of the contradictory Christian attitudes toward gender in the asceticism—often accompanied by antifeminism—of Hebraic, Hellenic (that is, Platonic, Aristotelian, Stoic, and Pythagorean), and Roman traditions, as well as in the Pseudepigraphia and in both the dogma of and reaction against Montanist, gnostic, Manichean, and Jovinian heresies. Still, the only indisputable conclusion is that it is as difficult to locate a single determining influence upon early medieval definitions of gender as to determine its originary moment. Indeed, given the multiplicity of possibilities, about all we can say with certainty is that the Mediterranean region of the early centuries of the Christian era offered a fertile milieu for what we have defined as a feminizing of the flesh, an estheticizing of the feminine, and a theologizing of esthetics. We find the glorification of the feminine in the Montanist, gnostic, and Jovinian heresies, while at the same time there is plenty of grist for the mills of asceticism in Platonic and Aristotelian thought. There is food for misogyny in Greek mythology and the Apocrypha. And the attempt to combat heresy, and especially the role of women in heretical movements, becomes practically synonymous with a reaction against the feminine. Although we have rounded up a good number of the usual suspects in the search for the sources of misogynistic thought in the West, we are left with little more than an almost limitless catalogue of overlapping proclivities and pressures that point more or less in the same direction. The attitudes toward gender that Christianity combines and crystallizes are to be found just about everywhere in the ancient world. No one source seems so compelling as to dismiss the rest; on the contrary, as soon as we distinguish one influence, another comes to mind. This means that in taking the identification of sources for explanation we risk—and herein lies the danger of misogyny as a citational mode—merely substituting for our object of study prior examples.

How and Why?

How then did Christianity's double attitude toward women come about? What were the historical, social, and even personal conditions under which the contradictory identifications of the feminine with the "Devil's gateway" and the "Bride of Christ" became mutually implicated and which allow us to understand the contradiction in a way not evident in the search for dates or sources?

These too are obviously what geneticists, in assessing the etiology of little understood chromosomal syndromes, term "multifactorial" problems. We can, nonetheless, distinguish among several groups of explanations—those scholars who view the antifeminism attached to Christian asceticism as a function of social reality; those who see it as a reaction to, or negative image of, social change; those who invest individual figures with primary responsibility; and those who tend, through some version of biology, to posit misogyny at the level of nature.

Among the realists, some historians point to overcrowded demographic conditions in the region, an explanation that makes Christian asceticism part of a collective unconscious effort at limiting population. Thus the condemnation of marriage and the praise of virginity were, in the view of David Herlihy, the ideological underpinnings of birth control and family planning. Indeed, John Chrysostom claimed in his treatise *On Virginity* that the population of the earth was sufficient to bring reproductive sex to an end.[41] Other realistically minded historians, in what is at once the most generally accepted and least examined explanation of the causes of misogyny, ascribe the Christian antimatrimonial thrust to the growth of the monastic movement from the second century on (including the ascetic sects, the Encatrites, Abeloïtes, and Syneisacts), whose campaign in favor of clerical celibacy was sustained rhetorically by the condemnation of the flesh and of woman.[42] The most sophisticated version of such an argument is that of Peter Brown who, in *The Body and Society: Men, Women and Sexual Renunciation in Early Christianity*, makes a forceful case for the early Christian discourse on sexuality as the principal ideological force behind a fundamental distinction between the old sexual order of the city and the new order of the desert, in which the body has been overcome.

Neither the thesis of overpopulation nor that of monastic deterrence is very far removed from what appears to be the millenarianism of the Roman world, the sense of civilization coming to an end (as in the coming of Christ) because of what is perceived to be the general moral laxity of the empire and the provision, by way of reaction, for such an eventuality.[43] Many historians, for example, insist upon the fact that homosexuality, which was tolerated to a greater extent in Greece and under the Roman republic, was condemned under the empire and in Christianity as an essential aspect of what can be seen as a resistance to decline. According to such a claim, Christian antifeminism represents one of the sublimated effects of the repression of the freer homosexual practices of both the Romans and Greeks.[44] Along the same lines, others cite the improvement of the legal and economic condition of women under the late empire, which, as in the combat against what was perceived to be the power of women in heretical movements, elicited a repressive response from the ruling patriarchy.[45] Elizabeth Schüssler Fiorenza, for example, considers Roman misogyny an expression of the resentment of middle-class men "whose psychic and economic reality were heavily determined by daily competition, and who therefore sought to maximize the 'natural' difference between women and men in order not to be replaced by women."[46] Here the assumption is that men rationalize subjugation through the disparagement of the subjugated, an idea that entails a certain logical inconsistency. For it implies the less tenable assumption that the more powerful woman is, the more she is feared, and the more feared she is, the more she is denigrated. Antifeminism, according to this logic, becomes a symptom not of disenfranchisement but of feminine power.

An important current of recent writings on the Roman and Hellenic period stresses changes in family structure that help to explain the transformation of the magical and cosmic misogyny of an earlier era into an antifeminism as everyday domestic annoyance in Juvenal and the church fathers. Paul Veyne, in particular, maintains that Christian attitudes toward gender reflect a more general change in the culture, which includes: (1) a shift away from personal forms of leadership and toward a professional bureaucracy; (2) a modification in family structure, beginning in the second century B.C., with the gradual decline of the patriarchal clan in favor of the nuclear family; (3) the constitution of the "couple" as master and mistress of the house, and of the household coextensive with a single living unit, along with the invention of a "new moral law" of conjugal love as part of the general displacement (interiorization) of statutory law by the concept of "virtue"; (4) the repression of concubinage and adultery, and of abortion, and the sacralization of the prohibition of incest; and most important (5) the generalization of marriage. The Christian era is synonymous with the passage "from a society in which marriage is not for everyone to a society where it is taken for granted that marriage is the fundamental institution of all societies and of the whole society."[47] Michel Foucault follows essentially the same line in the third volume of his *History of Sexuality, The Care of the Self,* which focuses upon the Hellenic as well as the Roman world and develops in greater detail than Veyne the consequences for the concept of person of the double evolution of marriage as a public institution and as a focus of private life.[48]

Veyne's and Foucault's tableau of the narrowing of the family to the dimension of the conjugal cell carries us a long way toward understanding one of the important elements of the "domestication" of misogyny. Within this context, it would appear to stem from the reduction of a once broader and freer model of sexuality to one of a "normality" defined by nature, a "heterosexuality of reproduction," and an increased burden placed upon the couple as an institution. Misogyny seen as domestic annoyance—complaint against petty jealousies, envy of neighbors, nagging, bragging, argument and contradiction, risks of birth, noises of the nursery, and disappointments of children—supports such a claim.[49] Peter Brown too insists that the *molestiae nuptiarum* are reflective of "the huge pain that any underdeveloped society places on the bodies of its fertile women" and that even the anticosmetic thrust of early Christianity can be seen in terms of a broader antipoverty campaign focused upon the conjugal cell.[50]

From the perspective of antifeminism as a sublimated form on an individual level of the attempt to resist women who are also, through its rhetoric, the object of subjugation, and from the perspective of antifeminism as essentially an expression of resentment of the nuclear family, we now move closer to psychohistorical explanations of medieval misogyny. Here we encounter, first of all, what one might think of as the "great men" theories of how the Christian position on sexuality came about. H. R. Hays, for example, explains Paul's attitude toward women in the following terms:

Paul, a Hellenized Jew with a Greek education, was a Roman citizen living in Tarsus. He was unattractive physically, small, somewhat deformed, with poor eyesight. He was also a prey to hallucinatory experiences, almost epileptic in character; in short he was the typical shaman. . . . From the psychoanalytical point of view, Paul was always struggling with father figures, the reflection of the harsh and blatantly male image of Yahweh. . . . In other words, social distress, grown more intense as society grew more complicated, reactivated basic male anxieties which we have been all along describing. And this is proved by the fact that the myth of the Fall became the central explanation of all evil.[51]

Claude Rambaux maintains that Tertullian's central role in the formulation of questions of gender in the West can be ascribed to his "obsessions and personal problems."[52] More recently, Elaine Pagels in *Adam, Eve, and the Serpent* attributes Christian attitudes toward sexuality to Augustine's personal struggle with the will, and more precisely to his attempt to repress the sexual adventures of his youth after conversion. Pagels maintains that this not only accounts for the invention of the concept of original sin, but also fell on fertile political ground in the era following Christianity's adoption as an official state religion.[53]

The "great men" theories, built implicitly upon a developmental model of object relations, assume what one might also think of as the generalized or naturalistic accounts of misogyny, in which the psychological borders upon the biological to produce explanations so broad as to make anti-feminism seem inevitable. This is the case of the psychoanalytic supposition that hatred of women stems from the male child's—every male child's—frustration and anger at his mother because he cannot possess her. The Freudian articulation of the Oedipal drama is, of course, the archetype of all such instances, but Freud is not the only one to explore the effects of separation anxiety upon later attitudes towards gender. Melanie Klein is even more explicit than the Viennese master:

> In the early anal-sadistic stage the child sustains his second severe trauma, which strengthens his tendency to turn away from the mother. She has frustrated his oral desires, and now she also interferes with his anal pleasures. It seems as though at this point the anal deprivations cause the anal tendencies to amalgamate with the sadistic tendencies. The child desires to get possession of the moth-

er's faeces, by penetrating into her body, cutting it to pieces, devouring and destroying it. Under the influence of his genital impulses, the body is beginning to turn to his mother as love-object. But his sadistic impulses are in full activity, and the hate originating in earlier frustrations is powerfully opposed to his object-love on the genital level. A still greater obstacle to his love is his dread of castration by the father, which arises in the Oedipus impulses. The degree in which he attains to the genital position will partly depend on his capacity for tolerating this anxiety. Here the intensity of the oral-sadistic and anal-sadistic fixations is an important factor. It affects the degree of hatred which the boy feels toward the mother; and this, in its turn, hinders him to a greater or lesser extent in attaining a positive relation to her.[54]

Katherine Rogers, who has written the most thorough historical study of misogyny, also adopts a version of the psychoanalytic hypothesis, according to which the projection of desire and fear are ultimately transformed into anger:

The underlying reasons for man's tendency to react against his own intense passion can probably be traced to the complex development of the human libido, as Freud analyzed it. He showed that sado-masochism, although it seems to be the antithesis of love, is normal in the erotic life of children and may persist into adult relationships. Furthermore, the prototype of a man's erotic relationships with women is his childish love for his mother, which necessarily includes some elements of frustration: the child's absolute dependence on her and her inevitable preference for another male.[55]

The difficulties with such an account should be obvious: first, every child, and not just little boys, has a mother. And yet, if one considers the effects upon girls by reversing the paradigm of frustration, one comes up neither with an analogous misogynistic response among women nor with a corre-sponding misandry, expressed in terms of hatred of the father, to equal the cultural effects of antifeminism.[56] Second, the psychoanalytic explanation tends to naturalize misogyny by universalizing it, since there can be no avoidance of the experience of separation assumed to frustrate every male child, who is as destined to dislike women as he is to pass through the Oedipus complex. The psychoanalytic model produces—and even the most contemporary thinkers can hardly be considered to be innocent—a version of the topos of the woman as the great other or as alien.[57] Finally, such an essentializing gesture can account for neither the historical nor the cultural manifestations of antifeminism, the diverse ways in which different societies at different moments have resisted, appropriated, assimilated, sublimated, or implemented the differing discourses of misogyny in terms of social practice.

If the late nineteenth century produced what remains the most individualized account of the origin of misogyny in the early childhood ambivalence toward the mother, it also witnessed the most collective explanation in the form of Engels's essay, *The Origin of the Family, Private Property, and the State*. Unleashing Marx upon Morgan's *Ancient Society*, Engels links the production of economic surplus at the transitional phase of culture between hunting and gathering and the domestication and breeding of animals to the creation of surplus wealth and to the constitution of the family as an economic unit, which in turn gave way to an entirely new order of relations between the sexes.[58] "Thus, on the one hand, in proportion as wealth increased it made the man's position in the family more important than the woman's, and on the other hand created an impulse to exploit this strengthened position in order to overthrow, in favor of his children, the traditional order of inheritance."[59] With the rise of some embryonic version of the nuclear family, the matriarchy of the phase of primitive communism gave way to both patrilineal inheritance and patrilocal residence.[60] "The overthrow of mother right was the *world historical defeat of the female sex*," writes Engels. This event, which took place well before Greco-Roman civilization, makes the misogyny of the ancients look mild by comparison: "The man took command in the home also; the woman was degraded and reduced to servitude; she became the slave of his lust and a mere instrument for the production of children. The degraded position of the woman, especially among the Greeks of the heroic and still more of the classical age, has gradually been palliated and glossed over, and sometimes clothed in milder form; in no sense has it been abolished."[61]

Engels's analysis of the subjugation of the female shares in the difficulties of the psychoanalytic model. Both situate a determining moment in the struggle between the sexes beyond consciousness and therefore out of reach of the will: the Freudian paradigm in the early development of the individual, and the Marxist paradigm in the prehistory of mankind. For those who follow Freud the Oedipal ambivalence and anger, located deep in the recesses of the unconscious, become the equivalent of fate, just as for Engels the definitive reversal of matriarchy, which predated the struggle between the classes, remains so distant temporally as to produce the assumption that it was almost always already there. Engels, no less than Freud, thus naturalizes that which he surely seeks to redress. And yet, *The Origin of the Family, Private Property, and the State* does point in the direction of a social analysis, and especially the analysis of family structure in relation to property rights—an issue that, I think it can be shown, is crucial to an understanding of the double Christian attitude toward gender.

The Biopolitics of Asceticism

Several socially oriented accounts of the origins of asceticism at the time of the late empire bring us closer to answering the question posed at the outset: How can Christianity at once affirm that woman is the "Bride of Christ" and the "Devil's gateway"?

Peter Brown, in *The Body and Society: Men, Women, and Sexual Renunciation in Early Christianity,* sees chastity as having provided the one thing missing from Paul's legacy—a distinctive mark by which converts might be identified and identify each other. Thus it functioned much like the sexual and dietary laws of Judaism. According to Brown (no doubt influenced by the first volume of Michel Foucault's *History of Sexuality*), sexuality was something that everyone shared within a heterogeneous community, "the one thing" that men and women from widely different social and religious backgrounds "had in common." Renunciation of the flesh thus became the principle that made Christianity a truly universal religion. It was "the great equalizer": "As Christians, women and the uneducated could achieve reputations for sexual abstinence as stunning as those achieved by any cultivated male. Total chastity was a gesture that cut through the silken web of decorum that swathed the public man: here was 'philosophical' restraint at its most drastic, now made open to all."[62] Asceticism served, at least at the outset, to define the struggling sects and to encourage their internal social cohesion.[63] Gradually, however, as the Roman world became increasingly divided between Christian and non-Christian, asceticism assumed, like the totem of the clans of a tribal village, a functional role in the definition of difference between the two cultures—one the secular culture of the city, of the body, of materialism, marriage, and women, and the other, the monkish culture of worldly renunciation. In a sophisticated version of antifeminism as a deterrent for clerics against the temptations of the flesh, misogyny constituted a "challenge to the city":

> Thus the studied misogyny of much ascetic literature did not reflect merely a shrinking away from women as a source of sexual temptation. It was mobilized as part of a wider strategy. It served to contain and to define the place of the ascetic movement in late Roman society. Faced by the perpetual threat of an asceticism so radical that it blurred the distinction between city and desert, even between men and women, the leaders of the churches, in Egypt as elsewhere, fell back on ancient traditions of misogyny in order to heighten a sense of sexual peril. In so doing, they insured that their heroes, the monks, remained in the prestige-filled, and relatively safe, zone of the desert. In fourth-century Egypt, fear of women acted as a centrifugal separator. It kept "world" and "desert" at a safe distance from each other. . . . They are separated by a "zone of silence."[64]

Finally, as Christianity became the official state religion and the original purpose of virginity as a social marker disappeared, asceticism continued to act, through Augustine's interpretation of Genesis, as the primary justification of the power of men over women and the vehicle of appropriation of the individual by the state.

A somewhat different view is taken by Elaine Pagels in *Adam, Eve, and the Serpent*. Pagels focuses upon the story of the Fall as a paradigm for the interpretation not only of church doctrine, but also of the individual's relation to his or her body. In the beginning asceticism, which reversed the reproductively oriented sexuality of the pagan world, represented a means to freedom, a denial of the notion of social destiny, "a way to gain control over one's own life." After Emperor Constantine's conversion, however, and the transformation of once rebellious sects into the hegemonic religion of empire, the principle of asceticism was adapted to new political realities. And where renunciation of the world had served as a defiant act of self-liberation, it became a dangerous doctrine harnessed, as in Brown's account, in the service of the state. Here too, the principal actor in the drama of social appropriation is Augustine, whose own struggle against temptation led to a radical freezing of the notion of the will and a condemnation as heretical of those who maintained its efficacy. The assumed original goodness of mankind characteristic of early Christianity was submitted to the Augustinian will and emerged as the

doctrine of transmittable original sin—living proof in every individual that
humans were ungovernable, in other words, were in need of strong political
control. Where, for example, according to Pagels, Chrysostom in reading the
story of Creation "proclaims human freedom, Augustine reads from the same
Genesis story the opposite—human bondage." This reading was in turn used
to rationalize the necessity of imperial rule.[65] Control over sexual impulse
becomes in this way the prototype of all modes of self-governance, including
the political.

Jack Goody approaches the issue of late Roman and early medieval family
structure from the perspective of the "historical materialist" and the "social
anthropologist." In his *Development of the Family and Marriage in Europe,* he
poses the question: "How was it that after about 300 A.D. certain general
features of European patterns of kinship and marriage came to take a different
shape from those of ancient Rome, Greece, Israel, and Egypt, and from those
of the societies of the Mediterranean shores of the Middle East and North
Africa that succeeded them?"[66] The answer to this question lies, Goody
maintains, not in the area of ideology—ethics or doctrine—rather, in the precarious economic situation of the early church and in the methods it
developed to attenuate the power of wealthy Roman families and thus to get
family property "flowing" in its direction. As would again be the case in the
twelfth century, as we shall see (chapter 7), the clergy sought ways of inserting
itself into the domestic life of converts through a series of "strategies of heirship" aimed at disrupting the devolution of the patrimony of the Roman clan.
Thus the church embarked upon a biopolitics of lineage predicated upon several actions.

1. The extension of the degrees of kinship within which marriage was
prohibited. This prohibition, which had been basic to the Arab world as well
as Greece and the Palestine of Jesus, weakened the family's ability to keep
property to itself through close or in-marriage, which was outlawed along
with polygamy.

2. Discouragement of the creation of "fictional" heirs by banning both
the Roman practice of adoption and the Germanic practices of wet-nursing
and fosterage.

3. The outlawing of concubinage, which among the Romans had had the
effect of creating offspring who, despite their illegitimacy, could nonetheless
inherit property.

4. The prohibition of divorce, which might have as an effect the creation
of progeny of a second bed when the first one was sterile.

5. The admonition against remarriage, which implies a second chance at procreation.

6. Affirmation of the principle of the consent of parties rather than paternal sanction where the choice of marriage partners is concerned.

7. The designation of celibacy as a virtue and the glorification of virginity as both a personal goal and a cultural ideal. This made it the duty of virgins to remain virgins, of those whose spouses had died to remain widows or widowers, and of those who had married to renounce within marriage further sexual relations.

For Goody the current of asceticism that was practically synonymous with Christian morality was but one of many strategies aimed at divesting the Roman family of its property. This was equally true of the issue of clerical celibacy. The church's "acquisitions, both real and personal, were of course exposed to much greater risk of dilapidation when the ecclesiastics in charge of its widely scattered riches had families for whose provision a natural parental anxiety might be expected to over-ride the sense of duty in discharging the trust confided to them."[67] The model of kinship proffered among the early sects in the first centuries of our era was aimed—consciously or not—at breaking up great family lineages, and thus great family fortunes, which instead began, through the practice of lateral donation as opposed to lineal legacy, to accumulate in the coffers of the spiritual brotherhood.

Many aspects of the ideology as well as the history of the first centuries of Christianity serve to substantiate Goody's claim that church policy was aimed at fragmenting the cohesiveness of the Roman gens. It is not hard, for example, to interpret the antiparental and antimarriage campaign of the apostles as an attempt to substitute the idea of spiritual family for the biological or even social kin-group, and this from the beginning. Jesus is reported to have said (Luke 14:26) "If any one comes to me and does not hate his own father and mother and wife and children and brothers and sisters, yes, and even his own life, he cannot be my disciple."[68] "But I would have you without carefulness," writes Paul. "He that is unmarried careth for the things that belong to the Lord, how he may please the Lord: but he that is married careth for the things that are of the world, how he may please his wife: There is a difference also between a wife and a virgin. The unmarried woman careth for the things of the Lord, that she may be holy both in body and in spirit: but she that is married careth for the things of the world, how she may please her husband" (1 Corinthians 7:32–34).[69]

As stated at the beginning of this chapter, one of the strong seductions of

Christianity in the early centuries was its appeal to women because of what is perceived by historians and theologians to this day to be its sexually liberating, egalitarian message. Christianity, and not just the primitive Christianity of Jesus, has from the beginning been understood as a religion that stresses the individual will as opposed to the subsuming notion of destiny or fate of the Greeks. More important, Christianity can be seen as a religion that held men and women accountable to the same rules where questions of marital fidelity, the penalties for adultery, the grounds for divorce, chastity, or virginity before marriage were concerned. In this it stands as a rejection of the blatantly inequitable double ethical standard of the Hellenic and Judaic world, the world of Palestine as well as of Rome.[70]

The church offered material advantages to those constrained by Roman family structure as well as to those isolated from the mainstream of Judaic religions and social life. More precisely, Christianity held the promise of escape from the patriarchy of the ancient world in which a girl of twelve might easily be married against her will to a man of fifty and would thus pass from the control of father to that of husband. "Forget also thine own people and thy father's house," Jerome, quoting Psalm 45, addresses Eustochium, "and the King [Jesus] shall desire thy beauty."[71] And at the same time, as some scholars have insisted, the sects of "brothers and sisters" extended to women opportunities from which they were otherwise excluded: advantages of travel (albeit as pilgrims), education and intellectual pursuits, relative freedom to control the fortunes left to them as daughters and widows, and, finally, the possibility of founding, participating in, and even directing religious institutions. Many religious foundations benefited from the disposition of feminine wealth. The clergy "welcomed women as patrons and even offered women roles in which they could act as collaborators," writes Peter Brown. "By 200 A.D., the role of women in the Christian churches was quite unmistakable. . . . Altogether the Christian intelligentsia of the age took the presence of women, as disciples and patronesses, absolutely for granted."[72]

Not only did the early sects of the faithful appeal to wives and daughters anxious to escape Roman tutelage, but also in the early church (that is, before its repatriarchalization) women functioned as prophets, missionaries, heroic martyrs, and leaders.[73] Anna and Mary played the role of prophets among the other female prophets mentioned in the second-century *Acts of Paul and Thecla*—Theonoe, Stratonike, Eubulla, Phila, Artemilla. The story of Thecla, like that of Mygdonia contained in the *Acts of Thomas*, illustrates woman's abandonment of family to follow the apostle and displays exemplary feminine missionary zeal.

By offering an alternative to the patriarchal family, to the tutelage of the Roman paterfamilias or the Jewish father, Christianity became in the phrase of Elizabeth Schüssler Fiorenza, a "role-revolt" that "advanced women's cultural-political emancipation,"[74] a "liberating choice," according to Rosemary Ruether.[75] It appeared as a "kind of women's liberation," says Robert Nisbet,[76] as a counter to the certain feminine disenfranchisement prevalent within marriage and in society at large. For the Christian community, understood in the light of Galatians 3:28, is rooted in an "egalitarian vision and in altruistic social relationships that may not," again in the words of Fiorenza, "be 'genderized'."[77]

The narrative iconography of the early church is filled with stories of the conflict between young martyrs who reject marriage and the claims of the family anxious to ensure survival of the family line.[78] Thecla is said to have refused a wealthy marriage after having heard Paul preach "the word of the virgin life." Her mother warns her fiancé that "all the women and young people go in to him" and that she is "dominated by a new desire and a fearful passion." Finally, the mother denounces Thecla to the governer, urging him to burn her daughter so "that all the women who have been taught by this man may be struck with terror!"[79] The third-century story of the life of Saint Anthony offers a male analogue to the legend of Thecla. The son of wealthy Egyptian parents, the orphaned Anthony, inspired by Jesus's words ("Go, sell what you have, and give to the poor, and you shall have treasure in heaven" [Matthew 19:21]), rejects both wealth and marriage.[80] Ambrose reports in *De virginibus* the story of a consecrated virgin who pleads before the altar of the church for protection against the claims of family. "When the others were silent, one burst forth somewhat roughly: 'If,' he said, 'your father were alive, would he suffer you to remain unmarried?' Then she replied with more religion and more restrained piety: 'And perchance he is gone that no one may be able to hinder me.'"[81]

To the legends of the virgin martyrs who refuse to marry are added those of the married women who, in opposition to family, choose to renounce marriage, as well as of the widows who reject remarriage. Vibia Perpetua, who is married and has a two-year-old child, refuses to sacrifice to the emperors and is thrown into prison where she endures a paternal plea: "Daughter . . . have pity on your father, if I deserve to be called your father, if I have loved you more than all your brothers; do not abandon me. . . . Think of your brothers; think of your mother and your aunt; think of your child, who will not be able to live once you are gone. . . . Give up your pride! You will destroy all of us." The father's attempt at dissuasion is echoed by the governor, who urges Perpetua before her execution "to have pity on her father's grey head; have pity on her infant son."[82] Less dramatic stories of refusal of marriage against the pressure of insistent relatives and spouses abound: in Macrima's desire to remain a virgin after the death of her fiancé; in Mygdonia's successful attempt, after hearing Thomas preach, to persuade her husband to live henceforth in a celibate marriage (*Acts of Thomas* 9, 88); in Olympias's refusal to remarry after being widowed at nineteen. Melania the Elder, after the deaths of her husband and two children, is opposed in her decision to embrace the ascetic life by "the whole force of her noble relatives."[83] Her granddaughter Melania the Younger has parents who forcibly "united her in marriage" at age fourteen to a man who, when she pleads for chastity, insists that they have two children to ensure the paternal succession.[84] "Why, mother, do you grudge your daughter her virginity? . . . Are you angry with her because she chooses to be a king's wife and not a soldier's? She has conferred on you a high privilege; you are now the mother-in-law of God," writes Jerome.[85]

Scholars may argue that martyrs, because of their exemplary status, are an exception to the lives of most Christians. Still, they agree that the ascetic campaign of the early church deeply disturbed the traditional patterns of marriage of the Roman patriarchy. "The clergy's new language of *ex voto* dedication," in the words of Peter Brown, "threatened in no uncertain manner to freeze the benign current of young girls that flowed from their parents' house so as to knit together the families of the locality."[86] Asceticism brought the life of cities as it had existed to an end: "And many other women besides fell in love with the doctrine of purity . . . and men too ceased to sleep with their wives. . . . So there was the greatest dismay in Rome" (*Acts of Peter* 34, 2).[87] Nor can such disruption be detached from the patterns of inheritance and the disposal of wealth of the gens. Whether by the refusal to marry or the practice of continence within marriage—house asceticism—the devolution of patrimony, which would normally pass to heirs, was at least potentially interrupted. More important, "bodies withdrawn in perpetuity from the normal ebb and flow," in Peter Brown's words, of the patriarchal family's marital policies did not mean the simple interruption of the capital exchange of a class, of the exchange of women and dowries as capital. It seems to imply a much freer disposition of property on the part of those who chose to practice asceticism.

If the ascetic campaign of the early church was based upon the principle of the consent of the parties to a marriage—the right of the unmarried to refuse to marry, the widowed to remarry, and the married to unmarry—this appeal, it must be remembered, was addressed primarily to woman. For women, who ordinarily would have been under the tutelage of fathers and husbands, the exercise of bodily self-control meant, by one of those curious paradoxes that permeate the early Christian articulation of gender, an added measure of control over wealth that ordinarily would have passed to their progeny.[88] This was an important factor in the economic life of the Christian community, given the greater longevity of women in the late Roman world, the fact that the majority of virgins were themselves daughters of widows, the fact that ascetic women were for the most part well-to-do,[89] and the fact that women—wealthy converts, young virgins, pious widows, benefactresses, prophets, exemplary martyrs, missionary coworkers, pilgrims, confidantes, and friends—were the greatest supporters of the communities of brothers and sisters. They were the children of God, who were encouraged, according to the apostolic model, "to leave mother and father," to become the "Brides of Christ," and to prefer spiritual kinship over blood ties—that is, to choose the family of ascetics who were "mothers," "fathers," "sisters," and "brothers" to each other. These were the women who endowed nunneries and monasteries, paid for pilgrimages, supported scholarly enterprises, and sustained the charitable undertakings of those who ministered to the poor.

Thus, Goody's theory, nourished by those of Castelli, Pagels, and Brown, goes a long way toward explaining the motivation of early Christianity to break the power of patriarchy by a series of social and institutional practices ideologically sustained by an ascetic campaign directed especially toward women. In this it points to a partial answer to the question posed at the beginning of this chapter, namely, that of the church's affirmation of the equality of the sexes alongside its condemnation of the feminine. But certain difficulties still remain. First, at the time of its campaign of renunciation the church also outlawed child abandonment, abortion, and homosexuality, practices of the Roman world whose continuation might have furthered the "strategies of heirship" aimed at inhibiting reproduction. Second, though much of the literature we have examined is assumed to appeal to women, there exists relatively little direct testimony to confirm its attractiveness to those to whom it was addressed. Jerome, for example, wrote many letters to Paula, Marcella, Asella, and Eustochium; John Chrysostom, to Olympias. We possess almost no letters of women written in response.[90] Third, and most important, although Christianity attracted women by offering them the freedom to travel, to study, to dispose of property, and to exercise power over the religious institutions they had a hand in founding, and although the church provided the possibility of escaping painful marriages and of becoming a "Bride of Christ" as an equal in the fellowship of God, nothing in all we have seen until now explains how fledgling Christian sects could logically hope to attract women by the renunciation of the flesh that is also gendered feminine. Elizabeth Castelli justly remarks that "it is not at all clear that the ideology of virginity was not as domesticating and circumscribing of women's sexuality as the ideology of marriage." On the contrary, we have seen that woman is allied with the body in the thinking of the early church fathers, so that "the demand to renounce passion is therefore more poignant when applied to women because passion has been located in the idea of female selfhood. . . . Therefore, for a woman to participate in the institution which calls for the negation of the feminine is . . . for her to participate in a profound self-abnegation, self-denial, even self-destruction."[91] To repeat, though the appeal of Christianity to women can be explained by their glorification as "Bride of Christ" within the order of redemption, it cannot be justified either by the alliance of the feminine with the flesh and the subsequent denigration of the flesh in terms so virulent as to eliminate the feminine altogether or by the copresence of conflicting topoi that make women alternately the "Bride of Christ" and the "Devil's gateway."

One possibility of a solution lies, I think, in how we understand the term *alternately*. For as long as we continue to view Christianity as a bundle of beliefs uniting disparate strands of preexisting cultures, we are liable to miss its uniqueness, which has nothing to do with the positing of a female redeemer, characteristic of much older fertility cults; with the recrudescence of asceticism, with its Stoic and even Jewish roots; or with the dissemination of the misogyny that can be found in different forms practically everywhere in the ancient Mediterranean world. As long as we continue to view the early church as embracing an attitude *either* sympathetic *or* antipathetic to women, its originality will remain hidden.

The uniqueness of Christianity has to do, as we have seen, simultaneously with a gendering of the flesh as feminine, an esthetization of femininity, and a theologizing of esthetics—all processes that can be found elsewhere, but not in quite this combination. The originality of Christianity consisted also in a repositioning of the feminine, such that the concept of woman came to occupy a central position in the "imaginary economy of the Church" (Peter Brown). The fathers—beginning with Paul, but even more intensely from Tertullian on—used the category of woman as a "tool to think with" (Claude Lévi-Strauss) that was every bit as charged and as fundamental to speculation in other areas of thought—the social, the moral, the metaphysical—as we have seen the realm of language and sign theory to be.[92] The questions of gender and of poetics become in the period under study enmeshed, analogous mediating terms for the understanding of the human being's place within the material and the spiritual world. Finally, the uniqueness of Christianity resides in the fact that it, unlike any of the cults and religions that can be identified as potential sources, not only makes women assume the burden of mediator but also holds conflicting sexual attitudes in simultaneous abeyance. Thus the message to women is not "you are the Bride of Christ," or "you are the Devil's gateway," or even "you can be either," "you have a choice." Rather, it says, "you are at one and the same time the 'Bride of Christ' and the 'Devil's gateway,' seducer and redeemer, but nothing in between." The effects of this coincident contradiction are powerful and far reaching indeed.

The simultaneously bivalent Christian attitude renders the feminine so abstract that woman (not women) can only be conceived as an idea rather than a human being. It polarizes the definition of the feminine to such an extent that women are pushed to the margins, excluded from the middle, in other words, isolated from history. Again, this is not to deny the importance of individual women within the early church, or the importance of women mystics of the late Middle Ages, such as Angelina of Foligno, Marguerite Porete, Hildegard of Bingen, or Bridget of Sweden (though here one does well to ask to what extent mysticism as the privileged territory of feminine religious experience is empowering or disenfranchising within the secular world).[93] Poised between contradictory abstractions implicated in each other, women are idealized, subtilized, frozen into a passivity that cannot be resolved. Thus we find the prevalence in our culture of the idea of woman as contradiction, which we have seen rendered throughout the Middle Ages in terms of woman as perpetual overdetermination—either too rich or too poor, too beautiful or not beautiful enough, too rational or out of her senses. And thus too arises the notion of woman as ambiguity, paradox,

enigma; woman as question; woman as a vehicle to be used for thinking;
and even the notion, at the cutting edge of some feminist theory, of woman
as theory. For the intractability of her doubleness under such a definition—
abstract, polarized, pacified—is the very stuff of a double bind that begins to
answer the question of Christianity's feminine appeal. It is, ultimately, the
definition of woman as neither the "Devil's gateway" nor the "Bride of
Christ" but both at once, neither seductress nor redeemer but both at once,
which constitutes a paradigm of subjugation as compelling for the relation
of power between the genders as the notion of original sin. Woman, at least
no real woman, can resolve the dilemma of the contradictory abstracted
double. She is, in a sense, as powerfully entangled as the story of the Fall
itself, entrapped by the logic of a cultural ideal that, internalized, makes her
always already in a state of weakness, lack, guilt, inadequacy, vulnerability.
The issue of vulnerability is crucial here, for it alone, as the end product of
the placement of women in the position of "both at once," allows us to see
that the strategy of Christianity at the outset was not simply to appeal to
women, which it could have accomplished much more readily by the elaboration of the seductiveness of the "Bride of Christ" motif alone, but to
appeal to women and to control them at the same time. The idea of woman
as simultaneously seducer and redeemer is therefore no contradiction at all
but a powerful ideological weapon by which women, along with the property attached to them, passed out of the possession of families and were
repossessed by the church. Individual women may have been freed from the
patriarchal order in the early centuries of Christianity, but they were liber-
ated only to be recuperated by the family of brothers and sisters in which
they assumed the burden, every bit as impossible as the old Roman tutelage,
both of carnality and spirituality, the agent—seducer and redeemer—
through which men were to find either perdition or salvation.

THE POETICS OF VIRGINITY

In this chapter we will explore several of the defining paradoxes at the center of the Christian definition of gender to see how the ideology of asceticism explored in chapter 3 is worked out in vernacular literary works written over a millennium after Paul or Tertullian. The first of these paradoxes is a corollary of the reversal of the hierarchy between the genders touched upon in the previous chapter, but nonetheless so complex as to seem intractable to reason: the price for women of liberation from the patriarchal clan is femininity itself. Only so long as a woman was willing to renounce sexuality—that is, to remain unmarried if she was a virgin, and not to remarry if she was a widow, or even to renounce sexuality within marriage ("house monasticism")—was she able to escape the tutelage of fathers and husbands, and indeed to become the equal of man; for, in the phrase of Ambrose, "if you conquer the home, you conquer the world."[1] In what seems like an Averroistic double truth *avant la lettre* the possibility of equality of which the fathers speak exists only within the order of redemption and not within that of creation, which is another way of saying that the original equality of the sexes, which was lost, according to the Philonian model, at the time of the Fall, can only exist outside marriage, which is not only a symptom of earthly incarnation but also, precisely because of the Fall, governed by the "household code."[2]

The irony of such a liberation leads to an even more pervasive paradox within the writings of the fathers: the seeming contradiction between the view, outlined in chapters 1 and 2, of woman as imperfection, as against the desire for wholeness expressed in the insistent theme of virginity. Related to asceticism, the concept of virginity serves to link the early Christian antimatrimonial spirit to medieval poetics and thus to bring us closer to that other face of literary gender in the Middle Ages—courtly love. One need only look at the titles of the essays of the early church fathers—Tertullian's "On the Veiling of Virgins," "On Exhortation to Chastity"; Ambrose's "Concerning Virgins"; Augustine's *On Holy Virginity;* Gregory of Nyssa's *On Virginity;* Cyprian's "The Dress of Virgins"; Novatian's "In Praise of Purity"; Chrysostom's *On Virginity, Against Remarriage;* Methodius's *Treatise on Chastity*—to realize what an obsession chastity was. Concomitantly, one need only look at the number of works in Old French alone that focus upon virginity to recognize the degree to which the patristic obsession passed into vernacular literary works of the High Middle Ages. It is no accident that Old French literature begins with the stories of two virgin martyrs: Eulalie, who resists the Emperor Maximilian's advances; and Alexis, who, looking at his bride on his wedding night, opts for chastity over marriage.[3] The courtly romance is, as we shall see, also related to the antimatrimonial ethos, just as the courtly lyric is structured by a version of the same medieval fixation upon chastity.

The question at hand is the following: If, according to the early Christian articulation of gender, woman is imagined to represent the flesh, or a flaw of the flesh insofar as she embodies embodiment as opposed to mind, how is it possible to imagine her virginity? To begin to answer what seems like yet another aporia of the medieval articulation of gender, we shall consider two thirteenth-century Arthurian fabliaux and Chaucer's "Physician's Tale."

The Arthurian Fabliau

Like the commingling of species on medieval versions of the robe of Nature, the Arthurian fabliau is a generic perversion whose scandalous indeterminacy has always disturbed medievalists. Specialists, anxious above all to maintain sharp distinctions between literary genres, are embarrassed by the promiscuity of a work belonging properly neither to high nor low, learned nor popular, tradition, one that seems to mix the idealistic with the lewd. Indeed, having written a book whose thesis is the popular origin of the comic tale, Joseph Bédier invents the category of *fabliau aristocratique* to describe what happens when the antifeminism of popular literature permeates the courtly ideology of the Arthurian world. Per Nykrog, who also wrote a book to prove the fabliau's aristocratic origin, opts instead for the term *lai burlesque.* Robert Dubuis describes the Arthurian fabliau as "une oeuvre hybride," just as Emmanuèle Baumgartner sees in them signs of "an unclassifiable Arthurian counterculture."[4]

If the hybrid scabrous Arthurian tale represents a scandalous excess, that excess is both thematized and pushed to its logical limit in a series of works involving an ordeal of feminine chastity. I am thinking of the chastity-testing motif contained in the first branch of the Welsh *Mabinogi*, in "Du Crône," in Ulrich von Lichtenstein's *Lanzelet*, in the *First Continuation of Perceval*, the *Livre de Caradoc*, the *Vengeance Raguidel*, the *Prose Tristan*, and, more specifically, of the ordeal of the mantel and horn of "Du Mantel mautaillié" and the "Lai du corn."

"Du Mantel mautaillié" is the story of a knight who arrives at King Arthur's court bringing an adventure and carrying a magic coat designed to fit only the woman who has been faithful to her husband or lover:

La fée fist el drap une oevre
Qui les fausses dames
   descuevre;
Ja feme qui l'afublé,
Se ele a de rien meserré
Vers son seignor, se ele l'a,
Ja puis à droit ne li serra,
Ne aus puceles autressi,
Se ele vers son bon ami
Avoit mespris en nul endroit
Ja plus ne li serroit à droit
Que ne soit trop lonc ou trop
   cort.

The fairy who made it put the power to discover false ladies in the cloth. If the woman who puts it on has betrayed her husband in any way, it will never fit correctly. And the same is true for maidens who have wronged their lovers; the coat will never fit but will be either too long or too short.[5]

As becomes painfully obvious in the course of more than one hundred public fittings in "Du Mantel mautaillié," the tailoring of the coat is assimilated to a certain monotonous misogynistic tailoring of the tale. One right fit and the tale is too short; too many wrong fits and it never ends. More important, beneath the magic garment, which is as potent a paradigm of what it is to make fiction (of representation) as the Middle Ages produced, lies the indiscretion of marital and courtly infidelity. And this at the highest level, since the anonymous author singles out Guinevere as the incarnation of unfaithfulness, the archetypal adulterer; her clever defense is intended to prove the deceitfulness of all woman:

La Roine se porpensa
S'ele fesoit d'ire semblant

The queen thought to herself that if she made a pretense of anger the shame

Tant seroit la honte plus grant;	*would only be greater; each one would*
Chascune l'aura afublé;	*have tried it on; she turned it into a joke.*
Si l'a en jenglois atorné.	*(Recueil,* vol. 3, 12)

The tale and the coat are linked in the assimilation of feminine deceit—trickery, infidelity, lies, hiding—to poetic invention, a link with which we are familiar from our earlier discussion of "La Rencontre du roi d'Angleterre et du jongleur d'Ely" and "La Rhiote del monde" (chapter 1).

An even more virulent form of the chastity-testing motif is to be found in Robert Biket's "Lai du corn." Here the disclosing instrument of transgression is a drinking horn that spills its contents upon the man whose wife has been unfaithful, has ever contemplated infidelity, or who himself has experienced jealousy.[6] And here too, as in the "Mantel mautaillié," Guinevere is designated as the archetypal unfaithful wife, the scandal of her conduct made manifest in the spiced wine that spills over Arthur:

Li rois Arzurs le prist	*King Arthur took and placed it to his*
a sa bouche le mist	*mouth, for he intended to drink; but it*
kar beivre le quida,	*poured over him from head to foot; and*
mes sour lui le versa	*he was sorely grieved.* ("Lai du corn,"
cuntreval desk'as pez:	vv. 291–96)
en fu li rois irrez.	

The "Lai du corn" turns around a play on the word *cors*—the drinking horn that reveals betrayal or jealousy, the woman's body that is at stake, and the horns that are the emblem of the cuckold. Beyond wordplay, however, the magic vessel becomes the defining principle of an all-pervasive guilt; for, again, there is no one at court who has not experienced jealousy, or whose wife has not been unfaithful or, according to the medieval equation of concupiscence with adultery, has not betrayed her husband in thought: "kar n'i est femme nee, / qui soit espousee, / qui ne eyt pensé folie" ("For there is no married woman who has not had a foolish thought" ["Lai du corn," vv. 309–11]). Like a totemic secret uniting Arthur's court, the complicity of cuckolds transforms the desire of woman into a scandalous excess that stains all who try to drink; or, as in the "Mantel mautaillié," all whose wives try to make the garment fit. This suggests that Guinevere, far from an exception, is the figure of everywoman. Both motifs imply an inadequacy of container and contained that comes to constitute a paradigm of exorbitance inherent to medieval articulations of the question of woman, which we discussed at the end of the last chapter in terms of a polarized, abstract overdetermination and in chapter 1 in terms of the association of femininity and riot. Every woman, according to this account, is either a virgin or the vehicle of universal guilt. More important, the search for the virtuous woman in "Du Mantel mautaillié," tends, through what seems like yet another antimatrimonial satire, to obscure the more serious question of where exactly virginity can be found—a question that obsessed the early church fathers and bears crucially, as we will see, upon the later courtly constitution of woman as an unattainable ideal.

Virginity

For the early church fathers virginity always carries a reference to Adam and Eve before the Fall, a time when, it was assumed, because of the absence of sexuality the sexes were equal.[7] Jerome, for example, speaks of the "paradise of virginity." "In paradise Eve was a virgin."[8] Jerome does not refer, of course, to a historical time or a geographical place, but to a theological state of man—the angelic, asexual state of apatheia akin to Augustine's notion of technical virgins who reproduce in Eden without desire or pleasure. Ambrose too claims that "in holy virgins we see the life of the angels we lost in paradise"; and, as Peter Brown has shown, the "abnormal" status of the virgin body made it, like the angels, a "mediator between the human and the divine"; virgins were "heroes of the soul."[9] Then too, the notion of virginity is all bound up in doctrinal reference to Mary, the virgin, who redeems Eve. "Death," Jerome writes, "came through Eve, but life has come through Mary. And thus the gift of virginity has been bestowed most richly upon women, seeing that it has its beginning from a woman."[10] Though Jerome asserts elsewhere that "God cannot raise a virgin once she has fallen," it is clear, according to the Christological model of salvation history, that redemption implies a return to the state of virginity, to the *vita angelica*—an eschatological abolition of sexuality. Methodius speaks of the "bliss of a new Eden," Gregory of Nyssa of a return to the time before the Fall: "Through this sequence of events, we, together with our first father, were excluded from paradise, and now, through the same sequence, it is possible to return to the original blessedness." "In the risen Christ," Gregory asserts, "there is neither male nor female."[11]

On the individual level one assumes, of course, that a virgin is a woman who has never slept with a man. Indeed, much of the imagery surrounding virginity focuses upon the notion of a bodily integrity that rhetorically holds out to the woman willing to renounce her sexuality the promise of escaping the consequences of the Fall.[12] Yet, as the fathers make abundantly clear, it is not enough merely to be chaste. As Methodius proves methodically, there can be no chastity merely of the sexual organs, for "it would be ridiculous to keep one's generative organs pure, but not one's tongue; or to keep one's tongue pure, but not one's sight, one's ears or hands; or to keep all these pure, but not one's heart, allowing it to consort with anger and conceit." And, conversely, there can be no control of the rest of the body that does not imply chastity: "For if a person endeavors to restrain his body from the pleasures of carnal love without controlling himself in other respects, he does not honor chastity; indeed, he rather dishonors it to no small degree by base desires, substituting one pleasure for another."[13]

The distinction between virgins in mind and chastity of the body is emphasized throughout, since there is no difference between desire and the act. Rather, the act is defined by the mental state of those who perform it. Thus, according to the *Glossa Palatina,* a couple could be said to practice chastity even while making love.[14] And, conversely, "one can commit an adultery only in the heart," writes Origen in his commentary on Matthew, "without going all the way toward realizing it. . . . The one who is guilty only in his heart will be punished for this adultery: . . . And if, on the contrary he has wanted to do it and has tried without succeeding, he will be punished as if he had sinned in act and not only in the heart."[15] A virgin, then, is a woman who not only has never slept with a man, but also has never desired to do so. "For there are virgins in the flesh, not in the spirit, whose body is intact, their soul corrupt," Jerome maintains. "But that virgin is a sacrifice to Christ, whose mind has not been defiled by thought, nor her flesh by lust." "There must be spiritual chastity," John Chrysostom insists, "and I mean by chastity not only the absence of wicked and shameful desire, the absence of ornaments and superfluous cares, but also being unsoiled by life's cares."[16] One might well ask how the absence of "superfluous cares" can be anything but the very superfluity it renounces; nonetheless, here we find the theme of a return to Eden via virginity combined with that of cosmetic theology to produce what is in the thinking of the fathers clearly a significant opposition.

We have seen, in relation to medieval sacramental theology, how powerful is the nostalgia for a return to the time before the Fall. Augustine, it will be remembered, posits as the goal of history the return of the Son to the Father, the Word to its Speaker, or the signifier to the signified, as the end point of a transcendence of the senses that signals a recuperation of the fantasized immediacy of Eden. Conversely, the Fall is related thematically to a loss of

[handwritten margin note: Why isn't sex seen as a return to a pre-Fall?]

virginity, to a loss of wholeness, of an immediate and natural relation of signifier and signified that would preclude altogether the necessity of what we
have termed the cosmetic theology of the fathers. The Fall implies a fall into
mediations, signs, representations that imply always a gap between inner and
outer, the body and its cover. Jerome equates decoration of the body with the
shameful "mantle of skins"; and if in paradise Eve was a virgin, "it was only
after the coats of skins that she began her married life," he states, implying
that clothes are less the sign than the cause of exile.[17]

Virginity is in some deep sense precisely the opposite of the cosmetic;
just as marriage is associated with ornamentation, virginity implies a lack of
ornament. "Let her very dress and garb remind her of Whom she is promised," Jerome admonishes in a letter to Laeta on a girl's education. "Do not
pierce her ears or paint her face consecrated to Christ with white lead or
rouge. Do not hang gold or pearls about her neck or load her head with
jewels, or by reddening her hair make it suggest the fires of gehenna."[18] So
too Methodius: "While guarding herself against those things which are intrinsically sinful, the virgin must not on the other hand be such things as
resemble or are equivalent to the same; for in that case, while conquering the
one, she would be overwhelmed by the other. Such would be the case if she
pampered her body with the textures of clothing, or with gold and precious
stones and luxury and other bodily finery—things which of themselves intox-
icate the soul."[19] And Cyprian: "what have such maidens to do with worldly
dress and adornments. . . . No one on seeing a virgin should doubt whether
she is one. Let her innocence manifest itself equally in all things, and her dress
not dishonor the sanctity of her body. Why does she go forth in public
adorned, why with her hair dressed, as if she either had a husband or were
seeking one? Let her rather fear to be attractive."[20] The virgin, adorned,
Cyprian warns, is no longer a virgin.[21]

Since the desire of a virgin is sufficient to make her no longer a virgin, and
since, according to the patristic totalizing scheme of desire, there can be no
difference between the state of desiring and of being desired, a virgin is a
woman who has never been desired by a man. Thus Cyprian, again: "But if
you . . . enkindle the fire of hope, so that, without perhaps losing your own
soul, you nevertheless ruin others . . . who behold you, you cannot be ex-
cused on the ground that your mind is chaste and pure. Your shameless
apparel and your immodest attire belie you, and you can no longer be num-
bered among maidens and virgins of Christ, you who so live as to become the
object of sensual love."[22] Or Tertullian: "For that other, as soon as he has felt

concupiscence after your beauty, and has mentally already committed (the deed) which his concupiscence pointed to, perishes."[23]

What's more, the fathers argue, since desire is engendered by, and indeed consists in, a look, a virgin seen is no longer a virgin.[24] Almost to a man they quote the dictum from Matthew 5:28, "Whosoever looketh on a woman to lust after her hath committed adultery," and are obsessed by public baths. "For it is required of thee, O believing woman," we read in the *Didascalia apostolorum,* "that thou shalt flee from the multitude of vain sights of the pride of eye which is in the bath."[25] It seems, Cyprian argues, that no amount of soap and water can cleanse the body sullied by being seen: "You gaze upon no one immodestly, but you yourself are gazed upon immodestly. You do not corrupt your eyes with foul delight, but in delighting others you yourself are corrupted. . . . Virginity is unveiled to be marked out and contaminated."[26] Origen equates the mind's adultery with the loss of virginity contained in a glimpse.[27] According to Tertullian, "marriage . . . as fornication is trans- acted by gaze and mind." "Seeing and being seen belong to the self-same lust."[28] And, in what is perhaps the most violent expression of the deflower- ing effect of the look, Tertullian insists that "every public exposure of an honourable virgin is (to her) a suffering of rape."[29] The founding thinking of the problem of desire in the first four centuries of the Christian era establishes a profound link, which will surface occulted in the twelfth century to domi- nate the Western love tradition, between the distortion implicit to the gaze and erotic desire. Hence the stipulation, found in the penitentials, that sexual intercourse should take place at night and the prescription of one in particular that a man should never see his wife naked.[30] And hence the phrase in the *Didascalia apostolorum,* "pride of eye," joined by a myriad similar figures of ocular sin: the "guilt in a look" (Ambrose); "unchastened gazing" (Chrysostom); the "concupiscence of the eyes" (Cyprian); or the "adultery of the eyes" (Novatian). A virgin, in short, is a woman who has never been *seen* by a man.

But not exactly, since, in condemning public baths, the locus par excel- lence of the gaze of the other, Jerome wonders if it is licit for virgins to bathe at all, for in seeing their own bodies, there is always the potential for desire. "For myself, however, I wholly disapprove of baths for a virgin of full age. Such an one should blush and feel overcome at the idea of seeing herself un- dressed."[31] And the author of the late thirteenth- or early fourteenth-century *Ancren Riwle* makes it clear that a woman's look upon a woman is just as dan- gerous as that of a man:

A maiden also there was, Jacob's daughter, it is told in Genesis, who
went out to see the strange women. Now, observe, it is not said that she
beheld men, but it says women. And what, thinkest thou, came of that
beholding? She lost her maiden honour, and was made a harlot.
Afterwards, for the same cause, were truces broken by high patriarchs,
and a great city burned, and the king and his son, and the men of the
city slain, and the women of the city led away; her father and her
brethren, such noble princes as they were, made outlaws. To this length
went her sight: and The Holy Spirit has caused the whole to be written
in a book, in order to warn women concerning their foolish eyes.[32]

Nor do things end here. Since desire resides in sight, and since it makes no
difference whether one sees or is seen, either by others or oneself, and finally
since sight does not reside entirely in the faculty of perception but is also a
faculty of the intellect, a virgin is a woman who is not thought not to be one in
the thought of another. The virgin is above suspicion. "Even though they
[men and women] may be separated by walls, what good is that?" John
Chrysostom asks. "This does not suffice to shelter them from all suspicion."
And Clement of Rome, supposedly the disciple of Peter, warns against sitting
next to a married woman, "lest anyone should make insinuations against
us."[33] Thus, the only true virgin is one who has never sat next to or been in the
presence of a member of the opposite sex, or, finally, who has not entered the
thought of another. "For," to quote Tertullian again, "a *virgin* ceases to be a
virgin from the time it becomes possible for her *not* to be one."[34]

"The Physician's Tale"

If the satiric "Du Mantel mautaillié" thematizes on the level of the popular
tale the difficulty of finding a chaste woman, which is not so different from the
high cultural articulation of the question of virginity among the fathers,
Chaucer's "Physician's Tale" explores from the opposite perspective the consequences of the virgin found, a virgin seen.

"The Physician's Tale" is the story of how a virgin named Virginia is es-
pied by a judge named Appius, who, through the compliant churl Claudius,
brings an indictment against her father Virginius, who in turn puts his
daughter to death rather than suffer the shame of her sequestration in Appius's house. Critics of "The Physician's Tale" have noted the poorly
developed motivation of this narrative account of yet another virgin martyr,

an inattention that accounts no doubt for the tale's relative critical disrepute and even neglect. Chaucer, or the narrator, does not seem highly motivated to begin, for the stultified moralizing prologue, in which he discusses Nature's creation of Virginia and the importance of parents' surveillance of their children, occupies 118 lines, or over one third of the whole. Once the poet does begin, that beginning itself participates to such an extent in the quality of the accidental—the "Once upon a time, it happened"—that one wonders about the relation between the prologue and the almost generic narrative start: "This mayde upon a day wente in the toun / Toward a temple, with hire mooder deere, / As is of yonge maydens the manere" (vv. 118–20).[35] Chaucer is, moreover, so anxious to end the tale that the compressed resuming action is more postulated than shown. A crowd appears out of nowhere, Appius is thrown into prison, Claudius is exiled, and everybody else is hanged—all in ten lines! (vv. 267–76).

The characters of "The Physician's Tale" act so inexplicably and even illogically that not even the weight of psychologistic Chaucerian criticism can recuperate their intent. The whole turns, of course, around what is possibly a conscious play on words—that the maiden must lose her head in order to preserve her maidenhead.[36] More important, Claudius's accusation is unclear and unconvincing on the level of plot,[37] as is Appius's refusal to hear Virginius's defense: "This cursed juge wolde no thyng tarie, / Ne heere a word moore of Virginius" (vv. 196–97). There is no internal debate or discussion when Virginius announces to his daughter that there are only two alternatives—"outher deeth or shame / That thou most suffre" (vv. 212–13). The father's sentence is, furthermore, as illogical as that of the judge—"For love, and nat for hate, thou must be deed"—all the more so since Virginius knows the accusation to be false: "Allas, that evere Apius the say! / Thus hath he falsly jugged the to-day" (vv. 227–28). It is implausible that with so little, and even contradictory, explanation, Virginia herself should beg for death. Nor is the sudden appearance of those who recriminate Appius after the fact, but not at the time of his false judgment, any easier to believe since we learn too late that the "false iniquitee" (v. 262) was known all along: "The peple anon had suspect in this thyng, / By manere of the cherles chalangyng, / That it was by the assent of Apius; / They wisten wel that he was lecherus" (vv. 264–67). Then too, one wonders at the end why Virginius, so uncompromising toward the beloved daughter for whom the notion of mercy never arises, is so quick to pardon Claudius, the instrument of the plot against her: "But that Virginius, of his pitee, / so preyde for hym that he was exiled" (vv. 272–73).

Most of all, however, it is Appius's instantaneous passion for Virginia, the love at first sight, that fatal attraction, which animates the rest of the tale but itself remains completely unexplained.

The incongruence between motivation and action has not escaped the eye of critics. Anne Middleton asserts that the "moral of the tale may be independent of the motives of any of the characters, and also independent of the point of view of the teller." Her reading of "The Physician's Tale" focuses appropriately upon the "passive sacrifice" of the virgin martyr, victimized by both justice and father, within a parable of passivity that extends even to the level of sentence structure: "Virginia is seen as an object, not a person; even when she is the grammatical subject of a sentence she is the sufferer of an action."[38] Charles Muscatine speaks of the "few essential details of plot handled so vaguely as to rob the tale . . . of any power it might have had to make us suspend disbelief."[39] Emerson Brown sees the Physician as "the literary projection of a mind incapable of dealing with causes" within a sick "world in which causes are at best imperfectly related to results."[40] Brian Lee concludes that "so good a character as Virginia is almost inevitably passive."[41] Almost all who have written on "The Physician's Tale" insist—as if Chaucer himself assumed a posture of passivity, in other words, as if Chaucer himself were innocent—that this is a story determined by a subsuming framing narrative. I refer not to the obvious framing occasioned by an acknowledged source ("There was, as telleth Titus Livius, / A knyght that called was Virginius" [vv. 1–2]), nor to the framing pretense at factual presentation (". . . for this is no fable, / But knowen for historial thyng notable; / The sentence of it sooth is, out of doute" [vv. 155–57]), but to the perception of some governing abstract design. Derek Pearsall speaks of a "moral imperative," Middleton of a "larger, operative philosophical context than his [Chaucer's] predecessors." Sheila Delany maintains that this context is intentionally apolitical—a pagan political narrative transformed into static Christian exemplum.[42]

It is, in fact, precisely something on the order of the exemplum sensed in "The Physician's Tale" that allows the critic at once to move so easily—and apparently logically—in the direction of allegory and to elide the narrative altogether in favor of personification. Patricia Kean maintains that "the *moralitas* indeed suggests that the 'historial thing' is being presented as an *exemplum*, in human terms, of the war of the vices against the virtues."[43] Middleton notes that the characters of "The Physician's Tale" act like allegorical figures, demonically possessed, without self-awareness; they embody ideas, are unidimensional, and lack freedom of will. Brian Lee speaks of "the undeviating rigor with which the characters adhere to the idea that animates them. . . . Apius is as ideal or allegorical a figure as Virginia herself, purely evil as she is purely good."[44]

There is no denying that "The Physician's Tale" is an allegory, or that Virginia, daughter of Virginius, is an allegorical figure in that her name is the quality that she embodies. Virginia's actions are, as Chaucer claims, a text: "For in hir lyvyng maydens myghten rede, / As in a book, every good word or dede / That longeth to a mayden vertuous, / She was so prudent and so bountevous" (vv. 107–10). Yet I would like to suggest that the fatality which seems to hang over "The Physician's Tale" has less to do with the model of the Christian martyr, with the constraints of history or a received story, or with moral allegory per se, than with medieval definitions of virginity, and with the relation of virginity, within the context of medieval poetics, to the specifically literary effects of a poetics of praise. Chaucer participates in a long tradition, most elaborately articulated by the church fathers, put into practice by the French vernacular poets, passed on through Jean de Meun and others, according to which the relation between sexual desire and poetic language was taken for granted and in which the concept of virginity occupied pride of place.

Put more simply, if we return to some of the conditions that, as we saw in relation to "Du Mantel mautaillié," render virginity impossible—Clement of Rome's woman who has never been in the presence of the opposite sex, Chrysostom's virgin as one who is "above suspicion," Tertullian's virgin as one who is not seen, or his formula that "a *virgin* ceases to be a virgin from the time it becomes possible for her *not* to be one"—it becomes clear that the stipulative restriction placed upon virginity becomes so universal as itself to become allegorized in a way that is the inverse of the Old French tale. For, if "Du Mantel mautaillié" underscores the difficulty of locating chastity, which is a version of the question of embodiment (which haunted the medievals), then "The Physician's Tale" explores the violence inherent in that location— the violence of perception, or, more specifically, of the look. Here we arrive at an interpretation of the key motivating moment of "The Physician's Tale," for the concept of virginity as elaborated by the church fathers bears directly, almost paradigmatically, upon Appius's fatal attraction for Virginia. The judge's fixation cannot be accounted for psychologistically in terms of his lechery or, in the phrase of one critic, his "blind lust," without adducing a conclusion that surpasses the sum of its parts. In simplest terms, that which motivates the action of "The Physician's Tale" is nothing more than the look. The fatality of Appius's attraction has nothing to do with Virginia per se and everything to do with the implicit transgressive sight of a virgin. Thus the passion that comes out of nowhere, that arrives accidentally in the course of a walk:

> And so bifel this juge his eyen caste
> Upon this mayde, avysynge hym ful faste,
> And she cam forby there as this juge stood.
> Anon his herte chaunged and his mood,
> So was he caught with beautee of this mayde,
> And so to hymself ful pryvely he sayde,
> "This mayde shal be myn, for any man!" (vv. 123–29)

And thus too the finality of the result, for Virginia is deflowered from the moment she steps into the street, or from the moment she crosses paths with Appius. Indeed, his name resonates with the deponent Latin verb *apiscor* (a rarer form of the compound *adipiscor*) meaning "to reach after," "to seize," "to get possession of," "to perceive," just as Claudius's name summons *claudo*, "to close," "shut," "hem in," which is also his function. What this means is that the shame Virginius offers his daughter as an alternative to death has already occurred in the moment that Virginia is perceived, since, as Tertullian holds, "every public exposure of a virgin is (to her) the equivalent of rape." And, as the author of *The Ancren Riwle* rules, every look recapitulates the biblical drama and is the prototype of the Fall: "Thus did sight go before and prepare the way for guilty desire; and death followed, to which all mankind is subject."[45] "Allas," Virginius laments, "that evere Apius the say!" (v. 227).

Chaucer's "Physician's Tale," a literary version of the medieval "theology of virginity" (James Brundage), is structured by the aporia of perception, which is in the Middle Ages a highly gendered issue.[46] For, as we have seen, woman is throughout the period in question associated with the cosmetic theology of the early church fathers, and the feminine is also synonymous with the realm of the senses. Philo, it will be remembered, states that "the most proper and exact name for sense-perception *is* 'woman'," who is allied with the sensitive (i.e., sensual) part of the soul as opposed to man who remains on the side of intellection. All of this suggests a series of paradoxes that serve to bring the idea of chastity into a relation with the feminine, with the senses, and with the material nature of representations in order to allow us, finally, to read the expressed impossibility of chastity as a contradiction not only within the Arthurian fabliau and the Middle English tale, but more generally within the medieval discourse on women.

First—and here the theologians are fully aware of the contradiction—
though virginity may represent the antithesis of the cosmetic, it remains an
adornment in its own right. Although Cyprian, for example, maintains that
"virgins, in desiring to be adorned . . . cease to be virgins" and that the only
proper adornment of the virgin is the wounds of the martyr, Jerome speaks of
continence as the "ornament of the inner man," and Methodius, of Christ as
"arming the flesh with the ornament of virginity."[47] There is, again, as we
have seen in relation to the attempt to discourage marriage, no way of dis-
suading the reader from ornamentation without becoming complicit with
that from which one pretends to dissuade.

Second, if woman is conceived to be analogous to the senses or perception, then any look upon a woman's beauty must be the look of a woman
upon a woman, and the male gaze is a non sequitur. And yet the fact remains
that in Western tradition, the transgression that lurks in a look remains reso-
lutely male. "Hence how often do we, from beholding a woman,"
Chrysostom warns, "suffer a thousand evils; returning home, and entertaining an inordinate desire, and experiencing anguish for many days. . . . The
beauty of a woman is the greatest snare. Or rather, not the beauty of woman,
but unchastened gazing!"[48] This is why the answer to Chrysostom's question,
"How is it possible to be freed from desire?" must be to be free of perception,
or from the body altogether.[49] Indeed, if to see is to be within the realm of the
senses while chastity implies a lack of perception, and if true chastity con-
notes a lack of desire that, as Clement of Alexandria maintains, goes beyond
even the self-renunciation of the Stoics,[50] then the will to escape perception is
indistinguishable from the desire to escape bodily incarnation. "The pursuit
of virginity," Gregory of Nyssa writes, "is a certain art and faculty of the more
divine life, teaching those living in the flesh how to be like the incorporeal
nature."[51] "Among the virgins whom the ardent desire of God has touched,"
Eusebius of Emesa maintains, "lust is dead, passion killed. Nailed to the cross
with its vices and desires, the body is like a stranger to them."[52]

Thus, if chastity implies transcendence of the corporeal, and if the corporeal is inextricably linked to the feminine, then the fathers' insistent
exhortations to feminine chastity can only be seen as a self-contradictory urging of the feminine to be something that it isn't. To urge a woman to chastity
is to urge her in some profound sense to deny her femininity, since to transcend the body is to escape that which is gendered feminine. Gregory, for
example, wonders if it is proper to call Macrina a woman since she "is above

nature," just as John Chrysostom is said to have maintained that Olympias was a man, "despite her physical appearance."[53] The thrust of such a paradox explains the prevalence of the motif of transvestism among the early fathers—of women disguised as monks for the purpose of hiding their identity, and also of surpassing the perceived limits of gender. Perpetua dreams of assuming a male body before her martyrdom. Thecla and Mygdonia cut their hair short and dress as men; Pelagia, in male garb, passes for a eunuch; Hilaria's breasts supposedly withered; and Apollonaria's body is said to have become "like the exterior of a turtle."[54] Basil of Ancyra urges not only that women avoid members of the opposite sex, but that they walk like men and adopt the tone of voice of a man as well as the "unnatural" brusqueness of a male demeanor.[55]

The logic of virginity thus leads syllogistically to an even deeper paradox, which I am not the first to notice. That is, if the feminine is elided to the side of the flesh such that the woman is the body of the man, and if renunciation of the flesh is the only means to equality, then woman is put in a position such that the only way she can be equal is to renounce the feminine or to be a man.[56] Thus the reply (*Gospel of Thomas*) of Jesus to Simon Peter, who demands that Mary Magdalene leave the circle of male disciples: "I myself shall lead her, in order to make her male, so that she too may become a living spirit, resembling you males. For every woman who will make herself male shall enter the Kingdom of Heaven"; and thus Mary's encomium to Jesus in the Gospel of Mary: "Praise his greatness, for he has prepared us and made us into men."[57] Where the exegetical tradition is concerned, Philo claims that "progress is nothing else than the giving up of the female gender by changing into the male."[58] Jerome too promises that the woman who leaves her husband for Jesus "will cease to be a woman and will be called man. . . . Let our souls cherish their bodies," the man who considers all Christians his children urges, "so that wives may be converted into men and their bodies into souls."[59] Asceticism, better than any modern-day surgical rearrangement of the anatomy, offered a way out of the gendered spirit-body dichotomy we encountered in previous chapters in what looks like Henry Higgins's query to Colonel Pickering in Shaw's *Pygmalion:* "Why can't a woman be more like a man?"

Third and finally, to the extent that chastity implies victory over the corporeal it betrays a deep longing to be rid of consciousness itself, and in this desire lies the unmistakable symptom of a death wish.[60] "While in the flesh let her be without the flesh," urges Jerome. "The virgin . . . both yearns for her death and is oppressed by life, anxious as she is to see her groom face to face and enjoy that glory," Chrysostom assures us.[61] "What is virginity," Novatian asks, "if not a magnificent contemplation of the afterlife?"[62] The fathers are, of course, highly conscious that if everyone practiced chastity, the human race would come to an end.[63] Virginity as absolute cannot, in other words, be absolute, but depends upon the difference it excludes. This is one of the persistent justifications for sexual intercourse—that in losing one's virginity one can always, as Jerome maintains, give birth to a virgin.[64] Nonetheless, celibacy generalized conspires with the end of human time, "for from marriage," warns Tertullian, "result wombs, and breasts, and infants. And when an end of marrying? I believe after the end of living!"[65]

In fact, a certain inescapable logic of virginity, most evident in medieval hagiography, leads syllogistically to the conclusion that the only real virgin— that is, the only true virgin—is a dead virgin. For Cyprian the only proper adornments of the virgin's flesh are the wounds of the martyr: "These are the precious jewels of the flesh; these are the better ornaments of the body."[66] Martyrdom is practically synonymous with virginity, as Ambrose insists in his tale of Saint Agnes's beheading: "What threats the executioner used to make her fear him, what allurements to persuade her, how many desired that she would come to them in marriage! But she answered: 'It would be an injury to my spouse to look on any one as likely to please me. He who chose me first for Himself shall receive me. Why are you delaying, executioner? Let this body perish which can be loved by eyes which I would not.' "[67] Again, the mutual exclusion of life and chastity serves as measure of the degree to which virginity is of necessity defined in terms of negative potential. The mere thought of losing it is sufficient to its loss. "For a *virgin* ceases to be a virgin from the time it becomes possible for her *not* to be one," Tertullian warns.

This implies one final paradox: to the extent that virginity is conceived as a quietude of the senses, an escape from desire, it itself becomes a source of desire: "true and absolute and pure *virginity* fears nothing more than itself," Tertullian observes. "Even *female* eyes it shrinks from encountering. Other eyes itself has. It takes itself for refuge to the veil of the head as to a helmet, as to a shield, to protect its glory against the blows of temptations, against the darts of scandals, against suspicions and whispers and emulations; (against) envy also itself."[68] Though virginity may hold the fantasy of an escape from desire, it cannot escape the logic of the desire to escape desire, which remains internal to desire itself. Nonetheless, we are drawn closer to a conclusion according to which there can be only two possibilities:

1. Virginity, as absolute, has no substance, does not exist. Thus the images of evanescence it engenders. Methodius speaks of the "ornament of virginity," and of virgins "clothed . . . in the brightness of the Word": "For her robe, she is clothed in pure light; instead of jewels, her head is adorned with shining stars. For their light is for her what clothing is for us. And she uses the stars as we do brilliant gems; but her stars are not like those visible to us on earth, but finer and brighter ones, such that our own are merely their copies and representations."[69]

2. The abstraction that virginity implies is destroyed by its articulation. This is another way of saying, again, that the loss of virginity implied in its exposure is analogous to the loss of universality of an Idea implicit to its expression; or, more simply, that there is no way of talking about virginity that does not entail its loss, since the universal is always veiled by the defiling garment of words. For if, as Tertullian maintains, the veil is the *sign* of the virgin, protecting her from both the gaze of others and her own gaze, then virginity itself can be nothing else but a veil; and, as veil, it falls within the material pale implicit to all embodied signs. There can be no difference between Tertullian's "veil of virginity," Jerome's "veil of chastity," and Methodius's "veil of letters." "With the word the garment entered," Tertullian assures us elsewhere. His statement can only be interpreted to mean that language is the ornament, the veil, which defiles the virgin by exposure, since the senses, equated with the body, have no direct access to an Idea, allied with the soul. "No one," Chrysostom writes, "has anywhere seen a soul by itself stripped of the body."[70] "Who could describe the pleasure [of the virgin's gaze upon God]?" he asks. "What expression could suggest the joy of a soul so disposed? It does not exist."[71]

Thus the category of virginity that so obsessed medieval theologians is, through a process of reduction analogous to that of the Arthurian fabliau, relegated to the realm of pure Idea; and this even beyond the obvious inherent tendency toward abstraction in the literature on chastity, such as Ambrose's claim that the integrity of the virgin's body is simply a sign of purity of character[72] or the portrayal of virginity as a "spiritual ornament" or the "ornament of the inner man." The process of reduction at work in relation to virginity surpasses the patristic displacement of the physical toward the spiritual, suggesting instead that the fathers, in their desire for the absolute (which, as absolute, is synonymous with virginity), are not satisfied until the concept of virginity, like that of woman, is also emptied of sense.

Authorial Complicity

This combination of a desire to transcend perception and the death wish has
particular meaning for our understanding of the literary texts with which we
began. For it suggests that the desire to locate the chaste woman in "Du Mantel mautaillié" and the "Lai du corn" represents a sexualized version of the
wish for transcendence, an embodiment of the desire to escape embodiment
altogether. And if the chastity of the women of Camelot seems, according to
the horn and mantle motif, an impossibility, it is because the very notion of
betrayal, imagined to consist in a woman's infidelity, in her desire to be unfaithful, and, finally, in her husband's imagining her desire, is a category
without substance. We might then focus our avowedly composite rendering
of the patristic notion of virginity upon the Arthurian fabliau to read: "The
reason that no one has seen a chaste woman is that to be seen is to be deflowered. If no woman is chaste, it is because embodiment itself is defilement."
In the example of "The Physician's Tale" such a conclusion implies not only
that Virginia is not a virgin from the moment she is seen, but that her death is
implied the moment she steps into the street. This, again, is why, as critics
have noted, there is so little give and take surrounding the father's taking of
his daughter's life. For, seen within the context of the concept of virginity
itself, the scholarly debate about whether or not Virginius loves Virginia, and
therefore whether he should have given her more room to protest, is mis-
placed; so too the rationalization that Virginia, because she was ravished, is
technically still chaste.[73] To repeat, Virginia is dead, at least as a virgin, the
minute she falls under Appius's gaze by which the action of the story, henceforth transformed into allegory, is complete.

Turned upon "The Physician's Tale," the theology of virginity inevitably
poses the question of Chaucer's own complicity in the act of despoliation
that he narrates through the Physician. That is, to the extent that we are
tempted to psychologize "The Physician's Tale," to explain the characters in
terms of Virginia's natural goodness and Appius's lechery, we must bear in
mind that the negative potential that Virginia as virginity embodies cannot,
by its very abstraction, fail to attract the attention of Appius as apperception;
together they stand as the two poles of an allegory, which is not so much that
of the virtues and vices as that of the genesis of the story itself. "The Physician's Tale," which contains no other action than the coming of a conception
into the purview of perception, is, at bottom, a parable of embodiment presented under the guise of the deflowering glance. The coming into

consciousness of something so abstract that it can only be conceived in terms of being, the breaking of the universality of the Idea implicit to material personification, is the very essence of the literary act. In other words, no narrative account of virginity can be other than the act of despoiling that which fiction presents as the possibility of virginal perfection.

My point is really very simple: that Chaucer, in exposing his tale, does to the characters exactly what Appius, under the guise of fiction, does to Virginia. He deflowers at the instant he depicts. And he does this prospectively by the rhetoric of excessive praise, absent both in Livy and Jean de Meun, which excites the desire of the reader before Appius even enters upon the scene. Chaucer, in the opening encomium to Virginia's beauty, issues— through the Nature he creates and who is invested with the power of creation—a challenge:

> Fair was this mayde in excellent beautee
> Aboven every wight that man may see;
> For Nature hath with sovereyn diligence
> Yformed hire in so greet excellence,
> As though she wolde seyn, "Lo! I, Nature,
> Thus kan I forme and peynte a creature
> Whan that me list; who kan me countrefete? (vv. 6–12)

By bringing Virginia under the gaze that is (to Tertullian) the equivalent of rape, Chaucer loses all pretense at innocence; he incites what the tale seems morally to denounce:

> And if that excellent was hire beautee,
> A thousand foold moore vertuous was she.
> In her ne lakked no condicioun
> That is to preyse, as by discrecioun.
> As well in goost as body chast was she;
> For which she floured in virginitee
> With alle humylitee and abstinence,
> With alle attemperaunce and pacience,
> With mesure eek of beryng and array. (vv. 39–47)

In praising Virginia, Chaucer, enmeshed in the paradoxical logic that would sing the virtues of perfect modesty and adorn excessively that which exists "with mesure eek of beryng and array," violates the virgin. For there is, again, no way of speaking about virginity that does not imply its loss, no poetics of praise that is not already complicit in the violence of rape, no magnification of the perfection of woman abstracted that is not a taking of possession. The Physician, or Chaucer for that matter, cannot avoid finding himself in the position of Appius, aping Appius: "This mayde shal be myn, for any man!" (v. 129). This assertion has enormous implications for another major component of the Chaucerian canon, *The Legend of Good Women,* where the same rhetoric of excessive praise is transformed into the equivalent of a genre. In "The Legend of Lucrece," for example, the boast that incites rape is explicitly thematized: "And lat us speke of wyves, that is best; / Preyse every man his owene, as hym lest, / And with oure speche lat us ese oure herte" (v. 1702–4). Thus Tarquin prepares the way for Collatine's complicity—again through a rhetoric of praise that solicits excess—in Lucretia's violation and death: "'I have a wif,' quod he, "that, as I trowe, / Is holden good of alle that evere hire knowe. / Go we to-nyght to Rome, and we shal se'" (vv. 1708–10).[74]

The translation of virginity into a pure Idea, into potential or absence, into pure negativity or a vacuum toward which man is drawn, offers a clue to the way we should understand Chaucer's attention to the fact "That thrugh that land they preised hire echone / That loved vertu, save Envye allone" (vv. 113–14). Perfection as a source of desire is, as we have seen, not only part and parcel of the paradox of virginity that cannot claim its transcendence of desire without at the same time creating a desire for such transcendence, but remains practically synonymous with the current of medieval antifeminism subsumed in the exhortation to chastity. It is also, as we shall see in the next chapter, an essential element of the courtly lay.

THE OLD FRENCH LAY AND
THE MYRIAD MODES
OF MALE INDISCRETION

 We explored in the preceding chapter one of the defining
paradoxes of medieval sexuality—the seeming contradiction
between the view of woman as imperfection as against the
desire for wholeness expressed in the insistent exhortation to virginity, which
is not only related to Christian asceticism but also serves to link the antimatrimonial spirit of the early Christian era to the poetics of the High Middle
Ages. In the present chapter we continue to shift our focus away from medieval antifeminism toward the phenomenon of courtliness, or rather toward
what I think can be shown to be a deep and significantly complicitous relation
between the phenomenon of courtly love and the discourse of asceticism as
we have defined it.

There are many superficial points of similarity between antifeminism and
courtliness as it is expressed in the love lyric, in the courtly romance to some
extent, but also as it is elaborated theoretically by Andreas Capellanus in the
Art of Courtly Love. We have seen, for example, that not only the senses but
also, more specifically, the gaze are central to what the church fathers conceive
to be the fatal attraction of women. For desire enters through the eyes, and
love is always love at first sight. "Hence how often do we, from beholding a
woman, suffer a thousand evils," writes John Chrysostom, "returning home,
and entertaining an inordinate desire, and experiencing anguish for many
days. . . . For the sake of the brief pleasure of a glance, we sustain a kind of
lengthened and continual torment."[1] Andreas Capellanus, some eight centuries later, defines love as "a certain inborn suffering derived from the sight
of and excessive meditation upon the beauty of the opposite sex."[2] Then too
the case can be, and has been, made that principled deferral of satisfaction
synonymous with courtliness represents a striving for spiritual purity that is
deeply beholden to a Christian notion of love, the poetic expression of a de-

sire deferred in this world because it is deflected toward the next. But the thematic resemblances between the idealizing Neoplatonic patristic distrust of the body and the courtly ideal of an always already impossible love relation, though important, should not distract us from what I think can be shown to be a deep structural identity of these two seemingly contrary fascinations with the feminine. To demonstrate the ways in which the discourses of misogyny and courtliness conspire with each other, we will first return to the question of virginity, before moving to the analysis of three courtly lais and passing from a poetics to what might be thought of as the politics of virginity.[3]

If the impossibility of locating virginity, which resides neither in the chaste body, nor in the body's desire, nor in the look, makes of it an abstraction equivalent to an Idea, the loss of virginity seems closest to what the medievals conceived as the loss of the universality of an Idea through its expression. And since the paradox of virginity is, in essence, that of representation, any expression will do. It is not necessary for chastity as Idea to be captured in graphic writing or speech, or even to be seen (much less touched) by the faculties of perception. It is sufficient for the question to enter consciousness as a thought, even an insinuation, in order for virginity to be impugned. The virgin is above suspicion; the virgin is one who is not thought not to be one in the mind of another. "No one," Chrysostom maintains, "has seen the soul stripped of the body." This is another way of saying that there is no way of thinking the question of virginity that does not imply its loss. Or, to make a less radical claim, there is no way of speaking about virginity that does not sully it. This leads to an extreme form of discretion not unrelated, I think it can be shown, to the ethos of courtly discretion (i.e., the prescription that "love uncovered cannot endure"), and to the dramatization of speech and silence that lies at the center of so many courtly works. They are, for example, keenly dramatized in the Old French poem, "La Chastelaine de Vergi."

"La Chastelaine de Vergi"

"La Chastelaine de Vergi" is a short narrative, which could be classified as a lai, even though there is something in it of a fabliau[4] devoid both of a precise interest in the body and of humor, a fabliau whose intractable internal logic and sudden reversals have gone awry to yield what one critic terms "a tragic mode."[5] It contains the story of a Burgundian knight who courts a chatelaine,

THE OLD FRENCH LAY AND

who surrenders her love with a warning that if he ever reveals it, it will disappear:

. . . la dame li otria	*The lady granted him her love under*
par itel couvenant s'amor	*such a covenant that he should know that*
qu'il seüst qu'a l'eure et au jor	*at the hour and day that their love*
que par lui seroit descouverte	*should be revealed by him, that he would*
lor amor, que il avroit perte	*have lost it—both the love and the gift of*
et de l'amor et de l'otroi	*herself that she had made to him.*[6]
qu'ele li avoit fet de soi.	

The chatelaine regularly signals their rendezvous by dispatching a little dog outside the garden wall. Meanwhile, the duke of Burgundy's wife also falls in love with the knight, and in one of the many medieval versions of Potiphar's wife denounces him to her husband when her advances are rebuffed. The duke threatens to exile what he thinks to be his treacherous vassal unless the vassal can prove that he loves someone else. The knight reasons that it is preferable to risk betraying the pledge not to disclose his affair than never to see his love again; and so, confessing his love for the duke's niece, the chatelaine, and making the duke promise not to tell a soul, he allows him to witness from a hidden vantage point the little scene of the dog in the orchard. Thus relieved, the duke is observed by his wife behaving cordially, one might even venture winking complicitly, toward the man she had denounced falsely for having made advances. In turn, eliciting a promise from the duchess not to tell, the duke is cajoled into recounting the truth of the knight's affair with his niece, dog and all:

. . . puis li conte	*. . . then he told her the whole tale about*
de sa niece trestout le conte,	*his niece as he had learned it from the*
comme apris l'ot du chevalier,	*knight—and how he was in the orchard,*
et comment il fu el vergier	*in the love nook where there were only the*
en l'anglet ou il n'ot qu'eus	*two of them when the dog came to them;*
deus,	(vv. 649–54)
quant li chienés s'en vint a eus;	

The wife cannot resist avenging the wrong that she feels the knight has done in originally rejecting her love, and so she recounts to the chatelaine the secret her husband has indiscreetly revealed. In a dénouement worthy of grand opera, the chatelaine dies of a broken heart, the knight kills himself, the duke kills his wife and then goes into exile.

"La Chastelaine de Vergi" is one of those bivalent short works of the thirteenth century which, like *Aucassin et Nicolette* or "Le Lai du corn," contains courtly elements mixed with others drawn from a less idealistic tradition. To the extent to which it presents the story of a man torn between two women instead of the more usual woman divided between two men (husband and lover), to the extent that the man in question prefers a woman of lower social standing to one of higher rank, and, finally, to the extent that the strictly unclassifiable tale is motivated by the machinations of a ruseful woman, it is atypical of a courtly work.[7] On the side of the courtly, however, we find the theme of illicit love in that the chatelaine is married,[8] which amounts to saying that love is presented as socially impossible; we are reminded repeatedly that such adulterous love thrives on jealousy and is threatened by indiscretion (an element to which we will return). "La Chastelaine de Vergi" displays the courtly types of knight, lady, and the so-called *losengiers,* the bad-mouthers or court gossips whose presence constantly menaces to expose what should be kept secret. The tale is set at the highest level of aristocratic society—at the court of Burgundy. The more specific decor, such as the garden of pleasure (*locus amoenus*) where the couple meets or the plenary court gathers, are thoroughly in keeping with the courtly ethos, as are the requisite motifs of the love request, the ritualized rendezvous, the lover's tribute to the joys of love, and complaint at the necessity of separation. The vocabulary of "La Chastelaine de Vergi" is drawn from the classic courtly semantic nexus, depending as it does on expressions like *otroier l'amor, semblant d'amors, amer de fin cuer, amer par amors, fine amanz,* and *fine amor.* Even the narrative form is, one senses, constantly menaced by the intrusion of the courtly lyric, a language of pure desire subtending the more historically mediated tale, and which does irrupt at the point at which the knight, torn between confession and exile, recites a strophe from the Châtelain de Coucy's "Par Dieu, Amors, fort m'est a consirrer" (v. 295). "La Chastelaine de Vergi" evolves toward the lyric *planctus* contained in the wronged lady's final lament (vv. 732–831), which has caused the whole to be characterized as a "story in search of a song."

The presence of a determining lyric subtext toward which all action within "La Chastelaine de Vergi" is inevitably drawn sets a mood of fatality that has broad implications for our understanding of the récit, since a relation can be established between the fatalism of this archetypal tale and the paradox of virginity we defined in the previous chapter. Further, once established, this relation permits a bridge between the discourse of antifeminism, of which virginity is in many respects a disclosing focus, and that of courtly love. The fatalism of the virgin exposed is, to state the matter in simplest terms, assimilable to that of the lover betrayed.

"La Chastelaine de Vergi" portrays a dark and tragic universe verging toward disaster without reprieve. The narrative itself is stark, remarkable in the mood of bleakness produced by a lack of description and of rhetorical elaboration. This is a work from which ornamentation seems to be absent, which lacks the allegorical, anaphrastic, antithetical, litotic, and hyperbolic figures characteristic of many more optimistically luxuriant courtly tales. Even the figure of repetition is reduced to a minimum in this simplified, rationalistic world of poetic minimalism. We never return to the same place within a narrative that refuses to linger, to dwell in a way that might have given the impression of respite from the unavoidable dilemma of decline.[9] The coldness of execution of unavoidable destiny, mechanically recounted, "with almost mathematical rigor," is of a piece with the bareness of a poetic universe that contains no poetry at all.[10] The refusal to name the lady, for example, in keeping with the courtly code, is here extended to the denial of names to all characters, who are thereby reduced to types, instruments of a machine of fate that, once set in motion, cannot be recalled—the duke, the duchess, the knight, the chatelaine. Once the knight's request for love has been accepted by the married chatelaine, it implies the necessity of secrecy, which means that the duchess's attempt at seduction can lead logically only to rejection. Once rejection has taken place, it produces inevitably denunciation to the duke, which in turn requires retaliation against the knight. Once retaliation has been posited in terms of an impossible choice (loss of love or exile), it calls necessarily for betrayal of the original prescription against revealing love. Once the chatelaine's secret has been betrayed, it leads to the duke's pardon of the knight, which is inevitably remarked by the duchess who, having managed to elicit the secret from her husband, is unable to resist again avenging herself, this time upon the chatelaine, whose death provokes that of the knight, whose death provokes that of the duchess, whose death leads—in a symmetry that is not without its tragic irony—to the self-imposition upon the duke of the penalty he originally offered the knight—exile.

The fatalism that suffuses "La Chastelaine de Vergi" makes it appear as the literary expression of a death wish in which everything conspires and toward which the narrative converges. Once the mechanism of desire has been set in motion, the characters, like the protagonists of a classical tragedy, are trapped by impossible choices, dilemmas from which there is no escape except transcendence. The knight must choose between betrayal of his lord and betrayal of his lady, or between exile and loss of his love; the duke must choose between the injustice done to a vassal, which in essence makes him a cuckold, and revealing his niece's adultery, which entails her death. The duchess is caught between rejection and betraying the man she apparently loves; and the chatelaine, between humiliation and death. The impotence of the characters, without names and therefore reduced to the cogs of a cruel machine of fate, is all the more evident in that "La Chastelaine de Vergi" is a work without action, except perhaps for that of dying. In the place of action, speech seems to seal the characters' fate the minute they open their mouth, a lack of objective activity transmitted by the récit's extremely weak verbal system.[11] There are essentially no verbs of action in "La Chastelaine de Vergi." Instead, the poem is ruled by verbs that signify taking and giving, going and coming, covering and uncovering (*celer* and *descouvrer*); by verbs having to do with osculation (*beser, rebeser, acoler*); by verbs of perception (*oïr, entendre, voir, decevoir, apercevoir*); verbs of affect (*amer, souffrir, haïr*); but it contains very few verbs capable of transmitting sensation, as if, again, the coldness of the destiny of the characters were reinforced by the dehumanization of a semantic universe incapable of transmitting emotion. The strongest verbal register in "La Chastelaine de Vergi" includes those which render speech and silence (*parler, estre meü, dire, conter, aconter, raconter, rasponer, prier, parjurer, desvoier, mentir, se taire, se plaindre, demander*), as if the predicative system of the work itself mirrored the drama of vows and revelations that is its most persistent theme. The only truly strong verbs of action are *ferir*, "to strike," and the now defunct active form of *morir*, "to kill," making it seem that the death sentence that hangs over the lay has penetrated even its verbal system. Thus the knight's confession and self-revenge:

"Mes je ferai de moi justise
por la trahison que j'ai fete."
Une espee du fuerre a trete
qui ert pendue a un espuer,
et s'en feri parmi le cuer:
cheoir se lest sor l'autre cors;
tant a sainié que il est mors

"But I will carry out justice upon myself for the betrayal for which I am responsible." He pulled a sword out of its scabbard which was hanging on a post and pierced himself through the heart: he allowed himself to fall on the other body and bled so profusely that he died.
(vv. 894–900)

The failure, or rather the absence, of action in "La Chastelaine de Vergi" is reinforced by the collapse of the dimension of time, as if the plane upon which events might occur had somehow vanished, abstracted and subtilized. Through the experience of love time seems literally to fold in upon itself:

Ne teus biens n'avient mie a toz,	*Nor do such good things happen to all for it is joy without pain and solace and*
que ce est joie sanz corouz	*pleasure; but the more there is, the*
et solaz et envoiseüre;	*shorter it lasts in the mind of the lover*
mes tant i a que petit dure,	*who has it; for it is never long enough, so*
c'est avis a l'amant qui l'a;	*pleasant is the life he leads, that even if a*
ja tant longues ne durera,	*night became a week, and a week became*
tant li plest la vie qu'il maine,	*a month, and a month a year, and a*
que se nuis devenoit semaine	*year three, and three years twenty, and*
et semaine devenoit mois,	*twenty years a hundred, at the moment*
et mois uns anz, et uns anz trois,	*at which the end approached, he would wish for another night still before the*
et troi an vint, et vint an cent,	*coming of day.* (vv. 447–60)
quant vendroit au definement,	
si voudroit il qu'il anuitast	
cele nuit, ainz qu'il ajornast.	

This passage reveals the occulted presence of the lyric just below the surface of the récit, for the wish for time's extension at the moment of separation is the very stuff of the medieval "dawn song" or *alba*. In "La Chastelaine de Vergi" the lyric voice lurks constantly in the background, ready to irrupt. Its menacing presence within the narrative of time is the symptom of a desire to escape time, or for death.

Si est en tel point autressi	*He is in the same position as the*
com li chastelains de Couci,	*Châtelain de Coucy whose heart*
qui au cuer n'avoit s'amor non,	*overflowed with love and who said in a*
dist en un vers d'une chançon:	*song:* By God, Love, it is so difficult to
Par Dieu, Amors, for m'est a consirrer	draw myself away from the sweet solace and the presence and the
du dous solaz et de la compaingnie	tendernesses of the one who was my
et des samblanz que m'i soloit moustrer	companion and friend: And when I remember her simple courtesy and
cele qui m'ert et compaingne et amie:	the sweet words she used to say to me, how can my heart remain in my
et quant regart sa simple cortoisie	body? When it doesn't burst out, it

et les douz mos qu'a moi soloit
parler,
comment me puet li cuers au cors
durer?
Quant il n'en part, certes trop est
mauvés.

shows itself unworthy.
(vv. 291–302)

It can, of course, be no coincidence that the lyric strophe actually imbedded in "La Chastelaine de Vergi" is identified as belonging to the Chatelain de Coucy: a poet whose legend, another fatalistic tale of discovery and disembodiment, was well known to the thirteenth century. For the Chatelain de Coucy, who died in the crusades, has his heart sent back to the woman he loves. Her husband, having learned of their adultery from the body part made into the textual body of illicit passion, has it served to his wife, who from then on refuses to eat and dies. The lyric insert contains, moreover, a play on the words *solaz* and *soloit,* culminating in a *soloit parler,* which suggests that the solace of love is somehow synonymous with the love of speech. Thinking about words, in other words, becomes the equivalent of an alienation of the heart from the body within a lyric in which death leads to cannibalism, and cannibalism to suicide. I return to the question of words because the dark fate that hangs over both the legend of "Le Châtelain de Coucy et la Dame de Fayel" and that of "La Chastelaine de Vergi" in which it is embedded, transforms, within the context of the structuring theme of revelatory speech, both récits into parallel dramas of language in which a certain linguistic fatalism is intimately bound to the wish for death.

"La Chastelaine de Vergi" turns around an ordeal of silence and speech, secrecy and discovery. And in this it is not unique, for many key works in Old French are similarly defined.[12] In *La Chanson de Roland,* for example, the debate about whether or not to sound the horn is, at bottom, a debate centering on the question of silence. In Chrétien de Troyes's *Erec et Enide* the breaking of silence is thematized in the famous involuntary speech act—Enide's denunciation of Erec's chivalric recreancy—as later in the ordeal of silence imposed by husband upon wife. "Should I speak and risk disobeying Erec or remain silent and risk losing the one I most love," the troubled Enide thinks to herself, trapped in a dilemma similar, as we shall see, to that of the lady of "Laüstic." Then too, Chrétien's *Perceval* turns at crucial moments around questions of silence and speech: first the mother's advice always to ask the name of one's companion, countered by the oblique father's injunction against speaking too much; then the silence at the Grail Castle, followed by his cousin's reproach: "If only you had asked the questions," she scolds, "you could have restored the king's lands and his power":

"A mal eur tu [te] teüsses,	*"It was an evil hour when you kept quiet,*
Que se tu demandé l'eüsses,	*since if you had asked the question, the*
Li riches rois, qui or s'esmaie,	*rich king who now suffers would have*
Fust ja toz garis de sa plaie	*been completely cured of his wound; and*
Et si tenist sa terre en pais,	*he would have held his land in peace,*
Dont il ne tendra point jamais."	*which he will now never hold."*[13]

In Marie de France silence is the defining issue of the "Prologue." Whether or not to break silence is the question posed in the first strophe of many courtly lyrics in which the topos of renascent nature and the birds' song is coterminous with the problem of how to begin.

The incipit of "La Chastelaine de Vergi" sets the terms of a drama of silence in the poet's warning about malicious gossip:

Une maniere de gent sont	*There are people who make a pretense out*
qui d'estre loial samblant font	*of being loyal and know well how to hide*
et de si bien conseil celer	*their true intent such that one is drawn*
qu'il se covient en aus fier;	*into confiding in them; and when it*
et quant vient qu'aucuns s'i	*happens that one opens oneself up to them*
descuevre	*about love, they spread it all around the*
tant qu'il savent l'amor et	*country so that people will joke and*
l'uevre,	*laugh.* (vv. 1–8)
si l'espandent par le païs,	
et en font lor gas et lor ris.	

At the time the chatelaine cedes her love to the knight she warns him that if it is ever known, he will lose it. Yet a promise, like a confession, can never be contained; it is made to be broken. And if the knight's pledge to keep his love for the chatelaine secret elicits a second promise on the part of the duke: "— Or n'en parlez ja, fet li dus; / sachiez qu'il ert si bien celé / que ja par moi n'en ert parlé" ("Don't ever mention it," said the duke, "know that it will be so well hidden that never will it be spoken of by me" [vv. 504–6]), the second promise becomes merely the condition of the transgression of the first. Yet a third promise, that on the part of the duchess to keep the secret told to the duke— "ainc n'oïstes grant ne petit / conseil que vous m'eüssiez dit, / dont descouvers fussiez par moi, / et si vous di en bone foi, / ja en ma vie n'avendra" ("You have never heard a big or little secret that you told me that I revealed; and I tell you for true that it will never happen as long as I live" [vv. 625–29])—is revealed when she informs the chatelaine that she knows of her little dog. The chain of confidences, broken at every link, returns to its point of origin.

To the extent to which the embedded oaths are successively violated, they raise a number of important questions. Is there something inherent to the secret that logically entails its revelation? If so, does this not mean that there is something specific to the secret that autonomously uncovers (*descuevrer*) that which language, or at least courtly language, cannot hide (and the word *celer* is used repeatedly)? If not, to what extent are those who promise, only to transgress the promise made, free to keep or break their oaths?[14]

The logic of the broken promise—which is not the same as the open secret—is, within the context of medieval poetics, that of courtly poetry itself. Courtly verse not only contains the story of love revealed, but also entails the ordeal of silence that it thematizes. Put another way, the poet, in speaking of illicit love, does to the protagonists of the drama exactly what the protagonists do when they successively denounce each other: he or she points the finger at hidden passion, and does so with an initial theoretical discussion of discretion no less binding, it would seem, than the promises elicited from the knight, the duke, or the duchess. "There are people," the poet assures us, "who make a pretense of being loyal and know well how to hide their true intent such that one is drawn into confiding in them; and when it happens that one opens oneself to them concerning love, they spread it all around the country so that people will joke and laugh. They then become crest-fallen when passion is uncovered." So too, the ending summary of the consequences of indiscretion seems only to confirm the commitment of the beginning:

Et par cest example doit l'en
s'amor celer par si grant sen
c'on ait toz jors en
    remembrance
que li descouvrirs riens
    n'avance
et li celers en toz poins vaut.
Qui si le fet, ne crient assaut
des faus felons enquereors
qui enquierent autrui amors.

This example proves that one should hide his love prudently, and one must keep in mind constantly that talking does no one any good and it is best to keep it hidden. If one acts thus, one need not fear the attacks of malevolent felons who spy on the love of others. (vv. 951–58)

Against this rogatory frame of discretion one does well to ask what in fact the storyteller does, if not, in the telling of the tale, to reveal hidden love. "The greater love is, the more saddened lovers are when one of them suspects the other of having revealed that which he or she should have kept secret. For often evil comes from it such that love ends in pain and shame, as it happened in Burgundy to a courageous and valiant knight and the lady of Vergi."[15] The fairytale-like "once upon a time in Burgundy" along with the story that follows constitute a structural equivalent to what the lay presents as theme and what the admonitory introduction and conclusion warn against—the telling of a tale of love that should remain hidden. Here we encounter a contradiction every bit as powerful as the paradox of virginity: that love only exists to the degree that it is secret; that secret love only exists to the degree that it is revealed; and revealed, it is no longer love. At the center of the courtly code of discretion and of almost every tale of so-called hidden love lies the logic of the poetry that transgresses what it posits, and not, as has been asserted, either a conflict of good versus bad lovers or a contradiction "imposed by the artificial code to which she [La Chastelaine] submits her very real love."[16] For if love must be kept secret to exist, then, as in the case of the virgin, there can be no way of speaking of it that does not imply its transgression. "La Chastelaine de Vergi" can, in a profound sense, be considered to be "La Chastelaine de Virginité" or "The Lady of Virginity."

Ignorance is Bliss: "Le Lai d'Ignauré"

Now let us consider another short narrative, "Le Lai d'Ignauré ou lai du prisonnier" by Renaut de Beaujeu. Unlike "La Chastelaine de Vergi" with its long-suffering dramas of devotion, "Ignauré" is the story of a knight who is having affairs simultaneously with the wives of twelve peers of Brittany, women who remain as ignorant of his involvement with the others as their husbands are of their infidelity:

A toutes douse s'acointa;
Et tant chascune l'en creanta
S'amour trestout a son voloir,
Et, s'[el] de li voloit avoir,
K'il seroit servis comme quens,
Chascune cuide k'il soit siens
Si s'en fait molt jolie et cointe.

He carried on with all twelve; to each he promised that if she wanted it she could have his love entirely and he would consider himself served as a count. Each believed he was hers and behaved most tenderly and graciously.[17]

The ladies, each of whom is convinced that her lover is the best, convoke a "love court" of the type seen elsewhere in "Flor et Blancheflor" or the "Concile de Remiremont." Retiring to a garden, they decide that each will reveal the name of her lover to one of them: "Chascune i voist, et se li die / Cui ele aimme, en confiession" ("Let each one go there and confess to her whom she loves, by way of confession" [vv. 90–91]). When the "mother confessor," who also loves Ignauré, reveals to the others the ignorance they have until then shared, they force him to choose one among their number. Thus restricted, Ignauré soon finds his love affairs discovered. He is captured by the league of husbands, who castrate him, kill him, and serve a stew composed of his genitals and heart to their unsuspecting wives:

Mangié avés le grant desir	*You have eaten the great desire that you*
Ki si vous estoit em plaisir	*used to hold to be such pleasure, for you*
Car d'autre n'aviés vous envie.	*desired no other. In the end you were*
En la fin en estes servie!	*served [by] it! I have killed and destroyed*
Vostre drut ai mort et destruit:	*your lover: you will all have shared the*
Toutes, partirés au deduit	*pleasure that women desire so much.*
De chou que femme plus	(vv. 567–73)
goulouse.	

As in "Le Châtelain de Coucy et la Dame de Fayel," the wives of the "Lai d'Ignauré" refuse henceforth to eat, and they die.

The "Lai d'Ignauré" can be read interestingly as a social drama of class conflict, and in this it seems to corroborate some of the most powerful sociological readings of medieval literature and culture.[18] Ignauré belongs, as Renaut de Beaujeu makes clear, to the lesser nobility of the region: "Ne fu mie de grant hauteche" ("He was not so high born" [v. 23]), which implies a lack of riches and property. The barons, on the other hand, are from the highest rank: "Chevalier erent preu et sage, / Riche erent de terre et de rente; / Chascuns ot femme biele et gente, / De haut linage, de grant gent" ("The knights were brave and wise and rich in lands and rent. Each had a beautiful and noble wife, of high lineage and great family" [vv. 40–43]). Ignauré's nobility is, then, more one of accomplishment than of birth: "Mais il fist tant, par sa proeche, / K'il n'avoit, en tout le païs, / Nul chevalier de si haut pris" ("But he did so many acts of prowess that there was no knight in all the land of such great worth" [vv. 24–26]). He also possesses nobility of soul, since he is endowed with the attributes of courtliness—beauty, generosity, musical talent, and a "gentle heart" ("le cuer gent" [v. 44]).

To the extent that it contains an intraclass conflict of upper versus lower aristocracy and, indeed, the values of an aristocracy versus those of a meritocracy, the "Lai d'Ignauré" can be understood from the point of view of lesser nobles as a parable of participation in the prestige and power of the high nobility—a dream of plenitude of desire and possession on the part of those whose real material base was progressively eroded in the course of the twelfth and thirteenth centuries. From the perspective of the great lords, Renaut de Beaujeu's lay, not unlike the Arthurian Round Table itself, can be seen to constitute a fantasy of social stability through parity. The men are equals, literally "peers": "Dedens le chastiel, a Riol / Avoit douse pers a estage" ("In the castle of Riol there were twelve peers lodged" [v. 37]). Their wives are, at least at the outset, equal in a situation without rivalry, jealousy, or conflict. That is, as long as their equality, mediated by Ignauré, Ignorance, or by their equidistant relation to him, remains unconscious.

It is through revelation, and not through the fact of adultery itself, that the social stability of Riol, guaranteed by a shared but unseen sexual transgression, is upset. The forced choice of one lady implies a preexcellence synonymous with Ignauré's downfall:

Mais or n'a c'une seule voie.	*But now there's only one way. He takes it*
Souvent i va, ki ke le voie.	*often, no matter who sees him. And by*
Par le trop aler fu dechus	*frequentation he was deceived and*
Et engigniés et percheüs:	*tricked and seen: A mouse which has only*
Soris ki n'a c'un trau poi dure.	*one hole does not live long.*
	(vv. 369–73)[19]

And yet, the necessity of choice is also synonymous with the dissolution of the *pax adulterii inter pares,* as is made clear in the remaining cuckold's simultaneously angry and prideful boast that Ignauré's election of his wife above all the other wives makes him the first among equals: "—Aeure Diu!, quant j'en suis sire, / Je vauc miex que li autre assés!" ("God be praised, when I am lord. I am worth more than the others!" [vv. 440–41]).

The social stability guaranteed by Ignorance can, Renaut's tale seems to say, only be restored by a collective murder and, in what resembles a totemic feast, by the ritual eating of the body. The story of Ignauré is, in essence, the story of a sacrifice—but only at a price. The totemic meal, intended to restore parity by reestablishing a relation of equidistance between peers, in fact smears, by the ingestion of the genitals, the difference between sexual and gastronomic appetites while, at the same time, through such cannibalism, it

dissolves the ultimate social difference for the medievals between man and
beast. The men restore peace among themselves only at the cost of the lives of
their wives. This lay seems, like "La Chastelaine de Vergi," to participate in a
fatal convergence toward death. In a sense the moral of the "Lai d'Ignauré" is
that Ignorance is bliss.

As in "La Chastelaine de Vergi," the only real action of the "Lai d'Ignauré" is a sacrifice caused by a series of revelations. First is the naming of
Ignauré, repeated to the "courtly priest" like a refrain. "Ignauré, the brave,
the wise, is the one to whom I have given myself," confesses the first lady. "His
name is Ignauré, the free," echoes the second. "I can name him, for he is the
most noble, Ignauré is his name, flower of chivalry," brags the third. "It's Ignauré, flower of chivalry," says the fourth.[20] This goes on until the confessor,
asked to declare whose lover is best, herself confesses: "Certes, chascune a dit
a mi / Le non d'un tout seul chevalier" ("Everyone has revealed to me the
name of a single knight" [vv. 204–5]). Further, Ignauré's choice of one lady
over the others engenders yet another denunciation, that of the *losengiers,* the
court gossips. "Is he a bourgeois or knight?" ask the anxious husbands, "give
us the name!" "It's a secret," replies the spy, "the vassal's name is Ignauré."
("—'Est chou bourgois u chevaliers? / Nomme le nous!'—'C'est tout con-
sans: / Ignaures a non li vassiaus'" [vv. 418–19]). This sentence, in its self-
contradiction—or rather, its performance of the contradictory relation between discretion and silence, on the one hand, and revelation on the other—
is significant. For it is as if Renaut de Beaujeu were saying that hidden love,
courtly love, exists only to be exposed. The secret endures only to be broken.

But how are we to distinguish between the confession of love on the part
of the twelve ladies and the denunciation of the court spy to their husbands
and, the implicit revelation on the part of the poet of a series of revelations?
This dilemma is emphasized from the start:

Cors ki aimme ne doit [repondre],	*He who loves should not keep quiet, but rather expose a tale by which others can*
Ains doit aucun biel mot despondre	*learn by useful example. For my part I can thus find honor but will never be*
U li autre puissent aprendre	*rewarded with riches. People are*
Et auchun biel example prendre.	*interested by gold and silver, and not by wisdom [sens] and knowledge. There is*
Bien [et] houneur i peuc avoir,	*no more generosity, no recompense for*
Mais ja n'i conquerrai avoir.	*anyone. Wisdom [sens] is lost if it lies*
Sens et savoir, or et argent,	*hidden. But if exposed, it can plant a*

A chou entendent mais le gent.　　*seed [semenchier] in another place.*
Tolu sont et remés li don　　　　(vv. 1–13)
Et nus hom n'ert mais
　　guerredon.
Sens est perdus, ki est couvers;
Cis k'est moustrés et
　　descouvers
Puet en auchun liu semenchier.

Renaut de Beaujeu participates in what is virtually a topos among courtly poets, one that we also encountered among the Latin satirists of the High Middle Ages—the impossibility of silence and the compulsion to reveal, as in Walter Map's "I am forbidden to speak, and I cannot keep silence" (chapter 2). "The one to whom God has given knowledge and the eloquence to speak," begins Marie de France in the "Prologue" to the *Lais*, "has no right to keep quiet nor to hide, but should willingly show himself." "The peasant often says in his proverb that one can, in not speaking, often hide by silence something that later will turn to good," Chrétien de Troyes concurs in the "Prologue" to *Erec et Enide*.[21] And to the extent that the poet uncovers that for which the tale ideologically prescribes silence, the action provokes a thematic intervention. The poet is an agent of indiscretion within the drama of speech and silence that the tale narrates around the figure of Ignauré, who represents on the level of theme an inscription of the genesis of the tale.

The "Prologue" to the "Lai d'Ignauré" is revealing in the identification it suggests between poet and protagonist, and which turns around the polysemic word *sens*. For this little syllable can mean "sense," as in "good sense," or as in "significance" (for example, Chrétien de Troyes's distinction between *sens* and *matière*), or it can mean "seed" or "semen," with the resonance (from the Latin *semino*) "to engender," "to procreate." In this sexualized reception the poet's duty to spread his meaning cannot be dissociated from his duty to spread his seed (*semenchier*), which is exactly what Ignauré, who assumes the figure of the poet, stands accused of doing. The poet/protagonist's daily routine, devoted to pleasure, includes jongleurs with musical instruments:

A l'ajornee se levoit;　　　　*At daybreak he got up and took five*
Cinq jougleres od lui menoit,　*jongleurs with him, flutists and reed*
Flahutieles et calimiaus:　　　*players. The bachelor went into the*
Au bos s'en aloit li dansiaus.　*woods.* (vv. 29–32)

Ignauré is, moreover, the object of universal desire only because he himself is the embodiment of the poetic voice:

Le mai aportoit a grant bruit.	*He brought back the May bush with*
Molt par estoit de grant deduit;	*great fanfare; pleasure was his everyday*
Chascun jour l'avoit a	*custom. Passionate love lit him and*
coustume.	*enflamed him. Women called him the*
Fine amors l'esprent et alume,	*Nightingale.* (vv. 33–37)
Femmes l'apielent Lousignol.	

This suggests, once again, not only that poetry seems less merely to express than to engender sexual desire, so that the lay excites the very thing its moral lesson appears to repress, but also that the "Lai d'Ignauré" is an allegory of ignorance not unrelated to the allegory of virginity we encountered earlier. The tale is not simply the innocent record of a drama of revelation, denunciation, and death; the violence and fatalism that haunt it and are its theme are finally connected in the medieval conception to a poetic voice that would reveal what it pretends to shroud in silence. The poet cannot speak without transgressing the discretion he or she prescribes; cannot speak without telling the tale he or she is presumed to ignore; cannot break silence, in other words, without breaking an implicit pact with Ignorance, without revealing the secret. This is the secret of the text: that it cannot tell its tale without transforming something universal and abstract, like the Idea of ignorance, into something particular and concrete; that the tale cannot be told without sacrifice; that the text, through writing, always silences a voice or, as in numerous medieval examples, puts the nightingale to death.[22]

For this is exactly what happens once the ladies have ingested the object of their desire. They transform the body, the life synonymous with the living voice, into a complaint:

En lor vivant complainte en	*In their lifetime they made a plaint: One*
fisent:	*lamented his beauty, his beautiful and*
Li une plaignoit sa biauté,	*well turned members so that all others*
Tant membres biaus et bien	*might seem ugly; thus they spoke of the*
molé	*young man. Another praised his great*
Que lait erent tout li plus biel;	*valor, and his noble body and his*
Ensi disent dou damoisiel.	*generosity; and the fourth his eyes, his*
L'autre plaignoit son grant	*flanks, which were so shiny and full of*
barnage,	*laughter. And another regretted his*

Et son [gent] cors, et sa
  largeche;
Et la quarte, les iex, les flans
K'il ot si vairs et si rians;
Et l'autre plaignoit son douch
  cuer:
Ja mais nul n'en ert de tel fuer.

sweet heart, of which none would ever be the equal. (vv. 588–98)

This passage makes it clear that we find in Ignauré the masculine equivalent of a rhetoric of excessive praise already encountered in Chaucer's "Physician's Tale" (see chapter 4). We have the impression that Ignauré is doomed from the moment he is seen, or from the moment his beauty is praised. Moreover, if the ladies, now literally composed of Ignauré for having eaten a piece of him, compose his lay, they too are transformed into a text by their own death: "D'eles douse fu li deus fais, / Et douse vers plains a li lais" ("Thus was the sorrow of the twelve, and the lay has twelve verses" [vv. 617–18]).

Thus we have seen in two examples, "La Chastelaine de Vergi" and the "La d'Ignauré," that promises are made only to be broken, that secrets exist only to be revealed. What's more, the theme of the broken pledge is not merely a popular literary motif but, within the ethos of mandatory courtly discretion, the inscription of a specific poetic effect—the disclosure of what is prescribed by the poet to remain secret. We encounter a paradox coterminous with courtly love itself, according to which the passion that is imagined necessarily to be secret is violated by expression. In other words, the code of courtliness stands in relation to courtly literature as any universal to its particular, or as an ideal to its embodiment. Its a priori violation is analogous to that of virginity which, as Idea, is also transgressed not only by some physical act, but by sight, speech, or even thought. The courtly relation does not exist any more than the virgin who is "no longer a virgin," in the words of Tertullian, "the moment that it is possible for her not to be one." What both examples suggest is that the paradox of so-called courtly—hidden, secret, adulterous—love is assimilable to the obsession with despoiling exposure encountered in our discussion of virginity, which is the essence of the misogynistic thinking of the question of gender.

The Lais *of Marie de France and the* Miracles de Notre Dame

The twelfth-century "Lai de Lanval" by Marie de France further substantiates the connection between the discourse of antifeminism and courtly literature.

"Lanval" is the story of a knight at Arthur's court who, although he participates in the royal campaign against the Picts and the Scots, is forgotten when
the time comes to distribute the booty of war:

Asez i duna riches duns	*He [King Arthur] gave rich gifts to*
E as cuntes e as baruns.	*counts and barons. To those of the Round*
A ceus de la Table Roünde—	*Table—and there were not such in all*
N'ot tant de teus en tut le	*the world—he distributed women and*
munde—	*lands, except to one who had served him:*
Femmes e teres departi,	*that was Lanval; he did not remember*
Fors a un sul ki l'ot servi:	*him nor give him any of his goods.*23
Ceo fu Lanval; ne l'en sovint	
Ne nuls des soens bien ne li	
tint.	

The neglected knight also happens to be far from home: "Fiz a rei fu, de haut
parage, / Mes luin ert de sun heritage!" ("He was a king's son, very high born,
but far from his ancestral lands!" [vv. 27–28]). He wanders off with his horse
into the countryside, where he encounters a series of marvelously beautiful
ladies before meeting the fairy princess of his dreams, a woman so rich that
"Queen Semiramis . . . and the Emperor Octavian himself together could
not buy the right panel of her tent" ("La reïne Semiramis / . . . Ne l'emperere
Octovïan, / N'esligasent le destre pan" [vv. 82–86]). She promises Lanval her
love, eternal fidelity, and as much wealth as his heart desires, under one condition—that he not reveal her existence:

"Amis, fet ele, or vus chasti,	*"Friend, she says, now I warn you, I*
Si vus comant et si vus pri:	*command and pray of you: Do not reveal*
Ne vus descovrez a nul humme!	*yourself to any man! For this will be the*
De ceo vus dirai ja la summe:	*result: you will have lost me forever, if*
A tuz jurs m'avrïez perdue,	*this love becomes known; never will you*
Si ceste amur esteit seüe;	*be able to see me nor have possession of my*
Jamés nem purrïez veeir	*body." (vv. 143–50)*
Ne de mun cors seisine aveir."	

Lanval, whose generosity to other knights as well as to jongleurs compensates
for Arthur's neglect, is able to maintain the secret of the source of his wealth
until Guinevere requests his love. When he refuses, she accuses him of homosexuality. The knight is only able to extricate himself with the boast of loving
someone more beautiful than the queen. Guinevere, in yet another rendering

of the Potiphar's wife motif like that of "La Chastelaine de Vergi," denounces him to her husband. Lanval realizes he has lost all: "Il s'esteit bien aparceüz / Qu'il aveit perdue s'amie: / Descovert ot la druërie!" ("He knows well he has lost his love: He uncovered loving" [vv. 334–36]). Arthur, meanwhile, like the duke of "La Chastelaine de Vergi," puts the wronged knight in a position of either proving the truth of his boast—which, as boast, prevents its own proof—or of being punished. The disconsolate Lanval, who contemplates suicide, is rescued at the last minute when, amid all the realistic trappings of his trial, the fairy maiden suddenly appears and is acknowledged to be the most beautiful: "La pucele entra el palais: / Unkes si bele n'i vint mais!" ("The maid entered the palace: Never before had such a beauty come there!" [vv. 601–2]). She carries him off to Avalon.[24]

If "Lanval" turns fatalistically around a certain logic of revelation, the promise made to be broken and the boast that denies the possibility of sub-stantiation, it is because both speech acts are so thoroughly enmeshed in the poetics of the lai as to make the transgression, rendered in terms of self-cancel-ing vows and conceits, the thematization of a broader paradox, which I have identified with the question of virginity, and which is comparable to the me-dieval thinking of the question of fiction itself. Lanval, after all, not only uses his new-found wealth to dress jongleurs, but also, like Ignauré, he is the figure of the poet. He is depicted as a loner, a dreamer, and, like the knight of "La Chastelaine de Vergi," is accused by the queen of being homosexual—a charge, as we know from Alain de Lille, that carried in the twelfth century an association with rhetoric.[25] Lanval's dilemma is, moreover, that of the poet who transgresses the unwritten rule of the courtly relation subsumed in the dictum "If you say it, you lose it," who violates what is imagined to be the integrity of an orality present to itself—and the fairy lady is just one version of such a fantasy of plenitude—every time he or she speaks. Put in the terms of medieval poetics, the voice associated with the presence of the body, or even of bodies, is transgressed by the lai, which is merely its trace, and by the act of articulation, transcription being merely the limit of such a transgres-sion.

There is no better example of the fatalistic mutual implication of writing and betrayal within the courtly lay than Marie de France's "Laüstic," the story of two knights who are neighbors, and of the wife of one who loves the other, another "bachelor."[26] It is unclear within the short narrative whether or not their love is consummated—in other words, whether or not the body ever attains to a presence. Nonetheless, the lovers communicate by looking at each other from adjoining rooms. Asked by her suspicious husband why she gets up so often at night, the wife replies: "There is no joy in all the world like hearing the nightingale."[27] The husband, jealous of his wife's pleasure, captures the nightingale by fashioning a *laz:* "N'i ot codre ne chastainier / U il ne mettent laz u glu, / Tant que pris l'unt e retenu" ("There was not a hazel or a chestnut tree on which they did not place a net or glue, until they trapped and held it" [vv. 98–100]). It is as if, and the reference could not be more explicit, the nightingale as voice is caught in Marie's own trap, which is the lay.

Even the word *lai* itself is a kind of linguistic trap, for no syllable demonstrates more explicitly the polysemic plasticity of the Old French language, or the sense in which the infinite semantic resources of orality are restrained by writing. In addition to the traditional acceptation of "melody" or "song," *lai* and its variants *lay, laye, laie, laiz, laes,* can be used as an adjective to connote the secular realm and as a substantive to designate a lay person. By extension, the word can refer to a member of the secular clergy,[28] to anyone not belonging to the university community, or, as a corollary, to someone considered ignorant.[29] *Lai* and its homonyms *laid, lait* are used variously as a synonym for the word *staddle,* for whatever is ugly, or, as so often in the *Miracles de Notre Dame,* to designate the Virgin Mary's milk. The adjectival homonyms *lé, ley, lay, let, lait, leit, laé, lede* specify that which is wide or large (> L. *latus*). *Lié, liet, leé, le* summon the idea of lightness, happiness, joy (> L. *laetus*); while *las, lax, lais* connote sadness, misery, or misfortune (> L. *lassus*). This tiny syllable becomes more interesting, however, when it signifies whatever is left over—not only fluvial deposits and manure, but any excess including the idea of a legacy or *legs* (as in the *Lais* of Villon). All of this suggests a link between the concept of a vestigial mark and the *Lais* as a written trace of preexisting song. Marie de France is aware that her writing not only constitutes the transcription or fixing of some more mobile, possibly oral, version of legend, but also that this transcription is already a rewriting of the written residues of a culture (the Breton one) that prefigures her own:

Les contes ke jo sai verrais,	*The tales—and I know they're true—*
Dunt li Bretun unt fait les lais,	*from which the Bretons made their* lais
Vos conterai assez briefment.	*I'll now recount for you briefly; and at*
El chief de cest comencement,	*the very beginning of this enterprise, just*
Sulunc la lettre e l'escriture,	*the way it was written down. I'll relate*
Vos mosterai une aventure	*an adventure that took place in Brittany*
Ki en Bretaigne la Menur	*in the old days.* ("Guigemar,"
Avint al tens ancïenur.	vv. 19–26)

The notion of the *lais* as a residue or mark connects such a legacy to the legit-imation of a place or *locus* (OF *leu*) from which to speak, or from which poetry becomes possible. "LA, *lai, lay,* adv., se dit d'un lieu qu'on désigne d'une man-ière précise," specifies Godefroy on p. 685 of volume 4 of his dictionary. Nor, in that same vein, is it an exaggeration to associate the *Lais* with the principle of poetic construction or binding subsumed under the rubric of the *laisse,* elaborated in Old Provençal as the process of linking verses (*lassar*). Christine de Pizan, describing the script of the letter found at her bedside in the *Dit de la rose,* equates this little syllable with the wrapping or binding of a book (*laz,* lace, from L. *laqueus*).[30] Finally, the word *lai* is used in its Old French forms *loi, lei, ley* to designate custom, usage, justice, or the law.

The dead bird, trapped in the net (*laz*) and thrown at the wife, makes a mark: "Sur la dame le cors geta, / Si que sun chainse ensanglanta / Un poi desur le piz devant" ("He threw the little body at his wife, and it bloodied her blouse, a little above her breast" [vv. 117–19]). The nightingale's body, the voice betrayed, is, in other words, presented as a form of writing upon the woman's body, and a message to be read. Indeed, the lady sends it to her lover like a letter to inform him of betrayal.

"Le laüstic li trametrai,   *"I will send the nightingale to him along*
L'aventure li manderai."   *with the adventure." She wrapped the*
En une piece de samit   *bird in a piece of silk embroidered with*
A or brusdé et tut escrit   *gold and written all around. She called*
Ad l'oiselet envolupé;   *her servant and charged him with her*
Un suen vaslet ad apelé   *message which she sent to her love.*
Sun message li ad chargié,   (vv. 134–41)
A sun ami l'ad enveié.

The lover, in turn, has the dead bird enshrined in a reliquary, which he carries with him as long as he lives.

We find in "Laüstic," as in "Lanval," the fantasy of a utopic plenitude or presence—here, however, explicitly identified with pleasurable orality.[31] For the supposed communication, which the proximity of houses makes possible ("Kar pres esteient lur repere" ["For their lodgings adjoined," v. 35]) is equa-ted with pleasure: "Delit aveient al veier, / Quant plus ne poeient aveir" ("They had the pleasure of seeing each other when they could have no more" [vv. 77–78]). It is worth stopping a moment at the word *delit* (pleasure or delight), since it is a key to the utopic presence associated with the body. The text *says* delight, but one may ask, delight at what? Certainly not presence, since Marie states categorically that "they had the delight of seeing each other *when they could have no more*" (emphasis added). The imagined pleasure of the body is a substitute for presence, a supplement, which is also synonymous with *délit* in the sense of the *flagrans delictum* in which the lovers are captured. For nowhere in the lai is the presence of a voice anything but a substitute for something else. The lovers are never present to each other, and the nightingale never sings to the lovers. It is itself nothing more than the sign of a ruse or lie told to calm the jealous husband's suspicions, an invention synonymous with the lai itself. The dead bird, encased in silk—literally "embroidered . . . and written" ("A or brusdé et tut escrit")—is sent like a poetic envoi to the lover, once consummation or the presence of bodies is no longer even imaginable. Nor was it ever; for such presence in the lai is always deferred. The deferral is, furthermore, analogous to the imagined pleasure we encountered in chapter 4, where John Chrysostom asks, "Who could describe the pleasure [of seeing "a soul by itself stripped of the body"]? What expression could suggest the joy of a soul so disposed?" and replies, "It does not exist."[32]

There is, in other words, no language of presence either in "Laüstic" or anywhere else adequate to render the coupling of bodies, such coupling being, as Marie makes clear in "Guigemar," a surplus that never enters language:

> Des ore est Guigemar a aise: *Now is Guigemar content. They lie*
> Ensemble gisent e parolent   *together and kiss and embrace often.*
> E sovent baisent e acolent.   *They would gladly welcome the rest of*
> Bien lur covienge del surplus   *that which lovers do!* ("Guigemar,"
> De ceo que li autre unt en us!   vv. 530–34)

An excess (*surplus*) that cannot be said, the presence of the body is excluded from the text. Which is not to imply that poets do not try all the time to capture the body; such attempts constitute the very essence of the poetic instance. Marie makes this clear in the general "Prologue," an *art poétique* that prescribes the making of texts as a series of rewritings, which, no matter how perfect, always leave a "surplus of meaning."[33]

This suggests that the body (and the voice), in the medieval understanding, is always deferred by the text that supplants it, transgresses it in a sense analogous to Lanval's betrayal of the fictional fairy. For the theme of betrayal dominates not only the lais of "Lanval" and "Laüstic," but also a great many

other so-called courtly works. In the chanson de geste betrayal takes the form
of broken oaths, apostasy, and treason, whereas in the courtly text—from
Béroul's *Tristan* and Chrétien's *Lancelot* to the prose romances of the thirteenth century—it is to be found in the theme of capture of the bodies of
lovers *in flagrante delicto*. Betrayal is a structuring principle of the courtly lyric
whose stock of characters includes the *losengiers,* liars, false speakers, and flatterers, but also denouncers of adulterers. So widespread, in fact, is the theme
of betrayal that both Lanval's and the lady of "Laüstic's" indiscretions, like
those of the knight, the duke, and the duchess of "La Chastelaine de Vergi,"
seem fated. The fatalism of the boast—whether of the most beautiful woman
or the greatest joy in the world—underscores the extent to which in medieval
texts the poetic and erotic are embedded in each other. For even the word
traire, like the word *lai,* is one of those polysemic markers that in its semantic
richness transgresses the premise of a plenitude inward to verbal signs, since
the ear can never hear as much or make as many distinctions as the eye can see.

At the beginning of "Guigemar," the hero who loves no one but is loved
by all—and who thus participates in a fantasy of plenitude or self-sufficiency,
of Being like unto itself—shoots a doe with antlers, a creature as sexually un-
defined as himself, and is in turn wounded by the arrow that is deflected back
in his direction: "Il tent sun arc, si trait a li, / En l'esclot la feri devaunt" ("He
holds his bow, he draws it to him; he struck the doe in the front hoof" [vv. 94–
95]).[34] The shooting of the arrow that is drawn to him ("trait a li") is, in
short, an inscription on the level of theme of what narrative elaboration is all
about. It remains indistinguishable from Marie's drawing of her own project:

Ki de bone mateire traite,   *He who fashions [draws, treats] good*
Mult li peise si bien n'est faite.   *material is very pained if it is not well*
Oëz, seignurs, ke dit Marie,   *done. Listen, lords, to what Marie says,*
Ki en sun tens pas ne s'oblie.   *she who in her time does not squander*
     her talent. ("Guigemar," vv. 1–4)

If *traire* (MF *tirer*) means "to shoot," it also means "to treat," "to draw out,"
or simply "to draw," as suggested by the "traits" of the portrait of Venus
painted on the wall of the lady's prison tower:

La chaumbre ert peinte tut   *The room was painted all around.*
  entur;   *Venus, the goddess of love, was well*
Venus, la deuesse d'amur,   *represented in the painting which showed*

Fu tres bien mise en la
   peinture;
Les traiz mustrout e la nature
Cument hom deit amur tenir
E lealment e bien servir.

her nature and her traits, how one
should carry on love, and loyally serve.
(vv. 233–38)

Then too, *traire* also signifies "to translate," "to transmit," or "to transform" and is the term for what any author does in extruding or drawing one text from another. Marie makes explicit in the "Prologue" the extent to which writing is an extrusion of prior writings; "Pur ceo començai a penser / D'aukune bone estoire faire / E de latin en romaunz traire" ("For this reason I began to think of making a few good stories and of translating them from Latin into romance" ["Prologue," vv. 28–30]).

As translation, *traire* implies the transformation of the same into the other; and if it means "to shoot," "to distance," or "to introduce difference," it is because such terms of alienation are the homonym of "to deceive." Indeed, given the fact that Old French, even though written, was intended for the ear (to be either recited or read aloud), there can be no difference between the words *traire* and *trahir*. "To draw or shoot" and "to betray" stand as proof of the treachery of a homophonic lack of difference in the sound of a word that can also mean "to differ."

The deflection of meaning obvious in Guigemar's treacherous arrow is also repeated in "Laüstic" in the logic of the lady's betrayal: she betrays her love in order supposedly to protect it, as if such self-betrayal were inevitable— as, according to a medieval sense of poetics, it is. For the poet in writing does exactly what the cardinal rule of courtly discretion prohibits. A transmitter of transgression through transcription, he or she reveals secret love affairs. Thus the fatality that hangs over "Lanval" and "Laüstic" from the beginning is that of the impossible equation that is poetry, which not only violates all the oaths of secrecy sworn by lovers, but disobeys Andreas's sanction against exposure as well. Just as desire revealed disappears, presence spoken is betrayed.

This is another way of saying that the lai is a liar, a deceiver, and that such deception cannot be divorced from the theme of adultery with which we began. Here there is no better proof than the story of "Eliduc," the tale with two names about the man with two wives, Guilliadun (the mistress) and Guildelüec (the wife): "D'eles deus ad li lais a nun / *Guildelüec ha Guilliadun.* / *Elidus* fu primes nomez, / Mes ore est li nuns remuez" ("From the pair of them the lay takes its name, *Guildelüec ha Guilliadun.* It used to be called

Elidus, but now the name has changed" [vv. 21–24]). Eliduc's bigamy is synonymous with ambiguity, the ambivalence of each woman's relation to him
being contained in the only partial perception of the existence of the other
rendered by the partial homophony of their names: Guilliadun "ne saveit pas
que femme eüst" ("did not know he had a wife" [v. 584]); and Guildelüec,
unaware of Guilliadun, wonders why her husband seems withdrawn: "Mut se
cuntient sutivement. / Sa femme en ot le queor dolent, / Ne sot mie que ceo
deveit; / A sei meïsmes se pleigneit" ("He acted quite withdrawn. His wife,
whose heart was greatly pained, did not know what to make of it; she la-
mented to herself" [vv. 717–20]). For the two women the bigamist is
ambiguity; and never more so, it turns out, than when he claims to be telling
the truth. "For I don't want," he claims, "to transgress my faith" ("Kar ne voil
ma fei trespasser" [v. 739]). Eliduc incarnates the paradox of the liar: "When
I tell you I'm telling the truth, I lie; and when I tell you I lie, I am telling the
truth." Which is no different, at bottom, from what the lai does when it denounces the very ambiguity it sanctions— "Kar n'est pas bien ne avenant /
De deus espuses meintenir, / Ne la *lei* ne deit cunsentir" (vv. 1128–30) which
can be read: "the law does not permit bigamy"; "the lai does not permit bigamy";
"the law does not permit ambiguity"; "the lai does not permit ambiguity."
Or, "When the lai tells you it does not permit double meaning, it means double." The law of the lai involves always—and here there can be no ambiguity—a betrayal, that of lovers, but also of univocal meaning, a presence or
plenitude in language that, as in the paradigmatic lay of "Lanval," is transgressed by expression. Put another way, the truth that poetry can never state
without transgressing its own status as fiction is that it is fiction. Thus
Lanval's trial is not only the trial of a despondent knight caught in an uncon-
scionable dilemma, but also the trial of fiction itself. That is, to the extent that
he wins his case and, in proving that his lady is best, proves that fiction is true,
he loses her; and to the extent that he fulfills the unwritten law of fiction (that
it may never be revealed as such) and thereby retains the fairy lady, he loses his
case. The legal case is, in essence, the case of literature as the medievals conceived it, and it is resolved only by Marie's own concluding ruse, the strategy
of the poet at one remove—to so confuse the distinction between what is to
be taken as real and what is not that the reader can no longer tell whether the
dream lady has come to life or reality has become a dream.

The word *traire* is also a synonym of *trover,* "to invent" in the sense of
poetic *inventio,* and "to discover" as in the betrayal of lovers. "Ce jur furent
aperceü / Descovert, trové et veü" ("That day they were perceived, dis-

covered, found, and seen" ["Guigemar, vv. 577–78]). This is Marie's phrase for the capture of lovers. To write or treat (*traire*) is to betray (*traire*). Put otherwise, to write immanence, whether figured as the body or the voice, is to betray it or, as in the case of the nightingale, to ensnare and contain it in a *laz*, to kill it, and ultimately to entomb the living voice in the dead letter of a text, to silence it.

This is why there are so many tombs in Marie's works. Whether the reliquary of the voice in "Laüstic," the father's tomb in "Yonec," the entombment at the end of "Chaitivel," the burial of lovers in "Deus Amanz," or the elaborate construction of the funerary chapel in "Eliduc," the lai as a vestige or legacy is the tomb of the voice and a monument to desire. Thus, in "Eliduc" the moment of the woman's burial and the hero's withdrawal from the world to the abbey is the moment he becomes a lyric poet: "Le jur que jeo vus enfuirai, / Ordre de moigne recevrai; / Sur vostre tumbe chescun jur / Ferai refreindre ma dolur" ("The day that I will bury you I will receive the holy order, and on your tomb every day I will refrain my sadness" [vv. 947–50]). Again, the lai as legacy is the site of mourning of a loss, more precisely, of a loss of imagined plenitude. "Nes voil tuz perdre pur l'un prendre!" ("I don't want to lose them all by taking one!" [v. 156]) laments the heroine of "Chaitivel," the feminine equal of Eliduc, the woman who would like to keep four men, and who is forced to choose. Her dilemma is thoroughly analogous to that of the poet, who must select a title for this lai from two alternatives.[35] "Because I have loved you so much," the woman says, "I want my pain to be remembered. Thus I will compose a lai, and *Quatre dols* will be its name" ("Pur ceo que tant vus ai amez, / Voil que mis doels seit remembrez; / De vus quatre ferai un lai / E *Quatre dols* le numerai" [vv. 201–4]). To repeat, the poet is the one who breaks the law by uncovering desire, who violates the fantasy of plenitude by choosing, and who thus places the presence of the voice in the tomb of writing.[36] Like the liar or Lanval, she cannot write of secret love without revealing it, cannot transcribe the presence of the voice without betraying it. She always loses something in "taking one." One always betrays, and even kills, something whenever one sings, boasts, or even talks about it.

Though such an assertion may seem on the surface unrelated to the theme of virginity discussed in chapter 4, it is, in the medieval articulation of the questions of language and gender, thoroughly implicated in it. For the notion of a loss incurred by any instance of writing, speech, or even thought is, on the basis of all that we have seen thus far, none other than that of the imagined loss of wholeness, analogous to a loss of chastity, implicit to the virgin seen or suspected, or, in the phrase of Tertullian, the "virgin who ceases to be a virgin from the time it becomes possible for her *not* to be one."

Readers will no doubt have sensed long before now the irony of the myriad oaths broken by men. For despite the fact that in the medieval thinking of gender woman is portrayed as verbal abuse—as garrulity, contention, and indiscretion (chapter 1)—the male protagonists are the ones who, having been warned, consistently transgress an implicit faith; break, like the knight and the duke, an explicit promise; or reveal, like Lanval, what is supposed to remain secret. This is another of the defining contradictions implicit to the discourse of misogyny. Regardless of the manifest attempt to establish and maintain sexual difference, according to which women assume the burden of indiscretion and men are assumed to be worthy of trust, and regardless of the association between femininity and the deceptive modes of representation synonymous with the literary, the possibility of clear gender distinction is obscured within the lay because of the opposition—not unlike that of the misogynist who uses rhetoric to denounce it—between what it says and what it does. The Old French récit could not state more explicitly the extent to which men are as implicated in the medieval alliance of gender and the literary as we have seen that women are thought to be. Nor is this association restricted to the secular genres that fall under the rubric of *le merveilleux païen*. For the broken promise of "Lanval," the archetypal lay, finds a structural analogue in another seemingly unrelated short form, the miracle narratives of the thirteenth and fourteenth centuries, and in particular the *Miracles de Notre Dame* of Gautier de Coinci. Though the *Miracles* belong in some respects to the religious literature of the High Middle Ages—and despite their vernacular status have traditionally been isolated from more secular texts—they contain numerous and important points of resemblance to the lay, and thus serve to link the courtly ethos both to the theme of violated virginity and to the antifeminist current of the early Middle Ages. Mary the Virgin is closer to Marie de France than conventional wisdom has historically held, and this is nowhere more apparent than in the longest "Miracle," entitled in Gautier's version "Comment Theophilus vint a penitance."

This is the story of a righteous cleric who, like Lanval, is wronged when a newly installed bishop, under the influence of evil counselors, unjustly withdraws from Theophilus the parish (*vidame*) he administers.[37] Understandably upset, Theophilus blasphemes.[38] With the aid of an accommodating Jew, he concludes a pact with the devil who, like a perverse version of the fairy queen of "Lanval," promises to restore his lost honors:

Li dyables respont atant:	*The Devil responds: "Because you beg me*
"Por ce que tu m'en prïez tant,	*so, if he without delay renounces his*
S'il renoie sanz demorance	*baptism and his faith, God and his*
Et son baptesme et sa creance,	*mother, male and female saints, I can*
Dieu et sa mere, sainz et saintes,	*still procure him many an honor.*
Encore li donrai honors	(vv. 373–78)
maintes.	

The Jew and the devil immediately draw up for Theophilus's signature a contract: "Bone chartre l'en a donnee / De son anel bien saelee" ("They give him a good charter sealed with his ring" [vv. 417–18])—which the blasphemer signs. As the Jew stipulates, it must remain secret:

Le gïux, qui assez savoit	*The Jew, who knew enough of the evil*
De la male malavanture,	*adventure, privily, by darkest night,*
Priveement par nuit obscure	*came to him often. "Sweetest of friends,*
Assez souvent aloit a lui.	*tell no one of our business, and I will do*
"Biauz tres doz sires, a nului	*more for you with my lord than you could*
Ne dire, fait il, nostre afaire.	*ever wish for. I can still help you out if*
A mon signor te ferai faire	*our dealings are kept quiet [hidden"].*
Plus que n'oseras soushaidier.	(vv. 460–69)
Encor t'i cuit je tant aidier,	
Se nostre affaire tres bien	
çoiles ["].	

Though the immediate result of Theophilus's secret pact with the devil is the bishop's change of heart and the restoration of his lost honor, the apostate, like Lanval after his boast, remains lost and blind: "Dyable ont si sa lampe estainte / Qu'il ne seit mais quel part il torne, / S'il anuite ne s'il ajorne" ("The devils have so put out his lamp that he does not know which way he turns, or whether it is day or night" [vv. 614–16]). Finally, disconsolate, deprived, and in near total despair, he is rescued by Mary, Notre Dame:

Theophilus quarante jors	*Theophilus remained in the house of*
En abstinences et en plors	*worship for forty days, in abstinence and*
Dedens le temple demora.	*in tears. He sighed there, he prayed*
Adez gemi, adez ora	*there, on bare knees and elbows. But the*
A nus genolz et a nus coutes.	*one in whom all sweetness resides, when*
Mais cele ou les douceurs sunt	*she sees that he has suffered so much,*
totes,	*fasted and prayed for so long, and that in*

Quant voit qu'il a tant travillié,   *his heart there is so much pain, appeared*
Tant geüné et tant villié   *to him toward midnight. Theophilus*
Et qu'en son cuer a tant d'anui,   *trembles and shakes now that he has seen*
Vers mienuit s'apert a lui.   *the vision of Notre Dame.* (vv. 921–33)
Theophilus tranble et tressue
Tot maintenant qu'il l'a veüe,
La vision de Nostre Dame.

Theophilus's repentance consists literally of a rewriting of the satanic charter: "Jamais nul jor n'iere asseür / Devant que je raie l'escrit / Qui ma mort devise et descrit" ("Never any day will I feel safe before I will have crossed out [erased] the writing which prescribes and describes my death" [vv. 1316–18]). The charter serves not only as a record—a vestige, a trace, a *legs,* a lai—of the secret diabolic pact, but is also, one can assume, the basis of Gautier's "Miracle" text.

This "Miracle de Notre Dame" and the secular lay of "Lanval" are similarly motivated by an initial tort. Both the neglected vassal (Lanval) and the divested cleric (Theophilus) consummate devilish pacts, the condition of which is secrecy. Both knight and apostate undergo loss, belated consciousness of loss, and eventual recovery. "Comment Theophilus vint a penitance" represents, it seems, a rewriting of the lay of "Lanval." Rather, they are translations of each other. And if Marie de France, for example, proposes to "translate stories she has heard from Latin into Romance" ("Et de latin en romaunz traire" ["Prologue," v. 30]), which carries the charge of translating from the discourse of theology to the secular realm, Gautier de Coinci translates in the other direction. Mary pulls the sinner from the devil and from his sin ("La mere Dieu, la debonaire, / De pecheürs de pechié traire" [vv. 1489–90]) by getting him to translate his charter; and she punishes the Jew in one decisive blow (*trait*): "Venez veoir le riche trait / Que la riche mere Dieu trait" ("Come see the powerful blow struck by the mother of God" [vv. 1503–4]). More important, both the Virgin and Lanval's fairy queen are presented as sources of abundance in what are conflicting, but nonetheless structurally identical, parallel versions of the rescuing female, or of redeeming femininity. Mary is the redeeming translator. As the mother of God she is there to rewrite the sin of Eve: "Grans preus nos en vint, ce me sanble, / Quant nous delivra tous ensanble / Del grant outraige et del forfait / Qu'Eve en la pomme avoit forfait" ("Great proof has come to us, it seems to me, when she delivers us all from the great outrage and sin that Eve did with the apple" [vv. 131–34])—just as she rewrites The-just as she rewrites Theophilus's charter, or the New Testament rewrites the history of the Jews, according to the process of figural representation.

The resemblance of the courtly text and the "Miracle" goes beyond mere thematic identity, however, precisely through what we have identified as the medieval paradox of virginity. "Lanval," like "La Chastelaine de Vergi" and the "Lai d'Ignauré," is built upon the issue of the broken promise, which thematizes the dilemma of the poet: "If you say it, you destroy it." This translates into the fairy's proposition: "If you reveal it, you lose it." It is also, because of the adulatory context of courtly literature, transgressed by over-praise of the beloved. "I love and am the friend of she who should have the prize among all those whom I know," boasts Lanval.[39] And what, it may be asked, is Lanval's boast but the essence of the courtly encomium—the excessive praise of the lady who surpasses all others? "Even her poorest maid," the indiscreet knight continues, "is worth more than the queen because of her body, her face, her beauty, her learning and her goodness."[40] The knight's boast is no different from that, say, of the troubadour Cercamon: "Compared to my lady, I would not value the most beautiful woman ever seen more than a glove."[41]

And what too is Lanval's suffering but that of the archetypal afflicted courtly lover, unable to obtain the beloved, faint, begging for mercy, alienated from himself, suicidal?

En une chambre fu tuz suls;	*In a room he was all alone, downcast and*
Pensis esteit e anguissus.	*anguished. He calls his friend often, but*
S'amie apele mut sovent	*that avails him not at all. He complains*
Mes ceo ne li valut neent.	*and sighs and faints every other hour;*
Il se pleigneit e suspirot,	*then he cries a hundred times for mercy,*
D'ures en autres se pasmot;	*that she should appear to her friend. He*
Puis li crie cent feiz merci,	*curses his heart and mouth. It's a*
Qu'ele parolt a sun ami.	*miracle that he doesn't kill himself.*
Sun quor e sa buche maudit;	(vv. 338–47)
C'est merveille k'il ne s'ocit!	

The only difference between Lanval and the eternally singing and suffering lover of the courtly lyric, which we will explore in the next chapter, is one of horizon: where the planctus is within the lyric presented in the first person "from within," from the perspective of the lyric "I," it is here presented from the point of view of a third party, as the narrative lay seems to propose a reading of the lyric by tracing the conditions and consequences of a rhetoric of excessive praise.

THE LOVE LYRIC AND THE PARADOX OF PERFECTION

In our last chapter we shifted the focus of discussion from the question of asceticism strictly speaking to the literary phenomenon of courtly love. More precisely, we linked a certain fatal vision in the medieval obsession with virginity, which lies at the heart of medieval antifeminism, to the fatalism of the look inherent to the courtly definition of love as an "inborn suffering derived from the sight of and excessive meditation upon the beauty of the opposite sex." Further, we recalled from previous chapters that virginity itself represents a universal or abstraction that is lost by embodiment or even perception. Finally, we compared the logical impossibility of virginity to the obsessive courtly theme within the Old French lay of love lost through just such gestures of discovery or indiscretion.

Bernart de Ventadorn

The connection between romantic love, virginity, and the ascetic impulse is even more apparent in the medieval lyric than in the short narrative form, as we can see in an archetypal canso from the end of the twelfth century, "Can vei la lauzeta mover" of Bernart de Ventadorn—the poet "in whom," Robert Briffault asserts, "the 'courtly' manner attains at a bound its full development": [1]

1. Can vei la lauzeta mover
de joi sas alas contral rai,
que s'oblid' e-s laissa chazer
per la doussor c'al cor li vai,
ai, tan grans enveya m'en ve

1. When I see the lark beat his wings for joy against the sun's ray, until for the sheer delight which goes to his heart, he forgets to fly and plummets down, then great envy of those whom I see filled with

de cui qu'eu veya jauzion,
meravilhas ai, car desse
Lo cor de dezirer no-m fon.

happiness comes to me. I marvel that my
heart does not melt at once from desire.

2. Ai, las, tan cuidava saber
d'amor, e tan petit en sai,
car eu d'amar no-m posc tener
celeis don ja pro non aurai.
Tout m'a mo cor e tout m'a me,
e se mezeis e tot lo mon,
e can se-m tolc, no-m laisset re
mas dezirer e cor volon.

2. Alas! I thought I knew so much about
love, but really, I know so little. For I
cannot keep myself from loving her from
whom I shall have no favor. She has
stolen from me my heart, myself, herself
and all the world. When she took herself
from me, she left me nothing but desire
and a longing heart.

3. Anc non agui de me poder
ni no fui meus de l'or' en sai
que-m laisset en sos olhs vezer
en un miralh que mout me plai.
Miralhs, pus me mirei en te,
m'an mort li sospir de preon,
c'aissi-m perdei com perdet se
lo bels Narcisus en la fon.

3. Never have I been in control of myself
or even belonged to myself from the hour
she let me gaze into her eyes:—that
mirror which pleases me so greatly.
Mirror, since I saw myself reflected in
you, deep sighs have been killing me. I
have destroyed myself just as the
beautiful Narcissus destroyed himself in
the fountain.

4. De las domnas me dezesper.
Ja mais en lor no-m fiarai,
c'aissi com las solh chaptener,
enaissi las deschaptentrai.
Pois vei c'una pro no m'en te
Va leis que-m destrui e-m
    cofon,
totas las dopt'e las mescre,
car be sai c'atretals se son.

4. I despair of women. No more will I
trust them; and just as I used to defend
them, now I shall denounce them. Since I
see that none aids me against her who
destroys me and confounds me, I fear and
distrust all of them, for I know very well
that they are all alike.

5. D'aisso's fa be femna parer
ma domna, per qu'e-lh o retrai,
car no vol so c'om deu voler
e so c'om li deveda, fai.
Chazutz sui en mala merce,

5. In such things my lady acts like a
woman, and for this I reproach her. She
does not want to do what she should, and
she does what is forbidden her. I have
fallen into ill-favor, and I have acted like

et ai be faih co-l fols en pon,
e no sai per que m'esdeve
mas car trop puyei contra mon.

the fool on the bridge; yet I do not know
how it happens to me, unless it is that I
tried to climb too high.

6. Merces es perduda, per ver,
et eu non o saubi anc mai,
car cilh qui plus en degr'aver
no-n a ges, et on la querrai?
A, can mal sembla, qui la ve,
qued aquest chaitiu deziron
que ja ses leis non aura be
laisse morir, que no l'aon.

6. Mercy is lost for good—although I
never knew it anyway—for she, who
ought most to have it has none at all. Yet
where shall I seek it? How sorry it must
appear, when one considers it, that she
lets this miserable, longing creature, who
has no good without her, perish without
helping him.

7. Pus ab midons no-m pot
   valer
precs ni merces ni-l dreihz
   qu'eu ai,
ni a leis no ven a plazer
qu'eu l'am, je mais no-lh o dirai.
Aissi-m part de leis e-m recre.
Mort m'a e per mort li respon,
e vau m'en pus ilh no-m rete,
chaitius, en issilh, no sai on.

7. Since neither prayers, pity, nor the
justice of my cause help me with my lady,
and since my loving her brings her no
pleasure, I will say no more to her. I leave
her and renounce her. She has slain me
and with death I shall answer her. Since
she does not retain me, I depart,
wretched, into exile, I know not whither.

8. Tristans, ges no-n auretz de
   me,
qu'eu m'en vau, chaitius, no sai
   on.
De chantar me gic e-m recre,
e de joi et d'amor m'escon.

8. Tristan, you shall have nothing more
from me, for I depart, wretched, I know
not whither. I forsake and renounce
singing, and I seek shelter from joy and
love.[2]

"Can vei la lauzeta mover" contains many of the elements we have seen in both the discussion of courtly love and that of antifeminism. Love is, first of all, practically synonymous with a dispossession not unlike that of the neglected knight, Lanval: "She has stolen from me my heart, myself, herself and all the world. When she took herself from me, she left me nothing but desire and a longing heart" (2). Further, the despoliation of the self that is the equivalent of desire is in the canso, as in both its courtly and ascetic context,

imagined to enter by the eye, to originate in what Andreas Capellanus terms
"sight of and excessive meditation upon the beauty of the beloved," and the
antifeminists, "adultery" or "pride of the eyes." "Never have I been in control
of myself or even belonged to myself from the hour she let me gaze into her
eyes," Bernart confirms (3). More important, "Can vei la lauzeta mover"
turns around a series of contradictions entailed by desire, which make it clear
that the lyric is as implicated in the global paradox of the misogynistic articulation of woman as paradox—simultaneously "the Devil's gateway" and
"the Bride of Christ"—as any of the more explicit antifeminist writings of the
early church fathers or Latin satirists.

Love is conceived as a paradox of knowledge and ignorance: "Alas!," the
poet laments, "I thought I knew so much about love, but really, I know so
little" (2). It is expressed as a paradox of coterminous joy and pain: the poet
who shares the joy of the lark beating its wings (1), and whose elation nonetheless remains inseparable from the destruction, misery, and wretchedness
of his departure (4–8). Bernart praises his lady as the source of all good for
him in stanza 6, and condemns her for having destroyed and confounded him
in stanza 4. He admits to loving and hating women at the same time: "I cannot keep myself from loving her," he confesses in stanza 2; "I despair of
women," he maintains in stanza 4. "Can vei la lauzeta mover" contains a profound drama of the will; rather, a conflict between knowledge and willpower
that is transmitted from the outset in the image of the high-flying bird so
taken with delight that it forgets to fly, which is picked up again in Bernart's
doubt (6) that he has "tried to climb too high." In short, the poet does not
have the power to obtain what he desires, a dilemma mirrored by the lady's
refusal to desire what she might obtain: "She does not want to do what she
should," the troubadour complains, "and she does what is forbidden her" (5).
"Mercy is lost for good—although I never knew it anyway—for she, who
ought most to have it has none at all (6)."[3]

The multiple contradictions contained in "Can vei la lauzeta mover" are
in some profound sense subsumed in the paradox of the poetic voice—that is,
in the articulation of a fear of speech, which is a common motif in the canso.
Cercamon, for example, maintains in "Quant l'aura doussa s'amarzis" to be
"so overcome that he doesn't dare to speak his desire" at the same time that he
alleges that his worst fear is "that he will die without daring to request" his
lady's love.[4] So too Bernart, in the lyric "Can l'erba fresch' e.l.h folha par,"
claims to fear his lady so passionately that he has never "dared speak to her of
myself."[5] In "Can vei la lauzeta mover" Bernart uses his voice to renounce

song. "I forsake and renounce singing" (8) is a phrase so contrary to the manifest presence of the song that one cannot help but notice the similarity between Bernart's amatory posture and the misogynist's "I am forbidden to speak. . . . Yet I cannot keep silence" (chapter 2). Nor can the paradoxical use of the song to renounce singing be separated from the poet's irreconcilable relation to his own desire. "I will say no more to her" (7) in the plaint directed to the lady is not essentially different from the threat "I leave her and renounce her" (7) and contradicts the original confession, "I cannot keep myself from loving her" (2).

Here we encounter an incongruence that can be considered as the global paradox of courtliness and that resides precisely in the fact that the poet continues to sing despite the intention to remain silent, that he continues to desire despite the hopelessness of desiring: "I cannot keep myself from loving her from whom I shall have no favor" (2).[6] One begins to wonder, in fact, if the poem gives expression to the futility of its own desire or if desire itself does not constitute the condition of poetic futility.[7] Nor is the paradox unlike that of virginity. Put in its simplest terms, the sine qua non of desire—that is, of a woman's being loved—is that she be perfect. Yet the condition of her perfection is that she be self-sufficient, self-contained, complete—or that, being desired, she herself should not desire. "The more I implore her," Bernart states elsewhere, "the crueler she is to me."[8] The perfection of the love object excludes or prevents her desiring. To be loved, according to the logic of the courtly relation, the woman must be indifferent, unattainable, unsullied—in short, a virgin. There is, in other words, no way of loving that does not imply the incongruity of persistent singing about dissatisfaction that "Can vei la lauzeta mover" makes explicit.

The paradox of the poet, according to the theoretical assumptions of the canso, which indeed seems like a vernacular elaboration of the doctrine of virginity of the church fathers, is that of an impossible enunciation, or rather of an impossible relation of speaker to voice. We encountered its narrative version in "La Chastelaine de Vergi" and in the lays of "Ignauré," "Laüstic," and "Lanval." The lover, despite claims to the contrary and despite the constant displacement of the blame for such revelations upon court gossips and false flatterers, is a revealer of secret affairs. "Lady," Bernart swears, "even if these false, envious men, who have stolen many good days from me, have been watching to find out how it is with us, you are still not lost through the chatter of base, knavish louts. For our love is not known through me; you may be well assured of that."[9] What's more, to the extent that the poet, like Lanval, exposes his desire or expresses it, it disappears or is at least debased. "The love which men boast about everywhere is not love, but pretense," Bernart maintains, "and he who does not respect what would be secret is base, villainous, and foolish."[10] According to this dilemma of language, which goes far beyond its mere thematic analogue in the courtly exhortation to discretion, the notion of an impossible virginity, destroyed by sight, thought, or even suspicion, resurfaces in a form that, for being unrecognized, is all the more compelling. It implies that every love song deflowers a virgin.

The paradox of the poet's singing to renounce song, of his desiring only that which by definition will not desire in return, the paradox, in sum, of the love of virgins, has several consequences for our understanding of the courtly phenomenon. First, it explains the easy movement within the lyric between so-called courtly love and the elements of antifeminism that transform the courtly poet into the fellow traveler of the misogynist. "I despair of women. No more will I trust them; and just as I used to defend them, now I shall denounce them. Since I see that none aids me against her who destroys me and confounds me, I fear and distrust all of them, for I know very well that they are all alike" (4). In fact, if we return to our definition of misogyny as a speech act such that the subject of the sentence is *woman* and the predicate a more general term (see the introduction), it becomes clear that there is a marked resonance between negative and positive qualifiers, between the reifying idealization of the abstract woman who is never named in the courtly lyric except as *domna,* and the condemnation of all women: "I despair of women. . . . for I know very well that they are all alike" (4). But with this difference: if the discourse of antifeminism is characterized by the speech act "all women are . . . ," that of the courtly lover is haunted by "this one woman is." Yet one wonders whether the woman as unique source of abstract virtues (the most beautiful, generous, courteous, kind), the woman as type, is really so different at all.

Even so cursory a reading of "Can vei la lauzeta mover" makes it clear that the deprecation of the feminine lurks just below the surface of the courtly idealization of woman. Nor is Bernart unique in this. Marcabru, whose biographer tells us that "he never loved any woman and was not loved by any" and that "he spoke ill of women and of love," is aware of the closeness of the connection between seemingly contrary images of gender.[11] Indeed, his poems are filled with practically all the topoi of antifeminism that we have encountered thus far: women are portrayed as licentious, fickle, unfaithful, duplicitous, and seductive.[12] "Not since the serpent lowered the apple branch have there been so many tricky women," he maintains.[13] More important, Marcabru, who is one of the few troubadours to show any awareness of the question of conception, portrays domestic life in terms of a constant masquerade of false paternity according to which fathers, thinking they can constrain their wives, raise and "nourish" the children of their rivals:

<table>
<tr><td>

D'autra manieira cogossos,
Hi a rics homes e baros
Qui las enserron dinz maios
Qu'estrains non i posca intrar
E tenon guirbautz als tisos
Cui las commandon a gardar

E segon que ditz Salamos,
Non podon cill perfors lairos
Acuillir d'aquels compaignos
Qui fant la noirim cogular,
Et aplanon los guirbaudos
E cujon lor fills piadar

</td><td>

There are some powerful and great
barons who imprison their wives in houses
so that no stranger can enter, and who at
the same time entertain the rogues to
whom they give the orders to guard them.
But according to the wisdom of Solomon
these lords could not offer hospitality to
worse thieves than this bunch that
bastardizes the race; and the husbands
caress little rogues thinking they are
covering their sons with affection.[14]

</td></tr>
</table>

Raimbaut d'Orange even goes so far as to suggest that only the misogynist, and not the courtly lover, is capable of success in love. "I wish to teach you even more with which you will conquer the best ladies," he promises. "Do everything with ugly words and hideous singing and boasting; and do honor to the worst women."[15]

Second, and this is just a corollary of the courtly abstraction of the feminine, the lyric seems to have very little to do with women at all. On the contrary, it bears more upon the poet's relation to himself than upon his relation with others.[16] Love in "Can vei la lauzeta mover" is born, as in the discourse of asceticism, through the gaze; but the gaze is not upon the woman so much as on the reflection of the man in her eyes: "Never have I been in control of myself or even belonged to myself from the hour she let me gaze into her eyes:—that mirror which pleases me so greatly" (3). At bottom, the poet's desire expresses, again in consonance with received antifeminist tradition, a deep-seated pessimism subtended by the death wish. This explains the pertinence of the myth of Tristan: "Tristan, you shall have nothing more from me, for I depart, wretched, I know not whither" (8). The dispossession of the self, the disembodiment implicit to the love of an abstraction, an ideal, an Idea that is destroyed by poetic embodiment, is self-inflicted. Thus the fatal attraction of seeing oneself in the eyes of the other, and thus also the attraction of the myth of Narcissus: "Mirror, since I saw myself reflected in you, deep sighs have been killing me. I have destroyed myself just as the beautiful Narcissus destroyed himself in the fountain" (3).

The self-inflicted annihilation of the self implicit to courtly love is nowhere more apparent than in Thibaut de Champagne's "Ausi conme unicorne sui," which contains many of the same motifs as "Can vei la lauzeta mover," but which makes the connection between desire, death, and virginity even more explicit. Thus Thibaut de Champagne, like Bernart de Ventadorn, is disembodied; his heart has been impounded:

Mes cuers aloit si tressaillant
Que il remest quant je m'en
   mui.
Lors fu menez sanz raençon
En la douce chartre en prison.
   [2]

My heart shook so violently [when I saw you] that it stayed with you when I left. Then it was captured without ransom and closed in the sweet prison. [2][17]

The poet has been seized—"Mult ont tost un honme saisi" ("They have quickly captured a man" [3])—or dispossessed, the word *saisi* being related to *saisine,* which is the literal equivalent of possession. Like Bernart, he desires his own interminable suffering: "Dame, je ne dout mes riens plus / Fors tant que faille a vous amer" ("Lady, I fear nothing more than failing to love you" [5]). Thibaut, moreover, recognizes the extent to which his own imprisonment is occasioned by a virgin, more specifically by the fatal effects of the look not only for a virgin, but for the one who looks upon her:

Ausi conme unicorne sui
Qui s'esbahist en regardant,
Quant la pucele va mirant.
Tant est lië de son ennui,
Pasmee chiet en son giron;
Lors l'ocit on en traïson.
Et moi ont mort d'autel
   senblant
Amors et ma dame por voir.
Mon cuer ont, n'en puis point
   ravoir. [1]

I am like the unicorn which is stunned in looking, fascinated, at the virgin. Happy with its torment, it falls into her lap; prey offered to the traitor who kills it. So it is with me: I am truly put to death by Love and my lady. They took my heart, and I cannot recover it. [1]

"Ausi conme unicorne sui" is as strong an illustration of the fatalism of the gaze upon the virgin as can be found in medieval literature. It stands as a parable of virginity, which underscores the overriding paradox of courtliness and of the courtly lyric.

Stated simply, to the extent that the woman of the lyric seduces but is never seduced, she represents a virgin. The prerequisite of her being desired is that she be perfect, ideal, complete unto herself, without imperfection or lack, and therefore without desire; the sine qua non of loving, therefore, is that one not be loved in return. The lady must be a virgin in order to be loved; the desire for the virgin represents an ideal or idea that we have identified elsewhere—in relation to the concept of misogynistic virginity—as a desire for the absolute, which in this case subtends a profound wish for identity with the other, for self-identity. Yet the very notion of self-identity, like the possibility of the embodied virgin, is undercut at every instant within the poem, since self-identity is never realizable, according to medieval sign theory, within the realm of language. The proof lies in the first line: "Ausi *conme* unicorne sui." "To be like" a unicorn is not "to be" a unicorn, language itself embodying the principle of such difference, or opening a space within the self each time one speaks or writes. This is, in essence, the meaning of the disincarnations contained in the poem: "They took my heart, and I cannot recover it" (1); "My heart shook so violently [when I saw you] that it stayed with you when I left" (2).

The alienation of the self from the self opened by the opening metaphor implies that something is the self which is not; that something is animate which is not; in other words, it implies personification. The culminating distance within "Ausi conme unicorne sui" is precisely that—personification allegory, the presentation of the self as abstraction, and conversely the presentation of abstractions as if they were animate. The pillars of the lover's prison are desire; the gates, contemplation; and the chains, good hope ("les piliers sont de désir, / les portes de contemplation, / et les chaînes, de bon espoir" [2]):

De la chartre a la clef Amors	*Love holds the key to the prison, and has*
Et si a mis trois portiers:	*placed there three guards: Sweet*
Biau Senblant a non li premiers,	*Seeming is the first, and then Beauty*
E Biauté ceus en fet seignors;	*which exercises its power. Danger has*
Dangier a mis a l'uis devant,	*been placed by the front gate, an ugly,*
Un ort felon vilain puant,	*stinking low felon, full of mischief and*
Qui mult est maus et	*spite. [3]*
pautoniers. [3]	

The question inevitably occurs, in reading a lyric like "Ausi conme unicorne sui," of where exactly to locate the allegorized drama that pits the principles of seduction (Biau Semblant) against those of inhibition (Dangier, Soufrir).

Does the conflict of psychologized abstractions belong to the woman, as C. S. Lewis has maintained in relation to the *Roman de la rose?* Or is it internal to the man? If one of the givens of the lyric is, by the very presence of the singing voice, a perpetually unsatisfied desire, what is the object of desire? Is it the woman who is never present? Is it, as suggested above, self-identity? Does the singing voice, as also has been suggested, desire language or the song itself? There is certainly ample evidence in other vernacular works to justify assimilating the gaps within language, what Marie de France calls its "obscurities," to a desire for meaning and for the text. Is the ultimate object of the poet's desire, as argued by Denis de Rougemont, desire itself? Thibaut's final strophe in which he asserts, "Lady I fear nothing more than failing to love you" (5), would certainly support such a claim. "Ausi conme unicorne sui," like "Can vei la lauzeta mover," makes it clear that the desire for suffering is indeed related to the desire for song and that this masochistic coupling transforms the poet's suffering into a relation less with the woman, never named, of whom it supposedly speaks, than with himself. Again, the terms of the lyric are those we have identified with the poetics of virginity. To wit, if the poet is like the unicorn who seduces himself with a fatal look, and if the representation in metaphoric language of that seduction implies an alienation of the poet from himself, then there is, finally, no way of separating the death wish attendant upon virginity from such use of metaphor. The prison of the poet is, in its medieval lyric reception, the "sweet charterhouse" of writing (*chartre*): "Lors fu menez sanz raençon / En la douce chartre en prison" ("Then it was captured without ransom and closed in the sweet charter, in prison" [2]).

This is another way of saying that there is less difference than is often assumed between the courtly love song, identified with the secular realm of the flesh, and the supposedly more spiritual genre of songs to the virgin—just as we have discovered a similarity between the secular lay of "Lanval" and the "Miracle," "Comment Theophilus vint a penitance." In a virgin lyric entitled "Tant ai amors servies longuement," for example, Thibaut seems to renounce the love of his lady in favor of devotion to the Mother of God. Yet he recognizes, at bottom, that love is always directed toward the unobtainable.

Mes bone amor ne let honme   *True love does not allow one to choose the*
apenser   *object of his thoughts. One prefers to love*

Ne bien choisir ou mete sa
pensee.
Plus tost aime on en estrange
contree,
Ou on ne puet ne venir ne aler,
Qu'on ne fet ce qu'on puet toz
jorz trover,
Ici est bien la folie provee. [5]

*in a foreign land where one cannot come
and go than to love what one can have at
home. The folly is well known. [5]* [18]

In the seemingly contrasting love lyric and the song to the virgin, Thibaut
underscores the coterminous paradox of courtliness and of virginity: to love,
one must love perfection, or a virgin; to love a virgin is to love an abstraction;
in loving an abstraction, one loves what is by definition unembodied; and,
finally, by giving expression to the love object, one destroys it. Whether one
desires the unattainable lady or the Holy Virgin, the object of desire is always
absent in order for desire to fix upon it. This is the point of several whole
subgenres of the lyric that are structured dramatically by the motif of departure—the *congé,* the dawn separation or *alba,* and, of course, the crusade song
of which "Tant ai amors servies longuement" represents but one example.
The premise of the love song is separation.[19] "With the season which rejuve-
nates the world and makes fields green again, I want to begin a new song
about a lady love whom I love and desire," confesses Cercamon, "but she is
so far away from me that I cannot attain her, and my words don't please her
anyway."[20]

Herein lies the profoundest sense of the famous "love from afar" (*amor de
lonh*) of the troubadours which, far from being an isolated subcategory of
courtly love, stands, in the phrase of Leo Spitzer, "paradoxically consubstan-
tial with the desire for union" and, in the terms of our analysis, as the purest
expression of the logic of virginity inherent to courtliness.[21] The *locus classicus*
is, of course, the case of Jaufré Rudel whose legendary *vida* offers a biographical analogue to the logic of the absent lover:

Jaufres Rudels de Blaia si fo mout gentils hom, princes de Blaia. Et
enamoret se de la comtessa de Tripol, ses vezer, per lo ben qu'el n'auzi
dire als pelerins que venguen d'Antiocha. E fez de leis mains vers ab
bons sons, ab paubres motz. Et per voluntat de leis vezer, et se croset e
se mes en mar, e pres lo malautia en la nau, e fo condug a Tripol, en un
alberc, per mort. E fo fait saber a la comtessa e ella venc ad el, al son leit
e pres lo antre sos bratz. E saup qu'ella era la comtessa, e mantenent

recobret l'auzir e-l flairar, e lauzet Dieu, que l'avia la vida sostenguda tro
qu'el l'agues vista; et enaissi el mori entre sos bratz. Et ella lo fez a gran
honor sepellir en la maison del Temble; e pois, en aquel dia, ella se
rendet morga, per la dolor qu'ella n'ac de la mort de lui.

> *Jaufré Rudel of Blaye was a very noble prince of Blaye. He fell in love with the
> countess of Tripoli without seeing her because of the good which he heard said
> about her by the pilgrims who came from Antioch; and he composed many songs
> (vers) about her, songs with good melodies but poor in rhyme. And out of a
> desire to see her, he took the cross and set out to sea. He fell sick in the ship and was
> taken to Tripoli, to an inn, like a dead man. The countess was informed; and
> she came to his bed and took him in her arms. He knew that it was the countess
> and immediately recovered the senses of sight and smell; and he praised God for
> having kept him alive long enough to have seen her. Thus he died in her arms.
> She had him buried with great honor in the house of the Temple. Then she
> became a nun on that same day, for the pain that she had of his death.*[22]

Jaufré's example is sometimes taken to be particular or idiosyncratic; yet it
points in the direction of several more general elements of the courtly song
whose logic is merely presented here in narrative form. First, in many love
lyrics, as well as many romances, love is kindled by rumor rather than by direct
contact. When desire, in other words, does not enter by the gaze, it arrives in
the form of hearsay.[23] Second, the *vida* makes clear the extent to which the
love lyric depends upon the absence of the lady as prerequisite to the poet's
song. For Jaufré's voyage toward her is ultimately fatal. Despite the fact that
she revives his senses of sight and smell, the meeting with the lady corresponds not only to the end of song, but to the end of life itself. The lady must
remain a virgin in order for singing to occur; and her own renunciation of the
world as a result of his death is symptomatic of the esthetics of virginity that
courtliness entails.

The *vida* underscores that which is evident in what is perhaps the most
famous of Jaufré's verses, the canso "Lanquan li jorn son lonc en may." Here
not just absence, but even the memory of absence is sufficient to engender
song:

| Lanquan li jorn son lonc en may | *When the days grow long, in May, the singing of birds pleases me; and when I* |

M'es belhs dous chans d'auzelhs de lonh,
E quan mi suy partitz de lay
Remembra-m d'un' amor de lonh:

leave off listening, I remember a faraway love.[24]

If absence is sufficient cause for song, its object seems to be the presence of the object of desire—to see the lady: "Be tenc lo Senhor per veray / Per qu'ieu veirai l'amor de lonh" ("I hold the Lord to be true through whom I shall see my faraway love" [5]). Also to be seen by her: "Ai! car me fos lai pelegris, / Si que mos fustz e mos tapis / Fos pels sieus belhs huelhs remiratz!" ("Oh, to be a pilgrim there such that my stick and my rough pilgrim's robe would be seen by her eyes" [2]). Yet, as Jaufré makes perfectly clear, to be in the presence of his lady would be to absent himself: "Iratz e gauzens m'en partray, / S'ieu je la vey, l'amor de lonh" ("Sad and happy, I would separate myself from her, if ever I see this faraway love" [4]). The condition of the poet's loving is, in other words, that he love and not be loved ("Qu'ieu ames e no fos amatz" [7]), in other words, that the woman remain unattainable.[25]

If Jaufré seems to desire an absent love but would renounce it in her presence, what, then, does he love? The traditional reading maintains that the poet loves her who is far away because she is the most difficult, and therefore the most worthy, object. Yet everything we have seen thus far pressures us toward another reading, according to which Jaufré's desire has little or nothing to do with the lady. On the contrary, what he desires is the distance that separates him from the possibility of presence, which, again in keeping with what we have defined as the paradox of virginity, would sully the purity of the "one whose value is so pure and perfect" ("Tant es sos pretz verais e fis" [5]).[26] Jaufré desires, above all, to keep the lady distant:

Ver ditz qui m'appella lechay
Ni deziron d'amor de lonh,
Car nuls autres joys tam no-m play
Cum jauzimens d'amor de lonh.

He speaks truly who called me "the one who desires distant love," for no other joy pleases me than the pleasure of a distant love. [7]

"Lanquan li jorn son lonc en may" participates in the pervasive poetics of virginity, according to which the poet loves finally an abstraction—the lady as long as she is kept at a distance, a hypostatic notion of perpetually unsatisfied love, or even his own voice—more than any concrete embodiment of the

avowed object of desire.[27] At an extreme, as the troubadour Guilhem de
Montanhagol recognizes, the love that ennobles ends necessarily in sexual renunciation: "Lovers must continue to serve Love, for love is not a sin, but a
virtue which makes the wicked good, and the good better, and puts men in
the way of doing good every day. Chastity itself comes from love, for
whosoever truly understands love cannot be evil-minded."[28]

This suggests that the paradox of the courtly lady, who is lovable as long
as she stays at a distance—remains, in other words, an abstraction—is but
a version of the paradox of the virgin who must remain unseen, unspoken,
and even unthought in order to remain a virgin. The impossibility inscribed at
the core of the invention of Western eroticism as we know it accounts for the
always present masochism of the poet and also explains the fatalism that hangs
over the courtly poetic production. It is not simply that love and death go together, or are bound in some kind of theologized notion of a desire for transcendence, mediated through the individual love object's being the same as
the desire to escape individual incarnation. On the contrary, the intimacy of
love and death in eroticism has to do, as we have seen in our analysis of the lay,
with the fact that one kills *something* whenever one desires—if nothing else,
the virginal purity that is conceived to be the sine qua non of loving. This
means that so-called courtly love is never very far from a poetics of virginity in
which the discourse of medieval antifeminism is subsumed. Indeed, all that
we have seen thus far indicates that the two dominant cultural discourses on
women, the deprecatory and the idealizing, are hardly contraries. For each is
as overdetermined as woman is herself assumed to be. Only recognition of the
closeness, even the identity, of the two can explain the mystery of William IX's
famous conversion from rude misogynist to the first courtly lover or, finally,
reconcile the opposing faces—courtly and misogynistic—of Andreas Capellanus's *Art of Courtly Love*.

William IX and Andreas Capellanus

One of the enduring questions attached to the origins of Western romantic
love turns around William IX, duke of Aquitaine (1071–1127), and his so-
called change of attitude toward women, from the crude songs characteristic
of what has been termed "chivalric love" to those in which courtly love is considered to have attained its founding expression. This "significant life change"
is accessible to us primarily through nonliterary accounts of the first troubadour's behavior.[29] William of Malmesbury (d. 1143), for example, reports

in the *Gesta regum anglorum* that the count's return from the First Crusade coincided with a time of great dissolution, which is practically synonymous with the impulse to entertain:

> There lived then William, the Count of Poitou, a foolish and shifty man who, after leaving Jerusalem . . . returned to loll in the slough of every vice. . . . Furthermore, coating his little bits of nonsense with a certain superficial charm [lit.: false beauty], he passed them off as wit, distending the jaws of his audiences with chuckling. . . . And [he] wildly proclaimed that he would establish this girl or that one, whom he named, all from famous brothels, as his abbess, his prioress, and his other officials.[30]

The legend of William's dissoluteness was nourished too by the infamy of an adulterous affair which, despite the attempt to have his marriage annulled (as was common) on the grounds of incest, earned him instead the anathema of the church. "Also, when he had driven away his legal wife," William of Malmesbury reports, "he carried off the wife of a certain viscount, whom he lusted after so much that he vowed to engrave the image of the strumpet on his shield, saying again and again that he would support her in battle just as she did him in bed."[31] William had the reputation of being a womanizer, a *vehemens amator feminarum* in the phrase of Geoffrey of Vigeois, who attributed his failure as a crusader to his libido.[32]

The poetic elements in the case for William IX's antifeminism are contained in songs 1, 2, and 5. Song 1 is the story of the poet's two horses, which are a veiled metaphor for two women:

Dos cavals ai a ma seilla ben e gen;	*I own two horses for my saddle in a good and noble manner;*
Bon son ez ardit per armas e valen,	*They are good and brave in battle and worthy,*
Mas no-ls puesc tener amdos que l'uns l'autre no consen.	*But I cannot keep them both, because the one does not tolerate the other.*[33]

Song 2 paints a picture of women as fickle, motivated by self-interest and greed:

Qu'eu anc non vi nulla domn'ab tan gran fei	*For I never saw any lady with such great fidelity.*

Qui no vol prendre son plait on sap mercei,	*Who would not take her case where she knows*
S'om la loigna de proessa, que ab malvastatz non plaidei.	*she can find clemency.*
	So that, if she is separated from Worthiness,
E si-l tenez a cartat lo bon conrei,	*she makes an accord with Baseness.*
Adoba-s d'aqeul que troba viron sei:	*If you keep good equipment from her by a high price,*
	She will equip herself with whatever she finds
Si non pot aver caval, ela compra palafrei. [5–6]	*around her:*
	If she cannot have a charger, she will buy a palfrey. [5–6]

Song 5, the famous "poem of the red cat," which one critic at least has identified as the first Old French comic tale or fabliau, is the story of the poet's meeting with the wives of two lords, his pretending to be mute, their testing him by dragging the cat's claws across his back, and, once assured he will not talk, their using him as a sexual object:

Tant las fotei com auziretz:	*How often I screwed them you will now hear:*
Cen e qatre vint et ueit vetz!	
Qe a pauc no-i rompet mos conretz	*One hundred and eighty-eight times!*
E mos arnes,	*So that my tackle almost broke*
	And my harness,
E no-us pues dir lo malaveig	*And I cannot tell you what great sickness*
Tan gran m'en pres. [14]	*Overtook me from all that. [14]*

The contrast between poems 1, 2, 5 and, say, song 9 is great indeed. For the cavalier lecher, who treats love in ribald fashion and women as interchangeable horses to be tricked and mounted until the point of exhaustion, is replaced by the timid courtly lover respectful, obedient, and even worshipful of the woman from afar. "Mout jauzens me prenc en amar" contains many of the elements that later will be associated with the setting and sentiment of courtliness. The poet, far from boastful as in the example above, emphasizes his own humility and, of course, praises the virtues of the lady:

Totz joys li deu humiliar	*Every joy should be humble*
E tota ricors obezir,	*And every wealth obeisant toward her,*
Midons, per son belh aculhir	*Milady, because of her beautiful welcome*

E per son belh, plazent esguar;	*And because of her beautiful, pleasing*
E deu hom mais cent ans durar	*face;*
Qui-l joy de s'amor pot	*And he would last another hundred*
sazir. [4]	*years*
	Who could seize the joy of her love. [4]

In song 9 William IX sounds most like Books I and II of *The Art of Courtly Love*, where Andreas Capellanus claims that love "makes a man shine with so many virtues," as opposed to the rude lover of the chivalric *vers:*[34]

Per son joy pot malautz sanar,	*Through her joy a sick man can become*
E per sa ira sas morir	*well,*
E savis hom enfolezir	*And through her anger a healthy man*
E belhs hom sa beutat mudar	*die*
E-l plus cortes vilaneiar	*And a wise man become foolish*
E-l totz vilas encortezir. [5]	*And a handsome man lose his beauty*
	And the most refined become boorish
	And the most boorish refined. [5]

The dichotomy visible in the production of William IX, combined with his *vida*, which describes him as "one of the most courtly men in the world and one of the greatest seducers of women," has led scholars since the nineteenth century to consider him a Janus-faced poet.[35] Karl Vössler claims his trajectory is marked by "progress from the obscene to the sublime"; Pio Rajna and Alfred Jeanroy call him two-faced. What's more, the count of Poitou's evolution is assumed not only to show moral progress, but also to be manifest in a stylistic evolution from the supposed quirky, clumsy, noncourtly versification of the works assumed to be earliest to a more refined style. Jeanroy finds the crudely composed lascivious poems replaced by graceful, delicate, exquisite verse.[36] Robert Briffault, in the tradition initiated by Gaston Paris, imagines that the first troubadour "changed his style completely and abruptly."[37] René Nelli follows suit: "given that the worst scabrous pieces are often the most archaic where style and versification are concerned, it is clear that their author effectively went from a crude eroticism to a more idealized one."[38]

Thus the critics assert that two moralities are expressed in two contrasting poetic styles, which also follow the biographical progress of the first troubadour. And yet, evidence concerning the chronology of the composition of the love songs of William IX is based entirely on the order contained in

Jeanroy's edition, which places the chivalric works before the courtly ones; this despite the fact that dating of the poems, as recent editors and critics have pointed out, is impossible.[39] Moreover, the sequence of the poems—which, after all, constitute the birth certificate of courtly, that is to say, Western, romantic love—derives not from historical information but from a fictitious moral order imposed according to nineteenth-century assumptions about the necessary biographical conversion to the wisdom of age from the folly of youth, "an internal crisis" ("crise intérieure") in the phrase of Reto Bezzola, on the part of a man about whom all that we can say with certainty is that he knew both folly and wisdom. William IX's moral trajectory can in no way be said to correspond to the supposed order of the composition of the poems which would have provided the basis for a biographical conclusion. "Unfortunately," writes Jean-Charles Huchet in his book *L'Amour discourtois,* "the order of the poems—which corresponds to the three ages of life—is not sustained by any of the manuscripts, none of which even contains the totality of the corpus. Only manuscript N ends with poem 11; C (which is by far the best and the most complete of the manuscripts) transcribes number 11 before numbers 1, 4, 6, 7 and 8, D places 11 before 6. The manuscript tradition," Huchet concludes, "thus maintains a confusion, mixing pleasurably courtly and obscene poems there where modern editors have tried to put them in order by isolating the crudely evocative pieces, fruits of frivolous youthful waywardness, in order to focus attention upon the poems considered to be the true origin of *fin'amors.*"[40]

This means that William IX's famous conversion, from which courtly love was supposedly born, is, due to the lack of textual evidence, no conversion at all. On the contrary, what emerges from the inconclusive documentation is that the relation of the first troubadour's two faces is more logical than chronological or biographical and that the copresence of misogynistic and courtly songs is better explained by the fact that the two medieval discourses on woman are not contraries but intermingling zones of a common conceptualization of gender. Antifeminism and the idealization of the feminine are mirror images of each other—coevally overdetermined visions of woman as overdetermined.[41]

Nor is the example of William IX, sometimes considered sui generis or idiosyncratic because it is the first, really that different from those of Marcabru, Bernart de Ventadorn, or Thibaut de Champagne, all poets in whose works, as we saw, conflicting attitudes are maintained in such close proximity—that is, within individual poems, and even within a single strophe—

that the contrasting elements of contradiction cannot be biographically detached. On the contrary, the fundamental bivalence of courtliness where the question of woman is concerned is there from the beginning, and the "two faces" of the first troubadour are the founding implicit articulation of a defining opposition that will simply appear to be more explicit in, say, the two portions of *Le Roman de la rose* with which we began, or in the two unusual motets of the *Chansonnier de Montpellier,* which alternate misogynistic and courtly strophes within a single lyric. Motet 126 deprecates all women in strophe 1 ("He who would like to test a woman will find no loyalty there, for she is ready to be false"), and praises the poet's love in strophe 2 ("I will wait patiently for favor, for she has a beautiful and noble body, and not so comely a one can be found between here and Ghent").[42] Then too, only a hypothesis that provides for the closeness of such seemingly contrary presentations of the feminine can account for the two distinct sections of Andreas Capellanus's *Art of Courtly Love,* which have perplexed scholars no less than William's seeming moral reversal.

We have already established in previous chapters the extent to which, according to the governing and irreducible incoherence of the discourse of antifeminism, women are portrayed as given to excessive speech by authors who themselves cannot keep quiet, as well as the extent to which women are imagined to be given to contradiction by authors whose work could not be more self-contradictory (see chapter 2). Andreas Capellanus is more explicitly conflicted still. Books I and II of *The Art of Courtly Love* seem to praise love as an ennobling force, a fountain of virtue for those whom it captures:

> Love causes a rough and uncouth man to be distinguished for his handsomeness; it can endow a man even of the humblest birth with nobility of character; it blesses the proud with humility; and the man in love becomes accustomed to performing many services gracefully for everyone. O what a wonderful thing is love, which makes a man shine with so many virtues and teaches everyone, no matter who he is, so many good traits of character![43]

And yet Andreas denounces love in Book III in terms reminiscent of the early church fathers' condemnation of the flesh and of woman as the source of universal ill:

> Chastity and the restraining of carnal desires are reckoned among the virtues, and so their opposites, lust and the delight of the flesh, must

necessarily be reckoned among the vices. . . . And for still another
reason we blame love; if you consider the thing rightly and trace it out
diligently, you will find that there is not a criminal excess that does not
follow from this same love. Now, it is admitted that homicide and
adultery very often come from it; perjury, too, comes from it, because
often when one betrays a woman with respect to love, he swears oaths
which according to the rules of the holy fathers are to be considered,
not as oaths, but rather as perjuries. That theft, too, comes from love is
shown by the seventh of the reasons for rejecting love that we have
already given. From it comes also false witness; there is no kind of lie
that lovers will not tell when compelled by the necessity of love. That
wrath, too, and likewise hate come from it is clear enough to everybody.
It is admitted, too, that incest very often comes from it. . . . Idolatry,
too, very clearly comes from love. . . . Love, moreover, regularly leads
men to deadly, inescapable warfare and does away with treaties of
perpetual peace.[44]

How are we to understand Andreas's *duplex sententia,* his love-hate relationship to love, his seeming conversion from a fascination with sexual
conquest to chastity?

One explanation has traditionally been to treat Book III of *The Art of
Courtly Love* as a palinode, a clerical renunciation of sexual desire on the part
of an author anxious to protect himself against the charge of promulgating
licentiousness. This, of course, is merely a version of the same kind of biographical speculation we have already seen in relation to William IX. Here,
however, the life of the "theorist" of courtly love is surrounded by none of the
minor certainties provided by the extraliterary witnessing of a William of
Malmesbury or a Geoffrey of Vigeois to allow even reasonable conjecture
concerning personal crisis and recantation. To the complete lack of documentation concerning courtly love as a historical phenomenon is added the
mystery of the persona of Andreas, who has been identified alternately as the
protégé of Marie de Champagne at Troyes or a chaplain at the royal court in
Paris.[45] Of the Latin satirist, his translator concludes, "we know almost nothing aside from his book." All of which means that the evidence for conversion
is purely circumstantial, and that we can conclude with certainty nothing
more than that someone in the position of a cleric, as Andreas's surname implies, can be assumed to have wanted to retract writings that might have been
considered to be licentious, as Books I and II of the *Art of Courtly Love* surely

would have been, despite the fact that no historical record of ecclesiastical condemnation has survived.[46]

A stronger version of the same thesis is to be found among the so-called Robertsonians who place Book III in a satiric relation to what precedes and more generally extend the principle of a distancing irony to all courtly production.[47] Then too, the relation between the two parts of Andreas can be seen as an example of an Averroistic double truth *avant la lettre,* or as an elaborate literary game in which the reader is challenged to choose between apparently irreconcilable opposites, and thus summoned, through the consciousness that such an aesthetic distance implies, to a higher moral plane.[48] At an extreme the incongruities of Andreas's text, in which are subsumed the inexhaustible possibilities of linguistic interpretation, become, via psychoanalysis, the basis of a hermeneutical challenge, the source of a self-sustaining pleasure in, and desire for, language that resembles nothing so much as, indeed seems to reproduce, the patristic entwining of woman and language as complementary facets of material imperfection.[49]

The key to the relation of Book III to Books I and II of *The Art of Courtly Love*—a work that, despite the enigma surrounding it, remains "one of those capital works which reflect the thought of a great epoch, which explain the secret of a civilization"—is not to be found in the realm of biography.[50] On the contrary, although the speculative biography of William IX, based upon a moral reconstruction, and the even more hypothetical biography of Andreas Capellanus, based upon clerical retraction, may contain the same opposing courtly and misogynistic elements, the order of these elements is reversed. Even if we were to admit the principle of conversion, its direction for the architect of courtly love is just the opposite of that for the first troubadour. In the one case we move from scabrous verse to delicate, distant subtilized desire; and in the other we move from virtuous courtliness to the rabid denunciation of women. Thus the two faces of William IX may be the same two faces as those of Andreas, but they face in opposite directions.[51]

What can be derived from the examples of William IX and Andreas Capellanus is, finally, the impulse to narrativize the relation of antifeminism to courtliness, to turn it into a story in which one element would come first, would be primary. In the case of the first troubadour misogyny comes before idealization; in the case of Andreas idealization precedes misogyny. And yet, as in the example of the simultaneous adoration and denigration of women among the church fathers, such contradictory images of the feminine will never be resolved in terms of the precedence of one over the other or, for that matter, in terms of equal but opposite forces of attraction and repulsion, which somehow cancel each other out. The specular relationship between a poetry "in which woman is treated as a pretext and vehicle for a statement of male prowess and social standing" and one in which she is idealized—the mirroring not only of William IX's *vers,* and Andreas's *Art of Courtly Love,* but of the two "halves" of the *Roman de la rose* with which we began—must be imagined in more logical terms.[52]

Indeed, held in abeyance, the terms of this opposition combine to function as a paralyzing paradigm of sexuality precisely because they maintain in such perfect balance the paradox of gender—gender as paradox. This is more than a question of positing, with the psychoanalysts, the eternal, Oedipal ambivalence of every male child's relation to his mother;[53] more than a question of asserting, with Jane Burns, a "fundamental ambivalence about females" among the troubadours;[54] more than the commonplace of contradictory antifeminist and courtly traditions in the Middle Ages;[55] more even than a question of yielding, with C. S. Lewis, to the naturalizing "truth" that " 'cynicism' and 'idealism' about women are twin fruits on the same branch . . . that . . . may be found anywhere in the literature of romantic love."[56] What I am suggesting, again, is that the simultaneous condemnation and idealization of woman and of love are not contrasting manifestations of the same phenomenon, opposite sides of the same coin. They are not opposites at all. Rather, antifeminism and courtliness stand in a dialectical rapport which, as we saw in our analysis of the copresent images of the "Devil's gateway" and the "Bride of Christ" among the early church fathers, assumes a logical necessity according to which woman is placed in the overdetermined and polarized position of being neither one nor the other but both at once, and thus trapped in an ideological entanglement whose ultimate effect is her abstraction from history. Courtly love *does* have a history, but its history is falsified by reduction to the level of a simple chronology that would undercut the assumption, dominant since the first centuries of the Christian era, of the ambiguity of gender, of gender *as* ambiguity. Nor is such a history merely biographical. For if we are to situate historically the advent of courtly love alongside the prevalent discourse of antifeminism that defines thought on gender throughout the early Middle Ages and well into the present era, we must turn to the legal, economic, and social institutions of twelfth-century France.

SEVEN

HEIRESSES AND DOWAGERS: THE POWER OF WOMEN TO DISPOSE

In the last chapter we connected what I had previously articulated as a poetics of virginity both to our discussion of antifeminism and to the birth, beginning in the twelfth century, of courtly love, from which our own notions of romantic passion ultimately derive. More precisely, we focused upon several founding figures in whom antifeminism and courtliness seem to intermingle: Bernard de Ventadorn, Jaufré Rudel, and especially William IX, the first troubadour, who is assumed to have undergone a conversion from the scabrous songs of his youth to poems that celebrate distant and even spiritual love. This "moral" evolution from antifeminism to a more refined sensibility is the opposite of that contained in Andreas Capellanus's *Art of Courtly Love,* whose third book, "The Rejection of Love," seems to deny the idealized portrayal of the effects of love in Books I and II. Placing William's trajectory from misogyny to courtliness next to Andreas's from courtliness to misogyny, we concluded that the relationship between medieval antifeminism and the idealization of the courtly woman is not biographical, that is to say, a moral order, but is one of logical necessity. The two dominant medieval cultural discourses on women are not as opposed to each other as they themselves pretend. On the contrary, each is as overdetermined by a model of gender put into place in the early centuries of Christianity as it assumes woman to be.

Here we confront a potentially dangerous paradox in our own thinking: as long as we are satisfied merely to assert the resemblance, or even the reciprocity, of the twin essentializations of woman as absolute evil and absolute good, our own analysis risks falling into the trap of a re-essentializing of the feminine, which has constituted from the outset our working definition of misogyny. One possible means of resistance to such an impulse lies in a historical understanding that would contextualize both the construction and the uses of gender in terms of social practice.

165

Marriage as Constraint

To begin to historicize the birth (and the endurance) of courtly love, we return to the lays of Marie de France, especially to the archetypal lay of "Lanval," beneath whose aura of the marvelous lurks a harsher material reality (see chapter 5). Lanval is the knight who is not only far from home, but who is impoverished as well. He has literally spent all he has: "Tut sun aveir ad despendu" (v. 30).[1] More serious, despite his participation in the king's wars against the Scots and the Picts, Lanval is forgotten when it comes to the distribution of gifts. Arthur "gives women and land to all those of the Round Table except to one who served him: his name was Lanval" ("A ceus de la Table Roünde— / . . . . Femmes e teres departi, / Fors a un sul ki l'ot servi: Ceo fu Lanval. . . ." [vv. 15–18]). And though Lanval is presented as being alone because of the king's neglect, his neglect can be considered to embody that of an entire caste of knights (including those who do receive gifts), dependent upon the generosity of those with the power of distribution. In this the lay is a mirror of social reality.

Inspired by work done by Marc Bloch in the 1930s, historians like Georges Duby and literary historians like Erich Koehler pointed in the 1950s and 1960s to the fact that around the middle of the twelfth century there occurred in France a schism within the knight-warrior class. This rift divided the great landholders and warlords, who were able to expand their own domains and to afford the strategic military advantage of private armies as well as stone castles, from the lesser nobles who, increasingly impoverished, were forced to alienate their own property, which went to enlarge the domains of higher aristocrats, many of whom became powerful enough to act like the king himself.[2] Thus there arose a more and more sharply defined hierarchy between the large landholders, possessed of the means of defense and support, and the petty landholders, who depended upon their lord economically and lived in ever greater numbers within the confines of his estate. All of which would have been less serious were it not for the fact that the class of dispossessed knights was at the same time menaced from below by the rise of an urban bourgeoisie—a class of literate bookkeepers, merchants, manufacturers, managers, and jurists, often allied not with aristocracy but with an increasingly aggressive monarchy which, beginning with the reign of Philip I, extended its own prerogatives and holdings in an evolution that would culminate in the thirteenth century with the alliance of kingship and sainthood in the figure of Saint Louis.

According to Erich Koehler, the doctrine of ennobling unhappy love emerged both as an idealization of the deteriorating situation of the lower nobility and as a forum for the resolution of potentially violent intraclass tension. The precarious position of both segments of an endangered chivalry produced a consciousness of their mutual class interest which, by occulting or idealizing the tension, prevented it from becoming an open conflict.[3] To the lower nobility, the *hobereaux* or squireens, courtliness offered the possibility of regaining a measure of lost prestige through the myth of an aristocracy of soul rather than birth; it also helped guarantee the material maintenance of the dispossessed knight by transforming the traditional feudal contract, by which the promise of loyalty and counsel on the part of the vassal was exchanged for material support and protection on the part of the lord, into the moral value of obligatory generosity or *largesse*.[4] To the upper nobility it offered the ideal image of a feudal king to whom the great horde of dispossessed knights remained loyal, even to the extent of being able to fantasize loving women of the upper aristocracy without actually being able to touch them; it transformed, as in the case of Jaufré Rudel and the troubadours, this distance between lover and lady (*l'amor de lonh*) into an ideal (see chapter 6).

Thus seen within the context of the material condition of the lower nobility, Lanval's wandering off into the countryside and his encounter with the fairy lady represent a dream of possession. The lady has all that Lanval lacks. Where he is an exile at court, she leaves her own country to find him. Where he is neglected by Arthur, she prefers him to all other knights. Where Lanval is impoverished, she is so rich that "Queen Semiramis and the Emperor Octavian himself together could not buy the right panel of her tent" ("La reïne Semiramis, / Quant ele ot unkes plus aveir / E plus pussaunce e plus saveir / Ne l'emperere Octaviän, / N'esligasent le destre pan" [vv. 82–86]). As the antithesis of Lanval's situation, and indeed in what could be read almost as a parody of topos of the damsel in distress rescued by the valiant knight, the fairy lady promises him eternal fidelity (in contrast to Arthur's neglect) and, more important, as much wealth as his heart desires:

Ore est Lanval en dreite veie!	*Now is Lanval on the right track! For she*
Un dun li ad duné aprés:	*gave him one final gift: never would he*
Ja cele rien ne vudra mes	*desire anything from this time on that he*
Que il nen ait a sun talent;	*would not have as much as he wanted.*
Doinst e despende largement,	*No matter how much he gave or spent,*
Ele li troverat asez.	*she would find enough. He is sitting very*
Mut est Lanval bien assenez:	*pretty: the more abundantly he spends,*

Cum plus despendra
 richement,
E plus avra or e argent!

the more gold and silver he will have!
(vv. 134–42)

The fairy lady is the source of unlimited riches, but under one condition—
that Lanval not reveal her existence, as if the prohibition, beyond its manifest
resonance with courtly discretion, were the prerequisite of an ideological prescription that the daydream of class unity might continue to function for as
long as nothing is said. She is the literary incarnation of a fantasized solution
to the material crisis of the class of unmarried, unendowed, and wandering
jeunes—an heiress whose riches are a reminder, as the French proverb still
holds, that "tout mariage est un heritage" ("every marriage is an inheritance")
within a matrimonial system that worked intrinsically against the interests of
women and younger sons.[5]

Though "Lanval" may contain only the fantasy of escape from a harsher
material reality, it points nonetheless toward the arcane area of medieval
family structure and marriage practice, which, I think it can be shown, holds
the key to a deeper understanding of the vexed issue of the relation of antifeminism to courtly love. At the very least it brings us closer to an explanation
of the conceptual closeness of the two—an answer to the question of how
courtliness came about when it did, and why it has endured as long as it has.
For it is generally accepted among historians of the postfeudal era that there
occurred, from the middle of the eleventh century, important shifts in the
shape and concept of the noble family, which bear significantly upon the topic
at hand. Specifically, the extended, so-called "horizontal" clan, descended
from a common ancestor and consisting of a loose mixture of agnatic and cognatic lines, but without a fixed residence, patronym, or sense of itself as a
dynastic group, began to shrink and to redefine itself along the lines of consanguineal rather than affinal kin. The growing consciousness of biological
relations in distinction to those of marriage was accompanied by a transformation of fiefs, which were at least theoretically revocable upon the death of a
vassal, into heritable *patrimoines*. The clannish kin group as a spatial extension
was displaced by the notion of the blood group distinguished by diachronic
progression, as the power of feudal princes, once established geographically,
produced a corresponding sense of the family as a linear series of successions
through time—consciousness, in short, of lineage. Beginning in what Duby
refers to as the "watershed years" of the eleventh century, "to be noble" becomes "to be able to refer to a genealogy."[6] As I have maintained elsewhere,

the radicalism of aristocracy's lineal "reorientation" in its representation of itself and in the management of its human and economic resources also implied what can only be termed a "biopolitics" of lineage.[7]

The genealogical family implied, first of all, the exercise of discipline with respect to marriage by the restriction of unions to the minimum necessary to assure the continuity of the family line. As Duby has demonstrated for the regions of Mâcon and the northwest, noble families permitted the establishment of only one or two households per generation, the rest of the unmarried sons being housed in monasteries and chapters, or simply remaining, as we have seen, unattached and disenfranchised.[8] The noble family husbanded its reproductive resources so as to produce sufficient progeny to ensure dynastic continuity without a surplus to deplete its wealth through the fragmentation of a patrimony divided among too many sons. Pierre Bonnassie confirms Duby's conclusions concerning the Mâconnais for the region of Catalonia; and Robert Hajdu calculates that in twelfth-century Poitou, the region of William IX, the number of married eldest sons exceeds that of married younger brothers by a factor of two.[9] And yet, the rule of primogeniture alone could not have guaranteed the integrity of lineage if it had not been accompanied by a model of marriage appropriate to the unilateral transmission of the fief and to the organization of feudal society as a series of alliances between landholders with mutual obligations.

Marriage represented in essence a treaty (*pactum conjugale*) to be negotiated between families. The complex web of kinship between the lineages of the postfeudal era depended upon the careful surveillance of marital ties. In particular, it assumed a matrimonial system—possibly from Germanic tradition—involving early betrothal (often at age seven or ten), early marriage (often at puberty), and, above all, the choice of partners to be made by the family or feudal lord.[10] Under normal circumstances, a marriage was concluded by the head of household (*caput mansi*) or the elders (*seniores*) of the lineage, and in their absence, by the relatives—the *amis charnels,* or mother, brother, sister, and uncle; when the potential spouse was an orphan, the marriage was arranged by the lord who exercised the right of wardship.[11] What matters most under this "lay aristocratic model of marriage" (Duby), is that the consent of parties mattered little, while that of parents and guardians was the sine qua non of a legal union. The question of who could marry whom was based upon a certain respect for canonical impediments and upon a careful husbanding of the paternal fief in accordance with an interlocking series of military, political, and social ties.

political marriage

There is ample evidence of such practice in twelfth-century hagiography and romance, where it constitutes a pervasive theme. Alexis's father in "La Vie de Saint Alexis" chooses his son's bride; and it is the son's gaze upon her in the nuptial chamber that pushes him toward sainthood (see chapter 4). Iseult's first thought, upon awakening from the effects of the love philter, which I have maintained elsewhere is the equivalent of an awakening of social conscience, is that she should live in society "in order to give ladies away to noble knights."[12] Or, to take other examples from Marie de France, the composite picture of medieval marriage that emerges from the condensed form of the lay is surprisingly similar to that of the historians whose conclusions supposedly derive from extraliterary accounts. This is true, of course, in "Lanval," where King Arthur's failure to endow Lanval with land and wife is the cause of the knight's alienation and daydream of recuperation. In "Fresne" it is a knight of Dol (meaning sorrow?) named Gurun, who falls in love with Fresne because of what he has heard about her ("De la pucele oï parler, / Si la comença a amer" [vv. 247–48]) but whose vassals force him to marry someone else:

Lungement ot od li esté,	*She had been with him a long time, so*
Tant que li chevalier fiufé	*long that his vassals considered it ill.*
A mut grant mal li aturnerent.	*They often asked him to marry a noble*
Soventefeiz a lui parlerent	*woman and to rid himself of this woman.*
Qu'une gentil femme espusast	*They would be happy if he were to*
E de cele se delivrast;	*produce an heir who could hold his lands*
Lié sereient s'il eüst heir	*after him. And they would be greatly*
Ki aprés lui peüst aveir	*grieved if he were to give up progeny with*
Sa terë e sun heritage.	*a lawful wife in order to stay with his*
Trop i avreient grant damage,	*concubine. They would no longer hold*
Si il laissast pur sa suinant	*him to be their lord nor serve him*
Que d'espuse n'eüst enfant.	*willingly if he did not do their will in this*
Jamés pur seinur nel tendrunt	*matter.* (vv. 313–27)
Ne volentiers nel servirunt,	
Si il ne fait lur volenté.	

"Les Deus Amanz" is a tale that turns around a jealous father's refusal to allow his daughter to marry;[13] just as "Milun" is the story of the imposition of a father's unhappy marital choice ("Sis peres li duna barun, / Un mut riche humme del païs" ["Her father gave her a baron, a very rich man of the region," vv. 124–25])—which is redressed by the son conceived out of wedlock.[14] In "Yonec" the lady of Carwent is given to her lord by her relatives whom she curses for "having married her to this old man's body."[15] Finally, "Eliduc" is, like "Lanval," the tale of a lord's neglect of a worthy knight ("Qu'amur de seignur n'est pas fiez" ["The love of a lord is not trustworthy" (v. 64)]) who wanders off in search of adventure and who, in spite of the fact that he is already married, falls in love with the daughter of another lord ready to dispose of her: "Vieuz hum e auncïens esteit; / Karnel heir madle nen aveit. / Une fille ot a marïer" ("He was an old, old man who had no male heir. He did have a marriageable daughter" [vv. 93–95]).

To the extent that the lay aristocratic marriages of the *Lais* are arranged, they are unhappy. Thus the theme, practically synonymous with the name of Marie, of the *mal mariée*—the woman constrained or literally imprisoned. "He was a very old man, and he had a wife," Marie describes the husband in "Guigemar." "She was of great nobility, honest, courteous, beautiful and wise. He was overly jealous. For, as nature has it, all old men are jealous, since no one likes to be a cuckold; and this is the way of old age! His surveillance of her was no joke: in an orchard, under the donjon, there was a wall all around. The walls were green marble, very thick and high! There was only one entry, which was guarded day and night. . . . An old wizened and white-bearded priest kept the key to the door. He had lost his lower parts; otherwise he would not have been trustworthy."[16] The wife in "Laüstic" is the object of close surveillance on the part of the husband whose suspicions lead, as we have seen, to the death of the bird, which is the symbol of her desire, and its eventual encasement in the reliquary, which is the symbol of desire's containment (see chapter 5). The jealous husband of "Yonec" behaves in a fashion similar to the one in "Guigemar": "Because she [his wife] was beautiful and noble, he put a lot of effort into keeping her. He had her locked in his tower, in a great tiled room. He had a sister; she was old and widowed, without a lord. He put her in with his wife in order better to keep her under guard."[17]

It is difficult to say, with respect to the *Lais,* if the woman's constraint is the cause or merely the embodiment of her unhappiness, but the two are practically synonymous. We have remarked that "Fresne" takes place in the land of Dol, a name that may, like Tristan's, contain a message of sadness. So too the action of "Yonec" is situated in Britain, in the city of Carwent, on the river Duëlas, a name that resonates with *dueil,* "grief." From the wife's point of view, marriage is the equivalent of pain:

"Lasse, fait ele, mar fui nee!   *"Alas," she says, "cursed be the hour I*
Mut est dure ma destinee!   *was born! My fate is so harsh! For I am*

En ceste tur sui en prisun,
Ja n'en istrai si par mort nun.
Cist vielz gelus, de quei se
     crient,
Que en si grant prisun me tient?
Mut par est fous e esbaïz! ["]

in prison in this tower and will only
escape through death. Of what is this old
jealous man afraid that he keeps me so
imprisoned? He is truly crazed and
senseless! ["] (vv. 68–74)

There is no tale of happy love in the *Lais*. Unhappiness is the lot of woman, though each is unhappy in her own way: the unhappily married wives of "Equitan" and "Chievrefoil"; the imprisoned wives of "Laüstic" and "Milun"; the wives married against their will of "Guigemar" and "Yonec"; the daughter prevented from marrying in "Les Deus Amanz"; the mistress scorned in "Fresne"; the spiteful wives of "Bisclavret," "Fresne," "Equitan," and "Lanval"; the woman unable to make up her mind of "Chaitivel"; the women fooled by a man in "Eliduc."

In their onerous constraint the unhappy women of the *Lais* come to resemble Lanval. And just as the neglected knight's fantasy of the bountiful woman can be taken to be the antidote to the real material disenfranchisement of the class of lesser nobles in postfeudal France, so too the women's discontent can be seen to engender the illusion of escape from the reality of aristocratic marriage. The daydream of the rescuing knight implies the fantasy of evading the lot of the *mal mariée*. Thus Guigemar's mysterious penetration of the guarded keep with only one entrance and the love idyll that lasts a year, or the evocation, on the part of the imprisoned wife of "Yonec," of "adventures" to distract the constrained:

Mut ai sovent oï cunter
Que l'em suleit jadis trover
Aventures en cest païs
Ki rehaitouent les pensis.
Chevalier trovoent puceles
A lur talent, gentes e beles,
E dames truvoent amanz
Beaus e curteis, pruz e vaillanz,
Si que blasmees n'en esteient
Ne nul fors eles nes veeient.

I have heard tell that in this country
there are marvels [adventures] which
raise the downfallen. Knights find
maidens to their liking, noble and
beautiful; and ladies find handsome and
courteous lovers, lovers valiant and
brave, so that they cannot be blamed,
and only they can see them.
(vv. 91–100)

If the imprisoned lady's wish of "Yonec" is the feminine version of that of Lanval, its fulfillment offers the fantasy of reversing the neglect which she, like the dispossessed knight, feels: "Quant ele ot fait sa pleinte issi, / L'umbre d'un grant oisel choisi / Par mi une estreite fenestre. . . ." ("When she had made her lament thus, the shadow of a large bird fell through the narrow window. . . ." [vv. 105–7]). And which fantasy exists under the same prohibition against revelation that we have identified elsewhere as characteristic of the virginal poetics of the lay:

"Dame, fet il, n'eiez poür:	*"Lady," he said, "do not be afraid: the*
Gentil oisel ad en ostur!	*sparrow hawk is a noble bird! And if*
Si li segrei vus sunt oscur,	*secrets are mysterious to you, make sure*
Gardez ke seiez a seür,	*we are secure, and make me your*
Si fetes de mei vostre ami! ["]	*lover! ["] (vv. 122–26)*

The imprisoned lady's secret is virtually identical to that of Lanval: "If you say it, it disappears." The bird that metamorphizes into a knight and the knight who changes into a bird is, as he makes clear, a false semblance ("La semblance de vus prendrai" ["I will assume your likeness," v. 161]), which, in the medieval thinking of such images, is akin to literature itself. The fantasy of escape through a fiction that remains intact as long as no one reveals the secret of its status as fiction, once again, is that of the literary instance, and more precisely that of courtliness, which traditionally has been understood as the expression of a collective literary daydream of escape from the reality of medieval marriage.

This, in any case, has been one of the significant traditionally accepted explanations for courtly, adulterous, secret love, which is, historically speaking, a purely literary phenomenon and produced no corresponding documentation within the historical domain. The *locus classicus* is, of course, *The Allegory of Love* (1936) of C. S. Lewis (via the ideas of Violet Paget), for whom courtly love is the direct logical consequence of a system of arranged marriages:

> Marriages had nothing to do with love and no "nonsense" about marriage was tolerated. All matches were matches of interest, and, worse still, of an interest that was continually changing. When the alliance which had answered would answer no longer, the husband's object was to get rid of the lady as quickly as possible. Marriages were frequently dissolved. The same woman who was the lady and "the dearest dred" of her vassals was often little better than a piece of property to her husband. He was master in his own house. So far from being a natural

channel for the new kind of love, marriage was rather the drab
background against which love stood out in all the contrast of its new
tenderness and delicacy. The situation is indeed a very simple one, and
not peculiar to the Middle Ages. Any idealization of sexual love, in a
society where marriage is purely utilitarian, must begin by being an
idealization of adultery.[18]

To hone Lewis's explanation just a bit, the invention of courtly love represents, at bottom, a clever ruse on the part of a licentious Germanic aristocracy, intent upon treating marriage as a bond to be honored only in the
breach. These nobles were under pressure from an increasingly assertive
church, anxious to extend its prerogative over marriage, a trend beginning
in the eleventh century with the Gregorian reform and culminating in the
twelfth with the transformation of the nuptial tie into a sacrament. The ideology of courtly love was invented, according to Lewis, in order that those in
power might avoid ecclesiastical censure and continue to act as they had done
in the past. Thus, for the great Cambridge medievalist, courtliness "arises as a
rival or a parody of the real religion and emphasizes the antagonism of the
two ideals."[19]

C. S. Lewis's thesis of courtly love as apologetics spawned a number of
books that had some influence in the period of World War II. Thus, Robert
Briffault maintains in *The Troubadours* (1945) that "love declared itself noble
in order that it not be declared scandalous"; Denis de Rougemont repeats almost verbatim in his *Love in the Western World* (1940) the theory of reactive
ruse: "The cultivation of passionate love," he writes, "began in Europe as a
reaction to Christianity (and in particular to its doctrine of marriage) by
people whose spirit, whether naturally or by inheritance, was still pagan."[20]
In de Rougemont, however, Lewis's notion of necessary adultery and religious parody are themselves parodied—that is, radicalized or carried to
their logical limit. For de Rougemont articulates explicitly that which remains implicit to *The Allegory of Love* and which works to undercut the
historical underpinnings of Lewis's claim, since the assumption that courtly
love is a reaction against increasingly strict Christian notions of marriage (as a
sacrament and therefore indissoluble) is itself based upon an understanding of
desire as the product of an attempt at containment, or desire as resistance.
This amounts to a positing of desire at the level of nature, since one is, if only
for the incest taboo, always more or less under the law; and in this specific
instance it also leads to a retheologization of the concept of impossible love,

which is thus relegated to the category of a universally signifying occulted expression of the wish, with which we are familiar, to escape embodiment. Indeed, concentrating upon the Tristan myth as the archetype of love in the West, de Rougemont seeks to answer the question of why the lovers seek obstacles to their love rather than simply setting up house in Morrois Forest when they have the chance, and living happily ever after.[21] He concludes that "what they need is not one another's presence, but one another's absence"; that "what they love is love and being in love"; that, finally, what they really seek is neither each other nor love, but death and transcendence: "In the innermost recesses of their hearts they have been obeying the fatal dictates of a wish for death; they have been in the throes of *the active passion of Darkness.*"[22]

In the alliance of romantic love with death de Rougemont brings us full circle from misogyny, through virginity, to courtly love—from the death wish that we associated with early Christian renunciation of the body to the eroticism that we equated with a seemingly asexual asceticism. Indeed, according to both de Rougemont and Georges Bataille, the link between eroticism and death is expressed in terms that extend beyond the relatively secularized association in ego psychology between love and hate[23] to a recognition of their "fundamental" and "decisive" relation.[24] Moreover, this relation is historical only insofar as eroticism appeared at precisely the same moment in the evolutionary development of mankind as a consciousness of death, which marks the anthropological difference between human and nonhuman worlds.[25] For Bataille, this crucial step, this fundamental link of eroticism and death, is predicated not upon the history of marital institutions, but upon the theological foundation of both. The necessity of courtly discretion, for example, cannot be reduced, as the thesis of Lewis suggests, to the banal bourgeois drama of a socially unacceptable and therefore secret passion; on the contrary, the secrecy of eroticism emanates from the sacredness of a religious interdiction.[26] At the July 4, 1939, meeting of the Collège de Sociologie, a gathering also attended by de Rougemont, Bataille presented the notion of love as an "annihilating expenditure" indissociable from religious sacrifice.[27] And his *L'Erotisme* (1957), translated into English with the subtitle *Death and Sensuality,* anthropologically extends the imbrication of eroticism, the wish for transcendence, and the poetic—which de Rougemont historicizes insofar as he localizes it in the founding myth of Tristan and Iseult—to virtually the entire cultural domain. Bataille is only tangentially fascinated by medieval examples of "joyous expenditure" in, say, the trial of Gilles de Rais, for he sees more generally in eroticism an expression of the desire of being for triumph over the contingency of individualism and for continuity, which is, finally, assimilable both to death and to the poetic. "If the union of two lovers is a consequence of passion, it calls for death. . . . Eroticism opens upon death. Death opens up to the negation of individual duration. . . . Poetry leads to the same point as every form of eroticism, to indistinction, to the blending of separate objects. It leads us to eternity, it leads us to death, and through death, to continuity: poetry is *eternity*."[28] The erotic is finally an instance of the sacred.[29]

The retheologizing of eroticism through an anthropological reading of Nietzsche on the part of de Rougemont and Bataille has recently received a fresh burst of energy in the writings of Julia Kristeva, who recognizes in courtly eroticism the most radical expression of the theology of renunciation as articulated by the church fathers, and which is most intensely focused upon the figure of the Virgin Mary. Love is, Kristeva maintains along with de Rougemont and Bataille, essentially necrophilic—"a death sentence that causes me to be." But where they posit the desire for transcendence in terms of a sociological mechanism that both founds and ensures the maintenance of culture, Kristeva pushes it in an other-worldly direction. She literally returns love to the domain of Christian mysticism, which, through the incantation of the courtly song, transforms rhetoric not into an instance of the sacred as in Bataille's "blending of separate objects" but into a religion:

> In point of fact, courtly songs neither describe nor relate. They are essentially messages of themselves, the signs of love's intensity. They have no object—the lady is seldom defined and, slipping away between restrained presence and absence, she is simply an imaginary addressee, the pretext for the incantation. . . . One should read it while hearing it and interpret it as a vast activity transposing univocal meaning outside of its limits, toward the two borders of *nonmeaning* and the mystical metaphysical totality of *Meaning*. This latter focus of incantation soon led to the inscription of courtly rhetoric into religion and changed the Lady into a Virgin Mary.[30]

The courtly lady is, according to Kristeva, merely another version of the Virgin Mary who represents the "prototype of a love relationship" in the West and "the focal point of men's desires and aspirations."[31]

The courtly lady as an avatar of the Mother of Christ is, of course, nothing new. Scholars ever since the nineteenth century have seen in courtliness a secular manifestation of medieval Mariology, pointing to the nostalgia of the lover for a distant ideal (*amor de lonh*), the attempt to spiritualize the physicality of the body along the lines of Cistercian mysticism, the glorification of suffering, the ecstasy of the lover, the woman as a source of redemption, and the infusion of religious terms within the semantic range of courtly sublimation.[32] And yet Kristeva is not content with mere analogy, or with a relationship between secular and Christianized virgins that might imply either reciprocity or the notion of discourses counterposed to each other. In *Tales of Love* she posits woman—or, more precisely, the mother—as an inexpressible biological principle manifest in different ways through disparate cultural fields (religion, psychoanalysis, and poetry), much as Bataille situates eroticism in a "beyond" of language surrounded by silence.[33] "The unspoken doubtless weighs first on the maternal body: as no signifier can uplift it without leaving a remainder, for the signifier is always meaning, communication, or structure, whereas a woman as mother would be, instead, a strange fold that changes culture into nature, the speaking into biology."[34]

What is the difference between the analogy I have established between the ascetic misogyny of the church fathers and courtly love as renunciation, and Kristeva's analogy between adoration of the Virgin Mary and courtly love as "the unconscious needs of primary narcissism," or attachment to the mother?[35] Just this: that where Kristeva seeks both the courtly lady and the Holy Virgin as aspects of a biologized maternal principle that must by its nature be the same everywhere, I have maintained throughout that they are the ideological representations of deeper cultural currents determined by material forces and interests (family structure, patterns of inheritance, control of patrimony) that cannot be confused with nature. For to mistake the culturally specific construction of gender with biology, to reduce it to the question of giving birth or even the "biosymbolic latencies of motherhood," is, finally, to fall into the trap of something like the Eternal Feminine, which has been from the start our working definition of misogyny. This, as Kristeva herself recognizes, is a dangerous move,[36] the historical consequences of which were realized in the flurry of writing on eroticism and love on the eve of World War II.[37]

One recognizes in the thought of de Rougemont, Bataille, and Kristeva the degree to which the notion we encountered in Lewis and Briffault of love as resistance (to the law, to the church) ends not only in an idealization of romantic passion—"love declared noble in order that it not be declared scandalous"—but in the universalizing glorification of love, and thus of woman, as a means of salvation. One recognizes too the extent to which the glorification of woman, whether consecrated virgin or redeeming mother, represents a version, the ultimate legacy, of the courtly abstraction of the feminine and, more important, the extent to which this abstraction works not to empower the woman it seems to elevate but to keep her at a distance from history and the world. The glorification of love and the sublimated elevation of both the feminine and the maternal work as effectively as the virginal misogyny of the fathers to cut woman off from a history that is only recuperable through a closer look at the extraordinary cultural and social nexus of twelfth-century Provence.

Robert d'Arbrissel and Fontevrault

The question of the cultural milieu in which courtliness was invented is crucial to an understanding of its relation to the hegemonic discourse of antifeminism that had dominated since the patristic period. Indeed, by the time of William IX there had been in southern France two generations of relative peace and material ease. The secular aristocracy of the region knew little of the ascetic Cluniac and Cistercian spirit of the north and had managed better than its northern peers to liberate itself from the tutelage of an insistently reform-minded clergy (which, according to the "resistance" theory of origins, should theoretically have obviated the need for reactive ruse). So advanced was the culture of the region considered to be that it has become customary even for historians to speak of the refinement of the "customs" of the south, by which they refer to the civilizing influence of Arabic culture due to contact with Catalonia and Aragon, to the renaissance of trade (and especially of trade in luxury items) across the Mediterranean Sea, to the organization of social life at courts (a social life in which women played a large part), and to the appearance of the troubadour lyric which, somewhat illogically, is in turn used as proof of the refinement of the very cultural milieu that supposedly spawned it.[38]

But let us assume that the historians of the Mediterranean littoral mean literally custom, in the sense of legal custom as well. Under such an assumption the most salient elements of refinement were both the relatively better social and legal position of women in the south as opposed to the north and what can only be termed the first feminist movement of the second feudal age, an institutional expression of feminine resistance to the disenfranchisement of women to be considered alongside the female convents and mystics that Caroline Bynum has discussed so brilliantly in the context of a later period and more northerly setting.[39] This movement crystallized around the turn of the twelfth century among the followers of Robert d'Arbrissel and the monastery, Fontevrault, which he founded in 1100 or 1101, and which eventually comprised affiliated houses in Poitou, the Limousin, Périgourd, Haute-Bruyère, Maine, Berry, Orléans, Toulouse, and Brittany. Fontevrault itself is estimated to have held three hundred nuns and sixty or seventy monks, and Suger, abbot of Saint-Denis, estimated its numbers in the decade of the 1140s at five thousand.[40] Robert, born around 1060 in Brittany, was one of the most powerful and seductive itinerant proselytizers of his time, was endowed by Pope Urban II with the title "apostolic preacher" and was followed in his wanderings, before the establishment of Fontevrault, by crowds, composed mostly of women, and women of all social classes. Robert's biographer, Baudri de Bourgueil, bishop of Dol and the author of the first and most complete vita, states that "the noble lady left her chateau, the peasant her cottage, the young girl her parents, the courtesan even her shameful pleasures to follow this 'divine sower of words'."[41] And, according to William of Malmesbury, Robert "was the most celebrated and eloquent preacher of these times: so much did he excel, not in frothy, but honeyed diction, that from the gifts of persons vying with each other in making presents, he founded that distinguished monastery of nuns at Font-Evraud, in which every secular pleasure being extirpated, no other place possesses such multitudes of devout women, fervent in their obedience to God."[42]

The view of Robert as the great liberator of women of the Middle Ages began with Michelet, whose judgment that "the restoration of woman took place primarily in the twelfth century" is refined to the extent of focusing upon d'Arbrissel as the catalyzing agent of liberation. "He reopened to women the bosom of Christ" ("Il rouvrit aux femmes le sein du Christ"), writes the Romantic historian in a phrase that reverberates in almost everything written since. Jean Pétigny, the scholar who in the nineteenth century did the most work on Robert d'Arbrissel, maintains that he had an "irresistible influence upon women." Reto Bezzola, author of the most complete study of courtly literature, speaks of Robert's "exaltation of woman" as "something unheard of in its time." For Régine Pernoud, Robert represents "the most perfect and convincing illustration of the new power of women which spread between the eleventh and twelfth centuries."[43]

In fact, the legend of Robert as a feminine liberator contains two separate components. The first, associated with the period of his wanderings and isolation in the Forest of Craon, belongs to the eremitic movement of the twelfth

century, which some consider to be predicated upon the model of the desert
fathers of the fourth century, and which is not without relevance to our discussion of early Christian asceticism. This period culminates narratively in the
famous episode of the *lupanar* of Rouen, recounted by Baudri, in which
Robert supposedly came into a house of ill-repute to warm his feet and ended
up preaching to the prostitutes who followed him out of the town into the
countryside. "Whereupon he drew them out of the town, he led them full of
joy to the desert, and there, having received their penitence, helped them to
pass from the demon to Christ," writes Michelet in a passage clearly meant to
ally Robert with the Syriac and Egyptian fathers of the church.[44] The second
period coincides with the cessation of itinerant preaching and the foundation
of Fontevrault.

Fontevrault itself represented an ensemble of convents dedicated to the
Virgin. In the tradition, again, of the mixed movements of early Christianity
(and perhaps also of the Celtic double houses), men and women lived together as equals at Fontevrault, which was governed by a woman. Robert
specified that, because of the knowledge of the world required to run a religious establishment, the abbess should be not a virgin but a widow:

> Petronilla, chosen by master Robert and constituted abbess by the
> common will and by the devoted request of the nuns as well as of
> the religious brothers, is to have and maintain the power of ruling the
> church of Fontevrault and all the places belonging to that church, and
> they are to obey her. They are to revere her as their spiritual mother, and
> all the affairs of the church, spiritual as well as secular, are to remain in
> her hands, or be given to whomever she assigns, just as she decides.[45]

Fontevrault was a place where a woman had power over women as well as over
men, a place whose particular brand of piety emphasized woman as the incarnation of the Mother of God. More important, it served an important social
function as a refuge for women, a "safe house" in which those seeking to escape marriage—either before or after—might find a haven. The list of women
who left husband or father to join Fontevrault reads like a *Who's Who* of the
nobility of the southern region as well as of Champagne and Anjou: Petronilla
of Anjou, Agnès de Craon, Hersende de Champagne, Agnès d'Aïs, Agnès de
Montreuil, Mathilde d'Anjou. Perhaps the most famous resident, however,
was Bertrade d'Anjou, daughter of Simon de Montfort, wife of Foulques le
Réchin, and mistress of Philip I, who arrived after the king's death. Philip was
excommunicated because of his affair with Bertrade and, as we shall see, was

defended at the Council of Poitiers by William IX, whose own wives and progeny were no strangers to Fontevrault. Two of William's wives—Ermengarde and Philippa—ended up there along with his daughter. His granddaughter Eleanor of Aquitaine went to Fontevrault after the death of Henry II, as did Eleanor's own daughter with Louis VII, Marie de Champagne.[46]

We cannot, of course, trace romantic love to Fontevrault, in the sense of a definitive identification of a unique source of a multifactorial literary and historical phenomenon, but we can say that the genealogy of those who passed through the double convent or who ended up there coincides remarkably with many of the figures we have encountered in the context of the creation of romantic love and its dissemination throughout France. Not only did William IX's two wives, daughter, granddaughter, and great-granddaughter end up there, but his granddaughter, Eleanor of Aquitaine is believed to have been accompanied by Bernart de Ventadorn when she went north to marry Louis VII. Eleanor's daughter Marie was largely responsible for the cultural life at the court of Champagne after her marriage to Henry the Liberal in 1164. It was there, in fact, that Andreas Capellanus's *Art of Courtly Love* is assumed to have originated sometime in the last quarter of the century.

Although courtly love cannot be said to have been "created" at Fontevrault, we can hypothesize that it came into being as a reaction to the ideas of Robert d'Arbrissel concerning the role of woman in the governance of the double convent and, by extension, her role in society at large. This is to conjecture that the reign of nuns, themselves drawn from the aristocracy, represented a reactive agent within a nurturing milieu, and provided the impetus to the inversion of the terms of antifeminism, characteristic of the early Middle Ages, into its conceptual courtly twin.[47] For it is clear that the presence of Fontevrault in the midst of France's rude macho peerage—men accustomed, like Foulque Nera, William's wife Ermengarde's father Foulque le Réchin, or William IX himself, to doing their will, no matter how outrageous, where marriage, adultery, or the repudiation of wives were concerned—represented a threat.[48] In the words of Jacques Dalarun, Robert d'Arbrissel "throughout his life represented a challenge to his times" ("posa, sa vie durant, question à son siècle").[49]

The relation of lay aristocracy to the convent was one of opposing misogynistic and philogynistic orders. Even Pétigny seizes this point, despite his own (perhaps unconscious) misogynistic rhetoric, when he compares Robert d'Arbrissel to Geoffrey of Vendôme (abbot of Vendôme, 1093–1132): "Robert felt for the weaker sex a sort of pious compassion and filial tenderness. Geoffrey of Vendôme, on the contrary, seems to have reserved for their sex in its entirety an implaccable hate; he cursed them as the organ of the Devil and the source of all evil in the world."[50] Fontevrault was the focal point of a rivalry between contending political camps united against each other around the question of woman. The attractiveness of the monastery shocked the Poitevin nobility where the issue of feminine power was concerned, and even troubled the regular clergy.[51] In the phrase of Bezzola, "a war was organized against this intruder" who was protected by many of William IX's rivals, including the bishop of Poitiers, Pierre II, as well as the pope. Yet the more Robert was opposed, the more he was feted by one element of the population, the women of Anjou and Périgourd, who showered him with pious gifts (which raises the question of the woman's right to dispose of property, to which we shall return below). Fontevrault was a locus of resistance, a place where woman became the battleground of an intense social and political struggle, "the stake in a fight," which was personal as well.[52]

Despite evidence to support the claim that William IX aided in the foundation of Fontevrault, and especially in choosing its site close to Poitiers,[53] William IX and Robert d'Arbrissel were enemies. During William's absence in 1098, when he aided the king of England against Philip I of France, his then wife Countess Philippa, left in charge of the town of Toulouse, made large concessions, at the urging of Robert d'Arbrissel, to the monks of Saint-Sernin.[54] The barons of Toulouse, in the presence of Robert d'Arbrissel, recognized the sovereignty of Philippa by swearing allegiance to her at the time of William's quarrel with the pope.[55] William and Robert opposed each other face to face at the Council of Poitiers, where King Philip was excommunicated for his adulterous union with Bertrade. William, afraid of himself being condemned, came to Philip's defense, railing so against the clergy that, according to one account, the fathers of the council fled in terror; only Robert and a handful of others braved his vituperative attack.[56] William's apprehensions were proven to be correct when Philippa, angered by her husband's affair with the viscountess of Châtellerault (and possibly at the urging of Robert),[57] withdrew to Fontevrault, thus escaping what could not have been a very warm and supportive home life—compensated only perhaps by the conversations that must have occurred between her and William's first wife Ermengarde whom she met there along with her daughter Audéarde.

But what does all this have to do with courtly love?

We are confronted, first, by a remarkable historical coincidence between the relative military calm of the turn of the twelfth century, the manifestation of a new social ideal more favorable to women than the patriarchal military-feudal ethos characteristic of an earlier period, and the appearance of the earliest courtly verse. This coincidence suggests further that the framing articulation of Western romantic love emanated dialectically from the rivalry between William IX, the "general spokesman of the aspirations of all of feudal society," and the "sower of divine words" of Fontevrault: "at that moment the miracle occurred" ("c'est à ce moment-là que le miracle se produit").[58] That miracle, akin to those of the Virgin Mary herself, represented an artful appropriation of the theme of the Virgin, which henceforth was transformed into the West's most enduring form of secular mysticism—the worship of an ideal lady, of a lady idealized, the worship of woman as ideal.[59] The opposite of a sacrament, it was an unholy transubstantiation of "the intimate aversion that this ascetic movement must have inspired in William IX and his peers" into the erotic adoration of the untouchable lady as *domna*.[60] Such an assertion is, of course, merely a personalized refinement of the theses of Lewis, Briffault, and de Rougemont, which holds courtliness to be a purposeful ruse. A licentious, antifeminist, patriarchal William IX, threatened by a competing cultural model, appropriated, transformed, and thus usurped the opposing ideology according to which woman is valued and even worshiped—and which had institutional expression at Fontevrault—by giving it a secular cast in terms of a veneration of woman who incarnates the Virgin and who also subsumes all earthly values. With this crucial difference: that where Lewis, Briffault, and de Rougemont see an opposition between two cultures played out or mediated through conflicting images of gender, I do not see divinized and secularized representations—or, for that matter, worship of the Virgin and adoration of the courtly lady—as opposite to each other at all. On the contrary, they are coconspiring manifestations of the same reifying abstraction of the feminine whose singular purpose can best be explained by changes in women's economic situation and, in particular, by a shift in women's relation to property, in the period and at the place under study.

Marriage and Consent

Readers will have noticed long before now that I have purposefully avoided the quicksand of the question of the specific doctrinal origins of courtly love, whether in Celtic folk rituals, Eastern religions, Albigensian heresy, Platonic philosophy, Arabic or Hispanic poetry, or even the cult of the Virgin. The courtly ideal, first expressed by the count of Poitiers, who was locked in a bit-

ter struggle with the founder of the double convent of Fontevrault, also
located near Poitiers, cannot be ascribed to any single cause. It was the result
of a rivalry between two orders of society over the question of woman: first, a
lay aristocracy whose power was based upon military force and whose wealth
was primarily based upon land, and which practiced a model of marriage that
reserved the choice of partners for parents, lord, or guardian in order to keep
the patrimony intact; second, an ecclesiastical culture which, if not more sympathetic to women, was at least more sympathetic to partners, and which,
beginning in the early twelfth century, possessed its own ideas concerning
marriage. For the quarrel between William IX and Robert d'Arbrissel can also
be seen to express the conflict between opposing models of medieval marriage. The first, based upon the choice of parents and practiced among the lay
aristocracy, worked, as we have seen above to disfavor women and younger
sons.[61] The second, on the other hand, was more favorable to partners and, in
particular, to the women who suffered the most under the feudal marriage
regime.

Evidence exists, beginning in the 1090s with Yves de Chartres, for an
ecclesiastical matrimonial model defined not by parental imposition but by
the consent of those involved. Actually, the importance of consent can be
traced back to the Roman prescription, "Nuptias non concubitus sed consensus facit" ("Consent and not coitus makes a marriage" [*Digest* 35, 1, 15]),
characteristic of the Justinian—that is, the Christianized—period. It was not
until the twelfth century, however, that the church, in extending its jurisdiction over all issues having to do with marriage, and also in making marriage a
sacrament, asserted the power to choose; it did this in two distinct ways.[62]

In the discourse of theology as it developed in the region of Paris, there
appeared a marked preference for the doctrine of "pure consensualism," that
is to say, for the belief that nothing other than the assent of parties is necessary to a valid bond. "The efficient cause of marriage is consent" ("Efficiens
autem causa matrimonii est consensus"), states Peter Lombard, who also stipulates that the words of consent must be stated in the present tense ("nec
futuro sed de praesenti") because marriage is, above all, an "obligation of
words."[63] The agreement of parents is not required at the time either of the
betrothal or of the actual wedding. Alongside the theological fixation upon
consent there developed at Bologna—among the canonists and especially in
the writings of Gratian—a doctrine according to which both consent and
consummation are required to make a matrimonial tie.[64] Here the model in-
voked is that of the sacrament: the union of Christ with the church, as applied

to the domain of matrimony, is not complete without both free choice and physical *unitas carnis* (uniting of the flesh). In reality, what Gratian meant was not that consent did not make a marriage, since he states explicitly that "the consent of those between whom the marriage is made is sufficient according to the law," but that the bond only became indissoluble once the *commixtio sexuum* (consummation) had occurred.[65] For Gratian there was a difference between a valid and a wholly licit tie, which difference resides in the distinction between nuptials (*conjugium initiatum*) and their confirmation in the *conjugium consummatum* or *ratum*. Only in the mingling of the flesh is the contract transformed into a bond whose sacramental status cannot be revoked.

Looking beyond Peter Lombard and Gratian, we find what is known as the great Alexandrian synthesis of 1163.[66] According to Pope Alexander III, as long as a vow is pronounced in the present tense (*per verba de praesenti*) or in the future tense (*per verba de futuro*) followed by consummation, it is legally binding. Alexander's ruling thus subordinates all public ceremony—the approval of parents, the formal request and negotiations between families, betrothal, bans, dowry, ecclesiastical sanction—to what Pollock and Maitland so elegantly term "a formless exchange of words."[67] This means that courtly love cannot adequately be explained in terms of constraint or as the result of arranged marriages as maintained in the theses of Lewis, Briffault, and de Rougemont. On the contrary, it comes into being at the very moment when the power of parents to dispose was contested by the power of children to choose. It was precisely in the decade preceding William IX's so-called conversion to courtliness that the doctrine of consent was articulated by Urban II, who, it will be remembered, met Robert d'Arbrissel in 1096.[68] And it is in the very decade of the Alexandrian synthesis that we find the classical Old French romances—those of Marie de France and Chrétien de Troyes, whose works read often like textbook cases of the will of children against parental precept (especially Chrétien's *Cligès*), or those of the *Tristan* poets, or of so many of the verse romancers of the thirteenth century whose protagonists marry under pressure from their vassals.

The proposition that women could accept proposals against the will of their parents, of course, never corresponded to the reality of social practice.[69] But even as an ideological position, it represented a threat not only to the traditional ways of nobility but also to its property, since the choice of a mate is so intimately bound to the future of a patrimony, the family fortune, its domain.[70] Further, the power to choose was particularly threatening in the region of the south, which was less feudalized than the north—that is to say, its independent fiefdoms or *allods* were often held freely, which removed them, strictly speaking, from the obligations of providing military tenure to an overlord. This is a point to which we shall return and which cannot be emphasized enough, since the detachment of landholding from the strict requirements of military service, which is another way of saying that the fief no longer must be held by a man, implies at least the possibility of a radically different relationship of women to land.

Matronymics, Inheritance, and Dowry

The picture of women and land is not a pretty one anywhere in Europe of the Middle Ages, and it varies enormously according to region, period, and social class. But for all this, woman's situation in the south in the era between the collapse of the Carolingian Empire and, say, the Albigensian Crusade was relatively better than elsewhere, as attested by (1) matronymics, (2) inheritance, and (3) dowry.

Matronymics

In the south women's names enter history more frequently than in other parts of what is now France. Pierre Bonnassie maintains that for neighboring Catalonia the given names in Romance that appear first and circulate most rapidly are feminine and that there is in the tenth century a certain tendency to favor the maternal over the paternal line in documentary representation.[71] David Herlihy shows that in the documents of southern France of the eleventh century we find twice the number of matronyms attached to land as in the north. To the 2 percent in Germany, and the 6 percent in other territories of France (as in Spain), we find 12 percent in the south to attest to the relative likelihood of women possessing land. A Poitevin charter from the reign of Guillaume V, seventh duke of Aquitaine (1039–58), for example, reads: "lord Count William, son of Countess Agnes, ruling."[72] There is little doubt that in the south women disposed of property more readily than elsewhere. "By a variety of legal resources," Herlihy contends, "the enterprising woman could, if she wished, render the tutelage [of her male relatives] more fictional than real, and even the woman under paternal power could eventually hold and manage property of her own."[73]

Not only does the matronym appear more frequently in southern acts, but also the percentage of documents involving transfer of property in which women's names appear in any capacity is also greater than in the north.[74] In addition, Robert Hajdu, Pierre Ourliac, and Penny Gold observe that the figures attesting to active participation in transfer of land, as opposed to simple consent, increase in the period during which courtliness takes hold. Between 1100 and 1300 the number of Poitevin noblewomen who simply consent to an action drops from 22.3 percent to 4.4 percent, while the number of co-actors triples from 5.1 percent to 17.5 percent, and the number of women acting independently of males increases fourfold from 3.2 percent to 12 percent. For the class just below, the simple castle holders or castellans of Poitou, the number of consenters in the same period drops dramatically from 30.2 percent to 1.9 percent, while the number of co-actors increases from none to 12.3 percent, and the number of women acting independently grows from 2.3 percent to 16 percent.[75] The overall figure in Anjou for women participating in acts of transfer in any capacity between 1100 and 1149 is 55.1 percent, reaching a peak of 65.3 percent specifically at Fontevrault; the participation of woman as consenters is also higher for Fontevrault than for other monasteries of Anjou.[76] Such ratios are significant within the context of the specific area in which courtliness first appeared, as opposed to other regions of what is now France.[77] In Picardy, by way of contrast, we find in the period between 1141 and 1300 that the number of noblewomen whose names figure as consenters drops by half, from 31.9 percent to 15.9 percent; the number of co-actors more than triples, from 5.3 percent to 16.4 percent; yet names of women as independent alienators or purchasers of land also drops slightly, from 6.4 percent to 5.8 percent. This last compares to a rise from 3.2 percent to 12 percent for the equivalent class in the south. Among the northern castellans in the same period, the number of female consenters drops dramatically from 26 percent to 6 percent, while the number of co-actors rises from none to 12 percent. The number of independent Picard castellans drops slightly from 7.8 percent to 6 percent, in contrast to the sevenfold increase from 2.3 percent to 16 percent in the south. The overall figure in Picardy for women participating in any capacity between 1100 and 1150 is 21 percent, which contrasts with the 55.1 percent of Anjou.[78]

Such figures are, of course, highly problematic. Given the variation over time, from region to region, and even between comparable institutions within a single region, generalization warrants caution.[79] It is, moreover, difficult to isolate the social and economic factors that might have contributed to such figures, much less to determine with certainty sufficient categories of analysis.

188 CHAPTER
SEVEN

The number of variables—changes in marriage arrangements, in inheritance patterns, in male/female population ratios, in the overall acceptability of group versus individual action where property transfers are concerned—complicate the issue even further. The figures may not necessarily mean that women were better off in Poitou and Anjou than elsewhere. The fact that fewer women are simply consenters to the alienation or acquisition of land and have become co-actors may, above all, attest to the fact that wives have replaced the husband's male relatives in contending for "second position in family affairs" as the family of the postfeudal era became oriented along the lines of lineage as opposed to the more horizontal cognatic group. Then too, in speaking of the property transfers involving women, we must not forget that we refer primarily to widows and not to daughters.

Although the number of factors involved in recovering from such a body of raw documentary data something on the order of "women's experience," or even "noblewomen's experience," should make us wary of generalization, the statistics do seem to attest, first, that women's relation to property, which is to say to male property, seems significantly different in the south than in the north; and second, that although most decisions over property were taken without a wife's permission, a woman of this region had a "somewhat greater share of decision making power over what was, or what would be hers."[80]

Inheritance

Where inheritance is concerned the situation in southern France again is special. For the region along the Mediterranean littoral, *Gallia togata* or the "land of written law," remained more heavily influenced by the vestiges of Roman practice than the northern "land of custom," where, for example, Salic Law (article LXII) prevented women, if not from inheriting altogether, at least from taking full possession of Salic land.[81] The law that remained as an influence was not, moreover, that of the republic, which, as in feudal custom, reserved the right of parents to choose their daughter's husband (the *confarreatio,* and later the *coemptio*) and the right of the husband to dispose of his wife's property, but that of the later, Christian period. Justinian's Code (528–533) limited the husband's right to his wife's dowry to that of *usufructus;* he could not claim ownership of it. More important, although the Roman woman might have been powerless in the public sphere, she did have the capacity to own and accumulate wealth, which she also inherited along with her brothers. Novelle 118, for example, provides specifically in the case of death *ab intestat* for the equal succession of all offspring.[82] The Theodosian Code (394–395), brought to southern France by the Visigothic invaders of the sixth century, gave sons and daughters an equal share of their father's estate; and the traces of such equality, though obviously not practiced, still appear in local custom over six centuries later.[83] The Custom of Montpellier, for example, specifies that "when a father dies without a will [*ses gazi*] his property shall be divided equally between his sons and his unmarried or undowered daughters."[84] The Visigothic Custom, which remains the most Romanized of the codes, reads: "If mother or father dies intestate, then sisters and brothers with full family status, and another impediment notwithstanding, inherit in equal parts."[85] And many of the documentary formulas found in wills of the time attest to a certain glimmer of a tendency toward equality between male and female heirs: for example, in 1010, "I Vermundus and my wife and my sons and my daughters give . . . "; "I give . . . to Raimondus and to Godefridus, his brother, and to their sons and daughters . . . "; "I Beatrix and my sons . . . and my daughter agree. . . . "[86] The *Vieux Coutumier de Poictou,* where real property or *propres* is concerned, reads: "the mentioned father or mother, or others, are not permitted by gift, either among the living or by testament, to favor one heir over another beyond the portion which is legitimate and customary."[87]

Although the question of inheritance is always vexed by the discrepancy between legal prescription and social practice, and the archival material from the region in question has by no means been fully explored, it is nonetheless clear from the evidence at hand that the system of primogeniture characteristic of northern France was weaker in the south,[88] and, where practiced, was extended to include, in the absence of sons, the eldest daughter as well.[89] The exceptional status of primogeniture was, again, a function of the relative independence of the area after the collapse of Carolingian sovereignty, or the inferior feudalization of the southern region where women continued to play an important political and even military role from the second half of the ninth century on.[90] In the south, due to the prevalence of *allods,* freeholdings less subject to the rigors of feudal service, women could inherit the domains from which they were virtually excluded in the north and west (that is, Normandy).[91] "Feudalism," in the words of Pollock and Maitland, "destroys the equality between husband and wife," which makes significant the fact that the exclusion of women from succession to property held by feudal tenure had disappeared in the south by the eleventh century at the latest; in such cases the husband served as a stand-in in the fulfillment of military service.[92] Here too, in contrast to Roman tradition, a widow could inherit from her husband and administer his estates post-mortem in his stead.[93]

By the tenth century a number of important southern fiefs were in the hands of women: Auvergne, Béziers, Carcassonne, Limousin, Montpellier, Nîmes, Périgourd, Toulouse.[94] Indeed, the history of the middle decades of the eleventh century is effectively that of an interregnum of either minor or weak counts of Poitou dominated by the toweringly competent figure of Agnès, the wife of Guillaume le Grand, and then—as if Guillaume le Grand were not grand enough—the wife of Geoffroy Martel. When Guillaume Aigret, son of Guillaume le Grand, became the fifth count of Toulouse and the seventh duke of Aquitaine in 1039, he was only sixteen. Agnès effectively ruled Poitou until he became a major, as attested by the recurrent formula of the charters of Saint-Maxent: "In the days when Countess Agnès was head of Poitou with her sons Guillaume and Geoffroy and vigorously administered the duchy, as much as it was in her power"; "in the time when Count Guillaume, his brother Guy, and the venerable countess Agnès their mother reigned in Poitou."[95] Guy-Geoffroy succeeded Guillaume and was also dominated by his mother until her death in 1068. The succession of William IX can, furthermore, be said to be haunted by the specter of the return of a woman's rule. At the time of Guy-Geoffroy's death in 1086 he had designated no successor, which meant that Poitou and Aquitaine would for a period of some five years have fallen into the hands of William's mother Audéarde, who was by no means as imperious a figure as Agnès, had the barons of the region not proclaimed the first troubadour's majority at age fifteen instead of the customary twenty-one.[96]

The political and military history of the second half of the twelfth century revolved around the question of whether or not Eleanor of Aquitaine, the daughter of William IX's oldest son and William's former mistress Maubergeonne, took her inheritance with her when she divorced Louis VII in order to marry Henry II. But of this there is no doubt—most of southern France did pass to Eleanor. And though her case may be typical of the way in which a woman might inherit but not enjoy full possession of land that was still controlled essentially by men, this does not lessen the fact that a woman's inheritance of land represented an enormous threat to the feudal equation of physical strength with land, and of land with power. Eleanor of Aquitaine, or Aliénor d'Aquitaine, is, as far as feudalism is concerned, the great alienator.

The inheritance of property by women may not attest at all to the independence or the social power of women but may simply be the sign of the shift

beginning in the eleventh century away from the horizontal clan—the soli-
darity of brothers that included both agnatic and cognatic relations—in favor
of the more vertically pitched consanguineal kin-group in which both males
and females theoretically have control over what is inherited from a lineage
and passed through a lineage according to the rule of *paterna paternis, mater-
na maternis.*[97] Individuals were, under such a law, more closely associated
with a specific piece of property. Conversely, each piece of property follows,
according to its lineal origin, its own course of descent—has, so to speak, its
own genealogy.[98] But with an enormous difference residing in the fact that
the forms of men's and women's property were different in kind. Against the
real estate—the *immobilier,* which passed through men and constituted a
propres that was a synonym of inheritance as well as of full possession—what
passed through women and was referred to in English law as chattel, were the
moveables practically synonymous with dowry. Woman's property consisted
of clothes, serving dishes, furniture (MF *meubles*), and, above all, of money.
For the economic evolution of which we speak is intimately connected to the
reintroduction, beginning in the twelfth century, of money, alongside the rise
of fairs, long-range markets, and towns, within the circuit of European economic exchange. Shared fortunes presuppose partible wealth.

Dowry

To this change in the mode of wealth associated with woman's inheritance alongside woman's greater participation in the control of actual
property under the regime of separate fortunes and the possibility of her inheritance can be added one final factor of our equation: a shift, beginning in
about the eleventh century, in the mode of exchange surrounding marriage.
We can identify three phases in this process.

First, in Rome consent to a marriage was almost always accompanied by a
dotal exchange, in which gifts from the groom were minimal and the wife's
dowry, which was in effect a condition of the legal recognition of a union, was
comparatively great.[99] Ancient Germanic culture, on the other hand, practiced a mode of marital exchange (*Kaufehe*) such that the husband's family
essentially purchased a wife from her family via the *morgengabe,* a gift presented on the "morning after."[100] In the centuries following the introduction of
Christianity and the invasions, however, both systems were transformed. Beginning about A.D. 200 the "flow of wealth" among the Romans changed
course, such that the burden of endowment, the *sponsalia largitas* or the

donatio ante nuptias, shifted from the family of the bride to that of the groom. Concomitantly, among the Germans the brideprice (*withrum*) was no longer paid to her parents or guardians but directly to the bride. And whether this reversal of the Mediterranean model along with the attenuation of that of the invading tribes was the product of contact of two civilizations or the result, as has been maintained, of a change in the sex ratio of available females to males, the fact remains, as David Herlihy observes, that "the dominant form of marital conveyance in Western Europe during the early Middle Ages, from the barbarian migrations until the twelfth century, was the reverse dowry."[101]

Second, in the centuries following the Germanic invasions and the fall of Rome a system evolved according to which the wife would receive from her husband a form of marriage gift (the *maritagium*) to be administered by him during her life but escheating to her if he should predecease her. "In general," Diane Owen Hughes writes, "the population of the western Mediterranean in the early Middle Ages, no matter what its ethnic origin, had adopted a system of marital assigns whose chief award was neither the dowry of the ancient world nor the brideprice of the ancient Germans but a grant that had grown out of the *morgengabe,* originally awarded to the wife as the price of her virginity."[102]

Third and finally, in the eleventh century, the *dos* in the classical sense of an endowment of the bride by her family reemerged in Italy, Catalonia, and southern France as the major marital award. The first medieval tract on the dowry dates from 1140 and repeats Justinian's prescription that gifts between the bride and groom had to be equal, or that the wife's contribution to the capital of the household had to equal that of the husband's *donatio.*[103] The return of the *dos* has been seen as the result of the reformist ecclesiastical effort to make marriages public or to protect the rights of wives, which tended to erode under customary law, or, as recent demographic studies have shown, as the consequence of marriage market pressures that restricted the supply of available men, or even as a manifestation of the crystallization in the postfeudal era of the vertical family or lineage. Still, the dotal world is, at bottom, one in which the woman depends less on the generosity of her husband (on the morning after) than on that of her own kin.

The dowry, unlike the land received by sons, consisted increasingly of moveable property, especially money. In spite of the fact that the dowry in Provence under special circumstances may have contained some real property, as when a father left only a daughter (whose husband might take her name as well as his father-in-law's family arms), it was, in the phrase of Diana Owen

Hughes, "shaped around a cash base."[104] The dowry represented, in essence, a "premortem inheritance" and the daughter's chief claim on her father's estate. Here we encounter the complicated issue, much discussed by medieval historians since Jean Yver's monumental *Egalité entre héritiers et exclusion des enfants dôtés* of 1966, of the exclusion of dowered daughters who were, especially in the region that concerns us, prevented from making future demands upon family property. The famous statue of Guillaume Forcalquier concerning dowered daughters (1162) is categorical: "the daughter or sister cannot come later or succeed to the father's goods, or the mother's, or the brother's, or the sister's."[105] And yet the exclusion of daughters, which seems on the surface to be a form of disinheritance, had just the opposite effect. Its prevalence in Anjou and Poitou may have worked, as far as the analysis of historical documents is concerned, to suppress further the apparent percentage of female inheritance in a land where women's right to a portion of the paternal domain was already greater than elsewhere; in other words, to hide what really was a legitimate share of paternal property behind the dotal instrument rather than the will. For the exclusion of dowered daughters has to be interpreted in the context of the *dos* and means nothing more than that the dowered daughter could not—as, say, in Normandy—"bring back" her dowry to be recalculated at the time of her parents' death in light of the division that would then occur between her other siblings. The Custom of Toulouse (Article 66) rightly characterizes the relation between the exclusion of daughters from their father's estate and their prior inclusion via the dowry: "If the father has provided a dowry for his daughter in land or money, this daughter shall not return for the division of the father's goods with her brothers, nor for the extra part of the legitimate heir, unless the father has specifically provided otherwise."[106]

The southern "rule of exclusion" has been variously interpreted as a reaction against the contemporaneous ecclesiastical effort to stop the alienation of church property to laymen, as a reaction against the fragmenting partition of patrimony due to the Roman principle of equality among heirs, and as merely an occulted version of the primogeniture characteristic of the more feudalized north—all "strategies to preserve and augment resources."[107] Yet this much is certain: the exclusion of dowered daughters did not necessarily divest women of land. On the contrary, it served preemptively to guarantee their rights of inheritance by a premortem partition over which they gained increased control.

Idealization and Appropriation

It may seem that we have come a long way from the topic of misogyny and courtly love. Yet when one considers that the appearance of the concept of romantic love as we know it took place at a specific time and place—in the first quarter of the twelfth century, in the region of Poitou—when one reckons that it involved specific individuals before whom one finds no trace of the notion of an ennobling erotic love that is also the source of suffering; when one takes into account the relation of Robert d'Arbrissel, the profeminist, to William IX, the antifeminist (or at least womanizer) turned troubadour; when one weighs the economic and social climate of southern France, more favorable to women than the north; and when one assimilates, finally, the emergence of a model of marriage and inheritance that contains the disruptive possibility of children choosing marital partners, and especially of endowed women disposing, according to their own predilection, of the paternal domain—when one takes stock of all this, then the distance we have traversed is, in reality, a circle. For the question is then no longer that of the resemblance of antifeminism and courtliness, nor of their conceptual identity, but of just how to articulate the dialectical relation of the secular denigration and idealization of the feminine as it occurred in the High Middle Ages and has endured ever since.

I am not the first to suggest that an amelioration in women's relation to property offered a nurturing matrix for the idealization that courtly love represents, or that it coincided historically with the political ascendancy of women. Socially minded students of the courtly lyric since Violet Paget's nineteenth-century study of medieval love have assimilated adoration of the elevated lady to the plethora of disenfranchised lesser nobles at the courts (and the mercy) of the wives of great lords.[108] Georges Duby identifies the theme of the wandering knight of chivalric romance with the lower nobility's quest for material support in the form of the wealthy dowager, which, as we saw, is powerfully rendered in the lay of "Lanval." Diane Owen Hughes points to the fact that the regions of the Mediterranean "where the dowry had made its most striking gains" and "the power of husbands over wives may have declined" are those that "glorify the gallant, popularize the cuckold, and give rise to a poetry of love."[109] Then too, the list of civilizing gains characteristic of eleventh- and twelfth-century southern France always includes, in greater or lesser detail, the appearance of the troubadour lyric alongside an improvement in general economic conditions, which implies a taste for decorative luxury and an enhanced role of women in the conduct of social and cultural life. These and other interpretations of courtliness as an idealization that is part and parcel, a mere reflection, of a real advance in women's proprietary rights are, at bottom, versions of courtliness as a liberating alternative to the antifeminism of an earlier age. They participate in the myth of the advent of romantic love as cultural progress, an antidote to ten centuries of misogyny, which is a view that dates to at least the nineteenth-century positivist belief. Michelet maintains that Robert d'Arbrissel is one of those who make history appear "as the progressive triumph of liberty." He sees the period under study as the century in which "God changed sex, so to speak . . . ; and just as woman reigned over heaven, she began to rule the earth."[110] Nor have we progressed very far from Michelet's founding articulation at the time that romantic love was rediscovered as part of the last century's Romanticism. "Psychologically and morally," writes Paul Imbs in our own time, "it is a question of the phenomenon of freeing the spirit and recognizing the right to happiness through the free disposition of one's body, a phenomenon whose first beneficiaries were the women of the South, who were more independent in relation to their husbands." Robert Miller speaks of the "civilizing influence" of courtly love: "In this quaint way, the western world was delivered from the Dark Ages." Charles Camproux is convinced of a "will toward the emancipation of women" ("volonté d'émancipation féminine"). Courtly love "celebrated woman as an ennobling spiritual and moral force, thus expressing a new feminism that contradicted both the antifeminism of the ecclesiastical establishment and the sexual attitudes endorsed by the church," writes Diane Bornstein, who, in *The Dictionary of the Middle Ages*, reinforces the accepted attitude concerning the invention of Western romantic love as a process of sexual textual liberation.[111]

By now it should be obvious that the danger of a conception of courtliness as a remedy to antifeminism is, first, a confusion of the idealization that courtliness contains with love itself and, second, a blindness to the profound identity of seemingly contrary but remarkably similar contending abstractions of the feminine—and thus a false ideological move inimical to any understanding of human sexuality as a superindividual or historical phenomenon. Moreover, the alternative—to view the invention of the troubadours not as remedy, but as reactive ruse, the thesis of Lewis, Briffault, de Rougemont, and Bezzola—is equally in need of revision. For all that we have seen thus far indicates that the conception of romantic love was not so much the product of ecclesiastical pressure upon a licentious aristocracy to respect the institution of marriage as it was a reaction on the part of a marriage-minded nobility against the increasing economic power of women; and this, again, precisely in the south where the hold of the church was reduced and the power of heiresses and dowagers implied, for the historical reasons outlined above, the greatest threat. Such a conclusion is the only one possible if we are to explain the idealization that courtliness entails as something other than a direct translation of the enhanced material condition of women, which it was not, given the fact that a courtly conception of love has lasted for over eight hundred years, while the economic gains for women that occurred beginning in the last quarter of the eleventh century were essentially lost in the last quarter of the twelfth.

The invention of Western romantic love represented, above all, a usurping reappropriation of woman at the moment she became capable of appropriating what had traditionally constituted masculine modes of wealth. This leads naturally to the question of why, if the improving material situation of women in southern France that gave rise to courtliness rapidly disintegrated beginning in the second half of the twelfth century, did the ideology of courtly love persist as long as it did?

The answer is simple: courtliness, not being recognized for what it is, is a much more effective tool even than misogyny for the possession and repossession of woman in what Julia Kristeva terms "the eternal war of the sexes." Stated in the simplest possible terms, a dialectical reading of courtly love, one that assumes idealization to be an inverted mirror and not simply the direct reflection of a material base, is just this: *As long as woman was property to be disposed of, she was deprecated in accord with received misogynistic notions of the feminine as the root of all evil; but as soon as woman became capable of disposing— and, more specifically, of disposing of property—she was idealized in the terms of courtly love.*

Although the discourse of courtliness, which places the woman on a pedestal and worships her as the controlling *domna*, seems to empower women along with an enabling femininity, it is yet another ruse of sexual usurpation thoroughly analogous to that developed in the early centuries of our era by the fathers of the church. No less than the discourse of misogyny does that of courtly love reduce woman to the status of a category; and no less than the discourse of salvational virginity does it place the burden of redemption upon the woman who, as in the double bind of Christianity's founding articulation of gender, finds herself in the polarized position of seducer and redeemer— always anxious, always guilty, never able to measure up, vulnerable. Misogyny and courtly love are coconspiring abstractions of the feminine whose function was from the start, and continues to be, the diversion of women from history by the annihilation of the identity of individual women, hidden behind the requirement of discretion and the anonymity of the *domna,* and thus the transformation of woman into an ideal. Courtliness is, at bottom, a competing mode of coercion that will, alongside misogyny, continue to hide its disenfranchising effects behind the seductions of courtesy, and thus to dominate the discourse of lovers in the West.

Courtly love is perhaps the best example of what Gisèle Halimi, in an anthology entitled *New French Feminisms,* terms "Doormat-Pedestal" tactics, which seek to elevate woman in order to debase her. To make her point Halami quotes Sacha Guitry who says, "I am willing to admit that women are superior to men as long as they do not seek to be equal," which is reminiscent of the Balzacian dictum: "Strictly speaking, woman is only an annex of man. She is a slave one must know how to place on a throne."[112] These may seem like frivolous remarks, but they contain more than a grain of historic truth in that the fear of women entering the public sphere—that is to say, the fear of their playing a role in history—has historically been associated with an elevation above the temporal that is synonymous with the very type of idealization of the feminine that courtliness represents.[113] "There are," writes Jean-Marie Aubert, "two ways of placing woman outside of all public life or refusing her the rights monopolized by men: one to consider her as an imbecile and to place her squarely in tutelage . . . the other to exalt her through a sublimation which renders her unworthy of all worldly tasks."[114] Here the possibilities—all versions of the Eternal Woman—are almost infinite, ranging from the psychoanalytic investment of the mother with omnipotence according to the Oedipal story, to her psychoanalytic positing as enigma, to the Lacanian version of the Woman as the Other, to the philosophical notion of woman as Truth in Nietzsche, or as Anti-Truth in Derrida, to her transubstantiation in theological discourse into the Holy Virgin, or, in the language of the love poets, into the revered *domna.*

INTRODUCTION

1. "Medieval Misogyny," *Representations* 20 (1987): 1–24. A series of responses to the original article appeared in the *Medieval Feminist Newsletter* 7 (1989): 2–16. My response to the responses appeared in the succeeding issue.

2. *Misogyny, Misandry, Misanthropy,* ed. R. Howard Bloch and Frances Ferguson (Berkeley: University of California Press, 1989), vii.

3. For an excellent survey of the varieties of feminism, see Janet Todd, *Feminist Literary History* (New York: Routledge, 1988); Jonathan Culler, *On Deconstruction: Theory and Criticism after Structuralism* (Ithaca: Cornell University Press, 1982), 43–64.

4. Elaine Marks and Isabelle de Courtivron, *New French Feminisms* (New York: Schocken, 1981), 222.

5. *Cité des Dames,* trans. Earl J. Richards, *The Book of the City of Ladies* (New York: Persea Books, 1982), 4. Thus too, Jean-Marie Aubert refers to "la monotone redite d'une même prétention mono-sexiste" (*La Femme: Antiféminisme et Christianisme* [Paris: Cerf Desclée, 1975], 10). Marie-Thérèse d'Alverny, in discussing the misogyny of the church fathers, insists upon their uniformity: "il ne faut pas espérer trouver chez eux des considérations originales; les moralistes répètent des lieux communs, dont l'antiquité vénérable ne permet guère de variations" ("Comment les théologiens et les philosophes voient la femme," *Cahiers de Civilisation Médiévale* 20 [1977], 105). Blanche Dow, who has written on women and the Quarrel of the *Roman de la rose,* notes that "what Aristotle has said of women for the ancient Athenian, what Ovid had said to the society of Augustan Rome, what Boccaccio expressed for the dawning of the Renaissance, and the resulting attitudes toward women were identical" (*The Varying Attitude Toward Women in French Literature of the Fifteenth Century: The Opening Years* [New York: Institute of French Studies, 1936], 48). See also Renate Blumenfeld-Kosinski, "Christine de Pizan and the Misogynistic Tradition," *Romanic Review* 81 (1990): 279–92; and Joan Kelly, "Early Feminist Theory and the *Querelle des Femmes,* 1400–1789," *Signs* 8 (1982): 4–28.

6. See, for example, Theodore Lee Neff, *La Satire des femmes dans la poésie lyrique française du moyen âge* (Paris: V. Giard & E. Brière, 1990); Katharine M. Rogers, *The Troublesome Helpmate: A History of Misogyny in Literature* (Seattle: University of Washington Press, 1966); Wulff, August, *Die Frauenfeindlichen Dichtungen in den romanischen Literaturen des Mittelalters bis zum Ende des XIII Jahrhunderts* (Halle: Max Niemeyer, 1914).

7. Dow, *Varying Attitude,* 260, 261.

8. "Il faut donc nous résigner à faire un exposé austère, illustré par des textes qui manquent de variété, et qui ne donnera qu'une image inexacte de l'attitude réelle des hommes que nous citerons" (d'Alverny, "Théologiens et philosophes," 105).

9. Rogers, *The Troublesome Helpmate,* xiii.

10. *Book of the City of Ladies,* 3.

11. Luce Irigaray writes incisively about the way in which men constitute woman as an enigma in what is assumed to be a patriarchal discourse: "So it would be the case of you men speaking among yourselves about woman, who cannot be involved in hearing or producing a discourse that concerns the *riddle,* the logogriph she represents for you. The enigma that *is* woman will therefore constitute the *target,* the *object,* the *stake,* of a masculine discourse, of a debate among men, which would not consult her. Which, ultimately, she is not supposed to know anything about" (*Speculum of the Other Woman,* trans. Gillian C. Gill [Ithaca, N.Y.: Cornell University Press, 1985], 13.

12. Cited in Theodore Stanton, *The Woman Question in Europe* (New York: Putnam, 1884), 6.

13. "Apart from the foundationalist fictions that support the notion of the subject, however, there is the political problem that feminism encounters in the assumption that the term *women* denotes a common identity. Rather than a stable signifier that commands the assent of those whom it purports to describe and represent, *women,* even in the plural, has become a troublesome term, a site of contest, a cause for anxiety. As Denise Riley's title suggests, *Am I that Name?* is a question produced by the very possibility of the name's multiple significations. If one "is" a woman, that is surely not all one is; the term fails to be exhaustive, not because a pregendered "person" transcends the specific paraphernalia of its gender, but because gender is not always constituted coherently or consistently in different historical contexts, and because gender intersects with racial, class, ethnic, sexual and regional modalities of discursively constituted identities. As a result it becomes impossible to separate out "gender" from the political and cultural intersections in which it is invariably produced and maintained" (Judith Butler, *Gender Trouble* [London: Routledge, 1990], 3).

14. Once again, Christine, who is careful to distinguish between these two ways of speaking, is aware that such a distinction implies, according to the individual case, even the possibility of a woman condemning another woman. Where there lurks an alienating generalization, speaking ill of one woman guarantees the integrity not only of one's own language, but of all women:

Et quant je di homs, j'entens famme	*And when I say man, I mean woman too,*
Aussi, s'elle jangle et diffame;	*if she rattles on and defames; for it is a*
Car chose plus envenimée	*more noxious thing which should be all the*
Ne qui doye estre moins amée	*more despised, that is the tongue of a*
	woman who either because of certain

N'est que langue de femme male	*knowledge or as a joke badmouths, mocks,*
Qui soit acertes ou par gale	*or teases another; and if ill comes of it, it is*
Mesdit d'autrui, moque ou	*a boon to the one used to it, for it is a vile*
ramposne;	*and ugly habit.* ("Le Dit de la rose,"
Et se mal en vient, c'est	*Oeuvres poétiques,* ed. Maurice Roy
ausmosne	[Paris: Firmin Didot, 1891], vol. 2,
A celle qui s'i acoustume,	29–48, vv. 464–73; my translation)
Car c'est laide et orde coustume.	

All translations are my own unless otherwise attributed.

15. Sheila Ryan Johansson, "'Herstory' as History: A New Field or Another Fad?" in *Liberating Women's History: Theoretical and Critical Essays,* ed. Berenice A. Carroll (Urbana: University of Illinois Press, 1976), 402, 403.

16. *Book of the City of Ladies,* 4.

17. It can be no accident, as Catherine Brown once pointed out in my seminar, that the discourse of misogyny, which represents an attempt to speak of the other through the voice of the other, is so closely allied with allegory, the literary form or register whose very name implies "speaking otherwise."

18. "French poets, in the eleventh century, discovered or invented, or were the first to express, that romantic species of passion which English poets were still writing about in the nineteenth century. They effected a change which has left no corner of our ethics, our imagination, or our daily life untouched, and they erected impassible barriers between us and the classical past or the Oriental present. Compared with this revolution the Renaissance is a mere ripple on the surface of literature" (C. S. Lewis, *The Allegory of Love* [Oxford: Oxford University Press, 1965], 4). So too Robert Briffault: "The sentimental idealization of the sex relation has thus assumed a character which is without equivalent in any other culture, and was unknown in the cradle of European civilisation in the Hellenic world" (*The Mothers: A Study of the Origins of Sentiments and Institutions* [New York: Macmillan, 1969], vol. 3, 506). Irving Singer concurs, but is somewhat more cautious: "The history of ideas about love did undergo a new development at the end of the eleventh and beginning of the twelfth centuries. A fresh approach to human relations arose in that early renaissance and it continued for hundreds of years, in some respects up to the present, as a recurrent phenomenon that can very well demand to have a title of its own. . . . Something of special significance did happen in the twelfth century, and those who see a continuity—even an evolution of ideas—developing for eight hundred years are not guilty of falsifying the facts" (*The Nature of Love* [Chicago: University of Chicago Press, 1984], vol. 2, 22).

19. The concept of "courtly love" was coined by Gaston Paris in an article on Chrétien de Troyes, "Etudes sur les romans de la table ronde: Lancelot du Lac," *Romania* 12 (1883): 459–534.

CHAPTER ONE

1. Jean de Meun, *Le Roman de la rose,* ed. Félix Lecoy, 3 vols. (Paris: Champion, 1966), v. 8531–40; hereafter cited in text as *Rose.*

2. Jerome writes: "A book *On Marriage,* worth its weight in gold, passes under the name of Theophrastus. In it the author asks whether a wise man marries" (*Adversus Jovinianum,* I,47, in *A Select Library of the Nicene and Post-Nicene Fathers,* 2d ser., ed. Philip Schaff and Henry Wace [Grand Rapids, Mich.: Eerdmans, 1952], vol. 6, 383). Latin text in J.-P. Migne, ed., *Patrologia latina* (Paris, 1844–55), vol. 23, 276; hereafter cited as *PL.* See Robert A. Pratt, "Jankyn's Book of Wikked Wyves: Medieval Antimatrimonial Propaganda in the Universities," *Annuale mediaevale* 3 (1962): 5–27; Charles B. Schmitt, "Theophrastus in the Middle Ages," *Viator* 2 (1971): 251–70. Jean Batany sums up the difficulty of intermediaries between Jean de Meun and Theophrastes, whom he identifies as a disciple of Aristotle: "c'est-à-dire qu'il [Jean de Meun] cite Théophraste au troisième ou au quatrième degré, à travers deux ou trois intermédiaires, attribuant même le texte de Gautier Map à un 'Valerius' qui n'a pas existé; il n'y a sans doute même un intermédiaire supplémentaire, si Saint Jérome n'a connu le libelle de Théophraste qu'à travers un ouvrage perdu de Sénèque" (*Approches du "Roman de la rose"* [Paris: Bordas, 1973], 61).

3. The source, again, is most likely Jerome, who sees domestic life as constant chatter and complaint: "Then come curtain-lectures the live-long night: she complains that one lady goes out better dressed than she" (*Adversus Jovinianum,* 383); *PL,* vol. 23, 276).

4. *Odyssey,* xii, 185–91. Hesiod's account of Pandora:

He told Hephaistos quickly to mix earth
And water, and to put in it a voice
And human power to move, to make a face
Like an immortal goddess, and to shape
The lovely figure of a virgin girl.
Athene was to teach the girl to weave,
And golden Aphrodite to pour charm
Upon her head, and painful, strong desire,
And body-shattering cares. Zeus ordered, then,
The killer of Argos, Hermes, to put in
Sly manners, and the morals of a bitch.
The son of Kronos spoke, and was obeyed.
The Lame God moulded earth as Zeus decreed
Into the image of a modest girl,
Grey-Eyed Athene made her robes and belt,
Divine Seduction and the Graces gave
Her Golden necklaces, and for her head

The Seasons wove spring flowers into a crown.
Hermes the Messenger put in her breast
Lies and persuasive words and cunning ways;
The herald of the gods then named the girl
Pandora, for the gifts which all the gods
Had given her, this ruin of mankind.

(Hesiod, *Works and Days,* ed. and trans. Dorothea Wender [London: Penguin, 1973], 61.).

5.

Worse still is the well-read menace, who's hardly settled for dinner
Before she starts praising Virgil, making a moral case
for Dido (death justifies all), comparing, evaluating
Rival poets, Virgil and Homer suspended
in opposite scales, weighed up one against the other.
Critics surrender, academics are routed, all
fall silent, not a word from lawyer or auctioneer—
Or even another woman. Such a rattle of talk,
You'd think all the pots and bells were being clashed together
When the moon's in eclipse. No need now for trumpets or brass: . . .

(Juvenal, *The Sixteen Satires,* trans. Peter Green [Harmondsworth: Penguin, 1974], 144)

6. John Chrysostom, *On Virginity, Against Remarriage,* trans. Sally Rieger Shore (New York: Edwin Mellen Press, 1983), 59; Jerome, *Adversus Jovinianum,* 367; *PL,* vol. 23, 249.

7. "Equality of Souls, Inequality of Sexes: Women in Medieval Theology," in *Religion and Sexism,* ed. Rosemary Ruether (New York: Simon & Schuster, 1974), 214.

8.

Il faut y joindre encore la
  revesche Bizarre,
Qui sans cesse d'un ton par la
  colere aigri
Gronde, choque, dément,
  contredit un Mari.
Il n'est point de repos ni de paix
  avec elle.
Son mariage n'est qu'une longue
  querelle.

One must add to the list the bizarre shrew who without cease, and in a tone of voice sharpened by rage scolds, shocks, rails, contradicts her husband. There is no rest or peace with such a one. Her marriage is one long quarrel. And does she let her husband breathe for an instant? Her servants are first off the object of her diatribes, and when she harangues them with a scornful tone, you should see with what words she

Laisse-t-elle un moment respirer son Epoux? Ses valets sont d'abord l'objet de son courroux, Et sur le ton grondeur, lors qu'elle les harangue, Il faut voir de quels mots elle enrichit la Langue. Ma plume ici traçant ces mots par alphabet, Pourroit d'un nouveau tôme augmenter le Richelet.	*enriches the language. My pen here* *tracing these words alphabetically might* *increase by a tome the Richelet Dictionary.* (Nicolas Boileau-Despréaux, *Oeuvres* *complètes,* ed. Antoine Adam [Paris: Gallimard, 1966], 71)

9. "En un mot elles ont déjà cette finesse qui caractérise leur sexe, ce tact délicat des convenances qu'on peut regarder en elles comme une faculté d'instinct, enfin ce talent particulier pour la conversation, qui doit assurer un jour leur empire, et auquel ells s'exercent incessamment" (*Dictionnaire de médecine,* vol. 6, 218).

10. Jules Barbey d'Aurevilly, *Les Bas-bleus* (Geneva: Slatkine Reprints, 1968), 303; P.-J. Proudhon, *De la Justice dans la Révolution et dans l'église* (Paris: Garnier Frères, 1858), vol. 3, 399.

11. Cesare Lombroso, *La Femme criminelle et la prostituée* (Paris: Felix Alcan, 1896), 183.

12. The original source of such a motif is, again, Jerome's *Adversus Jovinianum:* "To support a poor wife is hard: to put up with a rich one, is torture" (383; *PL,* vol. 23, 277).

13. Ibid.; Isidore, *De ecclesiasticis officiis,* 2. 20. 9; John of Salisbury, *Frivolities of Courtiers and Footprints of Philosophers,* ed. Joseph B. Pike (Minneapolis: University of Minnesota Press, 1938), 357.

14. John of Salisbury, *Frivolities,* 357.

15. "The Wife of Bath's Prologue: in *The Works of Geoffrey Chaucer,* ed. F. N. Robinson, (Boston: Houghton Mifflin, 1961), vv. 248–253.

16. Ce n'est pas merveille trop dure/ Se le mari nul temps ne dure/ Contre sa femme mal pitieuse,/ Envers la tençon rioteuse/ Que souvent li scet aprester ("It is no great wonder if the husband doesn't last very long against his pitiless wife, if he doesn't hold out against the riotous arguments that she knows how to prepare for him") (Jehan Le Fèvre, *Les Lamentations de Matheolus,* ed. A.-G. Van Hamel [Paris: Emile Bouillon, 1892], vv. 829–33.)

17. "Car um puet oyr sovent/ Um fol parler sagement./ Sage est que parle sage-ment" (*Recueil général et complet des fabliaux,* ed. Anatole de Montaiglon [Paris: Librairie des Bibliophiles, 1872], vol. 2, 256). Hereafter cited in text as *Recueil.*

18. *Adversus Jovinianum*, 383; *PL*, vol. 23, 276. Innocent III, *On the Misery of the Human Condition*, trans. Margaret Mary Dietz (New York: Bobbs-Merrill, 1969), 20; Latin text, *De miseria humane conditionis*, ed. Michele Maccarrone (Padua: Editrice Antenore, 1955), 23–24.

19. Victor Le Clerc, *Les Fabliaux*, in *Histoire littéraire de la France*, vol. 23 (Paris: H. Welter, 1895), 98.

20.

Et cil qui font le mariage,
si ront trop perilleus usage,
et coustume si despareille
qu'el me vient a trop grant
   merveille.
Ne sai don vient ceste folie,
fors de rage et de desverie.
Je voi que qui cheval achete
n'iert ja si fols que riens i mete,
conment que l'en l'ait bien
   covert,
se tout nou voit a descovert;
par tout le resgarde et espreuve.
Mes l'en prent fame sanz
   espreuve,
ne ja n'i sera descoverte,
ne por gaaigne ne por perte,
ne por solaz ne por mesese,
por ce, sanz plus, qu'el ne
   desplese
devant qu'ele soit espousee

And those who marry have a most unusual and dangerous way of operating that surprises me greatly. I don't know whence this foolishness can come except from madness and rage. For a man who buys a horse would not be so crazy as to put any money down if he had not seen it uncovered first, no matter how well covered it was in the first place. He looks it all over and tests it. But one takes a wife without testing, and neither for profit nor for loss, neither for pleasure nor for discomfort will she be uncovered; and for this reason alone—fear of displeasing before she is wed. (Rose, vv. 8631–47)

21. "Wife of Bath's Prologue," vv. 285–91. Jerome writes: "If she has a bad temper, or is a fool, if she has a blemish, or is proud, or has bad breath, whatever her fault may be—all this we learn after marriage. Horses, asses, cattle, even slaves of the smallest worth, clothes, kettles, wooden seats, cups, and earthenware pitchers, are first tried and then bought: a wife is the only thing that is not shown before she is married, for fear she may not give satisfaction" (*Adversus Jovinianum*, 383; *PL*, vol. 23, 277).

22. Innocent III, *Misery*, 20; *De miseria*, 23–24. The triad of the garrulous wife, smoky chimney, and leaky roof is also to be found in an antimarriage poem from the beginning of the thirteenth-century: "Fumus et mulier et stillicida/ Expullunt hominem a domo propria" ("De conjuge non ducenda," ed. Edelestand Du Méril, in *Poésies populaires latines du moyen âge* [Paris: Firmin Didot, 1847], 186). Chaucer repeats the topos: "Thow seyst that droppyng houses, and eek smoke,/ And chidying wyves

maken men to flee/ Out of hir owene hous" ("Wife of Bath's Prologue," vv. 278–80). It will be remembered too that Lombroso's *La Femme criminelle et la prostituée* contains a series of proverbs that show the degree to which John of Salisbury, Innocent III, and Chaucer were influenced by the folklore of the Middle Ages or the degree to which their writings have percolated to the level of modern popular culture. Thus Lombroso maintains that the Spanish are apt to say "Humo y gotera, y la muger echan al partera ombre de su casa fucra," which, he claims, recalls the English proverb, "from a smoking house and a scolding wife, Lord deliver us" (183). Nor is it too far-fetched to see in Barbey d'Aurevilly's notion of the woman writer as an inundating liquid whose style overflows its vessel a version of the topos of the leaky roof.

23. "Mais il n'est pas en cest païs/ Cil qui tant soit de sens espris/ Qui mie se péust guetier/ Que fame nel puist engingnier" (*Recueil*, vol. 1, 292).

Par example cis fabliaus dist	*By an exemplum this fabliau shows that*
Fame est fète por decevoir;	*woman is made to deceive. She makes a lie*
Mençonge fet devenir voir,	*seem true and the truth seem a lie. The one*
Et voir fet devenir mençonge.	*who composed this fable and these stories*
Cil n'i vout mètre plus d'alonge	*won't tarry any longer. Here ends the tale*
Qui fist cest fablel et ces dis.	*of the partridges.* ("Des Perdrix"
Ci faut li fabliaus des perdris.	[*Recueil*, vol. 1, 193])

"Par cest fable prover vous vueil/ Que cil fet folie et orgueil/ Qui fame engignier s'entremet;/ Quar qui fet à fame .I. mal tret,/ El en fet .X. ou .XV. ou .XX" ("By this fable I want to prove that he commits an act of folly and pride who undertakes to trick a woman; since, for each trick done to a woman, she does ten or fifteen or twenty back" ["Des .II. Changéors" (*Recueil*, vol. 1, 254)]). See Lesley Johnson, "Women on Top: Antifeminism in the Fabliaux," *Modern Language Review* 78 (1983): 298–307; Philippe Ménard, *Les Fabliaux* (Paris: Presses Universitaires de France, 1983), 116.

24. "Issi est suvent avenu:/ de plusurs femmes est seü,/ que si cunseillent lur seignur/ qu'il lur revert a deshonur;/ meinte femme cunseille a faire/ ceo dunt a plusurs nest cuntraire" (Marie de France, *Fables*, trans. Mary Lou Martin [Birmingham, Ala.: Summa Publications, 1984], 192).

25. ". . . et elle replique bien, quar elle se sent bien de bonne lignee, et lui remembre bien ses amis, qui aucuneffoiz lui en parlent, et sont en riote et jamés le bon homme n'avra joye. Il sera servy de mensonges et le fera l'en pestre" (". . . and she replies well, for she knows she's from a good family, and reminds him of her relations, who sometimes speak to him of her, and are riotous and never will the good man have joy. He will be served with lies and will graze upon them" [*Les Quinze joies de mariage*, ed. Jean Rychner (Geneva: Droz, 1963), 48]).

26.

Premiers commencerai au chief:
Ele est trecie par beubance,

D'un treçoir de fausse atraiance.
S'a .j. chapel de lasheté.
Et sa coiffe de fausseté
Paillolée de tricherie.
Sa crespe de mélancolie,
Et la robe qu'ele a vestue
N'est pas de soie à or batue,
Ainz est de fausse covoitise
Forrée à porfil de faintise
Qui ne lesse fère droiture.

("De Dame Guile," in Achille Jubinal, *Jongleurs et trouvères* [Paris: Merklein, 1835], 64).

27. "Par jangle de la pie/ Un vient à tromperie/ De gopil et de chat;/ Femme par parole/ Meynt homme afole/ Et ly rend tot mat" ("De la Femme et de la pye," in Achille Jubinal, *Nouveau receuil de contes, dits et fabliaux* [Paris: E. Pannier, 1842] vol. 2, 326). See Théodore Lee Neff, *La Satire des femmes.*

28. Schopenhauer continues, "For as nature has equipped the lion with claws and teeth, the elephant with tusks, the wild boar with fangs, the bull with horns and the cuttlefish with ink, so it has equipped woman with the power of dissimulation as her means of attack and defence, and has transformed into this gift all the strength it has bestowed on man in the form of physical strength and power of reasoning. Dissimulation is thus inborn to her. . . . To make use of it at every opportunity is as natural to her as it is for an animal to employ its means of defence whenever it is attacked. . . . A completely truthful woman who does not practice dissimulation is perhaps an impossibility" (*Essays and Aphorisms*, trans. R. J. Hollingdale [Harmondsworth: Penguin, 1970], 83). See also Schopenhauer's "Essay on Woman" in *Parerga und Paralipomena;* and H. R. Hays, *The Dangerous Sex: The Myth of Feminine Evil* (New York: G. P.Putnam's Sons, 1964), 209.

29. Friedrich Nietzsche, *Beyond Good and Evil,* trans. Walter Kaufmann (New York: Vintage, 1966), 163. "Mais si le mensonge est un vice très répandu dans toute l'humanité, c'est surtout chez les femmes qu'il atteint son maximum d'intensité. Démontrer que le mensonge est habituel, physiologique, chez la femme, serait inutile: cela est consacré par la croyance populaire" (Lombroso, *La Femme criminelle,* 135); "les femmes ont le mensonge instinctif" (*ibid.,* 137).

30. "Il est bien connu que pendant la menstruation la femme est plus menteuse, plus portée à inventer des calomnies et des contes fantastiques" (Lombroso, *La Femme criminelle,* 140).

31. I use the Vulgate version of the Old Testament since that was what was known in the Middle Ages. On the double Creation see Robert Alter, *The Art of Biblical Narrative* (New York: Basic Books, 1981), 140–47.

32. The canonical Hebrew Scriptures never appropriated Genesis 1:27. The early church fathers were aware of the existence of two versions. John Chrysostom, for example, explains away the priestly version in terms of the prescient vision of biblical authors who "speak of things not yet created as though already created. You see, since they perceive with the eyes of the spirit things due to happen after a great number of years, and accordingly view things as already laid out in front of their very eyes, they describe everything in this way" (*Homilies on Genesis 1–17,* in *Fathers of the Church,* trans. Robert C. Hill [Washington, D.C.: Catholic University of America Press, 1989], vol. 74, 132–33). See Mieke Bal, *Lethal Love: Feminist Literary Readings of Biblical Love Stories* (Bloomington: Indiana University Press, 1987), 104–31; Mary Cline Horowitz, "The Image of God in Man—Is Woman Included?" *Harvard Theological Review* 72 (1979): 175–206; Phyllis Trible, "Depatriarchalizing in Biblical Interpretation," *Journal of the American Academy of Religion* 41 (1973): 30–48; and Trible, *God and the Rhetoric of Sexuality* (Philadelphia: Fortress Press, 1978).

33. See my *Etymologies and Genealogies: A Literary Anthropology of the French Middle Ages* (Chicago: University of Chicago Press, 1983), 37–44.

34. Mary Nyquist, "Gynesis, Genesis, Exegesis, and Milton's Eve," in *Selected Papers from the English Institute, 1985,* ed. Marjorie Garber (Baltimore: Johns Hopkins University Press, 1987), 158; Margaret Miles, *Carnal Knowing* (Boston: Beacon Press, 1989), 17. Jean-Marie Aubert terms this passage "un des textes fondateurs du tout le sexisme chrétien" (*La Femme: Antiféminisme et Christianisme* [Paris: Cerf/Desclée, 1975], 86). Phyllis Trible, however, maintains that the original creational language implies neither derivation nor subordination, but simply difference. She translates Genesis 2:23 as "This, finally, bone of my bones and flesh of my flesh. This shall be called *'iššâ* because from *'iš* was differentiated this" (*God and the Rhetoric of Sexuality,* 102).

35. Katherine Rogers maintains that such a perspective explains the prevalence of misogyny from Paul's epistles to the *Catholic Encyclopedia* of 1912 (*The Troublesome Helpmate,* 11–14). Phyllis Trible sees the historical interpretation of this passage as crucial: "Over the centuries this misogynous reading has acquired a status of canonicity so that those who deplore and those who applaud the story both agree upon its *meaning*" (*God and the Rhetoric of Sexuality,* 73).

36. Philo, *On the Creation,* ed. F. H. Colson (London: Heinemann, 1929), 227; Chrysostom cited in France Quéré-Jaulmes, *La Femme: Les grands textes des Pères de l'Eglise* (Paris: Editions du Centurion, 1968), 178–79; Gratian cited in Aubert, *La Femme,* 88.

37. *Paradise Lost,* 8.496. So too Augustine, in describing the difference between the sexes in the Creation story, insists upon the difference between languages: "Vo-

cavit ergo mulierem suam vir, tanquam potior inferiorem, et dixit: *Hoc nunc os de ossibus meis, et caro de carne mea. Os de ossibus,* fortasse propter fortitudinem; et *caro de carne,* propter temperantiam. Hae namque duae virtutes ad inferiorem animi partem, quam prudentia rationalis regit, docenter pertinere. Quod autem dictum est. *Haec vocabitur mulier, quoniam de viro suo sumpta est;* ista origo nominis, et interpretatio in lingua latina non apparet. Quid enim simile habeat mulieris nomen ad viri nomen, non invenitur. Sed in hebraea locutione dicitur sic sonare, quasi dictum sit: Haec vocabitur virago, quoniam de viro suo sumpta est. Nam virago vel virgo potius habet aliquam similitudinem cum viri nomine; mulier autem non habet: sed hoc, ut dixi, linguae diversitas facit" (*De Genesi contra Manichaeos,* 2, 13 [*PL,* vol. 34, 206]. Or Jerome: "*Hoc nunc os ex ossibus meis, et caro de carne mea: haec vocabitur mulier, quoniam ex viro sumpta est.* Non videtur in Graeco et in Latino sonare, car mulier appelletur, quia ex viro sumpta sit: sed etymologia in Hebraeo sermone servatur. Vir quippe vocatur is (איש), et mulier ISSA (אישה). Recte igitur ab is, appellata est mulier ISSA. Unde et Symmachus pulchre etymologiam etiam in Graeco voluit custodire, dicens: Haec vocabitur ἀνδρὶς, ὅτι ἀπὸ ἀνδρὸς ἐλήθη., quod nos Latine possumus dicere: *Haec vocabitur virago, quia ex viro sumpta est*" (*Liber Hebraicarum quaestionum in Genesim* [*PL,* vol. 23, 942]. Isidore of Seville explains the difference between a maiden and a virago as that between one born of man and one who takes on manly deeds: "Inter virginem et viraginem. Virgo est quae virum nescit, virago autem quae virum agit, hoc est virilia facit" (*Differentiae* [*PL,* vol. 83, 68]).

38. "Vir nuncupatus, quia maior in eo vis est quam in feminis: unde et virtus nomen accepit; sive quod vi agat feminam. Mulier vero a mollitie, tamquam mollier, detracta littera vel mutata, appellata est mulier. Vtrique enim fortitudine et inbecillitate corporum separantur. Sed ideo virtus maxima viri, mulieris minor, ut patiens viri esset; scilicet, ne feminis repugnantibus libido cogeret viros aliud appetere aut in alium sexum proruere. Dicitur igitur mulier secundum femineum sexum, non secundum corruptionem integritatis: et hoc ex lingua sacrae Scripturae. Nam Eva statim facta de latere viri sui, nondum contacta a viro, mulier appellata est, dicente Scriptura (Genes. 2, 23): 'Et formavit eam in mulierem.' Virgo a viridiori aetate dicta est, sicut et virga, sicut et vitula. Alias ab incorruptione, quasi virago, quod ignoret femineam passionem. Virago vocata, quia virum agit, hoc est opera virilia facit et masculini vigoris est. Antiqui enim fortes feminas ita vocabant. Virgo autem non recte virago dicitur, si non viri officio fungitur. Mulier vero si virilia facit, recte virago dicitur, ut Amazona. Quae vero nunc femina, antiquitus vira vocabatur; sicut a servo serva, sicut a famulo famula, ita a viro vira. Hinc et virginis nomen quidam putant" (Isadore of Seville, *Etymologiarum sive originum,* ed. W. M. Lindsay [Oxford: Oxford University Press, 1911], vol. 2, XI, ii,17–20). See also d'Alverny, "Théologiens et philosophes," 113; John Fyler, "Man, Men, and Women in Chaucer's Poetry," in *The Olde Daunce:*

Love, Friendship, and Desire in the Medieval World, ed. Robert Edwards and Stephen Spector (Albany: SUNY Press, 1990), 154–76.

39. Innocent III, *Misery,* 10; *De miseria,* 13.

40. Augustine, *De libero arbitrio,* ed. J. H. S. Burleigh (London: SCM Press, 1953), 169; Latin text in *Opera omnia* (Paris, 1836), vol. 1, 990.

41. Cited in Thomas H. Tobin, *The Creation of Man: Philo and the History of Interpretation* (Washington, D.C.: Catholic Biblical Association of America, 1983), 14.

42. Boethius, *Arithmetica,* 1139, cited in Edgar De Bruyne, *Etudes d'esthétique médiévale* (Bruges: De Temple, 1946), vol. 1, 14.

43. Augustine, *De ordine,* ed. Jean Jolivet (Paris: Desclée de Brouwer, 1948), 307, 445, 306, 444.

44. Tertullian, "On Exhortation to Chastity," in *The Ante-Nicene Fathers,* ed. Alexander Roberts and James Donaldson (Buffalo: The Christian Literature Publishing Co., 1885), vol. 4, 54; also in *PL,* vol. 2, 922. Anselm's contempt-of-the-world book is *Cur Deus homo,* published in a French translation by René Roques, *Anselme de Canterbury, Pourquoi Dieu s'est fait homme* (Paris: Editions du Cerf, 1963), *Sources chrétiennes,* vol. 91. "The only necessary being is God, in whom resides all good; He is the Universal Good, total, alone, unique" (cited in Robert Bultot, *La Doctrine du mépris du monde* [Louvain: Nauwelaerts, 1964], vol. 4, 135).

45. Cited in Aubert, *La Femme,* 88.

46. The passage continues, "For when God looked upon man he was well pleased, for man was made in his image and likeness. . . . But at her creation woman partook of a mixture of the two (man and God); she is a different creature, created through another than God, ... The woman is therefore the creation of the man . . . and the man signifies the divinity, the woman the humanity, of the Son of God. The man therefore presides over the tribunal of the world, ruling all creatures, while the woman is under his mastery, and subject to him" (Hildegard of Bingen, *Liber divinorum operibus simplicis hominis* [*PL,* vol. 197, 885]). For a fine understanding of this passage, see Barbara Newman, *Sister of Wisdom: St. Hildegard's Theology of the Feminine* (Berkeley: University of California Press, 1987), 89–99; see also Shulamith Shahar, *The Fourth Estate: A History of Women in the Middle Ages* (London: Methuen, 1983), 57; Caroline Bynum, "'. . . And Woman His Humanity': Female Imagery in the Religious Writing of the Later Middle Ages," in *Gender and Religion: On the Complexity of Symbols,* ed. Caroline Bynum, Steven Harrell, and Paula Richman (Boston: Beacon Press, 1986), 261.

47. Augustine, *De libero arbitrio,* 163; *Opera omnia,* vol. 1, 985. This is also an important concept in the Aristotelian tradition, according to which in procreation man supplies the form and woman the matter; see in particular Aristotle, *De la Génération des animaux,* ed. Pierre Louis (Paris: Société d'Edition "Les Belles Lettres," 1961), 3–5, 39–43.

48. Rosemary Ruether writes: "Augustine assimilates maleness into monism, and this makes femaleness rather than bisexuality the image of the lower, corporeal nature. . . . When Eve is taken from Adam's side, she symbolizes this corporeal side of man, taken from him in order to be his helpmeet. But she is a helpmeet solely for the corporeal task of procreation, for which she alone is indispensable. For any spiritual task another male would be more suitable than a female as a helpmeet" ("Misogynism and Virginal Feminism in the Fathers of the Church," in *Religion and Sexism,* 156). Eleanor McLaughlin also shows how closely linked are the ideas of chronological priority and the spirit/flesh distinction: "The subordination and inferiority of Eve—and therefore of all womankind—to the male are thus established before the Fall in the order of God's original creation: first, by reason of the primacy of Adam's creation, who was not only first in time and the founder of the human race but also the material source of the first woman; and second, by reason of finality, for Adam displays the peculiar end and essence of human nature, intellectual activity, whereas Eve's finality is purely auxiliary and summed up in her bodily, generative function" ("Equality of Souls," 217).

49. Thus also Anselm: "Man should not bother in this world with the quest for these goods. Let him love the unique Good in whom are all other goods, and let that suffice. Let him love the perfectly simple Good, which is the totality of good, that is enough (cited in Bultot, *La Doctrine du mépris du monde,* vol. 4, 134). "C'est l'opposition augustinienne de l'Un et du multiple, et nous sommes au fondement ontologique du mépris du monde chez Anselme," Bultot remarks (*ibid.*).

50. "Femina vero a partibus femorum dicta, ubi sexus species a viro distinguitur. Alii Graeca etymologia feminam ab ignea vi dictam putant, quia vehementer concupiscit. Libidinosiores enim viris feminas esse tam in mulieribus quam in animalibus. Vnde nimius amor apud antiquos femineus vocabatur" (*Etymologiarum,* vol. 2, XI, ii, 24).

51. One can find this idea, for example, in the Middle Platonism (first century B.C.) of "Timaeus Locrus," *On the Nature of the World and of the Soul:* "The Idea is eternal, unchanging and immovable, indivisible and of the nature of the Same, intelligible, and a paradigm of things which are made and which are in flux. Matter is the impression, the mother and nurse and the one who brings forth the third kind of being. . . . The Form has the character of the male and father while matter has that of the female and mother" (cited in Tobin, *Philo,* 71–72).

52. John Chrysostom, "Letter to the Fallen Theodore, " in *A Select Library of the Nicene and Post-Nicene Fathers,* ed. Philip Schaff (Grand Rapids, Mich.: Eerdmans, 1956), vol. 9, 103. Greek text in J.-P. Migne, ed., *Patrologia graeca* (Paris, 1857–87), vol. 47, 298; hereafter cited as *PG.*

53. Innocent III, *Misery,* 6; *De miseria,* 8.

54. Here we encounter the far-reaching and culturally charged body of supersti-

tion attached in the Mediterranean world to the feminine natural processes and reaching back in Western tradition at least to classical natural history. "Hailstorms, whirlwinds, and lightnings even will be scared away by a woman uncovering her body while her courses are upon her," writes Pliny, who claims a menstruating woman is capable of souring new wine or fruit. "Hear now," Innocent continues, some thirteen centuries later, "on what food the child is fed in the womb: actually on menstrual blood, which ceases in the female after conception so that the child in her womb will be nourished by it. And this blood is reckoned so detestable and impure that on contact with it fruits will fail to sprout, orchards go dry, herbs wither, the very trees let go their fruit; if a dog eat of it, he goes mad. When a child is conceived, he contacts the defect of the seed, so that lepers and monsters are born of this corruption" (*Misery*, 9; *De miseria*, 11–12). Nor does Saint Thomas Aquinas ignore the misogynistic folklore attached to menstrual blood. "The gaze of a menstruating woman," the Angelic Doctor writes, "can dim and crack a mirror" (Aquinas, *Liber de veritate catholicae fidei contra errores infidelium seu summa contra gentiles*, vol. 3 [Rome: Marietti, 1961], 156).

55. Naomi Schor, *Reading in Detail: Aesthetics and the Feminine* (New York: Methuen, 1987).

56. "Autant l'homme considère l'espèce et les choses générales, autant la femme s'attache à l'individu et se fixe à des objets particuliers" (J. J. Virey, *De l'Influence des femmes sur le goût dans la littérature et les beaux-arts* [Paris: Deterville, 1810], 13, 14).

57. Hegel, *The Philosophy of Right* (cited in Schor, *Reading in Detail*, 25).

58. Proudhon, *De la Justice*, vol. 3, 356, 357, 358.

59. Jules Michelet, *Woman*, trans. John W. Palmer (New York: Carleton, 1866), 202.

60. "On trouve une autre preuve de l'infériorité de l'intelligence féminine dans sa moindre puissance d'abstraction, et dans sa grande préciosité. L'intelligence de la femme se montre défectueuse en ce qui est la suprême forme de l'évolution mentale, la faculté de synthèse et de l'abstraction; elle excelle au contraire en finesse dans l'analyse et dans la nette perception des détails" (Lombroso, *La Femme criminelle*, 180). "Il a été observé dans les collèges de jeunes filles que les occupations intellectuelles trop assidues, trop abstraites, produisent des aménhorées, de l'hystérisme, du névrosisme" (ibid., 181); also 183, 184.

61. Tobin, *Philo*, 146; also 150, 154, 159, 178. J. Daniélou, *Philon d'Alexandrie* (Paris: Fayard, 1958), 135; Elizabeth V. Spelman, "Woman as Body: Ancient and Contemporary Views," *Feminist Studies* 8 (1982): 109–31.

62. Philo, *On the Creation*, 227.

63. Ibid., 237, 249. See Richard Baer, *Philo's Use of the Categories Male and Female* (Leiden: E. J. Brill, 1970); Bynum, "'. . . And Woman His Humanity'," 257.

64. Ruether, "Misogynism," 156. See also d'Alverny, "Théologiens et philo-

sophes," 109, 113, 114, 119; John Bugge, *Virginitas: An Essay in the History of a Medieval Ideal* (The Hague: Martinus Nijhoff, 1975), 16; Henri Crouzel, *Virginité et mariage selon Origène* (Paris: Desclée de Brouwer, 1962), 136; Dom Jean Leclercq, *La Femme et les femmes dans l'oeuvre de Saint Bernard* (Paris: Téqui, 1982), 26. Here, as elsewhere within the sophistry of gender at which the fathers are so adept, we are witness to a slippery binary opposition, which simply shifts the frame of reference whenever logic would dictate the superiority or even the equality of the feminine. Thus, if man is associated with catalyzing activity or form and woman with passivity, then passivity is denigrated. Yet when activity is imagined to contain both a masculine and a feminine component, as in the act of procreation, the onus of carnality again shifts to the female side: "Our actions are feminine or masculine," writes the supposedly self-emasculated Origen. "Feminine, they are corporeal or carnal. If we plant a seed in flesh, the child of our soul is female, not male: but without nerves, soft and material. If we look toward the eternal, raising our intelligence towards the best, and if we fructify with the fruits of the spirit, all our children are male. All those who are brought before God, presented to the view of the Creator, are male, not female. For God does not deign to look at what is feminine and corporeal" (cited in Crouzel, *Virginité,* 136).

65. "'. . . And Woman His Humanity'," 257.

66. See Aubert, *La Femme,* 95; Quéré-Jaulmes, *La Femme,* 32; Ruether, "Misogynism," 157; Jo Ann McNamara, "Sexual Equality and the Cult of Virginity in Early Christian Thought," *Feminist Studies* 3 (1976): 146.

67. Cited in d'Alverny, "Théologiens et philosophes," 109; see also 119.

68. Thomas Aquinas, *Summa theologiae* (New York: McGraw-Hill, 1963), Part I, Qu. 92.; vol. 13, 37.

69. Page Du Bois, "'The Devil's Gateway': Women's Bodies and the Earthly Paradise," *Women's Studies* 7 (1980): 45, 47.

70. John Chrysostom, "Homily 15," in *A Select Library of the Nicene and Post-Nicene Fathers,* ed. Philip Schaff (Grand Rapids, Mich.: Eerdmans Publishing Co., 1956), vol. 9, 441. Novatian too sees the idolatry engendered by the gaze to be the central avenue of seduction leading to all other transgressions: "And anything else that draws the eyes and soothes the ears of the spectators has at bottom either an idol, or a demon, or some deceased person. You have only to look into its origin and foundation. Thus it was all devised by the devil because he knew full well that idolatry of itself is horrendous. He combined idolatry with spectacles so that idolatry would be loved through the pleasure that the spectacles afforded" ("The Spectacles," in *Fathers of the Church,* ed. Russell De Simone [Washington: Catholic University of America Press, 1974], 127; Latin text in *PL,* vol. 4, 785).

71. Thus a phrase, like that in Matthew 19:11–12, in which "to receive" is to un-

derstand what the reader must already know: "All men cannot receive this saying, say they to whom it is given. . . . He that is able to receive it, let him receive it."

72. I am grateful to Brian Stock for first pointing this out to me. It is also documented in his book, *The Implications of Literacy* (Princeton: Princeton University Press, 1983). See also Georges Duby, *Le Chevalier, la femme et le prêtre: Le mariage dans la France féodale* (Paris: Hachette, 1981), 117–21.

73. *De magistro,* ed. F. J. Thonnard (Paris: Desclée de Brouwer, 1941), 78, 82.

74. "For when we speak the truth, that is, speak of what we know," writes Augustine, "then the word which is born from the knowledge itself which we retain in the memory must be altogether of the same kind as that knowledge from which it is born. For the thought formed from that thing which we know is the word we speak in our heart, and it is neither Greek, nor Latin, nor of any other language" *The Trinity* [Washington: Catholic University of America Press, 1963], 476; Latin text in *PL,* vol. 8, 1071). Again Augustine: "It is just as if one were to write the name of the Lord in gold and ink; the former would be more precious, the latter more worthless, but the thing signified by both would be one and the same" (ibid., 116; *PL,* vol. 8, 880).

75. "Le Sort des Dames," in Jubinal, *Jongleurs et trouvères,* 186.

76. See my *Etymologies and Genealogies,* 12–20.

77. Jerome, *Adversus Jovinianum,* 394; *PL,* vol. 23, 297.

78. Ibid.

79. *The Trinity,* 223; *PL,* vol. 8, 936.

80. See *Etymologies and Genealogies,* 61–63.

81. "On the Veiling of Virgins" in *The Ante-Nicene Fathers,* ed. Alexander Roberts and James Donaldson (Buffalo: The Christian Literature Publishing Co., 1885), vol. 4, 30; *PL,* vol. 2, 894–95.

82. Ibid.; *PL,* vol. 2, 896.

83. Ibid., 31; *PL,* vol. 2, 898.

CHAPTER TWO

1. Sharon Farmer maintains that "because ancient and medieval societies were predominantly oral cultures, philosophers and theologians in those societies felt the full impact of speech as a sensuous and physical phenomenon, and they therefore associated speech with the physical realm and women. In the Middle Ages, moreover, the tendency to associate women with the power of speech was bolstered by the fact that there was a sharp division between the oral world of illiterate women and lay men and the textualized world of clerics" (Sharon Farmer, "Softening the Hearts of Men:

Women, Embodiment, and Persuasion in the Thirteenth Century," in *Embodied Love: Sensuality and Relationship as Feminist Values,* ed. Paula Cooly, Sharon Farmer, and Mary Ellen Ross [New York: Harper & Row, 1987], 116). I'm not so sure, however, that we can reduce the mistrust of women simply to a mistrust of the oral without at the same time naturalizing such a suspicion, since the assignment of women to the realm of the oral, which Farmer traces to the acquisition of a mother tongue ("women . . . as mothers or nurses had uttered the first words that these men had heard and mimicked") risks falling into the trap of the archetype of the garrulous female, which, as we saw in chapter 1, is one of the staples of misogynistic discourse from Greco-Roman times to the present. Nor can we reduce the antifeminist impulse merely to a question of lay versus clerical culture, since illiteracy, associated in the Middle Ages with "popular" as opposed to high or learned culture, certainly seems to have been no guarantee against misogynistic speech and attitudes (just consider the proverbs or examples of popular diction given in chapter 1), then or now.

2. Philo Judaeus, *On the Creation,* 237.

3. "Homily XV," in *Homilies on Genesis 1–17,* 198.

4. Methodius, *The Symposium: A Treatise on Chastity,* trans. Herbert Musurillo (Westminster: The Newman Press, 1958), 58.

5. Augustine, *De Genesi ad litteram,* ed. P. Agaësse and A. Solignac (Paris: Desclée de Brouwer, 1972), 462.

6. The metaphorical status of woman is not necessarily negative, for it is this possibility of interpretation that enables the Christian recuperation of the pagan past. Augustine, who distinguishes between "signs corporeally expressed" and "things intelligibly conceived" writes: "I have known a thing to be signified in many ways by the body that is understood in one way by the mind, and a thing to be understood in many ways by the mind that is signified in but one by the body. Consider sincere love of God and neighbor, see how it is expressed corporeally in many holy rites, and in innumerable languages, and in each language by innumerable turns of speech. Thus do the offspring of the waters increase and multiply. . . . Hence, if we think of the actual natures of things, not allegorically but properly, then the words, 'Increase and multiply,' hold for all things that are begotten from seed. But if we interpret these words as set down figuratively—and this I am inclined to think is intended by Scripture, for surely it did not needlessly ascribe this blessing only to the offspring of water animals and men—then we find multitudes among spiritual and among corporeal creatures." (Augustine, *Confessions,* ed. J. K. Ryan [New York: Doubleday, 1960], 358–59; Latin text in *Opera Omnia,* vol. 1, 400). See Marcia Colish, *The Mirror of Language: A Study in the Medieval Theory of Knowledge* (New Haven: Yale University Press, 1968), 11–79.

7. Marcia Colish, *The Stoic Tradition from Antiquity to the Early Middle Ages, II: Stoicism in Christian Latin Thought Through the Sixth Century* (Leiden: E. J. Brill, 1985), vol. 1, 27; also 28, 81–86, 246, 260; vol. 2, 48. See also Colish, "Cosmetic Theology: The Transformation of a Stoic Theme," *Assays* 1 (1981): 3–14.

8. "Do not adorn thyself so as to be seen by a strange woman and that she should desire thee." And if it happens that a woman is seduced, "She in truth was struck in her heart because thou art a youth, beautiful and good, and thou didst adorn thyself and make her desire thee. And thou art found guilty, that she hath sinned in regard to thee; for because of thine adornment it hath thus happened to her. . . . Thus again also let not the hair of thy head grow, nor comb it nor dress it; but shave it, and anoint it not, that it may not attract to thee such women as snare or are snared by lust. Also wear no beautiful garments nor even put on shows of lustful and contemptible workmanship, nor set signet-rings encased in gold upon thy fingers, because all these things are works of harlotry, and everything that thou doest which is beyond nature" (*Didascalia apostolorum,* trans. Margaret Dunlop Gibson [London: C. J. Clay & Sons, 1903], 4).

9. See, for example, chapter 5 of the "Testament of Reuben": "for the angel of the Lord told me, and taught me, that women are overcome by the spirit of fornication more than men, and in their heart they plot against men; and by means of their adornment they deceive first their minds, and by the glance of the eye instil the poison, and then through the accomplished act they take them captive. For a woman cannot force a man openly, but by the harlot's bearing she beguiles him. Flee, therefore, fornication, my children, and command your wives and your daughters, that they adorn not their heads and their faces to deceive the mind: because every woman who useth these wiles hath been reserved for eternal punishment" (cited in Bernard Prusak, "Women: Seductive Siren and Source of Sin? Pseudepigraphical Myth and Christian Origins," in *Religion and Sexism,* 101).

10. Claude Rambaux maintains that the difference between Tertullian and both preceding and surrounding currents of asceticism is that he systematized what until then had remained scattered (*Tertullien face aux morales des trois premiers siècles* [Paris: Société des Belles Lettres, 1979], 257). See also Herbert Preisker, *Christentum und Ehe in den ersten drei Jahrhunderten: Eine Studie zur Kulturgeschichte der alten Welt* (Berlin: Trowitsch, 1927), 196.

11. Jonathan Smith, in an essay entitled "The Garments of Shame," claims that this analogy is to be found in the pun in the Coptic *Gospel of Saint Thomas,* "between the Greek χόσμος meaning 'the world' and χόσμος meaning 'ornament'" (Jonathan Z. Smith, *Map is Not Territory: Studies in the History of Religion* [Leiden: E.J. Brill, 1978], 20). Clement of Alexandria as well, drawing upon the association between the sensuality of the Egyptian woman, makeup, and the sensible world, maintains that "one is

justified in treating them like courtesans since instead of faces they wear masks" (cited in Quéré-Jaulmes, *La Femme,* 165).

12. If readers are tempted to object that Tertullian is an idiosyncratic example, they should contemplate the assessment of Peter Brown, who writes: "Thus, far from representing the morose outpourings of a lonely genius, Tertullian's writings enable us to glimpse the conglomerate of conflicting notions on sexuality, and on the meanings that might be attached to its renunciation, that circulated in a major Latin church at the beginning of the third century" (*The Body and Society: Men, Women and Sexual Renunciation in Early Christianity* [New York: Columbia University Press, 1988], 76).

13. Tertullian, "On the Apparel of Women" in *The Ante-Nicene Fathers,* ed. Alexander Roberts and James Donaldson (Buffalo: The Christian Literature Publishing Co., 1885), vol. 4, 14; also in *PL,* vol. 1, 1305.

14. Here there is an association as well of woman with the Jews, for as the Jews come to represent the letter without the spirit, or understanding, women represent the superficially decorative. The passage from the Old Testament often cited by the church fathers is Isaiah 3:16–24, which deals with the "haughtiness of the daughters of Zion"; and that from the New Testament, 1 Timothy 2, which enjoins women "to adorn themselves in modest apparel, with shamefacedness and sobriety; not with broided hair, or gold, or pearls, or costly array."

15. See Colish, *Stoic Tradition,* vol. 1, 103. Quéré-Jaulmes, *La Femme,* 163.

16. "In a very convoluted argument, which can no longer be unraveled completely, Paul addresses several points for 'this custom' or hair fashion. The key to these points, in my opinion, however, is the opening statement praising the Corinthian pneumatics for having kept the traditions Paul has transmitted to them. These traditions are those of liberation, freedom, equality, and Spirit-empowerment in Christ or in the Lord" (Elizabeth Schüssler Fiorenza, *In Memory of Her: A Feminist Theological Reconstruction of Christian Origins* [New York: Crossroads, 1983], 228).

17. "On the Apparel," 16; *PL,* vol. 1, 1309.

18. Ibid., 23; *PL,* vol. 1, 1327.

19. Ibid., 16; *PL,* vol. 1, 1310–11.

20. "On the Pallium," in *The Ante-Nicene Fathers,* vol. 4, 9, 12.

21. From the *Paedagogus* 2, 12 (cited in Prusak, "Pseudepigraphical Myth," 101).

22. Tertullian, "On the Apparel," 21; *PL,* vol. 1, 1321.

23. Cyprian, "The Dress of Virgins," in *Treatises,* ed. and trans. Roy J. Deferrari (New York: Fathers of the Church, 1958), 44; *PL,* vol. 4, 455. Cyprian also writes, "The work of God and His creature and image should in no way be falsified by employ-

ing yellow coloring, or black powder or rouge, or, finally, any cosmetic at all that spoils the natural features" (ibid.; *PL,* vol. 4, 454–55).

24. Novation, "In Praise of Purity," in *Fathers of the Church,* ed. Russell De Simone (Washington: Catholic University of America Press, 1974), vol. 67, 175; *PL,* vol. 4, 826. "The wonder is, that there is no (open) contending against the Lord's prescripts! It has been pronounced that no one can add to his own stature. *You,* however, *do* add to your *weight* some kind of rolls, or shield-bosses, to be piled upon your necks! . . . . Nay, rather banish quite away from your 'free' head all this slavery of ornamentation" (Tertullian, "On the Apparel," 21; *PL,* vol. 1, 1323–24). One does well to think, or rethink, as well the association that runs throughout the Middle Ages between woman and weaving. The textile industry has, of course, been gendered as feminine due to the demographic fact of the presence of so many women workers (see Daniel Armogathe Naïté-Albistur, *Histoire du féminisme français du moyen âge à nos jours* [Paris: Edition des Femmes, 1977], 34–35; Andrée Lehman, *Le Rôle de la femme dans l'histoire de France au moyen âge* [Paris: Editions Berger-Levrault, 1952], 1980). The concept has even been anthropologized or universalized: "Civilization of course owes the textile industry to women. All over the world, a spindle with a little clay weight at the end dangled or still dangles from the woman's fingers as she ceaselessly manipulates the cotton or woolen thread. The oldest loom, still in use in Middle America, is attached at one end to the woman's belt and at the other to a tree or house post. The skill at counting and manipulating numbers is carried over from the more ancient and limited art of basketry into the charming patterns seen in the wraparound skirt of the contemporary Guatemalan Indian woman. From textiles came the art of the couturier. But even before that women were tailors" (Hays, *The Dangerous Sex,* 20).

25. "For withal the founders of the race, Adam and Eve, so long as they were without intelligence, went 'naked'; but after they tasted of 'the tree of recognition,' they were first sensible of nothing more than of their cause for shame. Thus they each marked their intelligence of their own sex by a covering" (Tertullian, "On the Veiling of Virgins," 34; *PL,* vol. 2, 904).

26. Tertullian, "On the Apparel," 17; *PL,* vol. 1, 1312.

27. Quéré-Jaulmes, *La Femme,* 162–64.

28. Tertullian, "On the Apparel," 20; *PL,* vol. 1, 1320.

29. Tertullian is aware of this paradox, which he simply turns into another seductive ruse. "'With speech,' says (my antagonist), 'you have tried to persuade me,—a most sage medicament.' But, albeit utterance be mute—impeded by infancy or else checked by bashfulness, for life is content with an even tongueless philosophy—my very *cut* is eloquent. A philosopher, in fact, is *heard* so long as he is *seen*" ("On the Pallium," 12; *PL,* vol. 2, 1049).

30. "On the Apparel," 17; *PL,* vol. 1, 1312.

31. Novation, "The Spectacles," 131; *PL,* vol. 4, 786.

32. Tertullian, "On the Apparel," 23; *PL,* vol. 1, 1328.

33. "For they who rub their skin with medicaments, stain their cheeks with rouge, make their eyes prominent with antimony, sin against HIM. To them, I suppose, the plastic skill of God is displeasing! In their own persons, I suppose, they convict, they censure, the Artificer of all things. For censure they do when they amend, when they add to, (His work); taking these, their additions, of course, from the adversary artificer. That adversary artificer is the devil" (ibid., 20–21; *PL,* vol. 1, 1321).

34. Ibid., 25; *PL,* vol. 1, 1332.

35. Compare Cyprian: "For God has not made sheep scarlet or purple, nor has He taught how to tint and color with the juices of herbs and with shell fish, nor has He made necklaces of precious stones set in gold, or of pearls arranged in chains with numerous joinings, wherewith to hide the neck which He has made so that what God has created in man may be covered, and what the devil has invented may be exposed to view. Has God wished that wounds be inflicted on the ears, by which childhood still innocent and without knowledge of the evil of the world may be tortured, so that later from the incisions and holes in the ears precious stones may hang—heavy, although not by their own weight but by their high prices? All these things the sinful and apostate angels brought in to being by their own arts, when, haven fallen into earthly contagion, they lost their heavenly power. They also taught how to paint the eyes by spreading a black substance around them, and to tinge the cheeks with a counterfeit blush, and to change the hair by false colors, and to drive out all truth from the countenance and head by the assault of their corruption" ("The Dress of Virgins," 43; *PL,* vol. 4, 452–54). See also Colish, *The Stoic Tradition,* vol. 1, 246; Marina Warner, *Alone of All Her Sex* (New York: Knopf, 1976), 73.

36. Ambrose, "Concerning Virgins," in *Nicene and Post-Nicene Fathers,* ed. Philip Schaff and Henry Wace (New York: Christian Literature Publishing Co., 1896), vol. 10, 367; *PL,* vol. 16, 207.

37. Ambrose, *Hexameron,* trans. John J. Savage, in *Fathers of the Church* (New York: Fathers of the Church, 1961), vol. 42, 260; *PL,* vol. 14, 260–61. See also John Chrysostom, *Les Cohabitations suspectes, comment observer la virginité,* ed. and trans. Jean Dumortier (Paris: Les Belles Lettres, 1955), 128, 135; *On Virginity,* 98; Jerome, Letters 38, 107, *Select Letters,* ed. F. A. Wright (Cambridge, Mass.: Harvard University Press, 1953), 163, 351; *Adversus Jovinianum,* 351.

38. Quéré-Jaulmes, *La Femme,* 162.

39. "Homily XV," 442. See also John Chrysostom, *Cohabitations suspectes,* 129; Saint Cyprian, "The Dress of Virgins," 41–42; *PL,* vol. 4, 450.

40. "Two Epistles Concerning Virginity," in the *Ante-Nicene Fathers,* ed. Alexander Roberts and James Donaldson (Buffalo: The Christian Literature Publishing

Co., 1886), vol. 8, 57. See also Clement of Alexandria: "For as covetousness is called fornication because it is opposed to contentment with what one possesses, and as idolatry is an abandonment of the one God to embrace many gods, so fornication is apostasy from single marriage to several" ("On Marriage" in *Alexandrian Christianity,* ed. and trans. J. E. L. Oulton and Henry Chadwick [Philadelphia: Westminster, 1954], 82).

41. *The Trinity,* 119; *PL,* vol. 42, 881. Or Clement of Alexandria: "The Word compels us to *not regard visible things but only invisible ones, for the visible have only one time, and the invisible are forever*" (cited in Quéré-Jaulmes, *La Femme,* 165). See also Bultot, *La Doctrine du mépris du monde,* vol. 4, 209.

42. Augustine, *The Trinity,* 105; *PL,* vol. 42, 874.

43. Tertullian, "On the Pallium," 8; *PL,* vol. 2, 1039.

44. "From that time forth she [Reason] found it hard to believe that the splendor and purity [of numbers] was sullied by the *corporeal matter of words.* And just as what the spirit sees is always present and is held to be immortal and numbers appear such, while sound, being a sensible thing is lost into the past" (emphasis mine; Augustine, *De ordine,* 435).

45. *De magistro,* 99.

46. *Etymologiarum,* I, ix.

47. Jerome, *Adversus Jovinianum,* 394; *PL,* vol. 23, 297.

48. Letter to Gontier Col, cited in Dow, *Varying Attitude,* 174.

49. See Enid McLeod, *The Order of the Rose: The Life and Ideas of Christine de Pizan* (Totowa, N.J.: Rowan & Littlefield, 1976).

50. Blanche Dow, in fact, sees the struggle between pro- and antifeminists in esthetic terms; see above p. 3 for the quotation which, after asserting the quarrel to be an eternal struggle between "the forces of naturalism and those of classicism," continues: "At the beginning of the seventeenth century Madame de Rambouillet and her followers will wage a similar battle in their attempt to 'dégasconner la cour', to refine the manners, to reform the speech, to rescue the purity of classical tradition from the inroads of what they account to be vulgarity and grossness. Christine is indeed a forerunner of the *Précieuses*" (*Varying Attitude,* 260). See also Pierre Darmon, *Mythologie de la femme dans l'ancienne France* (Paris: Seuil, 1983); Joan Kelly, "Early Feminist Theory," 4–28. A recent book by Jacqueline Lichtenstein suggests that the analysis we have made for the High Middle Ages and the late medieval period also holds for the relation between esthetic theory, painting, and literary representation in the seventeenth century (*La Couleur éloquente* [Paris: Flammarion, 1989]).

51. *Le Débat sur le "Roman de la rose,"* ed. Erik Hicks (Paris: Champion, 1977), 15.

52. Ibid., 34.

53. John Chrysostom, "Homily 3," in *A Select Library of the Nicene and Post-Nicene Fathers,* ed. Philip Schaff (Grand Rapids, Mich.: Eerdmans, 1956), vol. 9, 194.

54. Jehan Le Fèvre, *Les Lamentations de Matheolus.*

55. "Trop nuist son de femme qui tence;/ Car par la sensible excellence/ Est le sens d'omme corrompu:" "The sound of a quarreling woman is harmful indeed; for through the perfection of her senses is the mind of man corrupted" [1, vv. 1205–7]. This is a double paradox, for not only is woman, in the medieval discourse of misogyny, associated with the senses, but also she serves, as we see here, to corrupt them.

56. "The illness called 'heroes' (Eros) is a melancolic anxiety caused by the love for a woman.

"Cause. The cause of this disease is the corruption of judgment by means of the ardent attachment to form and figure. Whence as someone is seized by love for a woman: thus does he strongly meditate on her form and figure and manner, since he believes that she is better, more beautiful, more worthy of respect, more splendid and more well-endowed of body and of character than any other. And for that reason he burns with desire for her. And without bound or limit he thinks that if he could attain his goal, that this felicity and beatitude would be his" (Bernard of Gordon, *Lilium medicinae,* cited by John Livingston Lowes, "The Loveres Maladye of Heroes," *Modern Philology* 11 [1914]: 499). I am grateful to John Graham for pointing this out to me in his dissertation, "The Poetics of Interpretation: The Courtly Lyric as a Socially Symbolic Act" (Ph.D. diss., Yale University, 1989), 260. See also Mary Wack, "Imagination, Medicine, and Rhetoric in Andreas Capellanus' 'De Amore'," in *Magister Regis: Studies in Honor of Robert Earl Kaske,* ed. Arthur Groos (New York: Fordham University Press, 1986), 101–15.

57.

Si puet on par cest dist aprendre	*One can learn by this story that one should*
C'on ne doit blasmer ne reprendre	*blame neither lovers nor their friends; for*
Les amies ne les amanz,	*love has power and command over all, both*
Qu'amors a pooir et commanz	*men and women, and does its will with all*
Par deseur toz et deseur toutes,	*of them, and finishes all business with*
Et d'euls fet ses volentez toutes,	*honor. . . . This is the truth, and I tell it,*
Et tret a honor toz ses fez. . . .	*that love conquers all and will conquer all*
Veritez est, et je le di,	*as long as the world will exist.* Thus ends
Qu'amors vaint tout et tout vaincra	the lay of Aristotle. ("Le Lai
Tant com cis siecles durera.	d'Aristote," *Recueil,* vol. 5, 262)
Explicit li lais d'Aristote.	

58.

Que diront les logiciens
De leurs sophismes anciens,
Quant leur docteur et leur seigneur
Fu a confusion greigneur
Qu'onques mais ne fu fol tondu? . . . .
Las! Que dira philosophie,
Quant figure d'amphibolie
A le grant maistre deceü?
(1, vv. 1137–44)

59. "Celle qui parle et ne dit jamais rien" (Boileau, Satire X, in *Oeuvres complètes*, 79).

60. John of Salisbury, for example: "Grammar is the cradle of all philosophy. . . . It is called 'grammar' from the basic elements of writing and speaking. *Gramma* means a letter or line, and grammar is 'literal' "; "the twofold meaning of 'logic' stems from its Greek etymology, for in the latter language '*logos*' means both 'word' and 'reason' (*Metalogicon*, ed. Daniel D. McGarry [Berkeley: University of California Press, 1962], 37).

61. See Colish, *The Mirror of Language*, 225.

62. Compare Jehan's example of the woman who makes her husband believe that the moon is a cowhide: "A methe de fauls est mené/ Le fol mari mal assené;/ De femme ne se puet deffendre./ De la lune nous font entendre/ Par paroles et par revel/ Que soit une peau de veël" ("He is led to a fool's end, the crazy, unfortunate husband; he cannot defend himself against a woman. With her words and her riotousness she makes us believe that the moon is a cowhide" [1, vv. 1013–18]).

63. Andreas Capellanus, *The Art of Courtly Love*, ed. John J. Parry (New York: W. W. Norton, 1969), 201, 207.

64. It is perhaps ironic that the most univocal articulation of the essence of medieval poetry as doubling is contained in the "Prologue" to the *Lais* of Marie de France, France's first woman poet:

Custume fu as ancïens,
Ceo testimoine Precïens,
Es livres ke jadis feseient,
Assez oscurement diseient
Pur ceus ki a venir esteient
Et ki aprendre le deveient,
K'i peussent gloser la lettre
Et de lur sen le surplus
  mettre. . . .

As Priscian bears witness, it was the custom of the Ancients to speak obscurely enough in their books so that those who came afterward and would be obliged to teach [or learn] them would be able to gloss the letter and with their sense [meaning] fill in the rest. (Marie de France, *Lais*, ed. Jean Rychner [Paris: Champion, 1983], "Prologue," vv. 1–8)

65. Walter Map, *De nugis curialium*, ed. Montague James (London: Cymmrodorion Society, 1923), 160–61 (emphasis mine).

66. Andreas Capellanus, *The Art of Courtly Love*, 204.

67. Walter Map, *De nugis curialium*, 164.

68. Someone as rhetorically indulgent as Tertullian is, again, fully aware of the paradox (see above note 29).

69. *The Art of Courtly Love*, 204, 205.

70. Ibid., 210–11.

71. Ibid., 204.

72. Ibid., 206, 187.

73.

Je sçai, que c'est un texte où chacun fait sa glose: Que de maris trompez tout rit dans l'univers, Epigrammes, Chansons,Rondeaux, Fables en vers, Satire, Comedie; et sur cette matiere J'ay veu tout ce qu'ont fait La Fontaine et Moliere: J'ay leu tout ce qu'ont dit Villon et Saint-Gelais Arioste, Marot, Bocace, Rabelais, Et tous ces vieux Recueils de Satires naïves, Des malices du Sexe immortelles archives.	*I know that it is a text in which everyone makes his gloss: everything in the universe laughs at cuckolded husbands: epigrams, songs, rondeaux, fables in verse, satire, comedy; and speaking of this matter, I have seen all that La Fontaine and Molière have done with it; I have read all that Villon and Saint-Gelais have said, as well as Ariosto, Marot, Boccaccio, Rabelais, and all the old collections of early satires, which make up the immortal archives of the ills of Sex. (Oeuvres complètes, 64–65)*

74. Proudhon attempts to calculate the comparable physical, intellectual, and moral worth of the female versus the male in order to determine the proper ratio of their political representation: "Unconnected ideas, illogical reasonings, illusions taken for reality, empty analogies made into principles, a cast of mind fatally inclined toward destruction: this is the intelligence of woman. . . . And since where economic, political, and social life are concerned the body and mind work together, each increasing the effect of the other, the physical and intellectual worth of man compared to that of woman strikes a ratio of 3 x 3 to 2 x 2, or 9 to 4. Without doubt, if woman contributes to social order and social wealth to the degree that is appropriate for her, it is just

that her voice be heard; but where in the general assembly man's vote will count for 9, that of woman will count for 4: this is dictated by both arithmetic and Justice" (Proudhon, *De la Justice*, 348, 361).

75. "Against women there is no serious means of repression. Simple imprisonment is already a difficulty. . . . They corrupt everything, break everything; no closure is powerful enough. . . . They overturn justice, destroying all notion of it, causing it to be cursed and denied." The content of this passage, it must be said, is not as prejudicial as it may sound, since Michelet here argues against executing women because of their special mystery ("they are indeed responsible but not punishable"). The passage continues: "But to lead them to the scaffold, great God! A government guilty of such a stupidity guillotines itself. . . . In all the Revolution, I find them violent, conspiring, quite often guiltier than the men. But once one strikes them, one strikes onself" (*Histoire de la Révolution*, vol. 7, 2; cited in Roland Barthes, *Michelet* [New York: Hill & Wang, 1987], 168).

76. Charles Baudelaire, *Curiosités esthétiques* (Paris: Garnier, 1962), 492.

77. Ibid., 488.

78. *Oeuvres complètes* (Paris: Gallimard, 1975), 1272. Baudelaire's attitude toward woman is extremely complicated and sometimes seems no less contradictory than that of the thirteenth-century satirists discussed above. For the same poet who assimilates woman to her dress elsewhere denounces her for being on the side of nature—"la femme est naturelle, c'est-à-dire abominable"—which for the symbolist, as for the medieval theologian, is already the mask of a more essential reality.

79. *Oeuvres complètes* (Paris: Gallimard, 1945), 716–17.

80. Cited in Schor, *Reading in Detail*, 17.

81. Lombroso, *La Femme criminelle*, 180; Virey, *De l'Influence des femmes*, 17, 9, 16.

82. Baudelaire, *Curiosités esthétiques*, 470.

83. Friedrich Nietzsche, *Twilight of the Idols*, ed. Oscar Levy (London: T. N. Foulis, 1911), 5. Nietzsche too participates in the topical alliance of the feminine and the cosmetic: "Comparing man and woman on the whole, one may say: woman would not have the genius for finery if she did not have the instinct for a *secondary* role" (*Beyond Good and Evil*, 89).

84. Nietzsche, *Twilight of the Idols*, 24. See Sarah Kofman, *Nietzsche et la scène philosophique* (Paris: Union Générale d'Editions, 1979); Jacques Derrida, *Spurs/Eperons*, trans. Barbara Harlow (Chicago: University of Chicago Press, 1979). Further, Nietzsche maintains, if one of the feminine ruses is a pretense to the ideal, or to truth, this pretense ends necessarily in the anarchy of revenge. "By raising themselves higher, as 'woman in herself,' as the 'higher woman,' as a female 'idealist,' they want to lower the level of the general rank of woman; and there is no surer means for that than higher

education, slacks, and political voting-cattle rights" (Nietzsche, *Ecce Homo*, trans. Walter Kaufmann [New York: Vintage, 1969], 267).

85. The context is his commentary on (Mme.) Daniel Stern's *Histoire des Pays-Bas:* "Le lire, en effet, cette histoire, est manifestement un livre de femme, malgré toutes les peines que l'auteur se donne. Il est de femme par le manque d'aperçu, de profondeur, d'originalité, de vigeur enflammée; qualités viriles que les femmes n'ont pas, parce qu'elles en ont d'autres, la grâce, l'élégance, la finesse, le coloris doux, la tendresse, l'inattendu, la sensation vive que Mme Stern n'a pas non plus!" (Barbey d'Aurevilly, *Les Bas-bleus*, 79).

86. Ibid., 7.

87. Jules Michelet, *La Sorcière* (Paris: E. Denton, 1862), 131.

88. Ibid., 100.

89. Brunetière, to offer one prominent example, claims that the great writers of the sixteenth and seventeenth centuries submitted the poetry without poetry of the Middle Ages to the "rules of composition, the laws of style" (Ferdinand Brunetière, "L'Erudition contemporaine et la littérature française du moyen âge," in *Etudes critiques sur l'histoire de la littérature française* [Paris: Hachette, 1888], 49).

90. *De l'influence des femmes*, 23.

91. Proudhon, *De la Justice*, 378. Proudhon actually situates the great moment of effeminization of French literature in Rousseau: "Le moment d'arrêt de la littérature française commence à Rousseau. Il est le premier de ces *femmelins* de l'intelligence, en qui l'idée se troublant, la passion ou affectivité l'emporte sur la raison, et qui, malgré des qualités éminentes, viriles même, font incliner la littérature et la société vers leur déclin" (ibid., 379).

CHAPTER THREE

1. McNamara, "Sexual Equality and the Cult of Virginity," 145.

2. "Homily 13" on the Letter to the Ephesians in *A Select Library of the Nicene and Post-Nicene Fathers*, ed. Philip Schaff (Grand Rapids, Mich.: Eerdmans, 1956), vol. 4, 116; *PL*, vol. 62, 99.

3. See Miles, *Carnal Knowing*, xi; Caroline Bynum, *Jesus as Mother: Studies in the Spirituality of the High Middle Ages* (Berkeley: University of California Press, 1982), 203–9, 259–61.

4. Quéré-Jaulmes, *La Femme*, 211; *PL*, vol. 38, 1284–85.

5. Elizabeth Castelli perceptively makes just such a suggestion: "The demand to renounce passion is therefore much more poignant when applied to women because passion itself has been located in the idea of female selfhood. The construction of the

feminine as passion means that women, the embodiment or the cultural representation of the feminine, are erased by that repression of passion. Therefore, for a woman to participate in the institution which calls for the negation of the feminine is, on one level, for her to participate in a profound self-abnegation, self-denial, even self-destruction" ("Virginity and Its Meaning for Women's Sexuality in Early Christianity," *Journal of Feminist Studies in Religion* 2 [1986]: 88).

6. Quéré-Jaulmes, *La Femme*, 303; *PL*, vol. 39, 1990. One would certainly want to nuance the portrayal of Mary in terms of a liberator, for the Virgin and virginity are also thoroughly consonant, as we will see (chapter 5), with the growing asceticism of the second through fourth centuries, and it is arguable whether or not the denial of the flesh is beneficial to women.

7. Cited in Quéré-Jaulmes, *La Femme*, 230; *PG*, vol. 35, 789–817.

8. Ibid., 242; *PG*, vol. 46, 960–1000.

9. Cited in McNamara, "Sexual Equality and the Cult of Virginity," 149.

10. See Peter Brown, *The Body and Society,* 369; Elizabeth Clark, "Jerome, Chrysostom, and Friends," *Studies in Women and Religion* 2 (1979): 1–106; "Ascetic Renunciation and Feminine Advancement: A Paradox of Late Ancient Christianity," *Anglican Theological Review* 43 (1981): 252.

11. Cited in Quéré-Jaulmes, *La Femme*, 213; *PL*, vol. 38, 1284–85.

12. One solution certainly has been simply to accept literally the double truth of the orders of creation and redemption through the phrase "subordination and equivalence," which not only runs throughout the literature on early Christian attitudes toward gender, but also is elaborated in a volume whose title is its thesis (Kari Elisabeth Børresen, *Subordination and Equivalence: The Nature and Role of Women in Augustine and Thomas Aquinas* [Washington, D.C.: University Press of America, 1981]). But, while this particular formula allows us to reconcile texts that contradict each other by positing Averroistically the simultaneity of conflicting frames of reference and of understanding, I am not sure that it resolves the contradiction except in the most passive sense of repeating orthodox Christian doctrine; on the contrary, it is a reinscription of the problem of radically contradictory attitudes towards femininity and gender. See also Shahar, *The Fourth Estate,* 23; Miles, *Carnal Knowing,* 30.

13. See James A. Brundage, *Law, Sex, and Christian Society in Medieval Europe* (Chicago: University of Chicago Press, 1987), 59. Constance Parvey, "The Theology and Leadership of Women in the New Testament," in *Religion and Sexism,* ed. Rosemary Ruether (New York: Simon & Schuster, 1974), 136; Rogers, *The Troublesome Helpmate,* 11.

14. David Winston, trans. and introd., *Philo of Alexandria: The Contemplative Life, The Giants, and Selections* (New York: Paulist Press, 1981), 322; this is also the thesis of Tobin, *Philo.*

15. Elizabeth Schüssler Fiorenza, *In Memory of Her,* 256.

16. Rambaux, *Tertullien,* 257.

17. Warner, *Alone of All Her Sex,* 68–69.

18. Carolly Erickson, *The Medieval Vision: Essays in History and Perception* (New York: Oxford University Press, 1976), 194; Brundage, *Law, Sex, and Christian Society,* 2.

19. Elaine Pagels, *Adam, Eve, and the Serpent* (New York: Random House, 1988), 126–45.

20. Brundage, *Law, Sex, and Christian Society,* 9.

21. Paul Veyne, in fact, makes a strong case for a lack of difference between Christian attitudes towards sexuality and those of the evolving surrounding Roman milieu. See Paul Veyne, "La Famille et l'amour sous le haut-empire romain," *Annales* 33 (1978): 35–63; *A History of Family Life, I: From Pagan Rome to Byzantium* (Cambridge, Mass.: Harvard University Press, 1987), 217.

22. Hays, *The Dangerous Sex,* 81, 104; Warner, *Alone of All Her Sex,* 48.

23. Mary Hayter, *The New Eve in Christ* (Grand Rapids, Mich.: Eerdmans, 1987), 14–17.

24. Jean-Marie Aubert, for example, maintains that the Eve story is "le legs antiféministe le plus important du judaïsme transmis à la tradition chrétienne" (*La Femme,* 18). Pagels makes a similar claim in *Adam, Eve, and the Serpent,* xxi.

25. See Brundage, *Law, Sex, and Christian Society,* 65; Pagels, *Adam, Eve, and the Serpent,* 3.

26. Katherine Rogers writes, "In early Greek culture . . . traces of matriarchy are still apparent, and the reaction against women is consequently more bitter" (*The Troublesome Helpmate,* 41).

27. "The lover and the uxorious did not merely sink into a suspect state of emotional dependence on a woman; physiologically, their progressive loss of heat threatened to make them 'womanish'. . . . A powerful 'fantasy of the loss of vital spirit' lay at the root of many late classical attitudes to the male body. It is one of the many notions that gave male continence a firm foothold in the folk wisdom of the world in which Christian celibacy would soon be preached. . . . The most virile man was the man who had kept most of his vital spirit—the one, that is, who lost little or no seed" (Brown, *The Body and Society,* 19); see also Michel Foucault, *The History of Sexuality,* trans. Robert Hurley (New York: Vintage, 1988), 143.

28. Fiorenza, *In Memory of Her,* 256, 257.

29. See Brundage, *Law, Sex, and Christian Society,* 17, 75; Colish, *Stoic Tradition;* Rambaux, *Tertullien,* 56–58.

30. Soranus, *Gynecology,* ed. Owsei Temkin (Baltimore: Johns Hopkins University Press, 1956), 27.

31. See Erickson, *Medieval Vision*, 204.

32. See Robert D. Brown, *Lucretius on Love and Sex* (Leiden: E. J. Brill, 1987).

33. Prusak, "Pseudepigraphical Myth," 89–116.

34. Brown, *The Body and Society*, 99.

35. Brundage, *Law, Sex, and Christian Society*, 62.

36. Brown, *The Body and Society*, 113; also 112–19; Jorunn Jacobson Buckley, *Female Fault and Fulfillment in Gnosticism* (Chapel Hill: University of North Carolina Press, 1986); Pagels, *Adam, Eve, and the Serpent*, 59–77; Fiorenza, *In Memory of Her*, 271–74.

37. Clement of Alexandria, *Stromateis* 3.63 (cited in Fiorenza, *In Memory of Her*, 271); *Pseudo-Clementine Homilies* 2.15.3 (cited ibid.).

38. "And when he saw her, he said, 'It is you who have given me life: you shall be called Mother of the Living [Eve]; for it is she who is my Mother. It is she who is the Physician, and the Woman, and She Who Has Given Birth'" (cited in Pagels, *Adam, Eve, and the Serpent*, 66). See also Elaine Pagels, *The Gnostic Gospels* (New York: Random House, 1979), chap. 3.

39. Cited in Elizabeth Clark, "Devil's Gateway and the Brides of Christ: Women in the Early Christian World," in *Ascetic Piety and Women's Faith: Essays on Late Ancient Christianity, Studies in Women and Religion* 20 (1986): 35–36.

40. See Brown, *The Body and Society*, 377; Brundage, *Law, Sex, and Christian Society*, 84–85; Philippe Delhaye, "Le Dossier anti-matrimonial de l'*Adversus Jovinianum* et son influence sur quelques écrits latins du XIIe siècle," *Medieval Studies* 13 (1951): 65–86; Pagels, *Adam, Eve, and the Serpent*, 91; Pratt, "Jankyn's Book of Wikked Wyves," 5–27.

41. David Herlihy, *Medieval Households* (Cambridge, Mass.: Harvard University Press, 1985), 23–26.

42. Diane Boorstein, "Antifeminism," in *Dictionary of the Middle Ages*, ed. Joseph R. Strayer (New York: Scribners, 1982), vol. 1, 322; Pierre J. Payer, *Sex and the Penitentials: The Development of a Sexual Code: 550–1150* (Toronto: University of Toronto Press, 1984), 47.

43. William P. Le Saint, for example: "If her [the early church's] asceticism seems misguided and severe by modern standards, we may be helped to understand it by reflecting that it was, at least in part, a reaction of disgust at the degrading licentiousness of her pagan surroundings" (*Tertullian: Treatises on Marriage and Remarriage* [Westminster, Md.: The Newman Press, 1951], 4).

44. See Philippe Ariès, "Saint Paul and the Flesh," in *Western Sexuality: Practice and Precept in Past and Present Times*, ed. Philippe Ariès and André Béjin, trans. Anthony Forster (Oxford: Blackwell, 1985), 38; Aubert, *La Femme*, 60; John Boswell,

Christianity, Social Tolerance, and Homosexuality (Chicago: University of Chicago Press, 1980), 61-137; Foucault, *History of Sexuality,* vol. 3, 1-133; Hays, *The Dangerous Sex,* 108; Veyne, "La Famille et l'amour," 45; Paul Veyne, "Homosexuality in Ancient Rome," in Ariès and Béjin, eds., *Western Sexuality,* 26-35.

45. See Rogers, *The Troublesome Helpmate,* 41; Hays, *The Dangerous Sex,* 281.

46. *In Memory of Her,* 90; see also Parvey, "The Theology and Leadership of Women," 117-49; Ruether, "Misogynism," 150-83.

47. "Toutes les transformations de la sexualité et de la conjugalité sont antérieures au christianisme. Les deux principales font passer, d'une bissexualité de sabrage, à une hétérosexualité de reproduction; et d'une société où le mariage n'est nullement une institution faite pour toute la société, à une société où il 'va de soi' que 'le' mariage est une institution fondamentale de toutes les sociétés (croit-on) et de la société toute entière" (Veyne, "La Famille et l'Amour," 39). See also Veyne, "Homosexuality in Ancient Rome," 26-35.

48. "It appears that marriage became more general as a practice, more public as an institution, more private as a mode of existence—a stronger force for binding conjugal partners and hence a more effective one for isolating the couple in a field of other social relations" (Foucault, *History of Sexuality,* vol. 3, 77).

49. "There is pain always," writes Gregory of Nyssa, "whether children are born, or can never be expected; whether they live or die. One person has many children, but not enough means to support them; another feels the lack of an heir to the great fortune he has worked for. . . . One man loses by death a beloved son; another has a reprobate son alive; both equally pitiable, although one mourns over the death, the other over the life, of his son" (cited in Pagels, *Adam, Eve, and the Serpent,* 83).

50. "Even though they possessed a sophisticated medical tradition and were willing to practice contraception and abortion, the ruling classes of the Roman Empire could do little to alleviate pain and death in their wives" (*The Body and Society,* 25). "The successful running of a Christian household demanded the close collaboration of husband and wife. It assumed the dominance of the male within the family, of the husband over his wife, and of the father over his children. By successfully absorbing the young wife into his household, the husband would cut her off from the alluring 'vainglory' of civic life. Gently, but firmly, she was to be molded, 'like wax,' by her husband. . . . She would learn to cut back on her jewelry and dress; for she must not walk past the poor with the price of many dinners hanging from her ears" (ibid., 312).

51. Hays, *The Dangerous Sex,* 109. One should not, however, underestimate the importance of Paul: "It is possible to measure, in the repeated exegesis of a mere hundred words of Paul's letters, the future course of Christian thought on the human person. . . . The war of the spirit against the flesh and of the flesh against the spirit was a desperate image of human resistance to the will of God" (Brown, *The Body and Society,* 48).

52. "Dan le domaine sexuel, comme dans le domaine alimentaire, les théories et les prescriptions de Tertullien, s'accordent mieux avec ses hantises et ses problèmes personnels qu'avec l'Evangile, même considéré à travers les préférences que Paul n'a exprimées qu'une fois, à titre personnel, au début de sa carrière d'apôtre" (Rambaux, *Tertullien*, 258).

53. "For Augustine, the truth of his own experience (and so, he believes, of everyone's) involves, above all, human helplessness. Three primary experiences—infancy, sexuality, and mortality—offer, he believes, irrefutable evidence of such helplessness" (Pagels, *Adam, Eve, and the Serpent*, 139). Such personalized explanations of antifeminism also find later echoes in, say, the attribution of Milton's misogyny to unhappy experiences with women, or of that of Baudelaire to his mother's remarriage (Hays, *The Dangerous Sex*, 199–209).

54. Melanie Klein, "Early Stages of the Oedipus Conflict," *The International Journal of Psychoanalysis* 9 (1928): 170.

55. Rogers, *The Troublesome Helpmate*, 53. H. R. Hays writes: "All this can be related to the anxieties of the family situation. The sexually attractive mother and the competing, potentially dangerous father loom as all-powerful and both cause tensions in the helpless infant" (*The Dangerous Sex*, 35); see also Boorstein, "Antifeminism," 323; Du Bois, "'The Devil's Gateway'," 47, 51.

56. See Klein, "Early Stages of the Oedipus Complex," 173–78; Nancy Chodorow, *The Reproduction of Mothering* (Berkeley: University of California Press, 1978), 114–29.

57. "We must remember, however, that the male is dominant, he sets the pattern of the human being and the alien. His body and his biological processes are familiar and understandable and, by observation, he can see that other males are the same and therefore can be accepted into the category of the self versus the alien. But women are different. Despite a man's need for his mother's breast and his sexual attraction to her, she is not of his kind. . . . Woman, therefore, is alien, peculiarly filled with mana and, as we shall endeavor to show, a number of different situations combine to make him feel that her bad mana is more important than her beneficial potentialities" (Hays, *The Dangerous Sex*, 38).

58. "Here the domestication of animals and the breeding of herds had developed a hitherto unsuspected source of wealth and created entirely new social relations" (Friedrick Engels, *The Origin of the Family, Private Property and the State* [New York: International Publishers, 1972, rpt.], 117).

59. Ibid., 120.

60. "A simple decree sufficed that in the future the offspring of the male members should remain within the gens, but that of the female should be excluded by being transferred to the gens of their father. The reckoning of descent in the female line and

the matriarchal law of inheritance were thereby overthrown, and the male line of descent and the paternal law of inheritance were substituted for them" (ibid.).

61. Ibid.

62. *The Body and Society,* 61.

63. "As his [Justin's] *Apology* made plain, strict codes of sexual discipline were made to bear much of the weight of providing the Christian Church with a distinctive code of behavior. Sexual prohibitions had always distinguished Jews, in their own eyes at least, from the sinister indeterminacy of the gentiles. These were now asserted with exceptional vigor. Christian marital codes were rendered yet more idiosyncratic by a few novel features, such as the relinquishment of divorce and a growing prejudice against the remarriage of widows and widowers. Above the solid conglomerate of ancient, Jewish notions there now rose the peak of total chastity. Whatever exotic associations the gesture of continence might have had for the Christians themselves, outsiders could admire it as a form of physical heroism equivalent to the observed capacity of Christians to face down the chill fear of death" (ibid., 60).

64. Ibid., 243, 251.

65. Pagels, *Adam, Eve, and the Serpent,* 105. "The eventual triumph of Augustine's theology required, however, the capitulation of all who held to the classical proclamation concerning human freedom, once so widely regarded as the heart of the Christian gospel. By the beginning of the fifth century those who still held to such archaic traditions—notably including those the Catholics called Donatists and Pelagians—came to be condemned as heretics. Augustine's theory of Adam's fall, once espoused in simpler forms only by marginal groups of Christians, now moved, together with the imperially supported Catholic church that proclaimed it, into the center of western history" (Brown, *The Body and Society,* 126).

66. Jack Goody, *The Development of the Family and Marriage in Europe* (Cambridge: Cambridge University Press, 1983), 4.

67. Ibid., 81.

68. See also Luke 12:49–53.

69. Elizabeth Clark writes: "Once the women had given up those signs of the old world of 'structure,' namely husbands, children, and property, they were ready to be inducted into the new family of ascetics who were 'mothers,' 'fathers,' 'sisters,' and 'brothers' to each other. Jerome is as ready to adopt anyone as his own relative as he is to 'relate' his widows and virgins to other Christians. Thus he accepts Marcella's mother Albina as his own; he calls himself Blaesilla's 'father in the spirit, her guardian in affection'; all Christians are his children; and he urges Christian ascetics to view each other as foster-fathers, brothers, and so forth, depending on their age in relation to each other" ("Jerome, Chrysostom, and Friends," 54–55).

70. See Brown, *The Body and Society,* 23; Herlihy, *Medieval Households,* 11; McNamara, "Sexual Equality and the Cult of Virginity," 149.

71. Jerome, *Letters,* letter 22, 1, p. 22.

72. Brown, *The Body and Society,* 145, 152. See also Elizabeth Castelli, "Virginity and Its Meaning for Women's Sexuality," 61–88; Clark, "Ascetic Renunciation and Feminine Advancement," 240–57; R. Kraemer, "The Conversion of Women to Ascetic Forms of Christianity," *Signs* 6 (1980/81): 298–307; Pagels, *Adam, Eve, and the Serpent,* 88–89; Aline Rousselle, *Porneia: De la maîtrise du corps à la privation sensorielle, IIe–IVe siècles de l'ère chrétienne* (Paris: Presses Universitaires de France, 1983).

73. See *Women of Spirit: Female Leadership in the Jewish and Christian Traditions,* ed. Eleanor McLaughlin and Rosemary Ruether (New York: Simon & Schuster, 1979); John G. Gager, *Kingdom and Community: The Social World of Early Christianity* (Englewood Cliffs, N.J.: Prentice-Hall, 1975); Gerd Thiessen, "Itinerant Radicalism: The Tradition of Jesus Sayings from the Perspective of the Sociology of Literature," in *Radical Religion: The Bible and Liberation* (Community for Religious Research and Education, 1976), 84–93; Robin Scroggs, "The Earliest Christian Communities as Sectarian Movement," in *Christianity, Judaism and Other Greco-Roman Cults,* ed. Jacob Neusner (Leiden: E. J. Brill, 1975), vol. 1, 1–23.

74. "While the a-sexual and a-familial ethos of early Christianity is often misunderstood as antisexual and antiwomen, it actually is an indication of a 'role-revolt' which allowed women to 'legitimately' move out of the confines of the patriarchal family and to center their life around the spiritual self-fulfillment and independence that gave them greater respect, mobility, and influence" (Fiorenza, *In Memory of Her,* 90). "Insofar as the Christian movement rejected both sexual dimorphism and patriarchal domination as well [*sic*] broke down the rigid separation between the public and private religious spheres, it supported and advanced women's cultural-political emancipation" (ibid., 91). Marina Warner terms it a "revolution": "in spite of the misogyny that underpins the Christian religion, it offered women a revolution, as long as they subscribed to its precepts" (Warner, *Alone of All Her Sex,* 72). Elizabeth Clark writes: "It is one of the ironies of Christian history that the ascetic movement, which had so many features denigrating of women and marriage, became *the* movement that, more than any other, provided 'liberation' of a sort for Christian women" ("Devil's Gateway and the Brides of Christ," 19); See also Jane Tibbetts Schulenberg, "The Heroics of Virginity: Brides of Christ and Sacrificial Mutilation," in *Women in the Middle Ages and the Renaissance,* ed. Mary Beth Rose (Syracuse, N.Y.: Syracuse University Press, 1986), 41–42.

75. "What individuals find 'liberating' is relative, but perhaps the most important common denominator of the liberating choice is the sense of taking charge of one's own life; of rejecting a state of being governed and defined by others. One experiences the sense of moving from being an object to becoming a subject. I would argue that

asceticism could be and was experienced as that kind of liberating choice for women in the fourth century, for not only did it allow women to throw off the traditional female roles, but it offered female-directed communities where they could pursue the highest self-development as autonomous persons. It also offered security, for wealthy women endowed these communities for themselves and others. As a result, throngs of women were attracted to asceticism at this time, especially as the old Roman way of life was disintegrating" (Rosemary Ruether, "Mothers of the Church: Ascetic Women in the Late Patristic Age," in McLaughlin and Ruether, eds., *Women of Spirit,* 73). Peter Brown as well sees the choice of virginity, for men or for women, as a removal of the body from social control: "By the fourth century, such a view [dedication to virginity] had come to mean, in practice, that a number of young, well-placed persons, by deciding 'to make their bodies holy,' had, in fact, made plain that they considered that they had the right to dispose of their bodies as they pleased, by keeping them in their virgin state, out of circulation in society. Thus, the body itself was held to be no longer permeable to the demands that society made upon it" (Peter Brown, "The Notion of Virginity in the Early Church," in *Christian Spirituality: Origins to the Twelfth Century,* ed. Bernard McGinn and John Meyendorff [New York: Crossroad, 1985], 429).

76. "There is some ground in fact for regarding this religion during the first century in any event, as involved in a kind of women's liberation: from the powerful patriarchal and masculine orientation of the traditional family. To succeed in disengaging women from their family ties . . . it was necessary at one and the same time to denigrate the family and to proffer Christianity as itself a family—the highest of all types of families" (Robert Nisbet, *The Social Philosophers: Community and Conflict in Western Thought* [New York: Thomas Y. Crowell, 1973], 178). See also Naïté-Albistur, *Histoire du Féminisme français,* 12.

77. Fiorenza, *In Memory of Her,* 92. "Women who belonged to a submerged group in antiquity could develop leadership in the emerging Christian movement because it stood in conflict with the dominant patriarchal ethos of the Greco-Roman world. Therefore, the struggle and interaction of women in the Christian missionary movement can only be reconstructed as an integral part of the struggle between the emerging Christian movement and its alternative vision, on the one hand, and the dominant patriarchal ethos of the Greco-Roman world on the other. In this struggle women's leadership has become submerged again, transformed or pushed to the fringes of mainstream churches" (ibid.).

78. See Anne Yarbrough, "Christianization in the Fourth Century: The Example of Roman Women," *Church History* 45 (1976): 149–65.

79. *Acts of Paul and Thecla,* 7, 8, 9, 20 (cited in Pagels, *Adam, Eve, and the Serpent,* 18). For discussion of parental opposition to the choice not to marry, see Goody, *Development of the Family;* Brown, *The Body and Society,* especially 261–84, 343–46; Castelli, "Virginity and Its Meaning," 81–83; Pagels, *Adam, Eve, and the Serpent,* 18–22, 33–34.

80. Athanasius, *Life of Saint Anthony,* in *Early Christian Biographies,* ed. Roy J. Deferrari, vol. 15 of *Fathers of the Church* (Washington, D.C.: Catholic University of America Press, 1952), 133–224.

81. Ambrose, "Concerning Virgins," 373; *PL,* vol. 16, 218.

82. *Passio Sanctarum Perpetuae et Felicitatis,* trans. Herbert Musurillo, in *The Acts of the Christian Martyrs* (Oxford: Clarendon Press, 1972), 5, 6. See Mary Lefkowitz, *Heroines and Hysterics* (London: Duckworth, 1981), 53–58.

83. Francis X. Murphy, "Melania the Elder: A Biographical Note," *Traditio* 5 (1947): 65.

84. *Vita Melaniae Junioris,* trans. Elizabeth Clark, *The Life of Melania the Younger* (Lewiston, N.Y.: Edwin Mellen Press, 1984), vol. 1, 27–28.

85. Jerome, *Letters,* Letter 22, p. 30; *Select Letters,* 94.

86. *The Body and Society,* 261.

87. "Sexual renunciation might lead the Christian to transform the body and, in transforming the body, to break with the discreet discipline of the ancient city. By refusing to act upon the youthful stirrings of desire, Christians could bring marriage and childbirth to an end. With marriage at an end, the huge fabric of organized society would crumble like a sandcastle, touched by the 'ocean-flood of the Messiah' (*Acts of Judas Thomas* 31)" (Brown, *The Body and Society,* 31–32).

88. "The women of the Roman aristocracy pursued the genteel form of home asceticism without renouncing their wealth, though diverting it from the standard route of inheritance and thereby so disrupting the system of capital exchange within their class that eventually legislation was passed which prohibited such drainage of aristocratic holdings" (Castelli, "Virginity and Its Meaning," 83).

89. "The upper-class virgin was expected to be 'powerful in revenue, a mother to the poor'" (Brown, *The Body and Society,* 344).

90. See Castelli, "Virginity and Its Meaning," 62; Rousselle, *Porneia,* 231.

91. Castelli, "Virginity and Its Meaning," 85, 88.

92. For a brilliant discussion of the question of the use of women as objects of exchange, see Gayle Rubin, "The Traffic in Women: Notes on the Political Economy of Sex," in *Towards an Anthropology of Women,* ed. Rayna R. Reiter (New York: Monthly Review Press, 1975), 157–210.

93. See Bynum, *Jesus as Mother; Holy Feast and Holy Fast: The Religious Significance of Food to Medieval Women* (Berkeley: University of California Press, 1987).

CHAPTER FOUR

1. *PL,* vol. 16, 217.

2. See McNamara, "Sexual Equality and the Cult of Virginity," 153.

3.

Buona pulcella fut Eulalia,
Bel auret corps, bellezour anima.
Voldrent la veintre li Deo inimi,
Voldrent la faire diaule servir.
Elle no'nt eskoltet les mals
    conselliers,
Qu'elle Deo raneiet, chi maent
    sus en ciel,
Ne por or ned argent ne
    paramenz,
Por manatce regiel ne preiement;
Niule cose non la pouret omque
    pleier
La polle sempre non amast lo
    Deo menestier.
E por o fut presentede
    Maximiien,
Chi rex eret a cels dis soure
    pagiens.
Il li enortet, dont lei nonque
    chielt,
Qued elle fuiet lo nom christiien.
Ell' ent adunet lo suon element;
Melz sostendreiet les
    empedementz
Qu'elle perdesse sa virginitét;
Por os furet morte a grand
    honestét.

*A virtuous maiden was Eulalia, fair was
her body and fairer yet her soul. The
enemies of God would fain have vanquished
her, would make her serve the Evil One.
But she heeds not the wicked counsellors,
counselling her to renounce God who dwells
on high, nay not for gold or silver or fine
apparel nor a king's threats or pleading.
Nothing could ever bend her from steadfast
love for the service of her Lord. For this she
was brought before Maximian, who in
those days ruled over the pagans. He
exhorts her (but little does it reck her) to
flee the name of Christian. It does but
make her summon up her strength: rather
would she bear with persecution than that
she should lose her virgin innocence.*
(Alfred Ewert, ed. and trans., *French*
[London: Faber & Faber, 1933], 353)

Thus too, Alexis on his wedding night:

Quant an la cambra furent tut sul
    remés,
Danz Alexis la prist ad apeler:
La mortel vithe li prist mult a
    blasmer,
De la celeste li mostret veritét;
Mais lui est tart quet il s'en seit
    turnét.
"Oz mei pulcele! Celui tien ad
    espus

*When they were left all alone in the
chamber, sir Alexis began to upbraid her,
greatly did he begin to condemn this
earthly life, and shows her the truth of the
heavenly; but he is impatient to be gone.
"Hear me, maiden! Take him to spouse
who redeemed us with his precious blood. In
this world there is no perfect love: life is
frail, there is no lasting honour, this joy
turns to great sorrow." When he has told*

Ki nus raens[t] secle nen at parfit
amor,
La vithe est fraisle, n'i ad durable
honur;
Cesta lethece revert a grant
tristur."
Quant sa raisun li ad tute
mustrethe,
Pois li cumandet les renges de
s'espethe
Et un anel, a Deu l'(i) ad
comandethe.
Dunc en eissit de la cambre sum
pedre;
Ensur[e] nuit s'en fuit de la
contrethe.

*her his whole mind, then he commits to her
the baldric of his sword and a ring; he
commends her to God. Then he went forth
from the chamber of his father. During the
night he flees from the country.* (Ibid.,
357)

4. Joseph Bédier, *Les Fabliaux* (Paris: Champion, 1925); Per Nykrog, *Les Fabliaux* (Copenhagen: Munksgaard, 1957); Robert Dubuis, *Les Cent nouvelles nouvelles et la tradition de la nouvelle en France au moyen âge* (Grenoble: Presses Universitaires de Grenoble, 1973); Emmanuèle Baumgartner, "A Propos du Mantel Mantaillié," *Romania* 96 (1975): 315–32.

5. *Recueil*, vol. 3, 8. For a discussion of this tale, see my *Scandal of the Fabliaux* (Chicago: University of Chicago Press, 1986), 22–58.

6. " . . . cest corn fist une fee/ ranmponeuse, iree,/ e le corn destina/ que ja houm(e) n'i bev(e)ra,/ tant soit sages ne fous,/ s'il est cous ne gelous;" ("This horn was made by a mocking spiteful fairy who prescribed that, however wise or foolish, no man who has been a cuckold or jealous will ever drink from it") (*Mantel et Cor: Deux lais du xiie siècle*, ed. Philip Bennett [Exeter: University of Exeter Press, 1975], vv. 229–34).

7. McLaughlin, "Equality of Souls," 217.

8. Jerome, *Letters*, letter 22, p. 29; *Select Letters*, 92.

9. *De institutione angelica*, civ (cited in Bugge, *Virginitas*, 31; *PL*, vol. 16, 345). Brown, "Notion of Virginity," 433; see also Brown, *The Body and Society*, 187.

10. Jerome, *Letters*, letter 22, p. 30; *Select Letters*, 98.

11. Methodius, *The Symposium*, 39; see also 67; Gregory of Nyssa, *On Virginity*, in *Ascetical Works*, trans. Virginia Callahan (Washington: Catholic University of America Press, 1967), 46, 59. "La Virginité perfectionne donc le mariage mystique, sous ses deux formes. Union spirituelle, hors de la chair, elle est en ce bas monde la restitution de l'état paradisiaque, l'anticipation de l'état eschatologique, une conformation plus complète à la resurrection de Christ" (Crouzel, *Virginité*, 26).

12. See Warner, *Alone of All Her Sex*, 72–73.

13. Methodius, *The Symposium*, 150, 149. It is in this sense that virginity becomes a central virtue for the church fathers, the organizing principle of what Michel Foucault has analyzed in the third volume of the *History of Sexuality* in terms of the "techniques of the self" as they were set into place in the early centuries of Christianity. See also Michel Foucault, "Le Combat de la chasteté," *Communications* 35 (1982): 15–21.

14. *Glossa Palatina* to C. 31 q. 1 c. 11 v. *obtrectatores*, Trinity O. 10.2, fol. 55ra (cited Brundage, *Law, Sex, and Christian Society*, 366).

15. Comm. in Matt, xvi, 7–8 (cited in Crouzel, *Virginité*, 101). The "Penitential of Vinnian," however, states that the penance differs, depending on whether or not one has succeeded (see Payer, *Sex and the Penitentials*, 48).

16. Jerome, *Adversus Jovinianum*, 357; *PL*, vol. 23, 231. Chrysostom, *On Virginity*, 115.

17. Jerome, *Letters*, letter 22, p. 29; *Select Letters*, 92.

18. Jerome, *Letters*, letter 107, p. 191; *Select Letters*, 350. The disparagement of the ornamental extends logically even to the language arts. Jerome's admonishment of virgins to prefer grammar over decorated manuscripts amounts to a preference for grammar over rhetoric: "Let her treasures be not silks or gems but manuscripts of the holy scriptures; and in these let her think less of gilding, and Babylonian parchment, and arabesque patterns, than of correctness and accurate punctuation" (ibid., letter 107, p. 194; *Select Letters*, 364). Ambrose makes the same analogy between marriage and the cosmetic in speaking of wives: "And in this position spring up those incentives to vice, in that they paint their faces with various colours, fearing not to please their husbands; and from staining their faces, come to think of staining their chastity. What madness is here, to change the fashion of nature and seek a painting" ("Concerning Virgins," 367; *PL*, vol. 16, 207).

19. Methodius, *Symposium*, 87.

20. Cyprian, "The Dress of Virgins," 35; *PL*, vol. 4, 444–45. See also Yves-Marie Duval, "L'Originalité du *De uirginibus* dans le mouvement ascétique occidental: Ambroise, Cyprien, Athanase," in *Ambroise de Milan: XVIe centenaire de son élection épiscopale*, ed. Yves-Marie Duval (Paris: Etudes Augustiniennes, 1974), 26–27.

21. Cyprian: "hence virgins in desiring to be adorned more elegantly, to go about more freely, cease to be virgins" ("The Dress of Virgins," 48; *PL*, vol. 4, 459).

22. Ibid., 39; *PL*, vol. 4, 448.

23. Tertullian, "On the Apparel," 19; *PL*, vol. 1, 1318.

24. This despite the fact that virginity, as a means of transcending the distortions of perception that emanate from the senses, is supposed to lead to a clarity of vision. Gregory of Nyssa writes: "For, just as the eye cleansed from rheum sees objects shining brightly in the distance in the air, so also the soul through incorruptibility acquires the power to perceive the Light. The goal of true virginity and zeal for incorruptibility

is the ability to see God, for the chief and first and only beautiful and good and pure is the God of all, and no one is so blind in mind as not to perceive that even by himself" (*On Virginity*, 46). Still, a virgin is supposed to be recognized when seen; see Erickson, *Medieval Vision*, 190.

25. *Didascalia apostolorum*, 10. See also Brundage, *Law, Sex, and Christian Society*, 302.

26. Cyprian, "The Dress of Virgins," 47–48; *PL*, vol. 4, 458–59.

27. Crouzel, *Virginité*, 101.

28. "On the Veiling of Virgins," 34, 28; *PL*, vol. 2, 904–5; vol. 2, 891.

29. Ibid., 29; *PL*, vol. 2, 892. One finds the same idea in the *Ancren Riwle:* "Likewise Bathsheba, by unclothing herself in David's sight, caused him to sin with her. . . . You, my dear sisters, if any one is desirous to see you, never think favourably of him, but [rather] believe him the less. I would not that any man should see you except he have special permission from your superior; for all the three sins of which I have just now spoken, and all the evil with regard to Dinah of which spoke previously, did not happen because the woman looked forwardly upon men, but it happened through their uncovering themselves in the sight of men, and doing that which made them liable to fall into sin" (*The Ancren Riwle: A Treatise on the Rules and Duties of Monastic Life*, ed. James Morton [New York: AMS Press, 1968], 57).

30. See Brundage, *Law, Sex, and Christian Society*, 161.

31. *Letters*, letter 107, 194; *Select Letters*, 362.

32. *Ancren Riwle*, 55.

33. Chrysostom, *Cohabitations suspectes*, 130; Clement of Rome, "Two Epistles Concerning Virginity," in *The Ante-Nicene Fathers*, ed. Alexander Roberts and James Donaldson (Buffalo: The Christian Literature Publishing Co., 1886), vol. 8, 64.

34. Tertullian, "On the Veiling of Virgins," 34; *PL*, vol. 2, 904.

35. All quotations are from *Works of Geoffrey Chaucer*, 145–47. The accidental quality of the beginning of "The Physician's Tale" is to be compared with the beginning of "Du Mantel mautaillié" in which "it happened that a young knight appeared in the middle of the road" (*Recueil*, vol. 3, 5).

36. I am indebted to Lee Patterson for pointing this out to me.

37.

"To yow, my lord, sire Apius so deere,
Sheweth youre povre servent Claudius
How that a knyght, called Virginius,
Agayns the lawe, agayn al equitee,
Holdeth, expres agayn the wyl of me,

My servant, which that is my thral by right.
Which fro myn hous was stole upon a nyght,
Whil that she was ful yong; this wol I preeve
By witnesse, lord, so that it nat yow greeve.
She nys his doghter nat, what so he seye.
Wherfore to yow, my lord the juge, I preye,
Yeld me my thral, if that it be youre wille."
Lo, this was al the sentence of his bille.
(vv. 179–91)

38. Anne Middleton, "The *Physician's Tale* and Love's Martyrs: 'Ensamples Mo Than Ten' as a Method in the *Canterbury Tales,*" *Chaucer Review* 8 (1973): 14, 21.

39. Charles Muscatine, *Poetry and Crisis in the Age of Chaucer* (Notre Dame, Ind.: University of Notre Dame Press, 1972), 139.

40. Emerson Brown, "What Is Chaucer Doing with the Physician and His Tale?" *Philological Quarterly* 60 (1981): 134, 141.

41. Brian Lee, "The Position and Purpose of *The Physician's Tale,*" *The Chaucer Review* 22 (1987): 154.

42. Sheila Delany, "Politics and the Paralysis of Poetic Imagination in *The Physician's Tale,*" *Studies in the Age of Chaucer* 3 (1981): 47–60.

43. Patricia Kean, *Chaucer and the Meaning of English Poetry* (London: Routledge & Kegan Paul, 1972), vol. 2, 183.

44. Lee, "Position and Purpose," 142, 155.

45. "'Eve looked on the forbidden apple, and saw it fair, and began to take delight in beholding it, and set her desire upon it, and took and ate of it, and gave of it to her lord.' Lo! how Holy Writ speaks; and how, searching deeply into the cause and origin, it tells how sin began. Thus did sight go before and prepare the way for guilty desire; and death followed, to which all mankind is subject. This apple, dear sisters, betokeneth every thing that excites guilty desire and delight in sin. When thou lookest upon a man thou art in Eve's case; thou lookest upon the apple" (*Ancren Riwle,* 55).

46. Brundage, *Law, Sex, and Christian Society,* 83.

47. Jerome, *Adversus Jovinianum,* 351; *PL,* vol. 23, 221. Methodius, *Symposium,* 141. "But the ornament of virginity is not like this. It does not detract from the one wearing it because it is not corporeal but wholly spiritual" (Chrysostom, *On Virginity,* 99).

48. "Homily 15," 441. Novatian too sees the idolatry engendered by the gaze to be the central avenue of seduction leading to all other transgressions: "And anything else that draws the eyes and soothes the ears of the spectators has at bottom either an idol, or a demon, or some deceased person. You have only to look into its origin and

foundation. Thus it was all devised by the devil because he knew full well that idolatry of itself is horrendous. He combined idolatry with spectacles so that idolatry would be loved through the pleasure that spectacles afforded" ("The Spectacles," 127; *PL*, vol. 4, 783).

49. "Homily 17," 116.

50. "The human ideal of continence, I mean that which is set forth by Greek philosophers, teaches that one should fight desire and not be subservient to it so as to bring it to practical effect. But our ideal is not to experience desire at all. Our aim is not that while a man feels desire he should get the better of it, but that he should be continent even respecting desire itself" (Clement of Alexandria, "On Marriage," 66).

51. Gregory of Nyssa, *On Virginity*, 27. "How do you, the living, listen to the Crucified One, the Healer of sin, when He orders us to follow Him and to carry a cross as a banner against the Adversary, if you are not crucified to the world and have not taken on the death of the flesh" (ibid., 74).

52. *Homilia* 7, 13, in David Amand de Mendieta, "La Virginité chez Eusèbe et l'ascéticisme familial dans la première moitié du IVe siècle," *Revue d'histoire ecclésiastique* 50 (1955): 784. See also Brown, *The Body and Society*, 175.

53. As Elizabeth Castelli points out, "Many of the ascetic women whose stories remain are considered laudable because they escaped the bonds of their feminine nature" ("Virginity and Its Meaning for Women's Sexuality," 75; also 88). See Miles, *Carnal Knowing*, 55–56.

54. See John Anson, "The Female Transvestite in Early Monasticism: Origin and Development of a Motif," *Viator* 5 (1974): 1–32; Vern Bullough, "Transvestites in the Middle Ages," *American Journal of Sociology* 6 (1974): 1381–94; Marie Delcourt, "Female Saints in Masculine Clothing," in *Hermaphrodite: Myths and Rites of the Bisexual Figure in Classical Antiquity*, trans. Jennifer Nicholson (London: Studio Books, 1961); Evelyne Patlagean, "L'Histoire de la femme déguisée en moine et l'évolution de la sainteté féminine à Byzance," *Studi medievali* 17 (1976): 597–623.

55. See Brown, *The Body and Society*, 268.

56. See Paul, 1 Corinthians 7:32–34. Elizabeth Clark writes: "Thus all the differentiating factors of life in the world are stripped away, sexuality and family associations are removed. All that remains is for the women to transcend their femaleness, even to become 'men'; they will then be counted as equals with male ascetics. . . . In the eyes of our male writers, sex is not a differentiating characteristic applicable to these women, so far behind have they left their femaleness" ("Jerome, Chrysostom, and Friends," 55). See also her "Ascetic Renunciation and Feminine Advancement," 245. Elizabeth Schüssler Fiorenza concurs: "Like Philo (and Aristotle) the Fathers consider man to be the paradigmatic human being and maleness to be symbolic of the divine. Whereas their philosophical and theological conceptuality assumes the natural inferiority of women and sees the feminine as symbolic of earthly, bodily, carnal reality, the logic of

their Christian beliefs imposed on them a recognition of the fact that all the baptized are equals. Their theological problem was: how can a Christian woman who was made inferior by her nature, law, and the social-patriarchal order achieve in her life the Christian equality which belongs to her as a disciple of Christ? The Fathers answered this question by declaring that a Christian woman is no longer a *woman*" (*In Memory of Her*, 277). See also Bynum, "'. . . And Woman His Humanity'," 257–88.

57. *Gospel of Thomas* in James M. Robinson, ed., *Nag Hammadi Library* (San Francisco: Harper & Row, 1977), 130; 472. See Marvin W. Meyer, "Making Mary Male: The Categories 'Male' and 'Female' in the Gospel of Thomas" *New Testament Studies* 31(1985): 554–70; Dennis MacDonald, *There Is No Male or Female* (Philadelphia: Fortress Press, 1987), 98–102; Elizabeth Schüssler Fiorenza, "Word, Spirit and Power: Women in Early Christian Communities," in *Women of Spirit*, 45.

58. Philo, *Quaestiones et solutiones in Genesim*, I.8: cited in MacDonald, *There Is No Male or Female*, 99.

59. *PL*, vol. 23, 533, 53. For an excellent discussion of the masculinization of ascetic women, see Castelli, "Virginity and Its Meaning," 74–75; also Miles, *Carnal Knowing*, xii, 55; Schulenberg, "The Heroics of Virginity," 32.

60. I am not unaware of the fact that according to a certain Christological logic, virginity can also be said to triumph over death. Gregory of Nyssa: "Corruption has its beginning in birth and those who refrain from procreation through virginity themselves bring about a cancellation of death by preventing it from advancing further because of them, and, by setting themselves as a kind of boundary stone between life and death, they keep death from going forward. If then, death is not able to outwit virginity, but through it comes to an end and ceases to be, this is clear proof that virginity is stronger than death" (*On Virginity*, 48).

61. Jerome, *Letters*, letter 107, 194; *Select Letters*, 366. Chrysostom, *On Virginity*, 96.

62. Novatian, "In Praise of Purity," 170; *PL*, vol. 4, 823.

63. Novatian continues: "Virginity means victory over pleasure. Virginity does not have children, but what is more, holds them in disdain" (ibid.; *PL*, vol. 4, 823).

64. Jerome, *Letters*, letter 22, p. 30; *Select Letters*, 94.

65. Tertullian, "On Exhortation to Chastity," 55; *PL*, vol. 2, 925.

66. Cyprian, "The Dress of Virgins," 37; *PL*, vol. 4, 446. See Schulenberg, "The Heroics of Virginity," 38–39.

67. Ambrose, "Concerning Virgins," 364; *PL*, vol. 16, 201.

68. Tertullian "On the Veiling of Virgins," 36; *PL*, vol. 2, 910. Indeed, as an Idea, the pure potentiality of virginity as absence becomes translated into a pure negativity, or vacuum, to which man is drawn. The author of the *Ancren Riwle*, for example, transforms the seductions of negativity into a rule of nature such that it becomes difficult to

distinguish the purity of virginity from the negative potential of vice: "For this reason it was ordained by God in the old law that a pit should be always covered; and if any pit were uncovered, and a beast fell into it, he that uncovered the pit should make it good. This is a very terrible word to a woman who exposes herself to the view of man. She is represented by the person who uncovers the pit. The pit is her fair face, and her white neck, and her light eye, and her hand, if she stretch it forth in his sight. And, moreover, her word is a pit, unless it be the better guarded; and all that belongs to her, whatsoever it be, through which single love might sooner be excited, our Lord calleth it a pit. He commands that this pit be always provided with a lid and covered, lest any beast fall into it and drown in sin. . . . The dog enters gladly where he finds an open door" (*Ancren Riwle*, 59).

69. Methodius, *The Symposium*, 111; "My fair virgins, nothing can so help a person towards virtue as chastity. For chastity alone causes the soul to be guided in the noblest and best possible way and to be washed clean of the stains and impurities of the world. . . . But from the moment when Christ became man and armed the flesh with the ornament of virginity, the cruel despot that rules incontinence was overpowered; and peace and faith reign, and men are not so much given to idol worship as they were of old" (ibid., 141).

70. Chrysostom, "Letter to the Fallen Theodore," 104.

71. Chrysostom, *On Virginity*, p. 104.

72. "For a virgin, though in her also character rather than body has the first claim, puts away calumny by the integrity of her body" ("Concerning Widows," in *Nicene and Post-Nicene Fathers*, vol. 10, ed. Philip Schaff and Henry Wace [New York: Christian Literature Publishing Co., 1896], 395; *PL*, vol. 16, 255).

73. See Brown, "What Is Chaucer Doing," 138.

74. This too is how Shakespeare understood Collatine's boast of Lucrece's chastity and the desire it elicits:

> Happ'ly that name of "chaste" unhapp'ly set
> This bateless edge on his keen appetite;
> When Collatine unwisely did not let
> To praise the clear unmatched red and white
> Which triumph'd in that sky of his delight;
>   ("The Rape of Lucrece," 8)

"The poem understands Collatine's praise of Lucrece, his 'boast of Lucrece' sov'reignty' (29), as fundamental [*sic*] cause of Tarquin's rape of Lucrece; pointedly, it is not Lucrece's chastity but 'that name of "chaste"' that 'set/ This bateless edge on his keen appetite'" (Joel Fineman, "Shakespeare's *Will:* The Temporality of Rape," *Representations* 20 [1987]: 30).

CHAPTER FIVE

1. Chrysostom, "Homily 15," 441.

2. Andreas Capellanus, *The Art of Courtly Love*, 28.

3. The phrase is inspired by a chapter in Pagels's *Adam, Eve, and the Serpent* entitled "The Politics of Paradise."

4. There is some suggestion that in medieval poetics vernacular literary genres are specifically gendered, the lay being feminine and the fabliau masculine: "Les lais solent as dames plaire,/de joie les oient de gré/ qu'il sunt sulun lur volenté./ Li rei, li prince, li comtur, cunte, barun e vavassur/ aiment cuntes, chanceons e fables" ("Lays usually please women who listen to them willingly because they are to their taste. Kings, princes, counts, barons and vassals love tales, songs, and fables") (*La "Vie de seint Edmund le rei," poème anglo-normand du XIIe siècle*, ed. Hildung Kjellmann [Göteborg: Wettergren & Kreber, 1935], vv. 46–50.

5. Leigh A. Arrathoon, "The *Châtelaine de Vergi*: A Structural Study of an Old French Artistic Short Narrative," *Language and Style* 7 (1974): 168.

6. *La Chastelaine de Vergi*, ed. Frederick Whitehead (Manchester: Manchester University Press, 1944), vv. 22–28.

7. Though the knight himself may be of lower standing than the chatelaine, he prefers her to the duchess who uses her social status as a lure, vv. 60–98.

8. This is not obvious before she says to the duke's wife, upon learning that her affair has been revealed: "Je ne sai quel acointement/ vous penssez, ma dame, por voir,/ que talent n'ai d'ami avoir/ qui ne soit del tout a l'onor/ et de moi et de mon seignor" ("I do not know what liaison you have in mind, my lady, for truth; for I have no desire to have a friend who would not do honor to me and to my lord" [vv. 710–14]).

9. See Paul Zumthor, "De la Chanson au récit: La Chastelaine de Vergi," *Vox Romanica* 27 (1968): 84.

10. The phrase "mathematical rigor" is that of Whitehead in the second edition (Manchester: Manchester University Press, 1951), xviii.

11. See Jean Rychner, "La Présence et le point de vue du narrateur dans deux récits courts: le *Lai de Lanval* et la *Châtelaine de Vergi*," *Vox Romanica* 39 (1980): 86–103.

12. For a discussion of silence in Old French literature, see Peggy McCracken, "The Poetics of Silence in the French Middle Ages" (Ph.D. diss., Yale University, 1989); John Reinhard, *The Survival of Geis in Mediaeval Romance* (Halle: Max Niemeyer Verlag, 1933), 148–59; Volker Roloff, *Reden und Schweigen: Zur Tradition und Gestaltung eines mittelalterlichen Themas in der französischen Literatur* (Munich: Fink, 1973); and my "Silence and Holes: The *Roman de silence* and the Art of the Trouvère," *Yale French Studies* 70 (1986): 81–99.

13. Chrétien de Troyes, *Le Roman de Perceval*, ed. William Roach (Geneva: Droz, 1959), vv. 4669–74.

14. Jean Rychner writes, concerning the relationship between point of view, verbal system, and free will: "Pour eux [the characters], d'autre part, point de liberté. Je veux dire que l'analyse à laquelle ils sont soumis (serait-elle celle-là même de leur libre arbitre, comme elle l'est, en fait, quand elle porte sur le dilemme du chevalier) ne contribue pas à la création de personnages libres *vis-à-vis de leur créateur,* car ils sont pris tout entiers dans ses filets: rien d'eux n'est ailleurs" ("La présence et le point de vue," 87).

15. "Quar, tan com l'amor est plus grant,/ sont plus mari li fin amant/ quant li uns d'aus de l'autre croit/ qu'il ait dit ce que celer doit;/ et sovent tel meschief en vient/ que l'amor faillir en covient/ a grant dolor et a vergoingne;/ si comme il avint en Borgoingne/ d'un chevalier preu et hardi/ et la dame de Vergi. . . ." (vv. 11–20).

16. Emilie Kostoroski, "Quest in Query and the *Chastelaine de Vergi,*" *Medievalia et Humanistica* 3 (1972): 182.

17. Renaut de Beaujeu, *Le Lai d'Ignauré ou lai du prisonnier,* ed. Rita Lejeune (Brussels: Palais des Académies, 1938), vv. 45–51.

18. I am thinking, of course, of the work of Erich Koehler (see below, pp. 166–68).

19. Also: "La soris ki n'a c'un pertruis/ Est molt tost prise et enganee" ("The mouse with only one hole is quickly tricked and taken" [vv. 480–81]).

20. "Ignaures, li prus, l'ensaigneés/ C'est cil a cui je suis donnee" (vv. 114–15); "Il a non Ignaures li frans" (v. 136); "Nommer le puis, c'est li plus gens:/ Ignaure a non, [flours] de barnage" (vv. 154–55); "C'est Ignaures, flours de barnage" (v. 173).

21. "Ki Deus ad duné escïence/ E de parler bone eloquence/ Ne s'en deit taisir ne celer,/ Ainz se deit voluntiers mustrer" (Marie de France, *Lais,* vv. 1–4; "Li vilains dit an son respit/ que tel chose a l'an an despit/ qui molt valt mialz que l'an ne cuide;" ("Chrétien de Troyes, *Erec et Enide,* ed. Mario Roques [Paris: Champion, 1963], v. 1).

22. See Greg Stone, "The Death of the Grammatical Ego: Lyric Resistance to Individualism in Early Modern Narrative" (Ph.D. diss., Yale University, 1989).

23. "Lanval," in Marie de France, *Lais,* vv. 13–20.

24.

Fors de la sale aveient mis	*They had put outside of the room a great*
Un grant perrun de marbre bis,	*stone of dark marble on which heavy men*
U li pesant humme muntoent,	*mounted their horse before riding from*
Ki de la curt le rei aloent.	*court. Lanval got up on it; and when the*
Lanval esteit muntez desus.	*maid came out of the door, he jumped on*
Quant la pucele ist fors a l'us,	*the horse behind in a single bound!* (vv.
Sur le palefrei, detriers li,	633–40)
De plain eslais Lanval sailli!	

25. See my *Etymologies and Genealogies,* 133–36; Alexandre Leupin, "Ecriture naturelle et écriture hermaphrodite," *Diagraphe* 9 (1976): 119–41; Eugene Vance, "Désir, rhétorique et texte," *Poétique* 42 (1980): 137–55; Jan Ziolkowski, *Alan de Lille's Grammar of Sex* (Boston: Medieval Academy of America, 1985), 40–43.

26. See my "Dead Nightingale: Orality in the Tomb of Old French Literature," *Culture and History* 3 (1988): 63–78.

27. "Il nen ad joïë en cest mund/ Ki n'ot le laüstic chanter" ("Laüstic," in Marie de France, *Lais,* vv. 84–85).

28. "Je ne sai clerc, ne *lai,* ne prestre,/ Qui de fame puist consirrer," ("I know of no cleric, either secular or regular, who can do without a woman" ["Le Bien des fames," in Jubinal, *Jongleurs et trouvères,* 84]).

29. "Un gros example an porroit metre/ aux genz *lais* qui n'antandent letre" ("I could give an obvious example for ignorant people who do not know how to read" [*Rose,* vv. 17, 363–64]).

30. "Le *laz* en fu de soye azure,/ Et le seel de telle mesure/ Fut d'une pierre pre-cieuse/ Resplandissant et gracieuse" "The binding string was of azure silk, and the seal, of equal size, contained a precious stone, all shining and full of grace" [Christine de Pisan, *Dit de la rose,* vv. 580–83]).

31. In the abutment of the lovers' houses we find the fantasy of presence: "Kar pres esteient lur repere:/ Preceines furent lur maisuns/ E lur sales e lur dunguns;/ N'i aveit bare ne devise/ Fors un haut mur de piere bise" ("For their lodgings adjoined and their houses were close, and their living rooms and their dungeons. There was neither fence nor barrier except for a high wall of dark stone" [vv. 35–38]). Because of such proximity communication is envisaged as possible: "Des chambres u la dame jut,/ Quant a la fenestre s'estut,/ Poeit parler a sun ami/ De l'autre part, e il a li" ("From the window of the rooms in which the lady lay she could speak to her love; and, from the other side, he could do the same" [vv. 39–42]).

32. Chrysostom, "Letter to the Fallen Theodore," 104.

33.

Custume fu as ancïens,	*It was the custom of the Ancients, as*
Ceo testimoine Precïens,	*Priscian bears witness, to speak obscurely*
Es livres ke jadis feseient,	*enough in their books so that those who*
Assez oscurement diseient	*came after and would be obliged to learn*
Pur ceus ki a venir esteient	*[or teach] them might gloss the letter and*
E ki aprendre les deveient,	*add their surplus of sense.* ("Prologue, in
K'i peüssent gloser la lettre	Marie de France, *Lais,* vv. 9–16)
E de lur sen le surplus mettre.	

34. See my "Medieval Text—*Guigemar*—as a Provocation to the Discipline of Medieval Studies," *Romanic Review* 79 (1988): 63–73.

35.

Talent me prist de remembrer	*The urge came upon me to remember a lai*
Un lai dunt jo oï parler.	*which I had heard about. I will recount the*
L'aventure vus en dirai	*adventure, and I will name the city where*
E la cité vus numerai	*it came from and its name: one calls it*
U il fu nez e cum ot nun:	Chaitivel, *but many there call it* Les
Le Chaitivel l'apelet hum,	Quatre Deuls. ("Chaitivel," vv. 1–8)
E si i ad plusurs de ceus	
Ki l'apelent *Les Quatre Deuls.*	

See Leo Spitzer, "Marie de France—Dichterin von Problem-Märchen," *Zeitschrift für romanische Philologie* 50 (1930): 37–39.

36. This is exactly what Marie de France does in composing the *Lais:* "D'un mut ancïen lai bretun/ Le cunte e tute la reisun/ vus dirai . . ." ("I will recount to you the tale and the meaning of a very old Breton lai" ["Eliduc," vv. 1–3]); "Une aventure vus dirai,/ Dunt li Bretun firent un lai" ("I will tell you the adventure out of which the Bretons made a lai" ["Laüstic," vv. 1–2]); see also "Guigemar," vv. 19–24.

37. "Maintenant li noviaz evesques,/ Quant ordené l'ot l'arcevesques,/ A grant joie s'en repaira./ Maus consaus luez tant le maira/ Et tant le taria envie/ Theophilum sa signorie/ Toli et fist novial vidame" ("Now the new bishop, when ordered by the archbishop, with great joy took up residence there. Evil counsel took hold of him then and envy so struck him that he took Theophilus's jurisdiction away from him and named a new vicar") (Gautier de Coinci, *Les Miracles de Notre Dame,* ed. V. Frederic Koenig [Geneva: Droz, 1970], vol. 1, v. 115).

38. "Hahi! maufés, car aquer ore/ Et se me di en quel maniere/ A m'oneur revenrai arriere./ Ahi! maufez, car acorez!/ S'a cest besoing me secorés,/ Vostre hom et vostre clers serai/ E toz jors mais vous servirai" ("Ha! Devil, strike now and tell me how I can gain my power back. Ah! Devil, pierce to the heart! If you aid me in my hour of need, I will be your man and your clerk, and I will serve you always") (vv. 148–54).

39. "Mes jo aim e si sui amis/ Cele ki deit aveir le pris/ Sur tutes celes que jeo sai" ("Lanval," vv. 293–95).

40. "Tute la plus povre meschine,/ Vaut mieuz de vus, dame reïne,/ De cors, de vis e de beauté,/ D'enseignement et de bunté!" (vv. 299–302).

41. "Tota la genser qu'anc hom vis/ Encontra liey no pretz un guan;" (*Les Poésies de Cercamon,* ed. Alfred Jeanroy [Paris: Champion, 1922], 2).

CHAPTER SIX

1. Robert Briffault, *The Troubadours* (Bloomington: Indiana University Press, 1965), 83.

2. *The Songs of Bernart de Ventadorn,* ed. and trans. Stephen G. Nichols (Chapel Hill: University of North Carolina Press, 1962), 166.

3. True love presupposes the indifference of the lady, which is also apparent in "Can vei la flor, l'erba vert e la folha":

<table>
<tr><td>

Eu sec cela que plus vas me
  s'ergolha
e cela fuih que.m fo de bel
  estatge,
c'anc pois no vi ne me ni mo
  messatge,
per qu'es mal sal que ja domna
  m'acolha,
mas dreih l'en fatz** qu'eu m'en
  fatz fol parer,
car per cela que.m torn' en non-
  chaler
estauc aitan de leis que no la veya.

</td><td>

*I follow the woman who is most arrogant
towards me, while fleeing the lady who was
full of goodness. Never since her kindness to
me, has she seen me or my messenger—
whence it is a mistake for any woman to be
kind to me. But I make amends to her
when I let myself look like a fool by
remaining away where I cannot see her; all
on account of the other woman who is
indifferent to me.* (Ibid., 164)

</td></tr>
</table>

The editors note: "***mas dreih l'en fatz,* etc. The confused pronominal references make the sense of this passage difficult to follow. The demonstrative *cela* (1. 27) definitely refers to the lady mentioned in 1. 22 (the clause *que.m torn'en non-chaler* makes that clear). Whether the *leis* in 1. 28 refers to the whoman [sic] who is indifferent to the poet, or to the woman he has forsaken is not clear. However, the causal conjunction *car* (1. 27) leads one to expect that these last two lines of the stanza should be the explanation of 1. 26. In that case, the poet says he is playing the fool by staying away from the woman who *would* accept him, in order to court the lady who spurns him" (ibid., 187).

4. "Quan suy ab lieys si m'esbahis/ Quieu no . ill sai dire mon talan, . . . Tal paor ai qu'ieu mesfalhis/ No m'aus pessar cum la deman" (Cercamon, *Les Poésies,* 2).

5.

<table>
<tr><td>

Tan am midons e la tenh car
e tan la dopt'e la reblan
c'anc de me no.lh quer ni re no.lh
  man.
Pero ilh sap mo mal e ma dolor,
e can li plai, mi fai ben et onor,
e can li plai, eu m'en sofert ab
  mens,
per so c'a lais no.n avenha
  blastens.

</td><td>

*I love and cherish my lady so much, and I
fear and serve her so passionately, that I
have never dared speak to her of myself.
Neither do I seek or demand anything of
her. However, she knows my pain and grief,
and so, when it pleases her, she treats me
well and honorably; and when it pleases
her, I get along with less, so that blame will
not fall upon her.* (Bernart de Ventadorn,
Songs, 152)

</td></tr>
</table>

See also "En Cossirer et en esmai":

> E doncs pois atressi.m morrai
> dirai li l'afan que m'en ve?
> Vers es c'ades lo li dirai—
> no farai a la mia fe
> si sabia c'a un tenen
> en fos tot' Espanha mia;
> mais volh morir de feunia
> car anc me venc en pessamen.

And so, since I shall die anyway, shall I tell her of the suffering I undergo? Yes, I shall tell her at once. No, I shall not do it, by my faith, even if I knew all Spain would forthwith be mine for the telling. Indeed, I could die of chagrin for having allowed such a thought to cross my mind. (Ibid., 86)

6. Or, strophe 1 of "Lo tems vai e ven e vire":

> Lo tems vai e ven e vire
> per jorns, per mes e per ans,
> et eu, las, no.n sai que dire,
> c'ades es us mos talans.
> Ades es us e no.s muda,
> c'una.n volh e.n ai volguda
> don anc non aic jauzimen.

Time comes and goes returning through days, through months, and through years, and I alas, know not what to say, for my longing is ever one. It is ever one and does not change, for I want and have wanted one woman, from whom I never had joy. (Ibid., 129)

See also "Non es meravilha s'eu chan": "Ja Domnedeus no.m azir tan/ qu'eu ja pois viva jorn ni mes/ pois que d'enoi serai mespres/ ni d'amor non aurai talan" ("May God never hate me so much that I may live a day or a month longer, once I become a nuisance to others and lose all desire of love" [ibid., 132]).

7. I am aware, of course, that within the poetics of Bernart desire can also be seen to be its own reward as, for example, in "Ara no vei luzir solelh":

> Noih e jorn pes, cossir e velh,
> planh e sospir; e pois m'apai.
> On melhs m'estai, et eu peihz
>   trai.
> mas us bos respeihz m'esvelha
> don mos cossirers s'apaya.
> Fols, per que dic que mal traya,
> car aitan rich' amor envei,
> pro n'ai de sola l'enveya.

Night and day I think, worry and stay awake, weep and sigh; and then I am appeased. The better off I am, the worse I feel. But one good hope which eases my worry awakens me. Fool, why do I say that I suffer? Since I desire such a rich love, the desire itself is a reward. (Ibid., 60)

8. "On plus la prec, plus m'es dura" (ibid., 130).

9.

> Domna si'st fals enveyos
> que mainh bo jorn m'an estraih
> s'i metion en agaih

per saber com es de nos,
per dih d'avol gen tafura
non estetz ges esperduda;
ja per me non er saubuda
l'amors, be.n siatz segura.
("A, tantas bonas chansos" [ibid., 64])

That the poet is a revealer of secret love affairs is also evident in the *razo* connected to "Quan vei lalauzeta mover," for here it becomes absolutely clear that the poet places himself in the position of the *losengier* whom he denounces:

. . . E apelava la B[ernart] "Alauzeta", per amor d'un cavalier que l'amava, e ella apelet lui "Rai". E un jorn venc lo cavaliers a la dugessa e entret en la cambra. La dona, que.l vi, leva adonc lo pan del mantel e mes li sobra.l col, e laissa si cazer e[l] lieg. E B[ernart] vi tot, car una donzela de la domna li ac mostrat cubertamen; e per aquesta razo fes adonc la canso que dis: "Quan vei l'alauzeta mover . . ."

And Bernart called her "Alouette" because of a knight who loved her and whom she called "Ray." And one day the knight came to the duchess and entered her room. The woman who saw him then lifted the panel of her coat and put it on his neck; and she let herself fall upon the bed. And Bernart saw the whole thing, because one of the lady's servants showed it to him in secret; and he thus composed a song which goes: "Quand je vois l'alouette agiter . . ." (Jean Boutière and Alexander H. Schutz, *Biographies des troubadours* [Paris: Nizet, 1964], 29)

And this despite the fact that Bernart writes in the poem, "I hold that there is no vexation, vice, or villainy but that of the man who becomes the spy of other people's love" ("Non es enois ni falhimens/ ni vilania, so m'es vis,/ mas d'ome can se fai devis/ d'autrui amor ni conoissens" [*Songs,* 42]).

10. "c'amors, pois om per tot s'en vana/ non es amors mas es ufana/ et es enois, vilani' e foudatz/ qui no gara cui deu esser privatz" (ibid., 100).

11. "Que anc non amet neguna,/ Ne d'autra no fo amatz./ Trobaire fo dels premiers c'om se recort. De caitivetz serventes fez e dis mal de las femnas e d'amor" (*Poésies complètes du troubadour Marcabru,* ed. J.-M.-L. Dejeanne [Toulouse: Privat, 1909], 1).

12. "Non puosc dompnas trobar gaire/ Que blanch' amistatz no.i vaire" ("I cannot find any woman whose white friendship does not change into variegated colors" [Marcabru, *Poésies complètes,* 20]).

13. "Q'anc pos la serps baisset lo ram/ No foron tant enganairiz" (ibid., 24); "E non puesc mudar non gronda/ Del vostre dan moillerzin" (ibid., 50).

14. Ibid., 135. "Eyssamens son domnas trichans/ E sabon trichar e mentir,/ Per que fan los autrus enfans/ Als maritz tener e noyrir" ("Women are also tricky and they

know how to deceive and to lie; this is how they fool their husbands into keeping and feeding the children of others" [ibid., 166]); see also 50, 173. See my *Etymologies and Genealogies,* 109–13.

15. "Ancar vos vuelh mais ensenhar/ Ab que conquerretz las melhors./ Ab mals digz et ab lag chantar/ Que fassatz tut, et ab vanar;/ E que honretz las sordeyors./ Per lor anctas las levetz pars" (Raimbaut d'Orange, *The Life and Works of the Troubadour Raimbaut d'Orange,* ed. Walter T. Pattison [Minneapolis: University of Minnesota Press, 1952], 135).

16. Jane Burns writes concerning Bernart's "Ja mos chantars no m'er onors": "It is clear from this description that the 'real' (or womanly) side of the Lady refers to her frankly sexual being. But this 'woman' is no more real than her idealized and rarefied counterpart—the supportive, desexualized, object of adoration. Indeed the fantasy of narcissistic male desire . . . is perhaps more prevalent than has hitherto been acknowledged. In fact, every fact of the Lady as we see her in the *Canso* contributes to a myth of female sexual identity, a misreading of the feminine in terms of the masculine" ("The Man Behind the Lady in Troubadour Lyric," *Romance Notes* 25 [1985]: 263).

17. Thibaut de Champagne, *Poèmes d'amour des XIIe et XIIIe siècles,* ed. Emmanuèle Baumgartner (Paris: Union Générale d'Editions, 1983), 98.

18. Ibid., 198.

19. See Barbara Johnson, "The Lady in the Lake," in *A New History of French Literature* (Cambridge, Mass.: Harvard University Press, 1989), 627–32.

20. Ab lo temps qe fai refreschar/ Lo segle [els pratz] reverdezir? Vueil un novel chant comenzar/ D'un amor cui am e dezir;/ Mas tan s'es de mi loignada/ Q'ieu non la puesc aconseguir,/ Ni de mos digz no s'agrada" ("Ab lo temps qe fai refreschar," in Cercamon, *Les Poésies,* 4).

21. Leo Spitzer, *L'amour lointain de Jaufré Rudel et le sens de la poésie des troubadours,* University of North Carolina Studies in the Romance Languages and Literature (Chapel Hill: University of North Carolina Press, 1944), 21. The entire phrase, which takes Jaufré Rudel's "love from afar" as prototypical of the eroticism of the troubadours, reads as follows: "Tous, pas seulement Jaufré Rudel, interposent entre l'être aimant et l'être aimé l'obstacle' que conaissent les mystiques: cet obstacle est ce qui empêche en nous l'union mystique—l'éloignement est paradoxalement consubstantiel avec le désir de l'union."

22. Boutière and Schutz, *Biographies,* 16.

23. Love by hearsay may, in fact, be somewhat of a topos, found also in the *vida* of Raimbaut d'Orange: "Et el s'annamoret puis de la bona contessa d'Urgel, que fo Lombarda, filla del marques de Busca. Mout fon onrada e presada sobre totas las pros domnas d'Urgel; et Rambauz, senes veser leis, per lo gran ben que n'ausia dire, si s'enamoret d'ella et ella de lui. E si fez puois sas chansos d'ella; e si.1 manda sas chansos per

un joglar que avia non Rosignol, si con dis en una chanson" ("He then fell in love with the good countess d'Urgel, who was a Lombard and the daughter of the marquis de Busca. She was very honored and revered, more than all the noble ladies of Urgel; and, without seeing her, on the faith of all the good he heard say about her, Raimbaut was taken with her, and the lady with him. Also did he compose then his songs about her and sent them to her by a jongleur named Rossignol, as he tells it in a song" [Boutière and Schutz, *Biographies,* 441]).

24. *Les Chansons de Jaufré Rudel,* ed. Alfred Jeanroy (Paris: Champion, 1924), 12.

25. Thus too Cercamon in "Quant l'aura doussa s'amarzis": "Las! qu'ieu d'Amor non ai conquis/ Mas cant lo trebalh e l'afan,/ Ni res tant greu no.s covertis/ com fai so qu'ieu vau deziran;/ Ni tal enveja no.m fai res/ Cum fai so qu'ieu non posc aver" ("Alas, I have only gained anguish and pain from love, for nothing is obtained with as much difficulty as that which I desire the most, and nothing excites my desire more than that which I cannot have" [*Les Poésies,* 1]).

26. "L'*amor de lonh* ne vient-il pas chez Jaufré Rudel de cette 'mélancolie de l'imperfection', qui sent que 'quelque chose' manque toujours au bonheur absolu, et de cette auto-limitation volontaire, qui a besoin du lointain?" Spitzer asks (*L'amour lointain de Jaufré Rudel,* 16).

27. "Bien sai c'anc de lei no.m jauzi,/ Ni ja de mi no.s jauzira,/ Ni per son amic no.m tenra/ Ni coven no.m fara de si;/ Anc no.m dis ver ni no.m menti/ E no sai si ja s'o fara, a a" ("I know well that I have never had her, that she will never get off on me, nor have me for her lover, nor make me on her own account any promise; never does she tell me either the truth or a lie, and I don't know if she ever will" ["No Sap chantar qui so non di," *Chansons,* 17]). For an excellent discussion of the question of sexual desire and abstraction, with special reference to Jaufré Rudel, see Jean-Charles Huchet, *L'Amour discourtois* (Toulouse: Privat, 1987), 125–45; or Henri Rey-Flaud, *La Névrose courtoise* (Paris: Navarin, 1983), who writes: "Le désir du troubadour se pose ici dans son éternité, la femme n'étant donnée alors ni comme sa cause ni comme son objet, mais seulement comme son pôle hors d'atteinte. Car à l'atteinte est liée la menace. La réalisation du désir sous les traits de la Convoitise n'aurait pas pour effet l'extinction du désir, comme on l'a parfois soutenu, mais l'évanouissement de la femme. Si bien que la *fin'amor* illustre chez Jaufré Rudel une alternative sans issue: un sujet en attente ou un objet hors d'atteinte; un sujet en impasse maintenant un objet virtuel, ou bien un sujet désirant dont l'objet s'abîmerait au moment de l'advention" (27).

28. "Ben devon li amador/ de bon cor servir amor,/ quar amor non es peccatz,/ anz es vertutz qe.ls malvatz/ fai bons, e.ll bo.n son meillor,/ e met hom'en via/ de ben far tot dia;/ e d'amor mou castitaz,/ quar qi.n amor ben s'enten/ no pot far qe pueis mal renh" (*Les Poésies de Guilhem de Montanhagol,* ed. Peter Ricketts [Toronto: Pontifical Institute of Medieval Studies, 1964], 122).

29. See René Nelli, *L'Erotique des troubadours* (Toulouse: Privat, 1963); Leo Poll-

man, *Die Liebe in der hochmittelalterlichen Literatur Frankreichs* (Frankfurt: Klostermann, 1966).

30. *The Poetry of William VII, Count of Poitiers, IX Duke of Aquitaine,* ed. and trans. Gerald A. Bond (New York: Garland Publishing, 1982), 120.

31. Ibid., 128.

32. Cited ibid., xlvii.

33. Ibid., 2. All subsequent references are to the Bond edition and translation.

34. Andreas Capellanus, *The Art of Courtly Love,* 31.

35. "Lo coms de Peitieus si fo uns dels majors cortes del mon e dels majors tri-chadors de dompnas. . . ." (Boutière and Schutz, *Biographies,* 7).

36. Alfred Jeanroy, *Les Origines de la poésie lyrique en France au moyen âge* (Paris: Hachette, 1889), vol. 2, 7.

37. Briffault, *Troubadours,* 54.

38. "Etant donné que les pièces les plus 'gauloises' sont souvent les plus archaï-ques quant au style et à la versification, que leur auteur est effectivement passé d'une érotique grossière à une autre plus idéalisée" (Nelli, *L'Erotique des troubadours,* vol. 1, 156).

39. Gerald Bond, the editor of what is to date the most reliable version of the poems, writes: "No precise date between 1106 and 1119 has been determined for any of the other songs [all songs but song 11]. The only clues to their chronology comes from formal and internal evidence. In the *companho* songs, (1–3), lexical and formal similarities separate the first from the second and the third. The latter display a very similar monorhyme (*ei/es*), share a number of thematically important rhyme words (*conrei/conres; castei/casteis; lei/leis*), and introduce an epic caesura in the long line ending in *-a*. In the first song, on the contrary, none of these devices is present. A similar situa-tion is found in the rondeau songs (4–7). As already noted, a large number of formal and grammatical factors identify Song 5 as the least accomplished. Songs 4 and 7 share the same rhyme scheme and meter; in addition, there is an identical phrase at the rhyme (4.36 and 7.37), and both use a rare form of a verb as rhyme (4.41 and 7.17). Since in Song 7 the Count takes pains to praise his well-made words and music (7.37–42), as if they were new, one might assume that it is the model for the other, to which it is a kind of conceptual counterweight. . . . If increasing sophistication of a given form indicates a later date of composition, as appears logical, then one can establish the rela-tive order of these seven songs. Songs 1 and 5 were composed first. . . . Formal advances suggest a somewhat later date for Songs 2 and 3. The last is song 6, whose form builds upon that of 4 and 7. . . . an absolute date for any of the songs besides 5 and 11 would be helpful, but nothing definite has been proposed.") William of Aqui-taine, *Poetry,* lii–liii).

George Beech goes so far as to question whether, on the basis of the manuscripts, William IX is the author of the songs attributed to him ("L'Attribution des poèmes du comte de Poitiers à Guillaume IX d'Aquitaine," *Cahiers de civilisation médiévale* 31 (1988): 3–15.

40. Huchet, *L'Amour discourtois*, 63; see also Danielle Jacquart and Claude Thomasset, *Sexuality and Medicine in the Middle Ages* (Princeton: Princeton University Press, 1985), 96.

41. The only other critic who to my knowledge has explicitly suggested such a relation is, again, Huchet: "La misogynie—au même titre que l'amour—vise l' 'être' de la femme qu'elle essaie de réduire au paradigme insaturable de ses défauts et de ses vices" (*L'Amour discourtois*, 79).

42. "Qui voudroit feme esprouver/ N'i porroit trover loiauté,/ Car tot adès est preste de fauser"; "Deboinerement/ Atendrai merci;/ Cors a bel et gent,/ N'a si avenant/ De Paris dusqu'a Gant" (*Recueil de motets français des XIIe et XIIIe siècles*, ed. Gaston Raynaud [Hildesheim: Georg Olms Verlag, 1972], 22); see also no. 126, pp. 151–52. I am grateful to Sylvia Huot for bringing these to my attention.

43. Andreas Capellanus, *The Art of Courtly Love*, 31.

44. Ibid., 192, 193, 196.

45. John Benton, "Clio and Venus. An Historical View of Medieval Love," in *The Meaning of Courtly Love*, ed. Francis X. Newman (Albany: State University of New York Press, 1968), 19–42; Introduction to *Andreas Capellanus on Love*, ed. and trans. Patrick G. Walsh (London: Duckworth, 1982), esp. 17; Alfred Karnein, *De Amore in volkssprachlicher Literatur, Untersuchungen zur Andreas-Capellanus-Rezeption im Mittelalter und Renaissance, Germanisch-romanische Monatsschrift* (Heidelberg: Carl Winter, 1985), 23.

46. See Roger Boase, *The Origin and Meaning of Courtly Love* (Manchester: Manchester University Press, 1977), 111–14.

47. D. W. Robertson, *A Preface to Chaucer,* (Princeton: Princeton University Press, 1962), 391–503.

48. "The only successful issue from this problem that I can see is to take the first two books of the *De amore* as a literary fiction, a rhetorical construction that is not *immoral* but *amoral*, and to acknowledge that Andreas both creates and accepts it in this way. Such an interpretation recognizes that the text is not meant to be applied in practice, and hence lets Andreas off the hook that he would otherwise hang on. Andreas himself suggests in Book 3 that no one can be fully educated about love and its pains without being taught by *magister experientia* (3.23, p. 294): the text, in other words, does not really teach. Rather, it is the reader's responsibility to know what use to make (or, here, not to make) of the text" (Peter Allen, "*Assidua lectio* and the *duplex sententia:* Andreas Capellanus and the Rhetoric of Love" [unpublished paper]). See also Jacquart and Thomasset, *Sexuality and Medicine*, 96–110.

49. See, for example, Toril Moi, "Desire in Language: Andreas Capellanus and the Controversy of Courtly Love," in *Medieval Literature: Criticism, Ideology, and His-*

tory, ed. David Aers (New York: Saint Martin's Press, 1986), 11–33. In this article Moi affirms the relation we have been suggesting all along between the Middle Ages' distrustfulness of language and of women: "If the deceitful woman's language is indistinguishable from an honest woman's, the lover will never know whether he is listening to truth or deceit. He thus finds himself caught in exactly the same trap as the jealous lover: they are both in a situation where no amount of subtle interpretation will reveal the lady's true intention. Jealousy is indeed the essence of love; and Andreas's advice to Walter really amounts to saying that he ought to avoid *all* women, given the impossibility of distinguishing between them. Andreas conveniently represses the fact that he has unmasked a problem of general linguistic and epistemological importance (how can language convey truth?), and blames it all on the deviousness of women instead" (29).

50. Robert Bossuat, *Drouart la Vache, traducteur d'André le Chapelain* (Paris: Champion, 1926), 31.

51. Nor does the solution to the paradox of the palinode reside in what is, ultimately, a reinscription—via psychoanalysis—of the theological analogy between the "Otherness" of language and of woman. Huchet, for example, writes in a chapter section entitled "L'Autre": "Que l'auditoire (on peut en imaginer la composition) soit structurée autour de la *domina*, la châtelaine, permet de penser que chaque récitant parle à une femme de l'Autre-femme, à une femme de 'La Femme', non tant pour en approcher le mystère que pour se donner à désirer à travers ce débat avec le désir de 'je' pour 'elle', vient dès lors comme instrument d'une séduction dans le temps de la diffusion. Ne nous intéressera cependant—et c'est là un effet de la perte de l'oralité des textes—que 'elle', l'Autre, l'objet du chant" (*L'Amour discourtois,* 35). Such explanations are, again, either so general as to miss the historical specificity of the individual case or so specifically predicated upon specious biographical assumptions as to remain in the realm of pure conjecture.

52. William of Aquitaine, *Poetry,* lviii.

53. See Melvin Askew, "Courtly Love: Neurosis as Institution," *Psychoanalytic Review* 52 (1965): 19–29; Richard Koenigsberg, "Culture as Unconscious Fantasy: Observations on Courtly Love," *Psychoanalytic Review* 54 (1967): 36–50.

54. Burns, "The Man Behind the Lady," 254.

55. "Thus this work, which seems 'to present two points of view,' is a significant twelfth-century instance of a collocation of the two contradictory traditions which I have described. Andreas is at once the 'master of Courtly Love' and a master of Jeromean antifeminism. The two are merely different faces of the same coin" (Robert Miller, "The Wounded Heart: Courtly Love and the Medieval Antifeminist Tradition," *Women's Studies* 2 [1974]: 344).

56. Lewis, *The Allegory of Love,* 145.

CHAPTER SEVEN

1. All references to the *Lais* in this chapter are to Jean Rychner's edition.

2. The short discussion that follows is based upon material contained in my *Medieval French Literature and Law* (Berkeley: University of California Press, 1973), 98–100, 220–21. See also Marc Bloch, *Feudal Society* (Chicago: University of Chicago Press, 1964), vol. 2, 301; Georges Duby, *Medieval Marriage* (Baltimore: Johns Hopkins University Press, 1982); Duby, *Le Chevalier, la femme et le prêtre: Le mariage dans la France féodale* (Paris: Hachette, 1981); Duby, "Les 'Jeunes' dans la société aristocratique dans la France du Nord-Ouest du XIIe siècle," in *Hommes et structures du moyen âge* (The Hague: Mouton, 1973), 213–24; Erich Koehler, *Ideal und Wirklichkeit in der höfischen Epik* (Tübingen: Max Niemeyer, 1956); Koehler, *Trobadorlyrik und höfischen Roman* (Berlin: Rütten & Loenning, 1962); Koehler, "Observations historiques et sociologiques sur la poésie des troubadours," *Cahiers de civilisation médiévale* 7 (1964): 27–47.

3. "Artursreich und Arturskönigtum erweisen sich als dichterisch sublimierte Wunschbilder der feudalhöfischen Welt, und zwar als Wunschbilder, die die disparaten Interessen der verschiedenen adligen Schichten in sich aufzunehmen geeignet waren" (Koehler, *Ideal*, 38).

4. See ibid., 23–35.

5. "Lanval" can be read in light of the Marxist parable as a historically accurate tale of dispossession recuperated by the overly generous fairy; it is, in effect, the story of the wish fulfilment of an entire subclass. And yet, the fact that the redeemer is a woman is by no means neutral. For, as Duby in particular has shown, the one sure means to economic independence on the part of the knight without land is marriage to a woman whose dowry represents a potential source of income. Duby, in fact, takes the extreme position that the theme of the wandering knight in medieval literature is nothing more than a poetic expression of the historical quest on the part of the disenfranchised knights of the lower nobility to become "established" (see especially Duby, "Les 'Jeunes'").

6. Georges Duby, "Structures de parenté et noblesse dans la France du Nord aux XIe et XIIe siècles," in *Hommes et structures*, 283.

7. The argument that follows elaborates upon work contained in my *Etymologies and Genealogies*, 68–70, 161–63.

8. See Georges Duby, *La Société aux XIe et XIIe siècles dans la région mâconnaise* (Paris: Armand Colin, 1953), 418; Duby, *Medieval Marriage*, 10–12; Duby, "Les 'Jeunes'," 213–24.

9. Pierre Bonnassie, *La Catalogne du milieu du Xe à la fin du XIe siècle* (Toulouse: Publications de l'Université de Toulouse, 1975), vol. 1, 281; Robert Hajdu, "Family and Feudal Ties in Poitou, 1100–1300," *Journal of Interdisciplinary History* 8 (1977): 123.

10. "Les *fiançailles,* en droit germanique, sont une sorte de contrat d'achat passé entre le fiancé et le clan ou le curateur (*Vormund*) de la jeune fille; elles se rapprochent donc des fiançailles par gage que connaissait l'Orient. Le jeune homme offre en gage une certaine somme d'argent (*wadia*) et d'autres cadeaux de mariage; il s'oblige ainsi a prendre la jeune fille comme épouse et ă lui donner une partie de ses biens comme dot (*wittum*). Le 'procurateur' (*sponsor*) promet au jeune homme la jeune fille dont il est le 'tuteur' en lui offrant également un gage (*wadia*) symbolique. Le fiancé doit le rendre: par ce geste, il confie sa future femme jusqu'au jour de noces au détenteur du droit de tutelle (*mundium*) . . . . Les *noces* elles-mêmes commençaient par la confection de l'acte de mariage, où l'on établissait le montant de la dot (*wittum*) et le prix de la transmission de la tutelle (*mundium*)" (Edward Schillebeeckx, *Le Mariage* [Paris: Cerf, 1966], 229).

11. See Duby, *Medieval Marriage,* chap. 1; and Duby, *La Société,* 436; Charles Donahue, "The Policy of Alexander III's Consent Theory of Marriage," in *Proceedings from the Fourth International Congress of Medieval Canon Law* (Vatican: Biblioteca Apostolica Vaticana, 1976), 256, 257; Michael M. Sheehan, "Choice of Marriage Partner in the Middle Ages: Development and Application of a Theory of Marriage," *Studies in Medieval and Renaissance History* 1 (1978): 1–33; Juliette Turlan, "Recherches sur le mariage dans la pratique coutumière (XIIe–XIVe siècle)," *Revue historique du droit français et étranger* 35 (1957): 477–528.

12. "Tristan, the Myth of the State, and the Language of the Self," *Yale French Studies* 51 (1975): 61–81.

13.

Li reis ot une fille bele
E mut curteise dameisele.
Fiz ne fille fors li n'aveit;
Forment l'amot e chierisseit.
De riches hommes fu requise,
Ki volentiers l'eüsse prise;
Mes li reis ne la volt doner,
Kar ne s'en poeit consirrer."

The king had a beautiful daughter, and a very courteous maid. He had no other son or daughter, and he loved and cherished her. She was requested by rich men who would have willingly married her. But the king did not want to give her, because he could not do without her. (vv. 21–28)

14.

Milun ad a sun fiz cunté
De sa mere cum il l'ama,
E cum sis peres la duna
A un barun de sa cuntree,
E cument il l'ad puis amee
E ele lui de bon curage,
E cum del cigne fist message:

Milun recounted to his son how he came to love his mother, how her father had given her to a baron of that land, and how he had loved her afterwards, and she him, with true love, and how the swan played the messenger between them: so distrustful was he that the bird carried his letters. (vv.

Ses lettres li feseit porter,   488–96)
Ne s'osot en nul liu fïer.

15. "De haute gent fu la pucele,/ Sage, curteise e forment bele,/ Ki al riche hume fu
donee" ("The maid, from a very noble family, was wise, courteous, very beautiful, and
given to a rich man" [vv. 22–24]); "Maleeit seient mi parent/ E li autre communal-
ment/ Ki a cest gelus me donerent/ E de sun cors me marïerent!" ("Cursed be my
parents and the others with them, who gave me to this jealous old man and married me
to his body!" [vv. 81–84].

16.

Mult fu vielz hum, e femme aveit
Une dame de haut parage,
Franche, curteise, bele e sage.
Gelus esteit a desmesure,
Kar ceo purporte la nature
Ke tuit li vieil seient gelus—
Mult het chascuns ke il seit cous—:
Tels est d'eage le trespas!
Il ne la guardat mie a gas:
En un vergier, suz le dongun,
La out un clos tut envirun;
De vert marbre fu li muralz,
Mult par esteit espés e halz!
N'i out fors une sule entree:
Cele fu noit e jur guardee. . . .
Uns vielz prestres blancs e floriz
Guardout la clef de cel postiz;
Les plus bas membres out perduz,
Autrement ne fust pas creüz.
(vv. 210–24, 255–58)

17.

De ceo ke ele iert bele e gente,
En li garder mist mut s'entente;
Dedenz sa tur l'ad enserreie
En une grant chambre pavee.
Il ot une sue serur,
Veille ert e vedve, sanz seignur;
Ensemble od la dame l'ad mise
Pur li tenir mieuz en justise. (vv. 25–32)

18. Lewis, *The Allegory of Love*, 13. Violet Paget, "Mediaeval Love," in *Euphorion, Being Studies of the Antique and the Mediaeval in the Renaissance* (London: T. Fisher Unwin, 1884), vol. 2, 123–217.

19. Lewis, *The Allegory of Love*, 18.

20. Briffault, *Troubadours*, 96; Denis De Rougemont, *Love in the Western World* (New York: Fawcett, 1958), 77. "According to the theory officially received, courtly love arose as a reaction to the brutal lawlessness of feudal manners. It is well known that the nobles in the twelfth century made of marriage simply a means of enriching themselves, either through the annexation of dower estates or through the expectations of inheritance. When a 'deal' turned out badly, the wife was repudiated. . . . In order to counteract these abuses, which led to much quarrelling and to warring, courtly love established a *fealty* that was independent of legal marriage and of which the sole basis was love" (De Rougemont, *Love in the Western World*, 35). Actually, Briffault announces this thesis as early as 1927: "The transformation in the conceptions of romantic love, the idealisation of the relations between the sexes which is presented in the course of literary evolution from the primitive sagas of European peoples, from the first outburst of lyrical poetry in southern Europe to the dawn of the Renaissance, were not dictated by changes in public sentiment, but by the influence and by the pressure of the Christian Church" (Briffault, *The Mothers,* vol. 3, 505).

21. In what is perhaps the only humorous moment in a book darkly molded by fascism and the winds of war, de Rougemont urges us to "Just think of a Mme. Tristan!" (*Love in the Western World*, 46).

22. Ibid., 48.

23. "The relation of hate to objects is older than that of love. It is derived from the primal repudiation by the narcissistic ego of the external world whence flows the stream of stimuli. . . . it remains in constant intimate relation with the instincts of self-preservation, so that sexual and ego-instincts readily develop an antithesis which repeats that of love and hate" (Sigmund Freud, "Instincts and Their Vicissitudes," in *A General Selection from the Works of Sigmund Freud,* ed. John Rickman [Garden City, N.Y.: Doubleday, 1957], 85).

24. "N'y a-t-il pas dans les réactions obscures—immédiates—au sujet de la mort et de l'érotisme, telles que je crois possible de les saisir, une valeur décisive, une valeur fondamentale?" (Georges Bataille, *Les Larmes d'éros,* in *Oeuvres complètes* [Paris: Gallimard, 1970], vol. 10, 586).

25. "Nous l'avons vu, l'homme vraisemblablement velu de Néanderthal avait la connaissance de la mort. Et c'est à partir de cette connaissance que l'érotisme apparut, qui oppose la vie sexuelle de l'homme à celle de l'animal" (*Les Larmes d'éros,* 584). Bataille thus situates the development of eroticism beyond the reaches of genuine history in much the same way, as we saw, that Engels situates the development of

patriarchy beyond history. As equally unnegotiable prehistories, both are in effect naturalized.

26. "Pour des raisons qui ne sont pas seulement conventionnelles, l'érotisme est défini par le secret. . . . L'expérience érotique se situe en dehors de la vie ordinaire. Dans l'ensemble de notre expérience, elle demeure essentiellement retranchée de la communication normale des émotions. Il s'agit d'un sujet interdit" (Georges Bataille, *L'Erotisme,* in *Oeuvres Complètes,* vol. 10, 246).

27. "Beyond the common being met in their embrace, they [lovers] seek infinite annihilation in a violent expenditure where the possession of a new object, a new woman or new man, is only the pretext for an even more annihilating expenditure. In the same fashion, those who are more religious than others cease being narrowly concerned with the community for which sacrifices are performed. They no longer live for the community, they live only for the sacrifice. It is in this manner that, little by little, they are possessed by the desire to spread their sacrificial frenzy through contagion. In the same way that eroticism slips easily into orgy, sacrifice that becomes an end in itself lays claim, beyond the narrowness of the community, to a universal value" (*The College of Sociology,* ed. Denis Hollier, trans. Betsy Wing [Minneapolis: University of Minnesota Press, 1988], 339).

28. "Si l'union des deux amants est l'effet de la passion, elle appelle la mort . . . . L'érotisme ouvre à la mort. La mort ouvre à la négation de la durée individuelle"; "La poésie mène au même point que chaque forme de l'érotisme, à l'indistinction, à la confusion des objets distincts. Elle nous mène à l'éternité, elle nous mène à la mort, et par la mort, à la continuité: la poésie est *l'éternité*" (*L'Erotisme,* 26, 29–30).

29. "Le sacré est justement la continuité de l'être révélée à ceux qui fixent leur attention, dans un rite solennel, sur la mort d'un être discontinu" (ibid., 27).

30. Julia Kristeva, *Tales of Love* (New York: Columbia University Press, 1987), 287.

31. Ibid., 238, 245.

32. See Henry Adams, *Mont-Saint-Michel and Chartres* (London: Constable, 1950); Boase, *Origin and Meaning of Courtly Love,* 84–86; Myrrha Lot-Borodine, "Sur les Origines et les fins du *service d'amour,*" in *Mélanges Alfred Jeanroy* (Paris: Droz, 1928), 223–42; Leo Spitzer, *L'amour lointain de Jaufré Rudel.*

33. "Rien n'est interdit absolument," writes Bataille, "il y a toujours des transgressions. Mais l'interdit joue suffisamment pour que, dans l'ensemble, je puisse dire que l'érotisme, étant peut-être l'émotion la plus intense, dans la mesure où notre existence est présente en nous sous forme de langage (de discours), l'érotisme est pour nous comme s'il n'était pas. . . . En principe, l'experérience érotique nous engage au silence" (Bataille, *L'Erotisme,* 246–47).

34. Kristeva, *Tales of Love,* 259.

35. Ibid.

36. "Feminine perversion [*père-version*] is coiled up in the desire for law as desire for reproduction and continuity, it promotes feminine masochism to the rank of structure stabilizer (against its deviations); by assuring the mother that she may thus enter into an order that is above humans' will it gives her her reward of pleasure. Such coded perversion, such close combat between maternal masochism and the law have been utilized by totalitarian powers of all times to bring women to their side, and, of course, they succeed easily. And yet, it is not enough to 'declaim against' the reactionary role of mothers in the service of 'male dominating power.' One would need to examine to what extent that role corresponds to the biosymbolic latencies of motherhood" (Kristeva, *Tales of Love*, 260).

37. Indeed, the fascination of de Rougemont and Bataille with eroticism and death, which culminates in Kristeva's commitment to the woman as redeemer or a means of transcending death, ends logically in what is perhaps the most bizarre and disturbing modern book I have encountered in my research on either misogyny or romantic love, Gertrude von le Fort's *The Eternal Woman: The Woman in Time: Timeless Woman,* which appeared in Germany in 1934 as an apologetics (though it is never said) for the obligatory sacrifice on the part of every mother of a son in the cause of what the aristocratic poet must surely have sensed to be the imminence of war: "Sooner or later, concealed or unconcealed, the image of the Sorrowful Mother, the Pietà appears in the life of every mother" (Gertrude von le Fort, *The Eternal Woman: The Woman in Time: Timeless Woman,* trans. Marie Cecilia Buehrle [Milwaukee: Bruce Publishing, 1954], 100).

38. Indeed, Pierre Bonnassie, following a long tradition, suggests that a "kind of feminine tone" dominates southern society because of its proximity to what is now Spain: "On peut même dire qu'une sorte de tonalité féminine marque la société de l'époque" (*La Catalogne,* vol. 1, 277). See also Charles Camproux, *Joy d'Amor* (Montpellier: Causse & Castelnau, 1965), 29–32; Alfred Jeanroy, *La Poésie lyrique des troubadours* (Paris: Privat, 1934), 88; Moshe Lazar, *Amour courtois et 'fin 'amors' dans la littérature du XIIe siècle* (Paris: Klincksieck, 1964), introduction.

39. See Bynum, *Jesus as Mother;* Bynum, *Holy Feast and Holy Fast;* Bynum, "'. ... And Woman His Humanity'," 257–88.

40. Régine, Pernoud, *La Femme au temps des cathédrales* (Paris: Stock, 1980), 131.

41. Cited Jean de Pétigny, "Robert d'Arbrissel et Geoffroy de Vendôme," *Bibliothèque de l'Ecole des Chartes* 5 (1854): 6.

42. Cited Penny Gold, *The Lady and the Virgin: Image, Attitude, and Experience in Twelfth-Century France* (Chicago: University of Chicago Press, 1985), 103.

43. Jules Michelet, *Le Moyen âge,* in *Histoire de la France* (Paris: Laffont, 1981), 284; Jean de Pétigny, "Lettre inédite de Robert d'Arbrissel à la Comtesse Ermengarde," *Bibliothèque de l'Ecole des Chartes* 5 (1854): 221; Reto Bezzola, *Les Origines*

et la formation de la littérature courtoise en Occident (500–1200) (Paris: Champion, 1966), vol. 2, 286; Pernoud, *La Femme,* 129.

44. "A l'instant, il les fit sortir de la ville, il les conduisit plein de joie au désert et là, leur ayant fait faire pénitence, il les fit passer du démon au Christ" (Michelet, *Le Moyen âge,* 285). See also Jacques Delarun, *L'Impossible sainteté: La vie retrouvée de Robert d'Arbrissel (v. 1045–1116), fondateur de Fontevraud* (Paris: Editions du Cerf, 1985), 15, 121; Dalarun, "Robert d'Arbrissel et les femmes," *Annales E.S.C.* 39 (1984): 1142.

45. *PL,* vol. 162, 1083–84; translation Gold, *The Lady and the Virgin,* 99.

46. See Duby, *Le Chevalier,* 170; Pernoud, *La Femme,* 130–69; Ernst Werner, "Zur Frauenfrage und zum Frauenkult im Mittelalter: Robert v. Arbrissel und Fontevrault," *Forschungen und Fortschritte* 29 (1955): 274.

47. For a view of Robert as a social innovator see: Ernst Werner, *Pauperes Christi: Studien zu sozial-religiösen: Bewegungen im Zeit-alter des Reformpapsttums* (Leipzig: Koehler & Amelang, 1956); Tadeusz Manteuffel, *Naissance d'une hérésie: Les adeptes de la pauvreté volontaire au moyen âge,* trans. Anna Posner, (The Hague: Mouton, 1970).

48. "Wollte sich die Frau aus den Fesseln der feudal-patriarchalischen Herrschaft lösen, dann musste sie sich von der Gesellschaft absondern und auf sich selbst stellen, sich mit ihresgleichen verbinden, um sich von der überlieferten Bevormundung des Mannes zu emanzipieren. Ihren Ausdruck fand diese Emanzipationsbewegung in der Gleichstellung der Frau mit dem Manne im Rahmen religiöser Gemeinschaften" (Werner, "Zur Frauenfrage," 274). The philosopher Roscelin complained in a letter to his student Abelard that Robert refused to return recalcitrant wives to the husbands who claimed them (Jean-Marc Bienvenu, *L'Etonnant fondateur de Fontevraud Robert d'Arbrissel* [Paris: Nouvelles Editions Latines, 1981], 89). See also Duby, *Le Chevalier,* 171–72.

49. Dalarun, *L'Impossible sainteté,* 15.

50. Pétigny, "Robert d'Arbrissel et Geoffroy de Vendôme," 14. See also Dalarun, "Robert d'Arbrissel et les femmes," 1154.

51. Alfred Richard writes: "A la suite de ces événements une tranquillité relative régna dans le états du duc d'Aquitaine, mais si les guerres et leurs conséquences néfastes étaient pour le moment assoupies, un grand trouble continuait à agiter les esprits, en particulier dans les classes supérieures. Cette inquiétude se manifesta surtout par le mouvement qui entraîna les populations vers une nouvelle conception sociale, celle de l'émancipation de la femme, et comme il arrive dans toutes les réformes, le but fut tout d'abord dépassé. On ne se contenta pas de la considérer comme l'égale de l'homme, certains esprits voulurent qu'elle lui fût supérieure. L'apôtre de cette théorie risquée, Robert d'Arbrissel, ne cessait, par sa parole chaude, ses agissements hardis, de remuer la société, et de Fontevrault, devenu depuis 1099, sa résidence ordinaire, partaient journellement des bandes de disciples; on se demande si Guillaume, avec les

sentiments de curiosité raffinée qui étaient l'essence de sa nature, ne prenait point un réel intérêt à suivre les développements de cette oeuvre, dans laquelle la femme, à l'égard de qui il professait des sentiments moins purs et surtout moins élevés que ne le prêchait le réformateur, jouait le principal rôle" (Alfred Richard, *Histoire des comtes de Poitou, 778–1204* [Paris: Alphonse Picard, 1903], 446–47). See also Jeanroy, *La Poésie lyrique des troubadours,* vol., 1, 80–88.

52. Bezzola, *Les Origines,* vol. 2, 312, 311.

53. Bienvenu, *L'Etonnant fondateur de Fontevraud,* 73–74.

54. "La présence continue de la comtesse à Toulouse produisait de son côté les plus heureux effets; elle y régnait absolument en souveraine et, comme telle, elle disposait à son gré du domaine de ces ancêtres. . . . Ses inspirateurs, ceux dont elle avait pris conseil, étaient Munion, le prévôt de Saint-Sernin, et Robert d'Arbrissel, qui débutait dans la grande voie de propagande de ses doctrines et s'était créé dans Munion un adepte zélé" (Richard, *Histoire des comtes de Poitou,* 421); see also Bezzola, *Les Origines,* vol. 2, 278. For the history of Eleanor of Aquitaine's gifts to Fontevrault, see Pernoud, *La Femme,* 162–65.

55. "Pendant que ces événements se passaient en Poitou, d'autres de grande importance se produisaient à Toulouse. Les grands seigneurs du pays venaient l'un après l'autre reconnaître pour leur suzeraine la comtesse Philippie et lui prêter serment de fidélité. La plus importante de ces adhésions fut assurément celle de Bernard-Aton, vicomte de Béziers. Ce puissant personnage dominait directement ou indirectement sur le tiers du comté de Toulouse et particulièrement sur les six vicomtés de Carcassonne, de Razès, de Béziers, d'Albi, d'Agde et de Nîmes" (Richard, *Histoire des comtes de Poitou,* 469).

56. Pétigny, "Robert d'Arbrissel et Geoffroy de Vendôme," 7. See also Dalarun, "Robert d'Arbrissel et les femmes," 1145; Duby, *Le Chevalier,* 7–26, 135.

57. This is Richard's suggestion, *Histoire des comtes de Poitou,* 472.

58. Bezzola, *Les Origines,* vol. 2, 311, 312. Jacques Dalarun sees an analogy between the ethos of Fontevrault and that of *fin'amors* such that the latter would be latent in, ready to blossom within, the milieu of the former: "Que veulent, de leur côté, les soeurs? Très certainement être seulement obéies par les frères. Mais il serait tout aussi absurde de penser que ces femmes ont quitté le monde, ont supporté des conditions de vie pénibles, pour mieux laisser éclater un goût insensé du pouvoir. De Robert, elles acceptent un service qui les flatte. L'essor simultané de la 'fine amour,' dans le milieu même dont elles sont originaires, prouve que cette sensibilité est latente, prête à éclore à la cour ou au cloître" (Dalarun, "Robert d'Arbrissel et les femmes," 1150). See also his *L'Impossible sainteté,* 143–46.

59. "Er sah in der Frau das Symbol der Erlösung der Menschheit, die Personifizierung der Gottesmutter, unter deren Fuss die Schlange zertreten wurde" (Werner, "Zur Frauenfrage," 269).

60. Bezzola, *Les Origines*, vol. 2, 311. Thus too Bezzola's "great man" theory of the praise of women: "This 'imago' [of the Virgin] was born in Southwest France around 1100, by the genius-like intuition of a great lord who had the gift of expressing in poetry that which a part of the most advanced part of society vaguely felt, that which it always celebrated in another form, that of Mary, the 'domina' par excellence. The adoration of the Virgin herself would never again be extracted from the influences of this profane poetry that she had indirectly created" (ibid., vol. 2, 314).

61. Dalarun writes: "Robert est contemporain de Philippe Ier. Il se situe au coeur de l'intrigue que Georges Duby a choisie pour dater et illustrer le plus fort de la crise matrimoniale, née de l'affrontement de deux conceptions du mariage. Les femmes que rassemble Robert ont en commun d'être les victimes de cette crise.

"En premier lieu, elles sont victimes du mariage tel que le conçoivent princes, barons ou chevaliers: laissées pour compte, répudiées pour leur stérilité, abandonnées pour de plus belles alliances. Mais voici qu'elles s'éveillent à d'autres aspirations: elles fuient des maris par trop brutaux, grossiers, inconstants; elles ont soif de mysticisme, elles brûlent pour ces apôtres fascinants. A l'image de Pétronille, elles nourrissent d'autres ambitions que d'échapper à la coupe de leur père pour tomber sous celle de leur mari et d'échapper à la coupe du mari pour retomber sous celle du père" (Dalarun, "Robert d'Arbrissel et les femmes," 1144–45).

62. See Brundage, *Law, Sex, and Christian Society*, 137, 183–99; Pierre Daudet, *Les Origines carolingiennes de la compétence exclusive de l'église en France et en Germanie en matière de juridiction matrimoniale* (Paris: Sirey, 1933).

63. *Petri Lombardi, Libri IV Sententiarum* (New York: Saint Bonaventure, 1916), vol. 2, 917. See also Jean Dauvillier, *Le Mariage dans le droit classique de l'église depuis le décret de Gratien (1140) jusqu'à la mort de Clément V (1314)* (Paris: Sirey, 1933), 12–17; Duby, *Medieval Marriage*, 16–25; Adhémar Esmein, *Le Mariage en droit canonique* (Paris: Sirey, 1929), vol. 1, 131; Schillebeeckx, *Le Mariage*, 256.

64. See Dauvillier, *Le Mariage*, 23–29; Esmein, *Le Mariage*, vol. 1, 103; George E. Howard, *A History of Matrimonial Institutions* (Chicago: University of Chicago Press, 1904), vol. 1, 336; Schillebeeckx, *Le Mariage*, 258.

65. ". . . sufficiat secundum leges solus eorum consensus, de quorum conjunctionibus agitur . . ." (*PL*, vol. 187, 1392).

66. See Donahue, "The Policy of Alexander III's Consent Theory of Marriage," 251–81.

67. Frederick Pollock and Frederic Maitland, *The History of English Law* (Cambridge: Cambridge University Press, 1923), vol. 2, 372.

68. According to John Noonan, it was to Urban's rulings that Gratian turned in his answer formulated around 1140 to the question, "May a daughter be given in marriage against her will?" The first such ruling involved the marriage of Renaud Ridel, duke of Gaeta, to the daughter of Jourdain I, prince of Capua (d. 1090), whom the

pope, active in the affairs of the Norman conquerors in southern Italy, was anxious to please. The second concerned Sancho Ramirez, king of Aragon-Navarre, who, having pledged his niece to a marriage against her will, was relieved of the obligation to force her to comply on the basis that marriage should join those whose body is one in one spirit and on the basis that to counter this precept ran the risk of fornication: "Quorum enim unum corpus est, unus debet esse et animus, ne forte, cum virgo fuerit alicui invita copulata, contra Domini Apostolique preceptum aut reatum discidii, aut crimen fornicationis incurrat." See John Noonan, "Power to Choose," *Viator* 4 (1973): 420–21.

69. The claims of René Metz concerning the reflection of canonical prescription in social practice seem, for example, somewhat naïve: "Tout d'abord, le droit canonique s'est efforcé d'assurer peu à peu à la femme la plus complète liberté en matière de consentement. Ses efforts aboutirent, au milieu du XIIe siècle, à l'affranchir du consentement paternal, qui jusqu'à cette époque avait été une condition essentielle du mariage valide en droit romain comme en droit germanique. . . . La fille est libérée de l'autorité paternelle; elle peut contracter un mariage valide, même si les parents font opposition" (René Metz, "Le Statut de la femme en droit canonique médiéval," in *La Femme,* Recueils de la Société Jean Bodin 12 (Brussels, 1962), 86–87.

70. "Exogamy and indissolubility clearly emerged as hallmarks of Catholic marriage during this period and the papacy and the Church's courts both worked diligently to implement these ideals. As a consequence the laity, even at the highest social levels, lost much of its former control over the marriages of family members. The old-style capacity of families to arrange the marriages, divorces, and remarriages of their members was rapidly disappearing by the 1120s and 1130s" (Brundage, *Law, Sex, and Christian Society,* 225; see also 333).

71. Bonnassie, *La Catalogne,* vol. 1, 277.

72. Cited David Herlihy, "Land, Family and Women in Continental Europe," *Traditio* 18 (1962): 99. "The increased frequency with which women appear as owners of land after 950 does seem to correspond with a similar increase of matronymics for the same period. On a regional basis, Southern France is remarkable both for the extent of women's lands and the frequency with which the matronymic appears in our charters" (ibid., 108).

73. Ibid., 89.

74. Pierre, Ourliac, "L'Esprit du droit méridional," in *Droit privé et institutions régionales* (Paris: Presses Universitaires de France, 1976), 589.

75. Robert Hajdu, "The Position of Noblewomen in the Pays des Coutumes, 1100–1300," *Journal of Family History* 5 (1980): 126.

76. Gold, *The Lady and the Virgin,* 135. Also, ibid., 137: "For example, in Anjou the percentage of acts with women as consenters ranged from 30.8% to 49.5% over

the 250-year period. But the peak figure of 49.5% for the period 1100–1149 is the aggregate of the following figures from the three monasteries:

Le Ronceray d'Angers	29.2% of 137 acts
Saint-Aubin d'Angers	48.8% of 41 acts
Fontevrault	61.2% of 242 acts

77. Bonnassie maintains that for Catalonia out of 600 contracts of sale he examined from the tenth century, approximately half (49.3 percent) were signed by married couples. Of the rest, 117 were signed by men acting alone, 1 by a man accompanied by his children, for a total of 19.7 percent; 83 were signed by women acting alone, 32 by women acting with children, for a total of 19.2 percent (*La Catalogne*, vol. 1, 266).

78. These figures are taken from the tables that appear on p. 135 of Gold, *The Lady and the Virgin*, and p. 126 of Hajdu, "The Position of Noblewomen."

79. As Penny Gold has emphasized in her own analysis, the phenomenon of fluctuation is itself a significant element of women's experience (*The Lady and the Virgin*, 141).

80. Hajdu, "The Position of Noblewomen," 127. Bonnassie writes about Catalonia: "Ce qui frappe le plus dans la condition de la femme catalane aux alentours de l'an Mil, c'est son indépendance matérielle. Elle a reçu de ses parents une part d'héritage le plus souvent égale à celles de ses frères, quelquefois majorée, puisque les filles peuvent, au même titre que les garçons, bénéficier de la clause de *melioratio*. Mariée, elle conserve un pouvoir exclusif sur ses biens personnels: elle en dispose— pour les vendre, les donner, les mettre en gage—sans avoir à en référer à son époux. Et, de fait, le pourcentage de transactions opérées par les femmes, hors de toute tutelle et même de toute présence maritale, est sensiblement égal à celui des opérations effectuées par les hommes" (*La Catalogne*, vol. 1, 274).

81. According to François-L. Ganshof, "La Loi Salique dans son texte le plus ancien, tient les femmes pour complètement incapables de recueillir une succession immobilière et les en exclut d'une manière absolue . . . . 'De terra vero nulla in muliere hereditas est, sed ad virilem sexum qui fratres fuerint tota terra pertineant'" ("Le Statut de la femme dans la monarchie franque," in *La Femme*, Recueils de la Société Jean Bodin 12 [Brussels, 1962], 34–35). See also Roger Aubenas, *Anciens pays de droit ecrit: XIII–XVI siècle* (Aix-en-Provence: Librairie de l'Université, 1952); Lehman, *Le Rôle de la femme*, 47–48; Jo Ann McNamara and Suzanne Wemple, "The Power of Women Through the Family in Medieval Europe: 500–1100," *Feminist Studies* 1 (1973): 131; Naïté-Albistur, *Histoire du féminisme français*, 21.

82. See Roger Aubenas, "La Famille dans l'ancienne Provence," *Annales d'histoire économique et sociale* 42 (1936): 523; *Le Testament en Provence dans l'ancien droit* (Aix-en-Provence: Editions Paul Roubaud, 1927), 123; Jean Gaudemet, "Le Statut de la femme dans l'empire romain," in *La Femme*, Receuils de la Société Jean Bodin 11

(Brussels, 1962), 215; McNamara and Wemple, "The Power of Women," 127, 131.

83. "L'absence de tout droit d'aînesse, l'aptitude des femmes à succéder aux fiefs, tout au moins au début, les partages égaux ou à peu près égaux entre enfants, tels sont les principes dont l'application a conduit la féodalité provençale à l'état de faiblesse et d'instabilité qui est sa principale caractéristique au début du XIIIe siècle" (Aubenas, "La Famille dans l'ancienne Provence," 524). Bonnassie attests to the same equality in Catalonia due to Visigothic influence: "frères et soeurs sont tenus pour égaux par la loi, qui insiste même pour que ces dernières ne soient l'objet d'aucune discrimination. Dans la pratique, le comportement des parents semble répondre à cette prescription: le partage égal des patrimoines, qui est de droit en cas de succession *ab intestat,* est de même stipulé expressément par bien des testateurs, dont certains vont jusqu'à prévoir la part à réserver à leurs enfants posthumes. L'égalité de tous les fils et filles dans la division des héritages est donc, aussi bien en droit qu'en fait, la règle" (*La Catalogne,* vol. 1, 264).

84. Cited Meg Bogin, *The Women Troubadours* (New York: W. W. Norton, 1976), 22.

85. "Si pater vel mater intestati decesserint, tunc sorores cum fratribus in omni parentum facultate, absque alio objectu, aequali divisione succedant" Noël Didier, "Les Dispositions du statut de Guillaume II Forcalquier sur les filles dotées (1162)," *Le Moyen âge* 56 (1950): 255. See also Ganshof, "Le Statut de la femme," 40. "In contrast to Roman law, which provided equal rights of succession to the family's property by daughters and sons, the general principle upheld by the Burgundian, Alemannic, Bavarian and Ripuarian codes was that daughters could inherit only if there were no sons. Lombard law made similar provision, although it enabled fathers to give a third of their property to their daughters. Only the most Romanized of the Germanic codes, the Visigothic law, allowed equal rights of succession to daughters" (McNamara and Wemple, "The Power of Women," 131). Michelet, in what may be an exaggeration, maintains that the Capetian was the only house not recognizing the rights of women (*Le Moyen âge,* 286).

86. "Ego Vermundus et uxor mea et filii mei et filias meas donamus . . ."; "dono . . . Raimondo et Godefrido, fratri suo, et filiis et filiabus quos habent"; "ego Beatrix et filii mei . . . et filia mea . . . consentiamus" (Didier, "Les Dispositions," 255).

87. ". . . les dites père ou mère, ou aultres, ne peuvent faire par donaccion, soit entre vifz, pour cause de testament ou légat, l'un des héritiers meilleur que l'aultre oultre la part en porcion légitime et coustumière" (cited Jean Yver, *Egalité entre héritiers et exclusion des enfants dotés* [Paris: Sirey, 1966], 127).

88. "En Provence, si privilégié qu'il soit dans l'ordre politique, le fief, dans son régime économique, est soumis au droit commun. Rien, dans les lois, qui le protège et le sauvegaude; point de droit d'aînesse; dans les successions *ab intestat* ouvertes entre

nobles comme dans celles intéressant leurs censitaires, partage égale; point de droit de masculinité, les filles héritent à égal des fils" (Charles De Ribbe, *La Société provençale à la fin du moyen âge* [Paris: Perrin, 1898], 393). See also Aubenas, "La Famille dans l'ancienne Provence," 524; and Aubenas, *Le Testament en Provence,* 123. Jean Yver maintains that the system of primogeniture was particularly weak in Poitou; see "Les Caractères originaux du groupe de coutumes de l'Ouest de la France," *Revue historique du droit français et etranger* 30 (1952): 23. See also Marcel Garaud, *Les Châtelains de Poitou et l'avenèment du régime féodal: XIe et XIIe siècles* (Poitiers: Mémoires de la Société des Antiquitaires de l'Ouest, 1964), 75.

89. "Lorsque le *de cujus* n'avait laissé que des filles, l'aînée avait le principal manoir et le cinquième des fiefs. Son avantage était donc un peu moins important que celui de l'aîné mâle qui lui, prenait en plus, par préciput, le cinquième des terres roturières. . . . A défaut d'enfant mâle, la fille aînée a pour droit d'aînesse le manoir principal et ses dépendances, comme aurait pris l'aîné mâle, mais elle n'a pas droit à sa part avantageuse des deux tiers" (Paulette Portejoie, *Le Régime des fiefs d'après la coutume de Poitou* [Poitiers: Mémoires de la Société des Antiquitaires de l'Ouest, 1958], 134, 135). See also Yver, "Les Caractères originaux," 43.

90. See Lehman, *Le Rôle de la femme,* 136; Archibald Lewis, *The Development of Southern French and Catalan Society* (Austin: University of Texas Press, 1956), 170–73.

91. Yver, for example, contrasts Poitou and Normandy; see "Les Caractères originaux," 24–25, 48–49. Dom Vaissete's monumental *Histoire générale de Languedoc* contains the following prescription: "Les filles succédèrent non seulement aux fiefs ordinaires durant le xie siècle et le suivant, mais encore à ceux de dignité: la province en fournit divers exemples, entre autres ceux de Berthe, comtesse de Rouergue et marquise de Gothie, de Garseinde de Béziers et d'Ermengarde de Carcassonne" (*Histoire générale de Languedoc, par dom Cl. Devie et dom J. Vaissete* [Toulouse: Privat, 1874–92], vol. 3, 401). McNamara and Wemple correlate the freeholding and the capacity of women to inherit: "In addition to this growing freedom in disposing of royal fiefs, the aristocratic families of the ninth and tenth centuries were expanding their control of allodial—freehold—land by force and purchase and through land clearance. There were no serious restrictions on the family's power to distribute such land as it saw fit. Few families were inclined to exclude their daughters from the capacity to inherit allodial land. When such land came into the hands of a woman, it remained her property and did not pass to her husband or her husband's family unless she willed it to do so" (McNamara and Wemple, "The Power of Women," 134).

92. Pollock and Maitland, *The History of English Law,* vol. 1, 429; Hajdu, "The Position of Noblewomen," 133. Herlihy writes: "In Catalonia and southern France, it is evident from our charters that women were being widely admitted to feudal inheritances already from the tenth century" (David Herlihy, "Land, Family and Women in Continental Europe," *Traditio* 18 [1962]: 100).

93. "C'est ainsi qu'ils ont admis—chose qui eût certes scandalisé les Romains—une véritable *délégation de la puissance paternelle à la veuve:* c'est la veuve qui, souvent, et en vertu du testament même du mari, va succéder à la tête de la famille et de l'exploitation, c'est à elle que sera confiée l'administration de la fortune, c'est elle qui va gouverner, avec les pouvoirs les plus étendus. Que nous voici loin des idées romaines! La veuve, loin de tomber en tutelle, devient 'dame et administraresse', elle centralise entre ses mains toute l'autorité, elle a même le droit de chasser du foyer les enfants 'rebelles'; loin de déchoir, elle devient reine" (Aubenas, "La Famille dans l'ancienne Provence," 534).

94. See Herlihy, "Land, Family and Women," 100. The percentage of women mentioned in charters as being heiresses or as being holders of contiguous lands is in the tenth century 10 percent for southern France compared to 5 percent for the north; and in the eleventh century 11 percent in the south compared to 6 percent elsewhere in France (ibid., 105).

95. "Au temps où la comtesse Agnès était à la tête du pays de Poitou avec ses fils Guillaume et Geoffroy et administrait vigoureusement le duché, autant qu'il était en son pouvoir"; "alors que régnaient en Poitou le comte Guillaume, son frère Guy et la vénérable comtesse Agnès, leur mère" (Alfred Richard, ed., *Chartes et documents pour servir à l'histoire de l'abbaye de Saint-Maixent,* Archives Historiques de Poitou 16&18 [Poitiers, 1886], vol. 1, 123, 126). The heritage of William IX is equally marked (via marriage) by the example of Almodis de la Marche, countess of Toulouse, and the grandmother of William's wife Philippa. It was Almodis who ordered the codification of the Customs of Barcelona. See Bonnassie, *La Catalogne,* vol. 1, 509–11.

96. Richard, *Histoire des comtes de Poitou,* vol. 1, 382.

97. "La famille, elle-même, ne subit pas, semble-t-il, l'autorité inconditionelle d'un chef. On garde à la lecture des actes les plus anciens l'impression que tous les parents y participent également et que les femmes, dans tous les milieux de la société, jouissent d'une liberté qu'elles ne connaissent pas dans les pays coutumiers. Nobles, elles possèdent de bonne heure de très grands fiefs, Carcassonne, Narbonne, Aquitaine; héritières, elles peuvent, en Béarn, donner leur nom à leur mari et à leurs enfants; elles sont témoins dans les actes, gèrent leurs biens et en disposent entre vifs ou à cause de mort. Le régime matrimonial lui-même vise à maintenir égalité entre époux mais surtout à assurer le sort de la veuve. On peut croire que la brutalité des moeurs l'emportait sur la mystique des cours d'amour, mais il n'empêche que la femme avait une liberté qui lui était refusée ailleurs et, qu'à l'invers de ce que Monsieur Yver relève pour la Normandie, l'esprit du droit méridional était de faire prédominer le ménage sur le lignage" (Ourliac, "L'Esprit du droit méridional," 589).

98. See my *Etymologies and Genealogies,* 73.

99. See Brundage, *Law, Sex, and Christian Society,* 37, 88; Diane Owen Hughes,

"From Brideprice to Dowry in Mediterranean Europe," *Journal of Family History* 3 (1978): 264.

100. Brundage, *Law, Sex, and Christian Society*, 128; Goody, *Development of the Family*, 250–51.

101. Herlihy, *Medieval Households*, 77; see also 15, 21, 73–74; and Herlihy, "The Medieval Marriage Market," in *Medieval and Renaissance Studies*, ed. Dale B. J. Randall (Durham, N.C.: Duke University Press, 1974), 3–27.

102. Hughes, "From Brideprice to Dowry," 274.

103. See Herlihy, *Medieval Households*, 98; Hughes, "From Brideprice to Dowry," 276.

104. Hughes, "From Brideprice to Dowry," 282; see also Aubenas, "La Famille dans l'ancienne Provence," 526; Aubenas, *Le Testament en Provence*, 125; Didier, "Les Dispositions," 258. Dirty as money may seem in the post-Protestant era, and this is just an aside, the dowry oddly became linked in the period under study to the notion of feminine virtue. We find a "growing association between dowry and chastity"; and lack of a dowry is considered one path to prostitution. Then too, even after marriage, control of the dowry becomes a means of conjugal coercion in that a woman's dowry, under such an "economics of shame," escheated to her husband if she cheated or was unfaithful (Hughes, "From Brideprice to Dowry," 284–85).

105. ". . . filia vel soror non possit postea venire vel succedere in bonis patris, vel matris, vel fratris, vel sororis" (Didier, "Les Dispositions," 252). See also Yver, "Les Caractères originaux," 25–26, 55; Yver, *Egalité entre héritiers*, 127–72. Robert Caillemer is somewhat more cautious: "De même encore, et toujours comme conséquence de la force de l'organisation familiale, dès le XIIe siècle, en de très nombreux endroits de la Provence, les filles dotées sont exclues de la succession paternelle. Au milieu du XIIe siècle, la charte de consulat d'Arles, que M. Fitting rapproche cependant de notre Somme, le déclare expressément. Or, dans *Lo Codi*, non seulement on ne retrouve pas cette exclusion, mais le texte insiste d'une étrange manière sur le droit des filles à la succession de leurs parents, même quand elles ont été dotées; elles doivent seulement rapporter leur don à la masse héréditaire (VI, 101; VI, 26, 2)" ("Le Codi et le droit provençal au XIIe siècle," *Annales du Midi* 18 [1906]: 504–5).

106. "Si le père a baillé dot à sa fille en terre et argent, icelle fille ne viendra pas en partage des biens paternels avec ses frères, ni au supplément de légitime, sinon que le père en ordonnast autrement" J. Maillet, "De l'Exclusion coutumière des filles dotées à la renonciation à succession future dans les coutumes de Toulouse et Bordeaux," *Revue historique de droit français et etranger* 30 [1952]: 518). See also Didier, "Les Dispositions," 254; Hughes, "From Brideprice to Dowry," 279.

107. Herlihy, *Medieval Households*, 87.

108. See Paget, "Mediaeval Love"; Koehler, *Ideal;* Koehler, *Trobadorlyrik und höfischer Roman.*

109. "It is a process visible along the northern Mediterranean littoral as early as the twelfth century in the poetry of the troubadours, whose rise was contemporary with the decline of the husband's gift" ("From Brideprice to Dowry," 291).

110. *Le Moyen âge,* 285.

111. "Psychologiquement et moralement, il s'agit d'un phénomène de libération de l'esprit et de la reconnaissance du droit au bonheur par la libre disposition de son corps, phénomène dont les premières bénéficiaires furent les femmes du Midi, plus indépendantes à l'égard de leurs maris" Paul Imbs, "De la fin'amor," *Cahiers de civilisation médiévale* 12 [1969]: 266). Miller, "The Wounded Heart," 335, 336; Camproux, *Joy d'amor,* 101; *The Dictionary of the Middle Ages,* ed. Joseph R. Strayer, (New York: Scribners, 1983), vol. 3, 669.

112. Cited in Marks and de Courtivron, *New French Feminisms,* 222. Marks and de Courtivron go on to characterize the gesture, not unlike the above analysis, as "the Doormat-Pedestal tactics, or the tactics of 'kicking upstairs' to some honorary position someone who must be gotten rid of." The Balzac quotation is cited in Aubert, *La Femme,* 6: "La femme n'est à proprement parler qu'une annexe de l'homme. C'est un esclave qu'il faut savoir mettre sur un trône."

113. And this from the very beginning, according to E. Schüssler Fiorenza, who sees in Paul's injunction against women speaking in churches the Roman fear of women in public places, also to be found in the injunction of Livy: "As soon as they [women] become your equals, they will become your superiors" (Fiorenza, *In Memory of Her,* 232).

114. Aubert, *La Femme,* 110. See also Johansson, "'Herstory' as History," 400.

BIBLIOGRAPHY

Adams, Henry. *Mont-Saint-Michel and Chartres*. London: Constable, 1950.

Allen, Peter. "*Assidua lectio* and the *duplex sententia:* Andreas Capellanus and the Rhetoric of Love." French Department, Pomona College. N.d.

Alter, Robert. *The Art of Biblical Narrative*. New York: Basic Books, 1981.

d'Alverny, Marie-Thérèse. "Comment les Théologiens et les philosophes voient la femme." *Cahiers de civilisation médiévale* 20 (1977): 105–29.

Ambrose. "Concerning Virgins" and "Concerning Widows." In *Nicene and Post-Nicene Fathers,* ed. Philip Schaff and Henry Wace, vol. 10, 363–407. New York: Christian Literature Publishing Co., 1896.

The Ancren Riwle: A Treatise on the Rules and Duties of Monastic Life. Ed. James Morton. New York: AMS Press, 1968.

Andreas Capellanus. *The Art of Courtly Love*. Ed. John Jay Parry. New York: W. W. Norton, 1969.

Anselm. "Cur Deus Homo." In *Anselm de Canterbury, Pourquoui Dieu s'est fait homme,* ed. and trans. René Roques. Paris: Editions du Cerf, 1963.

Anson, John. "The Female Transvestite in Early Monasticism: Origin and Development of a Motif." *Viator* 5 (1974): 1–32.

Aquinas, Thomas. *Liber de veritate catholicae fidei contra errores infidelium seu summa contra gentiles*. Vol. 3. Rome: Marietti, 1961.

———. *Summa theologiae,* vol. 13. New York: McGraw-Hill, 1963.

Ariès, Philippe. "Saint Paul and the Flesh." In *Western Sexuality: Practice and Precept in Past and Present Times,* ed. Philippe Ariès and André Béjin, trans. Anthony Forster, 36–39. Oxford: Blackwell, 1985.

Aristotle, *De la génération des animaux*. Trans. Pierre Louis. Paris: Société d'Edition "Les Belles Lettres," 1961.

Arrathoon, Leigh A. "The *Châtelaine de Vergi:* A Structural Study of an Old French Artistic Short Narrative." *Language and Style* 7 (1974): 151–80.

Athanasius. *Life of Saint Anthony*. In *Early Christian Biographies,* ed. Roy J. Deferrari, 133–224. Vol. 15 of *Fathers of the Church*. Washington, D.C.: Catholic University of America Press.

Askew, Melvin. "Courtly Love: Neurosis as Institution." *Psychoanalytic Review* 52 (1965): 19–29.

Aubenas, Roger. *Anciens pays de droit ecrit: XIII–XVI siècle*. Aix-en-Provence: Librairie de l'Université, 1952.

————. "La Famille dans l'ancienne Provence." *Annales d'histoire économique et sociale* 42 (1936): 523–40.

————. *Le Testament en Provence dans l'ancien droit.* Aix-en-Provence: Editions Paul Roubaud, 1927.

Aubert, Jean-Marie. *La Femme: Antiféminisme et Christianisme.* Paris: Cerf/Desclée, 1975.

Augustine. *Confessions.* Ed. J. K. Ryan. New York: Doubleday, 1960.

————. *De Genesi ad litteram.* Ed. P. Agaësse and A. Solignac. Paris: Desclée de Brouwer, 1972.

————. *De libero arbitro.* Ed. J. H. S. Burleigh. London: SCM Press, 1953.

————. *De magistro.* Ed. F. J. Thonnard. Paris: Desclée de Brouwer, 1941.

————. *De ordine.* Ed. Jean Jolivet. Paris: Desclée de Brouwer, 1948.

————. *The Trinity.* Washington, D.C.: Catholic University of America Press, 1963.

Aurell, Marc. *Une Famille de la noblesse provençale au moyen âge: Les Porcelet.* Avignon: Aubanel, 1986.

Baer, Richard. *Philo's Use of the Categories Male and Female.* Leiden: E. J. Brill, 1970.

Bailey, Derrick. *Sexual Relations in Christian Thought.* New York: Harper, 1959.

Baker, Derek. *Medieval Women.* Oxford: Blackwell, 1978.

Barbey d'Aurevilly, Jules. *Les Bas-bleus.* Geneva: Slatkine Reprints, 1968.

Bal, Mieke. *Lethal Love: Feminist Literary Readings of Biblical Love Stories.* Bloomington: Indiana University Press, 1987.

Barnes, Timothy David. *Tertullian: A Historical and Literary Study.* Oxford: Clarendon Press, 1971.

Barthes, Roland. *Michelet.* New York: Hill & Wang, 1987.

Bataille, Georges. *L'Erotisme.* In *Oeuvres complètes,* vol. 10, 7–265. Paris: Gallimard, 1987.

————. *Les Larmes d'éros.* In *Oeuvres complètes,* vol. 10, 575–657. Paris: Gallimard, 1987.

Batany, Jean. *Approches du "Roman de la rose."* Paris: Bordas, 1973.

Baudelaire, Charles. *Curiosités esthétiques.* Paris: Garnier, 1962.

————. *Oeuvres complètes.* Paris: Gallimard, 1975.

Baumgartner, Emmanuèle. "A propos du Mantel Mautaillié. *Romania* 96 (1975): 315–32.

Bédier, Joseph. *Les Fabliaux.* Paris: Champion, 1925.

Beech, George. "L'Attribution des poèmes du comte de Poitiers à Guillaume IX d'Aquitaine." *Cahiers de civilisation médiévale* 31 (1988): 3–15.

Bell, Susan G. *Women from the Greeks to the French Revolution.* Belmont, Calif.: Wadsworth, 1973.

Bennett, Philip, ed. *Mantel et Cor: Deux lais du xiie siècle.* Exeter: University of Exeter Press, 1975.

Benton, John. "Clio and Venus: An Historical View of Medieval Love." In *The Meaning of Courtly Love,* ed. Francis X. Newman, 19–42. Albany: State University of New York Press, 1968.

Bernart de Ventadorn. *Songs of Bernart de Ventadorn.* Ed. and trans. Stephen G. Nichols. Chapel Hill: University of North Carolina Press, 1962.

Bezzola, Reto. *Les Origines et la formation de la littérature courtoise en Occident (500–1200).* 3 vols. Paris. Champion, 1966.

Bienvenu, Jean-Marc. *L'Etonnant fondateur de Fontevraud Robert d'Arbrissel.* Paris: Nouvelles Editions Latines, 1981.

Bloch, Marc. *Feudal Society.* 2 vols. Chicago: University of Chicago Press, 1964.

Bloch, R. Howard. "The Dead Nightingale: Orality in the Tomb of Old French Literature." *Culture and History* 3 (1988): 63–78.

———. *Etymologies and Genealogies: A Literary Anthropology of the French Middle Ages.* Chicago: University of Chicago Press, 1983.

———. *Medieval French Literature and Law.* Berkeley: University of California Press, 1973.

———. "Medieval Misogyny." *Representations* 20 (1987): 1–24.

———. "The Medieval Text—*Guigemar*—as a Provocation to the Discipline of Medieval Studies." *Romanic Review* 79 (1988): 63–73.

———. *The Scandal of the Fabliaux.* Chicago: University of Chicago Press, 1986.

———. "Silence and Holes: The *Roman de silence* and the Art of the Trouvère." *Yale French Studies* 70 (1986): 81–99.

———. "Tristan, the Myth of the State, and the Language of the Self." *Yale French Studies* 51 (1975): 61–81.

Bloch, R. Howard, and Frances Ferguson, eds. *Misogyny, Misandry, Misanthropy.* Berkeley: University of California Press, 1988.

Blumenfeld-Kosinski, Renate. "Christine de Pizan and the Misogynistic Tradition." *Romanic Review* 81 (1990): 279–92.

Boase, Roger. *The Origin and Meaning of Courtly Love.* Manchester: Manchester University Press, 1977.

Bogin, Meg. *The Women Troubadours.* New York: W. W. Norton, 1976.

Boileau-Despréaux, Nicolas. *Oeuvres complètes.* Ed. Antoine Adam. Paris: Gallimard, 1966.

Bonnassie, Pierre. *La Catalogne du milieu du Xe à la fin du XIe siècle.* 2 vols. Toulouse: Publications de l'Université de Toulouse, 1975.

Boorstein, Diane. "Antifeminism." In *Dictionary of the Middle Ages,* ed. Joseph R. Strayer, vol. 1, 322–25. New York: Scribners, 1982.

———. "Courtly Love." In *Dictionary of the Middle Ages,* ed. Joseph R. Strayer, vol. 3, 667–74. New York: Scribners, 1983.

Børresen, Kari Elisabeth. *Subordination and Equivalence: The Nature and Role of Women in Augustine and Thomas Aquinas.* Washington, D.C.: University Press of America, 1981.

Bossuat, Robert. *Drouart la Vache, traducteur d'André le Chapelain.* Paris: Champion, 1926.

Boswell, John. *Christianity, Social Tolerance, and Homosexuality.* Chicago: University of Chicago Press, 1980.

Boutière, Jean, and Alexander H. Schutz. *Biographies des troubadours.* Paris: Nizet, 1964.

Briffault, Robert. *The Mothers: A Study of the Origins of Sentiments and Institutions.* 3 vols. New York: Macmillan, 1969. Vol. 3.

———. *The Troubadours.* Bloomington: University of Indiana Press, 1965.

Brown, Emerson. "What Is Chaucer Doing with the Physician and His Tale?" *Philological Quarterly* 60 (1981): 129–49.

Brown, Peter. *The Body and Society: Men, Women, and Sexual Renunciation in Early Christianity.* New York: Columbia University Press, 1988.

———. "The Notion of Virginity in the Early Church." In *Christian Spirituality: Origins to the Twelfth Century,* ed. Bernard McGinn and John Meyendorff, 427–43. New York: Crossroad, 1985.

Brown, Robert D. *Lucretius on Love and Sex.* Leiden: E. J. Brill, 1987.

Brundage, James A. "Carnal Delight: Canonistic Theories of Sexuality." In *Proceedings of the Fifth International Congress of Medieval Canon Law,* ed. Stephen Kuttner and Kenneth Pennington, 361–85. Vatican City: Biblioteca Apostolica Vaticana, 1980.

———. *Law, Sex, and Christian Society in Medieval Europe.* Chicago: University of Chicago Press, 1987.

———. "Let Me Count the Ways: Canonists and Theologians Contemplate Coital Positions." *Journal of Medieval History* 10 (1984): 81–93.

Brunetière, Ferdinand. "L'Erudition contemporaine et la littérature française du moyen âge." In *Etudes critiques sur l'histoire de la littérature française,* 35–58. Paris: Hachette, 1888.

Buckley, Jorunn Jacobson. *Female Fault and Fulfillment in Gnosticism*. Chapel Hill: University of North Carolina Press, 1986.

Bugge, John. *Virginitas: An Essay in the History of a Medieval Ideal*. The Hague: Martinus Nijhoff, 1975.

Bullough, Vern L. "Medieval Medical and Scientific Views of Women." *Viator* 4 (1973): 485–501.

———. *The Subordinate Sex: A History of Attitudes Towards Women*. Urbana: University of Illinois Press, 1973.

———. "Transvestites in the Middle Ages." *American Journal of Sociology* 6 (1974): 1381–94.

Bullough, Vern L., and James A. Brundage. *Sexual Practices and the Medieval Church*. Buffalo, N.Y.: Prometheus, 1982.

Bultot, Robert. *La Doctrine du mépris du monde*. Louvain: Nauwelaerts, 1964. Vol. 4.

Burns, Jane. "The Man Behind the Lady in Troubadour Lyric." *Romance Notes* 25 (1985): 254–70.

Butler, Judith. *Gender Trouble*. London: Routledge, 1990.

Bynum, Caroline. *Holy Feast and Holy Fast: The Religious Significance of Food to Medieval Women*. Berkeley: University of California Press, 1987.

———. *Jesus as Mother: Studies in the Spirituality of the High Middle Ages*. Berkeley: University of California Press, 1982.

———. "' . . . . And Woman His Humanity': Female Imagery in the Religious Writing of the Later Middle Ages." In *Gender and Religion: On the Complexity of Symbols*, ed. Carolyn Bynum, Steven Harrell, and Paula Richman, 257–88. Boston: Beacon Press, 1986.

Caillemer, Robert. "Le Codi et le droit provençal au XIIe siècle." *Annales du Midi* 18 (1906): 494–507.

Camproux, Charles. *Joy d'amor*. Montpellier: Causse & Castelnau, 1965.

Castelli, Elizabeth. "Virginity and Its Meaning for Women's Sexuality in Early Christianity." *Journal of Feminist Studies in Religion* 2 (1986): 61–88.

Cercamon. *Les Poésies de Cercamon*. Ed. Alfred Jeanroy. Paris: Champion, 1922.

La Chastelaine de Vergi. Ed. Frederick Whitehead. Manchester: Manchester University Press, 1944.

Chaucer. "The Wife of Bath's Prologue." "The Physician's Tale," "The Legend of Good Women." In *The Works of Geoffrey Chaucer*, ed. F. N. Robinson, 76–88, 145–47, 480–518. Boston: Houghton Mifflin, 1961.

Chodorow, Nancy. *The Reproduction of Mothering*. Berkeley: University of California Press, 1978.

Chrétien de Troyes. *Erec et Enide*. Ed. Mario Roques. Paris: Champion, 1963.

———. *Le Roman de Perceval*. Ed. William Roach. Geneva: Droz, 1959.

Christine De Pizan. *The Book of the City of Ladies*. Trans. Earl J. Richards. New York: Persea Books, 1982.

———. *Le Dit de la rose*. In *Oeuvres poétiques*, ed. Maurice Roy, vol. 2. Paris: Firmin Didot, 1891.

Chrysostom, John. *Les Cohabitations suspectes, comment observer la virginité*. Ed. and trans. Jean Dumortier. Paris: Les Belles Lettres, 1955.

———. *Homilies on Genesis 1–17*. In *Fathers of the Church*, trans. Robert C. Hill, Vol. 74. Washington, D.C.: Catholic University of America Press, 1986.

———. "Letter to the Fallen Theodore," "Homily 3," "Homily 13," "Homily 15," "Homily 17." In *A Select Library of the Nicene and Post-Nicene Fathers*, ed. Philip Schaff, vol. 9, 91–111, 191–97, and 438–445; vol. 10. 115–23. Grand Rapids, Mich.: Eerdmans, 1956.

———. *On Virginity, Against Remarriage*. Trans. Sally Rieger Shore. Lewiston, N.Y.: Edwin Mellen Press, 1983.

Clark, Elizabeth. "Ascetic Renunciation and Feminine Advancement: A Paradox of Late Ancient Christianity." *Anglican Theological Review* 43 (1981): 240–57.

———. "Devil's Gateway and the Brides of Christ: Women in the Early Christian World." In *Ascetic Piety & Women's Faith: Essays on Late Ancient Christianity. Studies in Women & Religion*. 20: 23–60.

———. "Jerome, Chrysostom, and Friends." *Studies in Women and Religion* 2 (1979): 1–106.

———, trans. *The Life of Melania the Younger*. Lewiston, N.Y.; Edwin Mellen Press, 1984.

Clement of Alexandria. "On Marriage." In *Alexandrian Christianity*, ed. and trans. J. E. L. Oulton and Henry Chadwick, 40–92. Philadelphia: Westminster, 1954.

Clement of Rome. "Two Epistles Concerning Virginity." In the *Ante-Nicene Fathers*, ed. Alexander Roberts and James Donaldson, vol. 8, 53–66. Buffalo: The Christian Literature Publishing Co., 1886.

Colish, Marcia. "Cosmetic Theology: The Transformation of a Stoic Theme." *Assays* 1 (1981): 3–14.

———. *The Mirror of Language: A Study in the Medieval Theory of Knowledge*. New Haven: Yale University Press, 1968.

———. *The Stoic Tradition from Antiquity to the Early Middle Ages*. 2 vols. Leiden: E. J. Brill, 1985.

Crouzel, Henri. *Virginité et mariage selon Origène*. Paris: Desclée de Brouwer, 1962,

Culler, Jonathan. *On Deconstruction: Theory and Criticism After Structuralism.* Ithaca: Cornell University Press, 1982.

Cyprian. "The Dress of Virgins." In *Treatises,* ed. and trans. Roy J. Deferrari, 31–52. New York: Fathers of the Church, 1958.

Dalarun, Jacques. *L'Impossible sainteté: La vie retrouvée de Robert d'Arbrissel (v. 1045–1116), fondateur de Fontevraud.* Paris: Editions du Cerf, 1985.

————. "Robert d'Arbrissel et les femmes." *Annales E.S.C* 39 (1984): 1140–60.

Daniélou, Jean. *Philon d'Alexandrie.* Paris: Fayard, 1958.

Darmon, Pierre. *Mythologie de la femme dans l'ancienne France.* Paris: Seuil, 1983.

Daudet, Pierre. *Les Origines carolingiennes de la compétence exclusive de l'église en France et en Germanie en matière de juridiction matrimoniale.* Paris: Sirey, 1933.

Dauvillier, Jean. *Le Mariage dans le droit classique de l'église depuis le décret de Gratien (1140) jusqu'à la mort de Clément V (1314).* Paris: Sirey, 1933.

De Bruyne, Edgar. *Etudes d'esthétique médiévale.* Bruges: De Temple, 1946.

Delany, Sheila. "Politics and the Paralysis of Poetic Imagination in *The Physician's Tale.*" *Studies in the Age of Chaucer* 3 (1981): 47–60.

Delcourt, Marie. "Female Saints in Masculine Clothing." In *Hermaphrodite: Myths and Rites of the Bisexual Figure in Classical Antiquity,* trans. Jennifer Nicholson, 84–102. London: Studio Books, 1961.

Delhaye, Philippe. "Le Dossier anti-matrimonial de l'*Adversus Jovinianum* et son influence sur quelques écrits latins du XIIe siècle." *Medieval Studies* 13 (1951): 65–86.

De Ribbe, Charles. *La Société provençale à la fin du moyen âge.* Paris: Perrin, 1898.

De Rougemont, Denis. *Love in the Western World.* Trans. Montgomery Belgion. New York: Fawcett, 1958.

Derrida, Jacques. *Spurs/Eperons.* Trans. Barbara Harlow. Chicago: University of Chicago Press, 1979.

Didascalia apostolorum. Trans. Margaret Dunlop Gibson. London: C. J. Clay & Sons, 1903.

Didier, Noël. "Les Dispositions du statut de Guillaume II Forcalquier sur les filles dotées (1162)." *Le Moyen âge* 56 (1950): 247–78.

Donahue, Charles. "The Policy of Alexander III's Consent Theory of Marriage." In *Proceedings from the Fourth International Congress of Medieval Canon Law,* 251–81. Vatican City: Biblioteca Apostolica Vaticana, 1976.

Dow, Blanche. *The Varying Attitude Toward Women in French Literature of the Fifteenth Century: The Opening Years.* New York: Institute of French Studies, 1936.

Du Bois, Page. "'The Devil's Gateway': Women's Bodies and the Earthly Paradise." *Women's Studies* 7 (1980): 43–58.

Dubuis, Robert. *Les Cent nouvelles nouvelles et la tradition de la nouvelle en France au moyen âge.* Grenoble: Presses Universitaires de Grenoble, 1973.

Duby, Georges. *Le Chevalier, la femme et le prêtre: Le mariage dans la France féodale.* Paris: Hachette, 1981.

————. "Les 'Jeunes' dans la société aristocratique dans la France du nord-ouest du XIIe siècle." In *Hommes et structures du moyen âge,* 213–24. The Hague: Mouton, 1973.

————. *Medieval Marriage.* Baltimore: Johns Hopkins University Press, 1982.

————. *La Société aux XIe et XIIe siècles dans la région mâconnaise.* Paris: Armand Colin, 1953.

————. "Structures de parenté et noblesse dans la France du nord aux XIe et XIIe siècles." In *Hommes et structures du moyen âge,* 267–86. The Hague: Mouton, 1973.

Du Méril, Edelestand. *Poésies populaires latines du moyen âge.* Paris: Firmin Didot, 1847.

Duval, Yves-Marie. "L'Originalité du *De uirginibus* dans le mouvement ascétique occidental: Ambroise, Cyprien, Athanase." In *Ambroise de Milan: XVIe centenaire de son élection épiscopale,* ed. Yves-Marie Duval, 9–66. Paris: Etudes Augustiniennes, 1974.

Engels, Friedrich. *The Origin of the Family, Private Property and the State.* New York: International Publishers, 1972.

Erickson, Carolly. *The Medieval Vision: Essays in History and Perception.* New York: Oxford University Press, 1976.

Esmein, Adhémar. *Le Mariage en droit canonique.* 2 vols. Paris: Sirey, 1929.

Ewert, Alfred, ed. and trans. *French.* London: Faber & Faber, 1933.

Farmer, Sharon. "Softening the Hearts of Men: Women, Embodiment, and Persuasion in the Thirteenth Century." In *Embodied Love: Sensuality and Relationship as Feminist Values,* ed. Paula Cooly, Sharon Farmer, and Mary Ellen Ross, 115–33. New York: Harper & Row, 1987.

Ferrante, Joan M. "*Cortes'Amor* in Medieval Texts." *Speculum* 55 (1980): 686–95.

————. *Woman as Image in Medieval Literature from the Twelfth Century to Dante.* New York: Columbia University Press, 1975.

Fineman, Joel. "Shakespeare's *Will:* The Temporality of Rape." *Representations* 20 (1987): 25–76.

Fiorenza, Elizabeth Schüssler. *In Memory of Her: A Feminist Theological Reconstruction of Christian Origins.* New York: Crossroads, 1983.

Flandrin, Jean-Louis. *Familles: Parenté, maison, sexualité dans l'ancienne société.* Paris: Hachette, 1976.

Foucault, Michel. "Le Combat de la chasteté. *Communications* 35 (1982): 15–21.

———. *The History of Sexuality*. 3 vols. Trans. Robert Hurley. New York: Vintage, 1988.

Fyler, John. "Man, Men, and Women in Chaucer's Poetry." In *The Olde Daunce: Love, Friendship, and Desire in the Medieval World,* ed. Robert Edwards and Stephen Spector, 154–76. Albany: SUNY Press, 1990.

Gager, John G. *Kingdom and Community: The Social World of Early Christianity*. Englewood Cliffs, N.J.: Prentice-Hall, 1975.

Ganshof, François-L. "Le Statut de la femme dans la monarchie franque." In *La Femme*, 5–58. Recueils de Société Jean Bodin 12. Brussels: Société Jean Bodin, 1962.

Garaud, Marcel. *Les Châtelains de Poitou et l'avènement du régime féodal: XIe et XIIe siècles*. Poitiers: Mémoires de la Société des Antiquaires de l'Ouest, 1964.

———. "Le Viage ou le retour du vieux 'Coustumier de Poictou.'" *Bulletin de la Société des Antiquaires de l'Ouest* (1921): 747–88.

Gaudemet, Jean. "Le Statut de la femme dans l'empire romain." In *La Femme*, 191–222. Recuils de la Société Jean Bodin 11. Brussels: Société Jean Bodin, 1962.

Gautier de Coinci. *Les Miracles de Notre Dame*. 4 vols. Ed. V. Frederic Koenig. Geneva: Droz, 1970.

Gies, Frances, and Joseph Gies. *Women in the Middle Ages*. New York: Crowell, 1978.

Gold, Penny. *The Lady and the Virgin: Image, Attitude, and Experience in Twelfth-Century France*. Chicago: University of Chicago Press, 1985.

Goody, Jack. *The Development of the Family and Marriage in Europe*. Cambridge: Cambridge University Press, 1983.

Goody, Jack, Joan Thrisk, and E. P. Thompson. *Family and Inheritance, Rural Society in Western Europe 1200–1800*. Cambridge: Cambridge University Press, 1976.

Graham, John. "The Poetics of Interpretation: The Courtly Lyric as a Socially Symbolic Act." Ph.D. diss., Yale University, 1989.

Gregory of Nyssa. *On Virginity*. In *Ascetical Works*, trans. Virginia Callahan, 3–75. Washington, D.C.: Catholic University of America Press, 1967.

Guilhem de Montanhagol. *Les poésies de Guilhem de Montanhagol*. Ed. Peter Ricketts. Toronto: Pontifical Institute of Medieval Studies, 1964.

Hajdu, Robert. "Family and Feudal Ties in Poitou, 1100–1300." *Journal of Interdisciplinary History* 8 (1977): 117–39.

———. "The Position of Noblewomen in the Pays des Coutumes, 1100–1300." *Journal of Family History* 5 (1980): 122–44.

Hays, H. R. *The Dangerous Sex: The Myth of Feminine Evil*. New York: G. P. Putnam's Sons, 1964.

Hayter, Mary. *The New Eve in Christ*. Grand Rapids, Mich.: Eerdmans, 1987.

Hentsch, Alice. *De la littérature didactique du moyen âge s'adressant spécialement aux femmes.* Geneva: Slatkine Reprints, 1975.

Herlihy, David. "Land, Family and Women in Continental Europe." *Traditio* 18 (1962): 89–120.

———. *Medieval Households.* Cambridge, Mass.: Harvard University Press, 1985.

———. "The Medieval Marriage Market." In *Medieval and Renaissance Studies,* ed. Dale B. J. Randall, 3–27. Durham, N.C.: Duke University Press, 1974.

———. *Women in Medieval Society.* Houston: University of Saint Thomas, 1971.

Hesiod. *Works and Days.* Ed. and trans. Dorothea Wender. London: Penguin, 1973.

Hicks, Erik. ed. *Le Débat sur le Roman de la rose.* Paris: Champion, 1977.

Hollier, Denis, ed. *The College of Sociology.* Trans. Betsy Wing. Minneapolis: University of Minnesota Press, 1988.

Horowitz, Mary Cline. "The Image of God in Man—Is Woman Included?" *Harvard Theological Review* 72 (1979): 175–206.

Howard, George E. *A History of Matrimonial Institutions.* 3 vols. Chicago: University of Chicago Press, 1904.

Huchet, Jean-Charles. *L'Amour discourtois.* Toulouse: Privat, 1987.

Hughes, Diane Owen. "From Brideprice to Dowry in Mediterranean Europe." *Journal of Family History* 3 (1978): 262–96.

Imbs, Paul. "De la fin'amor." *Cahiers de civilisation médiévale* 12 (1969): 265–85.

Innocent III. *On the Misery of the Human Condition (De miseria humane conditionis).* Trans. Margaret M. Dietz. New York: Bobbs-Merrill, 1969.

Irigaray, Luce. *Speculum of the Other Woman.* Trans. Gillian C. Gill. Ithaca, N.Y.: Cornell University Press, 1985.

Isidore of Seville. *Etymologiarum sive originum.* Ed. W. M. Lindsay. Oxford: Oxford University Press, 1911, 2 vols.

Jacquart, Danielle, and Claude Thomasset. *Sexuality and Medicine in the Middle Ages.* Princeton: Princeton University Press, 1985.

Jaufré Rudel. *Chansons.* Ed. Alfred Jeanroy. Paris: Champion, 1924.

Jean de Meun. *Le Roman de la rose.* Ed. Félix Lecoy. 3 vols. Paris: Champion, 1966.

Jeanroy, Alfred. *Les Origines de la poésie lyrique en France au moyen âge.* 2 vols. Paris: Hachette, 1889.

———. *La Poésie lyrique des troubadours.* Paris: Privat, 1934.

Jehan Le Fèvre. *Les Lamentations de Matheolus.* Ed. A.-G. Van Hamel. Paris: Emile Bouillon, 1892.

Jerome. *Adversus Jovinianum.* In *A Select Library of the Nicene and Post-Nicene Fathers,*

2d ser., ed. Philip Schaff and Henry Wace, vol. 6, 364–416. Grand Rapids, Mich.: Eerdmans, 1952.

———. *Letters.* In *A Select Library of the Nicene and Post-Nicene Fathers,* 2d ser., ed. Philip Schaff and Henry Wace, Vol. 6. Grand Rapids, Mich.: Eerdmans, 1952.

———. *Select Letters.* Ed. F. A. Wright. Cambridge, Mass.: Harvard University Press, 1953.

Johansson, Sheila Ryan. "'Herstory' as History: A New Field or Another Fad?" In *Liberating Women's History: Theoretical and Critical Essays,* ed. Berenice A. Carroll, 400–430. Urbana: University of Illinois Press, 1976.

John of Salisbury. *Frivolities of Courtiers and Footprints of Philosophers.* Ed. Joseph B. Pike. Minneapolis: University of Minnesota Press, 1938.

———. *Metalogicon.* Ed. Daniel D. McGarry. Berkeley: University of California Press, 1962.

———. *The Statesman's Book.* Ed. John Dickinson. New York: Russell & Russell, 1927.

Johnson, Barbara. "The Lady in the Lake." In *A New History of French Literature,* 627–32. Cambridge, Mass.: Harvard University Press, 1989.

Johnson, Lesley. "Women on Top: Antifeminism in the Fabliaux." *Modern Language Review* 78 (1983): 298–307.

Jubinal, Achille. *Jongleurs et trouvères.* Paris: Librairie de J. Albert Merklein, 1835.

———. *Nouveau recueil de contes, dits et fabliaux et autres pièces inédites des XIIIe, XIVe, et XVe siècles.* Paris: E. Pannier, 1842.

Juvenal. *The Sixteen Satires.* Trans. Peter Green. Harmondsworth: Penguin, 1974.

Karnein, Alfred. *De Amore in volkssprachlicher Literatur, Untersuchungen zur Andreas-Capellanus-Rezeption im Mittelalter und Renaissance, Germanisch-romanische Monatsschrift.* Heidelberg: Carl Winter, 1985.

Kean, Patricia. *Chaucer and the Meaning of English Poetry.* London: Routledge & Kegan Paul, 1972.

Kelly, Joan. "Early Feminist Theory and the *Querelle des Femmes,* 1400–1789." *Signs* 8 (1982): 4–28.

Klein, Melanie. "Early Stages of the Oedipus Conflict." *The International Journal of Psychoanalysis* 9 (1928): 167–80.

Koehler, Erich. *Ideal und Wirklichkeit in der höfischen Epik.* Tübingen: Max Niemeyer, 1956.

———. "Observations historiques et sociologiques sur la poésie des troubadours." *Cahiers de civilisation médiévale* 7 (1964): 27–47.

———. *Trobadorlyrik und höfischer Roman: Aufsätze zur französischen und provenzalischen Literatur des Mittelalters.* Berlin: Rütten & Loenning, 1962.

Koenigsberg, Richard. "Culture as Unconscious Fantasy: Observations on Courtly Love." *Psychoanalytic Review* 54 (1967): 36–50.

Kofman, Sarah. *Nietzsche et la scène philosophique.* Paris: Union Générale d'Editions, 1979.

Kostoroski, Emilie. "Quest in Query and the *Chastelaine de Vergi.*" *Medievalia et Humanistica* 3 (1972): 179–98.

Kraemer, R. "The Conversion of Women to Ascetic Forms of Christianity." *Signs* 6 (1980/81): 298–307.

Kristeva, Julia. *Tales of Love.* New York: Columbia University Press, 1987.

Lacan, Jacques. "L'Amour courtois en anamorphose." In *Séminaire VII: L'éthique de la psychanalyse,* ed. Jacques-Alain Miller, 167–84. Paris: Seuil, 1986.

Lazar, Moshe. *Amour courtois et 'fin'amors' dans la littérature du XIIe siècle.* Paris: Klincksieck, 1964.

Le Clerc, Victor. *Les Fabliaux.* In *Histoire littéraire de la France,* vol. 23. Paris: H. Welter, 1895.

Leclercq, Dom Jean. *La Femme et les femmes dans l'oeuvre de Saint Bernard.* Paris: Téqui, 1982.

Lee, Brian. "The Position and Purpose of *The Physician's Tale.*" *The Chaucer Review* 22 (1987): 141–60.

Lefkowitz, Mary. *Heroines and Hysterics.* London: Duckworth, 1981.

Legrand, Lucien. *La Virginité dans la Bible.* Paris: Editions du Cerf, 1964.

Lehman, Andrée. *Le Rôle de la femme dans l'histoire de France au moyen âge.* Paris: Editions Berger-Levrault, 1952.

Lejeune, Rita. "La Femme dans les littératures française et occitane du XIe au XIIIe siècle," *Cahiers de civilisation mediévale* 20 (1977): 201–17.

Lemay, Helen Rodnite. "Some Thirteenth and Fourteenth Century Lectures on Female Sexuality." *International Journal of Women's Studies* 1 (1978): 391–400.

Le Saint, William P. *Tertullian: Treatises on Marriage and Remarriage.* Westminster, Md.: The Newman Press, 1951.

Leupin, Alexandre. "Ecriture naturelle et écriture hermaphrodite." *Diagraphe* 9 (1976): 119–41.

Lewis, C. S. *The Allegory of Love.* Oxford: Oxford University Press, 1965.

Lichtenstein, Jacqueline. *La Couleur éloquente.* Paris: Flammarion, 1989.

Lombroso, Cesare. *La Femme criminelle et la prostituée.* Paris: Félix Alcan, 1896.

Lot-Borodine, Myrrha. "Sur les Origines et les fins du *service d'amour.*" In *Mélanges Alfred Jeanroy,* 223–42. Paris: Droz, 1928.

Lowes, John Livingston. "The Loveres Maladye of Heroes." *Modern Philology* 11 (1914): 491–546.

MacDonald, Dennis. *There Is No Male or Female*. Philadelphia: Fortress Press, 1987.

Maillet, J. "De l'exclusion coutumière des filles dotées à la renonciation à succession future dans les coutumes de Toulouse et Bordeaux." *Revue historique de droit français et étranger* 30 (1952): 514–45.

Mallarmé, Stéphane. *Oeuvres complètes*. Paris: Gallimard, 1979.

Manteuffel, Tadeusz. *Naissance d'une hérésie: Les adeptes de la pauvreté volontaire au moyen âge*. Trans. Anna Posner. The Hague: Mouton, 1970.

Map, Walter. *De nugis curialium*. Trans. Montague James. London: Cymmrodorion Society, 1923.

———. *De nugis curialium*. Ed. Thomas Wright. London: Nichols & Son, 1850.

Marcabru. *Poésies complètes du troubadour Marcabru*. Ed. J.-M.-L. Dejeanne. Toulouse: Privat, 1909.

Marchalonis, Shirley. "Above Rubies: Popular Views of Medieval Women." *Journal of Popular Culture* 14 (1980): 87–93.

Marie de France, *Fables*. Trans. Mary Lou Martin. Birmingham, Ala.: Summa Publications, 1984.

———. *Lais*. Ed. Jean Rychner. Paris: Champion, 1983.

Marks, Elaine, and Isabelle de Courtivron. *New French Feminisms*. New York: Schocken, 1981.

McCracken, Peggy. "The Poetics of Silence in the French Middle Ages." Ph.D. diss., Yale University, 1989.

McLaughlin, Eleanor. "Equality of Souls, Inequality of Sexes: Women in Medieval Theology." In *Religion and Sexism*, ed. Rosemary Ruether, 213–66. New York: Simon & Schuster, 1974.

McLaughlin, Eleanor, and Rosemary Ruether, eds. *Women of Spirit: Female Leadership in the Jewish and Christian Traditions*. New York: Simon & Schuster, 1979.

McLeod, Enid. *The Order of the Rose: The Life and Ideas of Christine de Pizan*. Totowa, N.J.: Rowman & Littlefield, 1976.

McNamara, Jo Ann. "Sexual Equality and the Cult of Virginity in Early Christian Thought." *Feminist Studies* 3 (1976): 145–58.

McNamara, Jo Ann, and Suzanne Wemple. "The Power of Women Through the Family in Medieval Europe: 500–1100." *Feminist Studies* 1 (1973): 126–41.

Ménard, Philippe. *Les Fabliaux*. Paris: Presses Universitaires de France, 1983.

Mendieta, David Amandde. "La Virginité chez Eusèbe et l'ascéticisme familial dans la première moitié du IVe siècle," *Revue d'histoire ecclésiastique* 50 (1955): 777–820.

Methodius. *The Symposium: A Treatise on Chastity.* Trans. Herbert Musurillo. Westminster, Md.: The Newman Press, 1958.

Metz, René. "Le Statut de la femme en droit canonique médiéval." In *La Femme,* 59–113. Recueils de la Société Jean Bodin 12. Brussels: Société Jean Bodin, 1962.

Meyer, Marvin W. "Making Mary Male: The Categories 'Male' and 'Female' in the Gospel of Thomas." *New Testament Studies* 31 (1985): 554–70.

Michelet, Jules. *Le Moyen âge.* In *Histoire de la France,* books 1–17. Rpt. Paris: Laffont, 1981.

———. *La Sorcière.* Paris: E. Denton, 1862.

———. *Woman.* Trans. John W. Palmer. New York: Carleton, 1866.

Middleton, Anne. "The *Physician's Tale* and Love's Martyrs: 'Ensamples Mo than Ten' as a Method in the *Canterbury Tales.*" *Chaucer Review* 8 (1973): 9–32.

Migne, J.-P., ed. *Patrologia graeca.* 160 vols. Paris, 1857–87.

———, ed. *Patrologia latina.* 222 vols. Paris, 1844–55.

Miles, Margaret. *Carnal Knowing.* Boston: Beacon Press, 1989.

Miller, Robert. "The Wounded Heart: Courtly Love and the Medieval Antifeminist Tradition." *Women's Studies* 2 (1974): 335–50.

Moi, Toril. "Desire in Language: Andreas Capellanus and the Controversy of Courtly Love." In *Medieval Literature: Criticism, Ideology, and History,* ed. David Aers, 11–33. New York: Saint Martin's Press, 1986.

Montaiglon, Anatole de. *Recueil général et complet des fabliaux.* 6 vols. Paris: Librairie des Bibliophiles, 1872.

Morewedge, Rosemarie. *The Role of Woman in the Middle Ages.* Albany: State University of New York Press, 1975.

Murphy, Francis X. "Melania the Elder: A Biographical Note." *Traditio* 5 (1947): 59–77.

Muscatine, Charles. *Poetry and Crisis in the Age of Chaucer.* Notre Dame, Ind.: University of Notre Dame Press, 1972.

Naïté-Albistur, Daniel Armogathe. *Histoire du féminisme français du moyen âge à nos jours.* Paris: Edition des Femmes, 1977.

Neff, Theodore Lee. *La Satire des femmes dans la poésie lyrique française du moyen âge.* Paris: V. Giard & E. Brière, 1900.

Nelli, René. *L'Erotique des troubadours.* 2 vols. Toulouse: Privat, 1963.

Newman, Barbara. *Sister of Wisdom: St. Hildegard's Theology of the Feminine.* Berkeley: University of California Press, 1987.

Nietzsche, Friedrich. *Beyond Good and Evil.* Trans. Walter Kaufmann. New York: Random House, 1966.

———. *Ecce Homo.* Trans. Walter Kaufmann. New York: Vintage, 1969.

———. *Twilight of the Idols.* Ed. Oscar Levy. London: T. N. Foulis, 1911.

Nisbet, Robert. *The Social Philosophers: Community and Conflict in Western Thought.* New York: Thomas Y. Crowell, 1973.

Noonan, John. "Marital Affection in the Canonists." *Studia Gratiana* 12 (1967): 479–509.

———. "Power to Choose." *Viator* 4 (1973): 419–34.

Novatian. "The Spectacles" and "In Praise of Purity." In *Fathers of the Church,* trans. Russell De Simone, vol. 67, 123–33, 165–76. Washington: Catholic University of America Press, 1974.

Nykrog, Per. *Les Fabliaux.* Copenhagen: Munksgaard, 1957.

Nyquist, Mary. "Gynesis, Genesis, Exegesis, and Milton's Eve." In *Selected Papers from the English Institute, 1985,* ed. Marjorie Garber, 147–208. Baltimore: Johns Hopkins University Press, 1987.

O'Faolain, Julia, and Lauro Martines. *Not in God's Image.* New York: Harper & Row, 1973.

Ourliac, Pierre. "L'Esprit du droit méridional." In *Droit privé et institutions régionales,* 577–94. Paris: Presses Universitaires de France, 1976.

———. "Le Retrait lignager dans le sud-ouest de la France." *Revue historique de droit français et étranger* 30 (1952): 328–55.

Pagels, Elaine. *Adam, Eve, and the Serpent.* New York: Random House, 1988.

———. *The Gnostic Gospels.* New York: Random House, 1979.

Paget, Violet. "Mediaeval Love." In *Euphorion, being Studies of the Antique and the Mediaeval in the Renaissance,* vol. 2, 123–217. London: T. Fisher Unwin, 1884.

Parvey, Constance. "The Theology and Leadership of Women in the New Testament." In *Religion and Sexism,* ed. Rosemary Ruether, 117–49. New York: Simon & Schuster, 1974.

Passio sanctarum Perpetuae et Felicitatis. Trans. Herbert Musurillo. In *The Acts of the Christian Martyrs,* 106–31. Oxford: Clarendon Press, 1972.

Patlagean, Evelyne. "L'Histoire de la femme déguisée en moine et l'évolution de la sainteté féminine à Byzance." *Studi medievali* 17 (1976): 597–623.

Payer, Pierre J. *Sex and the Penitentials: The Development of a Sexual Code: 550–1150.* Toronto: University of Toronto Press, 1984.

Pernoud, Régine. *La Femme au temps des cathédrales.* (Paris: Stock, 1980).

Peter Lombard. *Petri Lombardi, Libri IV Sententiarum.* 2 vols. New York: Saint Bonaventure, 1916.

Pétigny, Jean de. "Lettre inédite de Robert d'Arbrissel à la Comtesse Ermengarde." *Bibliothèque de l'Ecole des Chartes* 5 (1854): 209–35.

_____. "Robert d'Arbrissel et Geoffroy de Vendôme." *Bibliothèque de l'Ecole des Chartes* 5 (1854): 1–30.

Petot, Pierre. "Le Statut de la femme dans les pays coutumiers français du XIIIe au XVIIe siècle." In *La Femme*, 243–54. Recueils de la Société Jean Bodin 12. Brussels: Société Jean Bodin, 1962.

Philo Judaeus. *On the Creation*. Ed. F. H. Colson. London: Heinemann, 1929.

Pollman, Leo. *Die Liebe in der hochmittelalterlichen Literatur Frankreichs*. Frankfurt: Klostermann, 1966.

Pollock, Frederick, and Frederic Maitland. *The History of English Law*. 2. vols. Cambridge: Cambridge University Press, 1923.

Pomeroy, Sarah. *Goddesses, Whores, Wives, and Slaves: Women in Classical Antiquity*. New York: Schocken, 1975.

Portejoie, Paulette. *Le Régime des fiefs d'après la coutume de Poitou*. Poitiers: Mémoires de la Société des Antiquaires de l'Ouest, 1958.

Power, Eileen. *Medieval Women*. Cambridge: Cambridge University Press, 1975.

Pratt, Robert A. "Jankyn's Book of Wikked Wyves: Medieval Antimatrimonial Propaganda in the Universities." *Annuale mediaevale* 3 (1962): 5–27.

Preisker, Herbert. *Christentum und Ehe in den ersten drei Jahrhunderten: Eine Studie zur Kulturgeschichte der alten Welt*. Berlin: Trowitsch, 1927.

Proudhon, P.-J. *De la justice dans la Révolution et dans l'église*. 3 vols. Paris: Garnier Frères, 1858.

Prusak, Bernard. "Woman: Seductive Siren and Source of Sin? Pseudepigraphical Myth and Christian Origins." In *Religion and Sexism*, ed. Rosemary Ruether, 89–116. New York: Simon & Schuster, 1974.

Quéré-Jaulmes, France. *La Femme: Les grands textes des pères de l'église*. Paris: Editions du Centurion, 1968.

Les XV. joies de mariage. Ed. Jean Rychner. Geneva: Droz, 1963.

Raimbaut d'Orange. *The Life and Works of the Troubadour Raimbaut d'Orange*. Ed. Walter T. Pattison. Minneapolis: University of Minnesota Press, 1952.

Rambaux, Claude. *Tertullien face aux morales des trois premiers siècles*. Paris: Société des Belles Lettres, 1979.

Recueil de motets français des XIIe et XIIIe siécles. Ed. Gaston Raynaud. Hildesheim: Georg Olms Verlag, 1972.

Reinhard, John. *The Survival of Geis in Mediaeval Romance*. Halle: Max Niemeyer, 1933.

Renaut de Beaujeu. *Le Lai d'Ignauré ou lai du prisonnier*. Ed. Rita Lejeune. Brussels: Palais des Académies, 1938.

Rey-Flaud, Henri. *La Névrose courtoise*. Paris: Navarin, 1983.

Richard, Alfred. *Histoire des comtes de Poitou, 778–1204*. Paris: Alphonse Picard, 1903.

———, ed. *Chartes et documents pour servir à l'histoire de l'abbaye de Saint-Maixent*. 2 vols. Archives Historiques de Poitou 16 & 18. Poitiers, 1886.

Robertson, D. W. *A Preface to Chaucer*. Princeton: Princeton University Press, 1962.

Robinson, James M., ed. *Nag Hammadi Library*. San Francisco: Harper & Row, 1977.

Rogers, Katharine M. *The Troublesome Helpmate: A History of Misogyny in Literature*. Seattle: University of Washington Press, 1966.

Roloff, Volker. *Reden und Schweigen: Zur Tradition und Gestaltung eines mittelalterlichen Themas in der französischen Literatur*. Munich: Fink, 1973.

Rose, Mary Beth. *Women in the Middle Ages and the Renaissance: Literary and Historical Perspectives*. Syracuse, N.Y.: Syracuse University Press, 1986.

Rousselle, Aline. *Porneia: De la maîtrise du corps à la privation sensorielle, IIe–IVe siècles de l'ère chrétienne*. Paris: Presses Universitaires de France, 1983.

Rubin, Gayle. "The Traffic in Women: Notes on the Political Economy of Sex." In *Towards an Anthropology of Women*, ed. Rayna R. Reiter, 157–210. New York: Monthly Review Press, 1975.

Ruether, Rosemary. "Misogynism and Virginal Feminism in the Fathers of the Church." In *Religion and Sexism*, ed. Rosemary Ruether, 150–83. New York: Simon & Schuster, 1974.

———. "Mothers of the Church: Ascetic Women in the Late Patristic Age." In *Women of Spirit: Female Leadership in the Jewish and Christian Traditions*, ed. Eleanor McLaughlin and Rosemary Ruether, 71–98. New York: Simon & Schuster, 1979.

Rychner, Jean. "La Présence et le point de vue du narrateur dans deux récits courts: le *Lai de Lanval* et la *Châtelaine de Vergi*." *Vox Romanica* 39 (1980): 86–103.

Schillebeeckx, Edward. *Le Mariage*. Paris: Cerf, 1966.

Schmitt, Charles B. "Theophrastus in the Middle Ages." *Viator* 2 (1971): 251–70.

Schopenhauer, Arthur. *Essays and Aphorisms*. Trans. R. J. Hollingdale. Rpt. Harmondsworth: Penguin, 1970.

Schor, Naomi. *Reading in Detail: Aesthetics and the Feminine*. New York: Methuen, 1987.

Schulenberg, Jane Tibbetts. "The Heroics of Virginity: Brides of Christ and Sacrificial Mutilation." In *Women in the Middle Ages and the Renaissance*, ed. Mary Beth Rose, 29–72. Syracuse, N.Y.: Syracuse University Press, 1986.

———. "Word, Spirit and Power: Women in Early Christian Communities." In *Women of Spirit: Female Leadership in the Jewish and Christian Traditions*, ed. Eleanor McLaughlin and Rosemary Ruether, 29–70. New York: Simon & Schuster, 1979.

Scroggs, Robin. "The Earliest Christian Communities as Sectarian Movement." In *Christianity, Judaism and Other Greco-Roman Cults,* ed. Jacob Neusner, vol. 1, 1–23. Leiden: E. J. Brill, 1975.

Shahar, Shulamith. *The Fourth Estate: A History of Women in the Middle Ages.* London: Methuen, 1983.

Sheehan, Michael M. "Choice of Marriage Partner in the Middle Ages: Development and Application of a Theory of Marriage." *Studies in Medieval and Renaissance History* 1 (1978): 1–33.

Singer, Irving. *The Nature of Love.* Chicago: University of Chicago Press, 1984, vol. 2.

Smith, Jonathan Z. *Map Is Not Territory: Studies in the History of Religion.* Leiden: E. J. Brill, 1978.

Soranus. *Gynecology.* Ed. Owsei Temkin. Baltimore: Johns Hopkins University Press, 1956.

Spelman, Elizabeth V. "Woman as Body: Ancient and Contemporary Views." *Feminist Studies* 8 (1982): 109–31.

Spitzer, Leo. *L'Amour lointain de Jaufré Rudel et le sens de la poésie des troubadours.* University of North Carolina Studies in the Romance Languages and Literature. Chapel Hill: University of North Carolina Press, 1944.

―――. "Marie de France—Dichterin von Problem-Märchen." *Zeitschrift für romanische Philologie* 50 (1930): 29–67.

Stanton, Theodore. *The Woman Question in Europe.* New York: Putnam, 1884.

Stock, Brian. *The Implications of Literacy.* Princeton: Princeton University Press, 1983.

Stone, Greg. "The Death of the Grammatical Ego: Lyric Resistance to Individualism in Early Modern Narrative." Ph.D. diss., Yale University, 1989.

Stuard, Susan M. *Women in Medieval Society.* Philadelphia: University of Pennsylvania Press, 1976.

Tavard, George. *Women in Christian Tradition.* Notre Dame, Ind.: University of Notre Dame Press, 1973.

Tertullian. "On the Pallium," "On the Apparel of Women," "On the Veiling of Virgins," and "On Exhortation to Chastity." In *The Ante-Nicene Fathers,* vol 4. Ed. Alexander Roberts and James Donaldson. Buffalo: The Christian Literature Publishing Co., 1885.

Thibaut de Champagne. In *Poèmes d'amour des XIIe et XIIIe siècles.* Ed. Emmanuèle Baumgartner. Paris: Union Générale d'Editions, 1983.

Thiessen, Gerd. "Itinerant Radicalism: The Tradition of Jesus Sayings from the Perspective of the Sociology of Literature." In *Radical Religion: The Bible and Liberation,* 84–93. Berkeley, Calif.: Community for Religious Research and Education, 1976.

Tobin, Thomas H. *The Creation of Man: Philo and the History of Interpretation.* Washington, D.C.: Catholic Biblical Association of America, 1983.

Todd, Janet. *Feminist Literary History.* New York: Routledge, 1988.

Topsfield, Leslie T. *Troubadours and Love.* Cambridge: Cambridge University Press, 1975.

Trible, Phyllis. "Depatriarchalizing in Biblical Interpretation." *Journal of the American Academy of Religion* 41 (1973): 30–48.

———. *God and the Rhetoric of Sexuality.* Philadelphia: Fortress Press, 1978.

Turlan, Juliette. "Recherches sur le mariage dans la pratique coutumière (XIIe–XIVe siècle)." *Revue historique de droit français et étranger* 35 (1957): 477–528.

Vaissete, Dom Joseph. *Histoire générale de Languedoc, par dom Cl. Devie et dom J. Vaissete.* 3 vols. Toulouse: Privat, 1874–92.

Vance, Eugene. "Désir, rhétorique et texte." *Poétique* 42 (1980): 137–55.

Van Hoecke, Willy, and Andries Welkenhuysen. *Love and Marriage in the Twelfth Century.* Louvain: Leuven University Press, 1981.

Verbeke, Gerard. *The Presence of Stoicism in Medieval Thought.* Washington, D.C.: Catholic University of America Press, 1983.

Veyne, Paul. "La Famille et l'amour sous le haut-empire romain." *Annales* 33 (1978): 35–63.

———. *A History of Family Life, I: From Pagan Rome to Byzantium.* Cambridge, Mass.: Harvard University Press, 1987.

———. "Homosexuality in Ancient Rome." In *Western Sexuality: Practice and Precept in Past and Present Times,* ed. Philippe Ariès and A. Béjin, trans. A. Forster, 26–35. Oxford, 1985.

La *"Vie de seint Edmund le rei," poème anglo-normand du XIIe siècle.* Ed. Hildung Kjellmann. Göteborg, 1935.

Virey, J. J. *De l'influence des femmes sur le goût dans la littérature et les beaux-arts.* Paris: Deterville, 1810.

Von le Fort, Gertrude. *The Eternal Woman: The Woman in Time: Timeless Woman.* Trans. Marie Cecilia Buehrle. Milwaukee: Bruce Publishing, 1954.

Wack, Mary. "Imagination, Medicine, and Rhetoric in Andreas Capellanus' 'De Amore.'" In *Magister Regis: Studies in Honor of Robert Earl Kaske,* ed. Arthur Groos, 101–15. New York: Fordham University Press, 1986.

Walsh, Patrick G., ed. and trans. *Andreas Capellanus on Love.* London: Duckworth, 1982.

Walther, Johannes von. *Die ersten Wanderprediger Frankreichs: Studien zur Geschichte des Mönchtums, I: Robert von Arbrissel.* Leipzig: T. Weicher,1903.

Warner, Marina. *Alone of All Her Sex.* New York: Knopf, 1976.

Werner, Ernst. *Pauperes Christi: Studien zu sozial-religiösen: Bewegungen im Zeit-alter des Reformpapsttums*. Leipzig: Koehler & Amelang, 1956.

———. "Zur Frauenfrage und zum Frauenkult im Mittelalter: Robert v. Arbrissel und Fontevrault." *Forschungen und Fortschritte* 29 (1955): 269–76.

Westermarck, Edward. *The History of Human Marriage*. London: Macmillan, 1925.

William IX of Aquitaine. *The Poetry of William VII, Count of Poitiers, IX Duke of Aquitaine*. Ed. and trans. Gerald A. Bond. New York: Garland Publishing, 1982.

Winston, David, trans. and introd. *Philo of Alexandria: The Contemplative Life, The Giants, and Selections*. New York: Paulist Press, 1981.

Wulff, August. *Die Frauenfeindlichen Dichtungen in den romanischen Literaturen des Mittelalters bis zum Ende des XIII Jahrhunderts*. Halle: Max Niemeyer, 1914.

Yarbrough, Anne. "Christianization in the Fourth Century: The Example of Roman Women." *Church History* 45 (1976): 149–65.

Yver, Jean. "Les Caractères originaux du groupe de coutumes de l'Ouest de la France," *Revue historique du droit français et étranger* 30 (1952): 18–79.

———. *Egalité entre héritiers et exclusion des enfants dotés*. Paris: Sirey, 1966.

Ziolkowski, Jan. *Alan de Lille's Grammar of Sex*. Boston: Medieval Academy of America, 1985.

Zumthor, Paul. "De la Chanson au récit: La Chastelaine de Vergi." *Vox romanica* 27 (1968): 77–95.

INDEX